EVERYDAY STRENGTH

Praying the Bible,

as you read through the Bible

Mark D. Partin, D. Min.

Contents

Contents

JANUARY

IN THE BEGINNING GOD
Genesis 1:1

Have you ever given consideration what was before Genesis 1:1? There was no heaven. There was no earth. There was only God and that was all that was ever needed. The account in Genesis 1 tells us that God created the heavens and the earth. How? He is Elohim, the creating God, He thought creation into being. He spoke and it was. Man is so unlike God. Man can make things by mixing this with that, or by combining things together. Oh, but God creates with nothing but His word.

You find the phrases in Genesis 1 that "God created," "God said," "God saw," "God called," "God made," "God set," and "God blessed." In the beginning there was only God, and Eternal God is more than sufficient to meet your needs. It is the desire of God to communicate with man. All of His creation: His creating, speaking, and blessing were so that man could know God and have a relationship with Him.

You are told of Jesus Christ in Revelation 13:8 that He was the "lamb slain from the foundation of the world." So what happened before Genesis 1:1? Jesus Christ, the Lamb of God, was sacrificed for you so that you may be saved. Jesus gave His life so that you can come into a relationship with Holy God and live for His glory.

Prayer and Praise:

Lord, thank You. Before creation ever took place, You were thinking of how to redeem me. You are God Elohim and I exalt You. All through creation Your desire was to bless man, to bless me. Not to bless me with the abundance of things that distracts me from You, but to bless me with Your presence and to bless me with Your Word. Thank You. In the mighty name of Jesus Christ, my Lord. Amen.

FINDING GRACE IN THE EYES OF THE LORD
Genesis 6:8-9

In Genesis 6:8-9, you see for the first time the word grace. Many times you have heard people say that "the New Testament is the beginning of God's grace." As you read the Bible, the first place you find the word grace is in Genesis 6:8. This was before the law ever came into being and yet you discover a man finding "grace in the eyes of God."

The word grace has been defined as the "free and unmerited favor of God." In the Hebrew, it comes from the word chanan'el, meaning, "to bend or stoop in kindness to an inferior." God, your Creator, stooped in kindness to inferior, frail, limited, sinful man, so man could find grace in His eyes. Noah found grace; he found favor and he gained the acceptance of God.

How did Noah find grace in the eyes of God? In Genesis 6:8-9, you are told, "But Noah found grace in the eyes of the Lord ... Noah was a just man, perfect in his generations. Noah walked with God." You find three reasons why Noah, or anyone else, can find grace in God's eyes. Noah was just, perfect in the idea of complete, and he walked with God.

What does it mean to be just? Habakkuk 2:4 tells us, "The just shall live by his faith." Noah lived by faith in Holy God. What does it mean to be perfect or complete? He was upright. He lived correctly in an incorrect world. He lived to the divine standard because he lived by faith. What does it mean to walk with God? He actively chose to be with God. He ordered his life and his lifestyle around God.

Do you live by faith? Does obedience to God's work, God's Word, and God's will flow from your life? Do you live by God's divine standard? Are you upright? Do you actively organize your life around God, or do you try to fit God in when it is a convenient time? Have you found grace in God's eyes?

Prayer and Praise:

Lord, I praise You for Your grace. I praise You for allowing me the gift of faith that I can place in You. I praise You for the enablement of grace to live upright in a world that is not upright. Father, every day, let me adjust my life to Your schedule. Let me organize my life around You. Use me for Your honor and glory. Let my life reflect You just as Noah's life did. In the mighty name of Jesus Christ, my Lord. Amen.

GOD SHUT HIM IN
Genesis 7:16

A preacher was preaching on Noah's Ark. When he got to the sixteenth verse of Genesis 7, the preacher paraphrased and said, "And God shut the door." To illustrate this, the preacher went to a side door, opened it, and stepped outside. He slammed the door shut after him. To his surprise the door locked and he was stuck outside. The preacher ran around the building and came in the front door and says, "But when God shuts the door, there will be no other door to come in through."

In Genesis 6:3, you are told, "My Spirit shall not strive with man forever." From this you understand that time will run out for a person to come to Christ. Time can run out for a person to get right with God. You must be careful not to waste your time, to squander your time, or to live frivolously. When Jesus Christ, by the Holy Spirit, brings conviction of sin to a person's life, that is God inviting that person to be saved. That is what the Bible teaches us in John 6:44, "No one can come to Me (Christ) unless the Father who sent Me draws him."

You live in a society that thinks a person can come to Christ any time he or she wants to. This is not consistent with the Word of God. A person can only come to Christ when God invites him or her by conviction of sin and unrighteousness. To ignore the convicting of God's Holy Spirit is to risk having the door of heaven closed for all eternity. God chooses the time of one's salvation, not man. Be careful with the time you have. Respond to God when He draws you.

These verses also show us how God "shuts in" His people. When God shut the door on the ark He was shutting His people in from the destruction of the storm. Getting in the ark was not a spur of the moment decision. Noah and his family had spent 120 years building the ark and preparing for the storm. Because Noah lived a life of daily obedience, he was ready when the storm came. Are you?

Noah and his family sailed in the ark safely while the storm raged outside. Make no mistake, they faced the storm, but they were safe as they abided in the ark. I am glad God so loves me that He has provided a shelter in the storms of life. The wind blows, the rain falls, and the lightening may strike, but as long as you abide in Christ, you have been "shut in" for God's glory. The ship may toss and take on water, but our heavenly Father has it in His care.

Prayer and Praise:

Lord, I thank You for loving me so much You shut me in unto Your care. I praise You in the storms of life because You are my God and You are in control. As Noah obeyed You in the building and the boarding of the ark, let me obey You in the routine of life. I exalt You. In the Mighty name of Jesus Christ, my Lord. Amen.

THE CALL OF GOD
Genesis 12:1-2

How was it possible for a man who was raised in pagan darkness to come to faith in God, and no one witnessed to him? You are told in Romans, if there is no verbal witness, everyone is still responsible to respond to God because creation testifies to God's glory. God spoke to Abram and called him to Himself without a human witness, and Abram responded to the call of God.

God told Abram to arise and leave his home and homeland and go to a place He would show him. Upon hearing God speak, Abram obeyed God, he responded. God told Abram that He would make him a great nation and bless him. God would bless those that bless Abram and curse those that cursed Abram. In Abram, all the families on the earth would be blessed. In this we see the purpose of God. All people are to know Him as God and Father and to remake that which has been marred by sin.

You are so blessed. You not only have men who preach and teach God's Word. You also have individual believers willing to share their faith in Christ so others can hear. You have missionaries, pastors, evangelists and regular believers who witness of Christ. It is comforting to know that God comes to you. He cares so much for you and loves you that He witnesses of Himself to you.

When God speaks to you, do you rise in obedience to all that He says? Do you adjust your life to God's Word, work, and will? Failing to respond to God's call creates the capacity for you to mess up your life for years to come.

It was only as Abram obeyed that he could know the blessing of God on his life. It is only as you obey God that you can experience God's best and blessing in your life. As Abram obeyed God, he entered into the purpose of God. I am thankful God gives our lives meaning and purpose beyond the ordinary things of life as we obey God.

Prayer and Praise:

Lord, I praise You for calling me just as You did Abram. I thank You for giving me direction one step at a time, and I thank you for the purpose You give my life. Continue to speak to me and guide me. When I hesitate to obey you quickly, speak stronger to me. I love You. In the mighty name of Jesus Christ, my Lord. Amen.

ESTABLISHING COVENANT
Genesis 15:9-18

In Genesis 15, God and Abram entered into covenant. A covenant is a binding agreement between two parties. When a couple marries, they enter a covenant, but sadly many do not take it seriously. A covenant is costly.

When Abram entered this covenant with Almighty God, we find sacrifice, blood, death, even horror and great darkness as Abram fell asleep. In verse thirteen, God foretold Abram of Israel's Egyptian captivity. In verses seventeen and eighteen we read, "It came to pass when the sun went down and it was dark, that behold, there appeared a smoking oven and a burning torch that passed between those pieces. On the same day the Lord made a covenant with Abram." A covenant is cut, a covenant is binding, and this covenant is permanent. The covenant allowed Abram to receive revelation knowledge.

When you came to faith in Jesus Christ, you entered a covenant relationship with the triune God. There was sacrifice, blood, death, horrors and darkness, but thanks be to God, He initiated and established covenant with you. Because of your relationship with Christ, you also can have revelation knowledge of God's Word. The key to revelation knowledge is abiding in Christ. You have been sealed and are secure in Christ. It is your responsibility to remain in Christ and not follow your own will or way. Failure to adjust one's life daily to Christ and the Word of God, causes a lack of revelation. Without revelation from God, you will not know what to be about and you will fail.

If you fall, get back up and return to Christ quickly. Come back to Christ confessing your sin, seeking fresh cleansing from the Father, and asking Him to once again fill you with His Holy Spirit so you can abide in Him.

Jesus Christ paid it all so that you can know Him in intimacy. Realize the covenant you are in with Christ—it cost Christ His life. Please do not take that for granted.

Prayer and Praise:

Lord, I exalt You. You are my shield and my exceedingly great reward. Teach me how to abide in You. Continue to show me how costly and important covenant is with You. Use me, speak to me, let me have revelation knowledge so I can serve You faithfully to the very end. In the mighty name of Jesus Christ, my Lord. Amen.

INTERCESSION
Genesis 18:16-33

In Genesis 18 we find the story of God's preparing to destroy Sodom and Gomorrah. Verse seventeen says, "And the Lord said, 'Shall I hide from Abraham what I am doing?'" God told Abraham His plan to destroy these cities because their sin was very great. We are told that Abraham stood before the Lord (v. 22). Abraham interceded on behalf of the righteous people that might live in these cities.

To intercede on behalf of another means to pray with an earnestness and intensity of the request. It means to plead on behalf of one in difficulty or trouble. Have you ever interceded for someone with such earnestness? Have you interceded for your community and country?

As Abraham interceded with God, he asked God questions. He asked God if He would spare these cities for fifty righteous people. Sodom and Gomorrah was made up of five cities and the population has been estimated from six hundred to twelve hundred people. God agreed. Then Abraham went all the way down to forty-five, and then forty, then down to ten righteous people. God said He would not destroy the cities for even ten righteous people.

Abraham was interceding based on the righteousness of the people, and God was honoring his intercession. However, they could not find even ten righteous people to stop the judgment of God from falling. Have you ever thought of how many truly righteous people it takes to stay God's hand of judgment in your town? Have you ever considered that your community may not be experiencing the judgment of God because of the righteousness of a few?

If there were twelve hundred people in these cities, ten is around one percent. One percent can impact an entire town. Sadly, they could not find one percent in Sodom and Gomorrah. Was Abraham's intercession in vain? No. Intercession is as much about pleading in the presence of God as it is about the answer. When you intercede, you are sharing the burden of God. Do you know the burden of God?

Prayer and Praise:

Lord, as Abraham came before You, as You shared Your burden with him, let me come before You knowing Your burden for my community. O Father, let men and women pursue righteousness. Let men and women understand the importance of living in Your righteousness. I pray, Father, that even as You preserved Lot, You will preserve others who are righteous in the day of Your judgment. In the mighty name of Jesus Christ, my Lord, Amen.

THE DANGER OF LINGERING
Genesis 19:12-24

Have you ever known God's will, yet you did not hurry to fulfill it? Have you ever heard God speak a command to your heart and you waited to obey? To presume on the mercy and grace of God is a dangerous thing. It can be very costly.

When Lot was warned by two angels of the destruction of his town, he lingered. The word lingered means that he hesitated. He delayed doing what he was told to do. His life, his family—all were in jeopardy—and Lot hesitated to obey God. What would cause a person to linger in a time of danger, in a time of urgency? The pull of the world had overtaken Lot. Lot had pitched his tent toward Sodom (Genesis 13:12); however, he ended up living in Sodom (Genesis 14:12). Be very careful what you position yourself toward in life. Finally, Lot was sitting in the gate of Sodom (Genesis 19:1), a place of leadership for a community.

Lot simply wanted the good life. He wanted the best for his family, and the lights of the city of Sodom seduced him slowly to the place where he became a part of Sodom. Are there things in your life that compromise you with the world? When God speaks because of these things, it is easy to ignore the voice of God and resist the Word of God.

How do you know if you are lingering in the wrong place? When God's Word is preached, taught, or read, and it challenges something in your life, if you refuse the Word of God, you are lingering. Lingering can be costly.

Lot, his wife, and two daughters had to be grabbed by the hands and led out of Sodom by angels. You may not be as fortunate. As Christians, we have the indwelling Holy Spirit to prompt us and lead us, but have to yield daily to the Spirit in order to be so directed.

It is so easy to get accustomed to this world and the things of the world. It would be better never acquiring so many things in life, knowing they will rival our faith in Christ. Be very careful what you give yourself to.

Prayer and Praise:

Lord, show me anything I allow to rival my faith, my love, and my devotion for You. Let me be careful to examine my life as to what will cause me to lose my focus on You. Long before I make a move toward the world, bring a strong rebuke to my heart and soul. Oh Father, let me not be impressed by the world but keep me close and clean before You. In the mighty name of Jesus Christ, my Lord I pray. Amen.

GOD'S TESTING
Genesis 22:1-14

How are you at taking tests? In school you had tests over material that had been taught. The tests were to see if you learned the lessons. God also gives tests. God gives tests not to defeat us or hurt us, but to prove us and to further build us in faith and His Word. Tests come to see if we have learned how to live by faith.

Genesis 22 begins with these words, "Now it came to pass after these things...." After what things? After times of faithfulness to the Lord. Abraham was not tested because he was unfaithful, but because he was faithful to the Lord.

When God called Abraham to offer Isaac as a sacrifice, Abraham obeyed. Is that not amazing? Abraham rose up early, heading out in obedience to God's Word. There was no discussion or hesitation. When Abraham left his servants in verse five, he told them, "Stay here with the donkey; the lad and I will go yonder and worship, and we will come back to you." The phrase, "we will come back to you," is a statement of faith. Do you have such faith? This kind of faith only comes through testing and tough times.

How does a believer come through this type of testing? We need to note that this type of test came closer to the end of Abraham's life and not at the beginning. Testing seems to be progressive for the believer. We will never come to the place where we do not have testing of our faith.

First, expect testing times. Do not be surprised when they come. Secondly, you must love the Lord supremely. Love is a matter of your will, not an emotion or feeling. Without loving God supremely, we will fail. Third, exercise a steadfast faith. Abraham said with confidence, "We will come again." Then he took the wood, the knife, and Isaac, leaving nothing behind. There would be no excuses or delays.

Finally, recognize the spiritual potential of testing times. As Abraham offered Isaac, his focus was completely on God. So often, you make mistakes and sin because your focus is on self. Abraham teaches you to focus on God's promises and not an explanation. Focus on God's power and not human resources. Focus on God's purpose and not personal desires.

Prayer and Praise:

Lord, I thank You that You know what is best for me and You have not left me to my own ideas and plans. Thank You for testing times that are intended to build my faith and increase my love, confidence, and my devotion to You. Enable me to be found faithful. As Abraham left nothing behind, let me leave nothing behind as I walk in obedience to Your Word. Teach daily how to die to self and live in obedience to You. In the mighty name of Jesus Christ, my Lord I pray. Amen.

BUILD YOUR ALTAR
Genesis 26:25

"So he built an altar there and called on the name of the Lord, and he pitched his tent there; and there Isaac's servants dug a well" (Genesis 26:25). Everyone needs to mark this verse in your Bible because many people do the exact opposite. Most people build their tents and pitch their altar. They have their priorities backwards. Remember, this is not all there is to life; you are just passing through. In the process of passing through life, you will have to make decisions. These decisions will affect you and your family, even your grandchildren.

The Bible says Isaac built an altar, and he pitched his tent. The altar is priority. The altar is eternal. The altar is what will last for you and your family forever as you get and stay connected to your eternal Father.

It is so easy to do the opposite. You build your tents, and then you try and pitch your altar. A tent implies temporary housing as you are just passing through. There is nothing wrong with a nice tent. However, you must be sure you do not pitch your altar and build your tent.

The last part of the verse says, "Isaac's servants dug a well." How does this apply to you? Here are the essentials of life: an altar, a tent, and a well. As you build your altar to God with priority and you pitch your tent as you pass through life, you also dig wells of water. How did Isaac know to dig a well? His daddy had dug a well (Genesis 21:30). Dads, teach your children by example how to dig wells of refreshment.

Can you imagine watching your father pray and receiving a fresh word from God, following God, and handling the crises of life by trusting God? Isaac saw his dad in crisis, and Isaac learned from his dad how to build an altar, how to pitch his tent, and how to dig a well. What are you teaching your children and grandchildren?

Prayer and Praise:

Lord, You are my God. You have allowed me to build an altar and to pitch my tent. Please do not let me get confused in this. It is so easy to get caught up in living that I fail to maintain the altar. Help me to recognize the teachable moments in life for my children, even when they are grown. Let me provide wells of refreshing to future generations. I praise You for Your love, direction, and provision. In the mighty name of Jesus Christ, my Lord, Amen.

THE AWESOME PRESENCE OF GOD
Genesis 28:17

The word awesome means dreadful, terrible, awful, great and fearsome. Jacob was in the presence of God, the manifest presence of God, and Jacob was overwhelmed. The place became known as Bethel, the House of God.

In Daniel, we find Daniel was terrified by that awful, dreadful, awesome presence, and he said, "I prayed to the Lord my God...the great and awesome God..." (Daniel 9:4). In Isaiah 8:13, you read, "The Lord of hosts, Him you shall hallow; let Him be your fear, and let Him be your dread." The Hebrew word for fear is "reverence." He is telling you to let God grip your heart with His terrible holiness.

You have become so familiar with God and that he is a loving Father who calls you to come boldly before the throne of grace. You have made God like one of yourself. You have made Him to be a man of flesh and bone. But God is Spirit, He is high and holy. Yes, He is good, loving, and kind. But He is not one like us. We must recognize Him as holy.

John, on the Isle of Patmos, was the one who leaned his head on the breast of Jesus Christ, but now, when Jesus appeared He had fire in His eyes and a sword coming out of His mouth. His countenance shone and John fell on his face as a dead man (Revelation 1:14-17). No one would be able to stand in His presence.

I pray that you are seeking the manifest presence of God in your life, your home, and your church. Oh, that God's presence would come down in such a way that the church and the Christian would experience conviction of the sins of his life, sins such as slothfulness and irreverence. Just as Jacob had fear and a holy dread because he was in the place of God, so should we.

Prayer and Praise:

Lord, You are my God and I praise You for Your majesty and glory. Keep me ever aware that You are God and I am not. Keep me ever aware that Your ways are not my ways and Your thoughts are not my thoughts. Keep me aware of Your holiness and righteousness. Father, as I approach You, let me have a reverence for You. You are my God and I bow before You. In the mighty name of Jesus Christ, my Lord, Amen.

SUBSTITUTES FOR PRAYER
Genesis 32:1-11

Is prayer your first priority or your last resort? Oftentimes when a believer goes through trials, challenges, and difficulties, he tries a lot of things. He will ask advice of friends and family. He will resolve to do better. He may even become more involved in church or a ministry. Why does he not pray? If you asked him he would say, "Oh, I have prayed about it." So why does he keep struggling and planning to fix the situation?

Prayer is more than telling God what you want and when you want it. Prayer is more than telling God what you are going to do. Prayer is humbling oneself and seeking God. You seek His face, His will, or you tell Him what your plans are, expecting Him to bless them. It appears many have tried to turn prayer into a magic formula, but it does not work that way.

In our passage, Jacob has left his father-in-law Laban's house and herds, slipping away in the night to get a head start before Laban came after him. After Laban caught up with him and a treaty was agreed upon, Jacob and all his family and possessions go on their way. We are told he was met by angels of God, and he named the place Mahanaim, or "double camp." The place was the camp of the angels and the camp of the people.

In the first eleven verses of Genesis 32, we see five substitutes Jacob makes for prayer: 1) knowledge is a substitute for prayer. Jacob was going in "his way" (v. 1); he believed he had knowledge to do the best thing, but he did not pray; 2) next, Jacob resorted to numbers (v. 3). He sends "messengers before him to Esau." He felt numbers would impress his offended brother, but he did not pray. 3) Jacob sent Esau riches (v. 5); he sent him a large number of animals; riches would not win over an offended brother, yet he did not pray; 4) Jacob organized (v. 4, 7); he divided the people and the flocks, but he did not pray. 5) Jacob finally prayed (v. 9-11).

When you are facing a situation or a challenge, how long does it take before you pray? What do you do first before calling out to God for help, grace, and direction? Have you learned to be still in the presence of God and wait? Prayer is not to be our last resort, but rather our first response to any situation in life. Prayer takes time. Prayer is not a one-sided conversation where you do all the talking. You have to learn to be still and listen. You have to learn to be in the Word of God. Do not make substitutes for prayer.

Prayer and Praise:

Lord, You are my God. You are not my errand boy or my magic genie. You are my God and I am Your servant. Enable me to realize the necessity of being still before You and listening to You. You are under no obligation to bless my plans or my best efforts. Help me be like the psalmist as he tells us, "Be still and know that I am God." (Psalm 46:10). Thank You, I praise you in the mighty name of Jesus Christ, my Lord. Amen.

GOING BACK
Genesis 35:1

In Genesis 28, as Jacob was on his way going to his uncle Laban's home, he camped in a place that was ultimately named Bethel. The word Bethel means "house of God." This was the place the ladder came down from heaven and God made promises to Jacob. At Bethel, Jacob was experiencing God, the promises of God, the blessings of God. In chapter twenty-nine, verse one Jacob went on his journey, on to Laban's house.

The question we must ask is, why did Jacob leave the presence of God? We find no command for him to go, we find no indication that God sent him on his way. Why did Jacob leave the House of God, El Bethel?

So many times in life we get headstrong in a direction and we ignore, we leave, we pursue our own wants and desires more than God. Without a word from God we "go on our journey." We try to maintain a relationship with the Father, but we have moved away from intimacy with Him. That is how we find Jacob in this passage.

Nearly thirty years had passed since this first encounter, and now God gave a specific and direct command to Jacob. "And God said to Jacob, 'Arise, go up to Bethel and dwell there; and make there an altar unto God'."

The subtleness of sin impacts one greatly. The way back to God is always the same. The point of departure is the point of return. Going back requires acknowledgment that you have left the place of God. Going back requires putting away functioning idols that you have picked up along the way. Going back to God requires purification from sin.

What is it going to take for you to get back to God's presence? Do you recognize your point of departure? Do you know when it was that your walk with God began to cool down and you began going through the religious motions and routines? Do you know when it was that other things became more important to you than God?

If you will ask, God will tell you when, how, and why you "went on your journey." God longs to restore and forgive. God longs to receive you back into fellowship. Will you respond to God?

Prayer and Praise:

Lord, You are God and God alone. You call me back when I go astray. Help me obey quickly. Lead me, Father, back to Your presence. Lead me back to vital spiritual union with You. Just as Jacob received Your Word, let me receive it also in obedient faith. In the mighty name of Jesus Christ, my Lord, Amen.

THE BLOODY COAT
Genesis 37:31-35

Have you ever been told a word from someone and it hurt your feelings? Someone tells you something and you believe it. For weeks, months, even years you believe what you have been told. Finally, you discover none of it was true. That is a "bloody coat."

The story of Joseph is familiar to most Christians. It is the story of how Jacob played favorites with his sons, and he gave Joseph a coat of many colors. He would then send Joseph out to check up on his brothers, and they hated Joseph for that. God then gave Joseph dreams, and Joseph shared his dreams with his brothers and his parents. Dreams that said, one day I will rule over you all and you will bow down before me. Guess what? Nobody was impressed with Joseph's God-given dreams.

The brothers so hated Joseph, when he came to check up on them, they plotted to kill him. They put him in a pit and planned their scheme. In God's amazing providence, a caravan of Ishmaelite traders came by, and they sold Joseph to them and Joseph was taken to Egypt.

The brothers killed a goat, put the goat's blood on Joseph's coat, and proceeded to let their father believe a lie as they laid the bloody coat in Jacob's lap. The brothers asked, "Is this Joseph's coat?" Jacob presumed the worst, Joseph was dead. He spent the next twenty-two years grieving, sorrowing, all because he made an assumption, all because he was led to believe a lie, all because he made a wrong presumption. .

Has someone laid a bloody coat in your lap? You have heard things, even seen some things when you think "how could it not be true?" The Devil has many bloody coats that he wants to lay in your lap. He wants to get you to grieve and be sorrowful, to be consumed with a lie.

That is why we are commanded in the Scriptures about "bringing every thought into captivity to the obedience of Christ" (2 Corinthians 10:5). Are there any bloody coats you are hanging on to? It is time to lay them down. Maybe you have placed a few bloody coats in someone's lap. It is time to make things right.

Prayer and Praise:

Lord, I thank You for giving me Your Word. Oh Father, expose any bloody coats I have received and let me be free in You. Show me any bloody coats I have placed on others and help me remove them. Do not let me waste weeks, months, or even years assuming wrongly and being in sorrow. Let me know Your deliverance. In the mighty name of Jesus Christ, my Lord. Amen.

WHEN PEOPLE FORGET YOU
Genesis 40:21-23

Have you ever thought, If I only knew the right person that would help me in my situation. It could help me get the job, the promotion, the advancement. If I only had the right connection. If that is how you think, be very careful. Hoping that people will help you advance can be very dangerous because it breeds "living in the flesh," and by the world's standards, and not living by faith in Almighty, Omniscient God.

Joseph was in a pharaoh's prison for a crime he did not commit. He was in a situation not pleasant or enjoyable in the eyes of man. However, Joseph was exactly where God wanted him for this time of his life. God was with him. You must never forget God will never leave you or forsake you if you are His child.

While in prison, Joseph was used to interpret the dreams of the imprisoned butler and the baker of the Pharaoh. Even in a less than perfect situation, Joseph used his gifting to help others. Joseph told them the butler was restored to his position and the baker would be executed. The butler promised Joseph he would remember him, he would help him as soon as he got restored. However, he forgot Joseph.

People will let you down and disappoint you, but our hope and faith is not in people, it is in our Lord and Savior, Jesus Christ. Listen to Psalm 105:16-20,

Moreover He called for a famine in the land; He destroyed all the provision of bread. He sent a man before them—Joseph—who was sold as a slave. They hurt his feet with fetters, He was laid in irons. Until the time that his word came to pass, the word of the Lord tested him. The king sent and released him, the ruler of the people let him go free.

The word of the Lord tested Joseph. It tried his faith, and when the word of God had completed its work in Joseph's life for this time period, God brought Joseph out. God did more for Joseph than any man could have ever accomplished. You have to trust God's Word (the Bible) and God's timing. Even when people forget you, God knows exactly where you are and how and when to bring you out.

Prayer and Praise:

Lord, thank You for knowing everything about me. You know where I am and what I need. You have it all under control. As I wait for Your timing and Your Word to complete its work in me, give me strong confidence in You. Let me be found faithful, just as Joseph was, using the gifts you have given me to point others to Christ. In the mighty name of Jesus Christ, my Lord. Amen.

WHEN HE SAW THE CARTS
Genesis 45:27-28

One of the names of God we discover in Scripture is Jehovah Jirah, which means "the Lord our provider." We first are introduced to that name in Genesis 22:14, in the story of Abraham offering Isaac on Mount Moriah. Just as he began to drop the knife, God stopped him and a ram was provided. Abraham called the name of the place Jehovah Jirah, The-Lord-Will-Provide.

It is a challenge at times to wait for the Lord's provision. It requires faith, trust, confidence, and obedience to the Word of God. Our flesh, the world, and the Devil scream in our ear, "You'd better deal with it yourself. God is not going to provide this time." If we listen to the voice of doubt, wherever it comes from, it costs us our faith being real and active.

When Joseph revealed himself to his brothers, he told them he would provide for them and for them to go and get his father. Joseph told them not to be concerned about bringing their things; he would provide for them all they needed. He sent wagons loaded with supplies and good things.

When they returned to Canaan and told their father Jacob that his beloved son was alive and he was governor over all of Egypt, Jacob did not believe. "And Jacob's heart stood still, because he did not believe them (Genesis 45:26)." It is a terrible thing not to believe the word of God.

Jacob did not believe. Why? Years ago a bloody coat was laid in his lap, and he assumed a lie was the truth. He should have clung to the word of God that Joseph had spoken when he told him his God-given dreams. Genesis 37:11 tells us after he shared the dreams, "his father kept the matter in mind." After twenty years of believing a lie, he had a difficult time believing the truth.

"When he saw the wagons (carts) which Joseph had sent to carry him, the spirit of Jacob their father revived. Then Israel said, 'It is enough. Joseph my son is still alive. I will go and see him before I die'" (Genesis 45:27-28).

When he saw the wagons, when he saw the provision of the king, when he saw the bountiful supplies, his heart revived. Oftentimes God sends provisions and it seems they are ignored, yet they are from God. God gives you a word, and the farther away you get from seeing it come to fruition, the more difficult it is to hang on to. Oh, that God would allow you to have eyes of faith to see the wagons when they are sent for you.

Prayer and Praise:

Lord, You are my provider. You are Jehovah Jirah, and I thank You. Father, let Your Word ever be present in my mind. Thank You for Your grace and mercy. Thank You for the wagons of benefits You supply. In the mighty name of Jesus Christ, my Lord. Amen.

WHEN GOD SPEAKS
Genesis 46:2

Have you ever heard God speak to you? If you are a Christian, you have had to have heard God speak to you. God had to speak to you in order for you to be saved. No one can come to God apart from the Holy Spirit's drawing him. "No one can come to Me (Jesus) unless the Father who sent Me draws him" (John 6:44).

Hearing God speak to you personally is crucial if you are to live a life of faith in Jesus Christ and glorify God. The purpose you are here for is to glorify God. You are not here to make a name for yourself or to establish a great business or ministry, though God may use these things. You exist to glorify Holy God.

Jesus said in John 10:27, "My sheep hear My voice, and I know them, and they follow Me." If you have trouble hearing God's voice, you are in trouble at the very heart of your faith. If you are not hearing God speak, you must ask yourself, why is God not speaking to me? Is there sin in my life? Am I doing the last thing God told me to do? Is the stewardship of my life in agreement with the Word of God? Am I holding bitterness and unforgiveness in my heart toward someone? Am I living in agreement with Scripture? Am I in a season of waiting upon the Lord? Have I taken things into my power to fix certain issues?

Hearing God speak is crucial. God still speaks to His children. He speaks primarily through His Word. Is there any area in which you are violating God's Word? He speaks by the Holy Spirit. The Holy Spirit impresses the Word of truth in our lives. What was the last thing God told you? Have you obeyed that Word? Are you still obeying that Word?

In this passage God spoke to Israel, and Israel responded immediately to God's voice (Genesis 46:2). When God speaks, He expects an immediate response of obedience from you. Do you respond immediately to the Word of God and the voice of God? Jacob responded, and God continued to speak to him. God assured Jacob, and God gave a promise to Jacob. Jacob obeyed God, having full confidence in God.

When you hear God speak, God gives revelation and His Word builds your faith, so that you can live with full confidence in God. If you refuse God's voice or ignore God's Word, your faith will suffer. The Bible tells us, "Whatever is not from faith is sin" (Romans 14:23).

Prayer and Praise:

Lord, thank You for speaking to me. Thank You for Your precious Word and Your Holy Spirit. Let me be attentive to Your Word and not ignore it, put it off, or refuse it. Move in my heart with strong conviction if I fail to heed Your Word. Oh Father, Your Word is precious, it is life giving. In the mighty name of Jesus Christ, my Lord. Amen.

REUBEN
Genesis 49:3-4

Last words are important. Standing at the bedside of a loved one who will soon pass on into eternity, you listen intently for any last word. You want to know their wishes and what they may be seeing, experiencing, or anticipating.

A Christian man, many years ago, told me that he had asked his dying wife to tell him what she saw, if she was able, right before she died. As she lay in a coma for a week and the time drew short for her to pass into eternity with Christ, it looked as if she would not be able to tell him what she saw. The man said right before she breathed her last breath, "her eyes opened wide and she extended her arms and hands toward heaven and she went to be with her Lord Jesus Christ." Without a word being spoken, she told him what she saw. Amen.

In this passage of Scripture, Jacob was giving his last words. He was coming to the end of his life, and the final words that he uttered may be the best words he ever spoke. The imposter was now inspired. The cheater was now the convincer. The player was now a prophet. On his death bed, he spoke to bless his sons. Even though Jacob was blind, he saw more clearly than he ever had.

Reuben was his firstborn. He was a man who had everything, but ended up with nothing. He was a man with a guilty secret. Reuben had unconfessed sin. Reuben had slept with his father's wife, Bildad, and he thought no one knew. Now it was exposed for all to see.

Jacob told Reuben, "You are ... unstable as water, you shall not excel (Genesis 49:4)." Water is a wonderful thing, but it is not stable. Water has no foundation. You spill it and you cannot recover it; it will evaporate and disappear. Jacob was telling Reuben he was unstable, lacked character, lacked courage, and lacked conviction.

Many people are like that. They say one thing and do another. You cannot rely on them. Is that your character? Oftentimes we think and act as if this life is all there is, but it is not. Jesus Christ will have the last word as we each stand before the judgment seat of Christ. What will He say of you? Is there any unconfessed sin in your life? Maybe it was twenty or more years ago. Maybe you think it is no big deal and nobody knows. Jesus Christ knows and sin is a big deal. It was because of your sin Jesus died on the cross. Get honest with God and deal with your sin.

Prayer and Praise:

Lord, I thank You for dying on the cross and shedding Your blood to atone for my sin. Father, I ask You to bring to my mind any sin that I have not dealt with in honest confession. Wash me anew and cleanse me afresh with the blood of Christ. In the mighty name of Jesus Christ, my Lord. Amen.

THE BURNING BUSH
Exodus 3:2-4

Moses had a miraculous intervention in his life as a child. He was born a Hebrew slave, but raised in the palace of the pharaoh. When he came to age or maturity of understanding, he chose the suffering of the people of God and the cause of Christ (Hebrews 11:25-26). By faith, he left Egypt and went to the backside of the desert. Moses spent forty years in Egypt and then the next forty years in the desert.

After forty years in the desert, Moses heard God speak to him through the burning bush. The bush was burned with fire but not consumed, and Moses stopped and turned aside to see this amazing sight. The Bible tells us, "So when the Lord saw that he turned aside to look, God called to him from the midst of the bush and said, 'Moses, Moses!' And he said 'Here am I.'"

What does it take for you to get still so God can speak to you? What is required of you to get away from the distractions of the world and everyday life so you are in a position to hear God? Every day we make choices. Someone said we make a minimum of five thousand choices every day. Many of these are trivial, but many of these will determine your life's direction.

Each day you choose if you will spend time in the Word of God and prayer. If you do not make this a priority, it will soon vanish away. Good intentions mean nothing. Typically, you get up in the morning and you are rushed. Maybe you stayed up late and have overslept. Maybe you were up several times in the night for babies crying, sick children, or a host of other things, but you fail to get up early enough to spend time alone with God.

When you arrive home, you are weary and all you want to do is sit down and relax. Your mind is exhausted, and you have too many chores to do, so you do not get alone with God. I have been there, and it is easy to overextend your time and energy and not have a time alone with God that is meaningful. It is easy to let a week go by and you have missed your daily quite time.

Your daily quiet time with God must be just that, daily—you need a set time and a set place to get alone with God. This is not a luxury; this is a necessity for a Christian to walk with God. When you fail to walk with God, it can cost you.

Do not miss the moment when God calls your name. Do not let trivial activities rob you of the joy of your salvation and your divine purpose in life.

Prayer and Praise:

Lord, just as You called Moses by name, let me hear You when You speak my name. Let me respond to You. Let me hear Your voice when You speak. In the mighty name of Jesus Christ, my Lord. Amen.

WHEN THINGS GET WORSE
Exodus 5:17-21

Have you ever found yourself in a situation where you have been obeying God and a difficult situation results from your obedience? Have you discovered that in the Christian life you can abide in Christ, while obeying God with the stewardship of your life, things can still go wrong? Have you lived long enough to realize that obedience to Christ is not a guaranteed blanket of protection from difficulty or adversity?

In this passage we find Moses obeying the will of God. He goes back to Egypt and faithfully delivers God's message to his Israelite brothers and to Pharaoh. We are even told the Israelites believed the word from God that Moses told them (Exodus 4:31). After Moses told God's Word to Pharaoh, Pharaoh told the Egyptian taskmasters not to give the Israelites straw for making their quota of bricks. Yet, they were to have the same quota, but now they had to gather their own straw.

God's children were beaten by the taskmasters because they were not meeting the brick quota. When they met Moses and Aaron, they were not pleased with them, and they complained to Moses. Things had gotten worse. Things had gotten worse because Moses obeyed God.

What do you do when your obedience allows for things to get worse? Do you grumble? Complain? Do you stop obeying God's Word? How do you react to the difficulties that come because you obey God?

You must do as Moses did; he returned to the Lord and he prayed (Exodus 5:22-23). Moses asked God why. There is nothing wrong with asking God why, as long as you do not ask God with an accusative voice or tone. You can ask God questioningly why, but only with a submissive attitude to His will. Moses asked why, and God answered him (Exodus 6:1).

When you pray, have you learned to listen for what God has to say? God told Moses His purpose, and Moses continued in the path of obedience. Oh that you would continue in the path of obedience, even when things get worse.

Prayer and Praise:

Lord, You are my God and I want to obey You regardless of the cost. I want to obey even when misunderstood by Your own people. I want to obey You, no matter what. I ask You to teach me to bring my questions and concerns to You and to listen to Your response. In the mighty name of Jesus Christ, my Lord. Amen.

HARDNESS OF HEART
Exodus 7:3, 8:15

It is baffling how the sun can be so hot that it bakes a dry river bed and mud turns to into solid masses of dirt. Yet that same sun beating down on a tub of butter melts it to liquid. Why is that? It is because of the makeup of the material being exposed to the sun's heat. It is the same way with a person's heart. People can sit in the same service, hear the same message from God's Word, and one leave hardened and indifferent, while another person completely melted or broken before God.

Exodus 7:3 reads, "I will harden Pharaoh's heart." That was God speaking. When Moses came to Pharaoh with the words of God, Pharaoh resisted and refused to yield. Then in Exodus 8:15 you find, "He hardened his heart." That was in reference to Pharaoh. Is this a contradiction? No.

When God hardened Pharaoh's heart, it was for a greater purpose to be revealed. God was going to expose the false gods of Egypt. In doing so, all of Egypt would recognize the greatness and the supremacy of Almighty God.

As the plagues continued, Pharaoh hardened his own heart as he resisted the word and the work of God. When a person refuses or resists God's Word, and the convicting power of the Holy Spirit is ignored, that person's heart grows hard. Having a hard heart toward God and the things of God is a dangerous position to be in.

Has God spoken to you about any area of your life and you have refused submission to God? If so, your heart is hardened. You can still go to church, read your Bible, and pray, but you have allowed a callous to cover your heart, and now you are less sensitive to the Holy Spirit and the Word of God.

How do you overcome this? The point of departure is the point of return. You have to go back to the time, the issue that God spoke to you about and deal with that specific sin. You have to surrender to God everything He has spoken to you. If you refuse, the callous continues to grow on your heart and life.

Prayer and Praise:

Lord, show me again any area I have ignored when You spoke to me. Move again with strong conviction and let Your Word penetrate my life so I can respond in faith and obedience to You. Father, I do not want to just feel better because I have had an emotional release of tears. Oh God, I want to be clean and right with You, my sins cleansed and forgiven. Speak to me again and I will adjust my life to You. In the mighty name of Jesus Christ, my Lord. Amen.

WHEN GOD EXPOSES FALSE GODS
Exodus 11:1-10

Today's society is filled with false gods, many of which are worshiped every day as people give them their time, their talents, and their attention. They are functioning idols, things you cherish that give a sense of fulfillment, things you make priority in your life, but they rival your relationship with Jesus Christ. It robs you of time spent in the Word of God studying and memorizing. It robs you of time spent bending in prayer before Almighty God. Yet, it is so easy to be caught up in these things and not even recognize it. False gods are still among us, and they seem to meet a need in one's life. They are very subtle and deceptive.

When Moses came to Pharaoh asking him to let God's people go so they could worship and serve the living God, Pharaoh refused, mocking the God of Israel. God began to send plagues upon Egypt. These plagues were not just terrible things, but each plague was an attack on an Egyptian god. The plagues were aimed at the gods of Egypt.

When God sent all these plagues, He completely wiped out the confidence of the Egyptians in their false gods. What is it you place before God? What will God have to send to destroy your confidence in those functioning idols?

Prayer and Praise:

Lord, thank You for being the true and living God. Thank You for sending Jesus Christ, Your only Son, to die for me and make a way possible that I can know You as Lord of my life. Show me anything I have in my life that rivals Your position as my God. Show me any person, pastime, or pleasure I need to forsake. In the mighty name of Jesus Christ, my Lord. Amen.

THE LORD LEADS YOU THE LONG WAY
Exodus 13:17-22

You live in an age and a society that wants instant everything. You want instant breakfast, instant success, instant ability to perform, and even instant spiritual maturity. You do not have to live very long to realize that most things do not come overnight or easily. You can grow a mushroom overnight, but it takes years and years for an oak tree to grow and develop.

Even in your walk with Christ, you find yourself wanting to do "something" and be instantly spiritually mature. That is one of the dangers of some groups of believers. They give the impression and idea if you have a certain experience, you are instantly spiritually mature. That is not true. Sanctification is a progressive work of the Holy Spirit in your life, and it takes years and years, and even then, you will never arrive to the place where you are finished maturing this side of heaven

In the passage you read for today, you find God leading the children of Israel the long way. In Exodus 13:17, you are told, "God did not lead them by the way of the land of the Philistines, although that way was near." Why not go the shortest route, taking the closest way? Because God always has your good in mind, and He will do nothing to compromise you. The shortest route was through the land of the Philistines, Israel's enemy. If they went this direction and they faced a physical conflict with these people, the Israelites could "change their mind" and turn back to Egypt.

In God's purposeful foresight, He takes them the long way to avoid such a temptation. That is how He works in your life as well. He sees what is ahead of you, and He guides you in a direction that will enable you to gain maturity in your faith and deeper confidence in Almighty God. The crucial issue is you must follow wherever He leads. In time, there will be conflicts and battles, but God only allows these as you have been given the opportunity to have your faith developed.

Do not waste opportunities and do not waste your time being distracted with the world. Be very careful of time robbers, those things that consume time and energy from following Jesus Christ.

To gain spiritual maturity, you must abide daily and deeply in Jesus Christ. You must adjust your life and your lifestyle to the Word of God and the will of God. When those long detours come, realize it is for your benefit and protection.

Prayer and Praise:

Lord, thank You for leading me the long way. Thank You for knowing where I am spiritually and what I am capable of and going before me, making the way known to me. I praise You. Let me constantly be aware that I have not "arrived." Let me live daily in dependency on You. In the mighty name of Jesus Christ, my Lord. Amen.

WHEN THE ENEMY COMES TO FIGHT
Exodus 17:8-16

Have you ever been striving to live for the Lord, are doing everything you know you are supposed to do, but even so, opposition comes? In Mark's gospel Jesus told the disciples to get in a boat and go to the other side, and as soon as they were on their way, a storm came up. That is how the Christian life is. You will regularly face opposition and trials.

In the section of Scripture you read for today, not long after the Israelites crossed the Red Sea and began their journey, the Amalekites come to fight. These enemies of God's people come to prevent the Israelites from following after God. Israel had just experienced a mighty move and provision of God. They drank water from the rock. They had been refreshed and readied, and the enemy came to fight.

You will face times in life when God works on your behalf. He will refresh you and equip you for what lies ahead. Often, you think it is for only your satisfaction and you do not connect it with your faith to enable you to fight. Whenever God makes provision, He not only supplies the need of the moment, but He is also preparing you for what is getting ready to happen next.

Once Israel was on the battlefield, Moses, Aaron, and Hur are up on the mountain in a position to watch, but more so, in a position to intercede. The outcome of the battle does not depend upon the strength and planning of Joshua, but it depended on the intercession of Moses, Aaron, and Hur.

The conflict was determined on two separate but united fields. Joshua and the Israeli army were on the battlefield engaging the enemy, as Moses, Aaron, and Hur were on the mountain engaging God the Father. It takes both modes to have victory. You must have private devotion before you will have public steadfastness. Before you will succeed publically, you must succeed privately. You must be willing to station yourself on the side of a mountain, communing with God in prayer.

As you pour yourself out in prayer, you will grow weary and your hands will tire. That is why you must have others praying for you, lifting your hands to the Father. If you do not, you will grow weary, lax, and will lose the battle. The only way to stand publically is to make sure privately you are faithful to God. Life's battles are won or lost in the place of prayer.

Prayer and Praise:

Lord, I praise You for being my ever-sufficient God. You see the beginning and the end. You know every opposition and attack of the enemy before it arrives; thank You. Enable me to understand the times of refreshing are times of preparation for the fight. Teach me that battles are won or lost on my knees. I praise You. In the mighty name of Jesus Christ, my Lord. Amen.

THE LAW
Exodus 20:1-17

As God led His children out of bondage from the world (Egypt), He led them for three months through the wilderness to Mount Sinai. As God's people camped at the foot of this mountain, "Moses went up to God." While on this mountain, away from the distractions of everyday life, God spoke to Moses. Do you have a place you go to be alone with God to get away from the distractions of life?

It was on this mountain God gave Moses the Ten Commandments, the Law. The Ten Commandments were given for God's people to govern how they were to live. They were to live in harmony with God, God's Word, and God's Law. The Commandments reveal the character of God, the very glory of God. To break even one of the commandments means you have missed the mark, you have sinned and have fallen "short of the glory of God" (Romans 3:23).

The Ten Commandments were given to you to show and teach you what God demands. Yet you cannot keep the Law perfectly, you fall short. The Law was given to show you that you cannot do it by yourself. The Law of God exposes your sin, your failure, and your inability to do what you are supposed to do. That is why you have the Law.

The good news is Jesus said, "Do not think that I came to destroy the Law or the Prophets. I did not come to destroy but to fulfill." The Law was given to reveal the character and glory of God. Man sinned and fell short of God's glory, God's character. Therefore the Law exposed man's sin. However, Jesus died for your sin. Jesus paid the penalty for your sin. Jesus Christ lived in complete obedience to the Law, fulfilling the Law.

When a person places his or her faith in Jesus Christ, trusting His death, burial and resurrection for salvation, that person is born again by Almighty God. The Holy Spirit of God comes into that person's life, saving and sealing him or her. The demands of the Law have not changed, but the resources that equal the demands of the law have been made available in and through Jesus Christ.

Only Jesus Christ can live the Christian life. It is not a technique or a discipline; rather, it is a relationship with Christ that is abiding and real. Christ then lives in you, and it is Christ that lives the Christian life through you.

Prayer and Praise:

Lord, Your Law reveals who You are and what You expect of me. Let me be ever aware that apart from an abiding and real relationship with Christ daily, I will continue to miss the mark and fall short of Your glory. In the mighty name of Jesus Christ, my Lord, Amen.

COME UP HIGHER
Exodus 24:9-18

In this passage of Scripture you find God telling Moses to "come up" to Him on the mountain. Moses, Aaron, Nadab, Abihu, and seventy of the elders of Israel went up and worshipped. God still gives invitations for you to worship Him. Do you take advantage of every opportunity?

Moses built an altar. There they had sacrifices, offerings, and the shedding of blood. Moses read the Book of the Covenant to the people. They responded, "All that the Lord has said we will do" (Exodus 24:7). They prepared themselves to come into God's presence. Do you?

When Moses and the others went up into the mountain to meet with God and worship Him, the Scripture says, "They saw the God of Israel." I do not understand that fully, but I accept it. They saw God and they had a meal with Him (Exodus 24:11). They sat in His presence and had fellowship. That is amazing. Never be too busy with life that you fail to obey when God gives you a word of direction. Think what you could miss by ignoring the will of God. Think what you could forfeit by delaying to obey God.

Then Moses heard an additional word from God, "Moses, Come up to Me on the mountain and be there." Moses was told to come up higher, to go deeper. You think it cannot get any better than that, but it can. Do not ignore the voice of God.

"Then Moses went up into the mountain, and a cloud covered the mountain. Now the glory of the Lord rested on Mount Sinai, and the cloud covered it six days. And on the seventh day, He called to Moses out of the midst of the cloud ... So Moses went into the midst of the cloud and went up into the mountain. And Moses was on the mountain forty days and forty nights" (Exodus 24:15-16, 18).

Would you wait six days on the Lord? Could you be still and wait patiently upon God? If you are to go up higher you have to learn to wait upon the Lord. Life is about God's timetable and not yours. Moses not only went up into the mountain, he went into the very cloud of God. Oh that God would call you into His cloud and for weeks you could know the very glory of God in and on your life. Hallelujah!

Prayer and Praise:

Lord, You are God and You have all glory, power, and honor. I praise You. Thank You for calling me higher and deeper into Your glory. Thank You for giving me fellowship and communion with You. Let me ever be faithful to prepare to come into Your presence. In the mighty name of Jesus Christ, my Lord. Amen.

MAKE AN ALTAR
Exodus 27:1

Do you have a personal altar? A place you go regularly to and get low and alone before God? Did you build this altar? Or is it merely a place you go to and slip away from the world and the distractions of life? An altar is a place you meet with God.

The Old Testament word for altar means "a place of sacrifice," or "a place of putting to death." It a place of surrender and sacrifice to Almighty God. It is the place you will meet with God. In chapter 27, God gave Moses the instructions for building the altar. As you read this section, you see that God goes into great and explicit detail about how the altar was to be built. Have you ever wondered why such detail? God knows man cannot approach Him any way he chooses. God set forth a particular path you are to walk. God sets forth how He is to be approached, so that He can be worshipped by you.

Have you lived long enough as a Christian to learn that not everything done under the banner of worship is true worship? Not everything that is done by Christians is acceptable to God. You must be very cautious. It is easy to get caught up in the excitement of the music, the drama, the motivational messages, and still miss God.

Jesus walked the hill of Calvary bearing the cross, sacrificing for your sin. Jesus lived the cross-style life, and everything about Christ was for you to be able to approach God. It was not so you could have the best life possible now. Nor was it to ensure you merely not to go to hell. Jesus lived, died, resurrected, and ascended to the Father so that you can come before God humbly so you can surrender and sacrifice to Him. It is so you can know God.

An altar does no good if you do not use it for its purpose. How long has it been since you knelt before your altar and surrendered afresh to Christ? How long has it been since God met with you at the altar?

Prayer and Praise:

Lord, I thank You for taking the cross and making the only sacrifice whereby men can be saved. Enable me, Father, to daily bend my knee before You, to daily slip away to the altar and surrender afresh. Oh God, meet me at the altar. Speak to me there and direct my life for Your glory. In the mighty name of Jesus Christ, my Lord. Amen.

THE ANOINTING
Exodus 30:22-25

In Exodus 30, you find the command and the ingredients that God gave to Moses to make His anointing oil. God told Moses how to make it, what and whom to anoint. It was holy anointing oil, and man was not to try and duplicate it by making it for his own use. If he did, he would be cut off from God's people. He would be lost forever.

How does one understand anointing? When someone is under the anointing of God, that means God is resting powerfully on the person for a purpose. The anointing depends on God. It does not come with college degrees or the length of a sermon. When God anoints, He pours forth life.

When God gave instructions on how to make this holy anointing oil, you need to understand the ingredients. As you understand the ingredients, you can understand your part in living with the anointing of God on your life. You do not have to be a preacher or a missionary abroad to know the anointing of God. It is available to every child of God.

The first ingredient is myrrh, and myrrh is always associated with death. To know the anointing of God you must know death to self. To know the anointing of God, to minister resurrection life, you must live the crucified life (Galatians 2:20).

The second ingredient is cinnamon. Cinnamon expresses sweetness. Your life is to have a fragrance, a sweet aroma. You are to have the fragrance of Christ. You are to bring refreshment to others.

The third ingredient is sweet calamus, or cane. It is found in the miry clay on the edge of river banks or marshes. It is taken, dried, and then beaten and ground to a powder. In this powder form, it is useful. To become useful, we will have to experience seasons of dryness and brokenness. It is a refining process.

The fourth ingredient is cassia. Cassia is a tree that is taken and split, and the bark is scraped off for medicinal purposes. This tree grows in high elevations and you have to climb to get there. God wants to take you higher and higher, but it takes time.

Finally, olive oil is the last ingredient. All these ingredients by themselves cannot stick together, but the olive oil enables them to stick, or adhere to each other. The olive oil speaks of the Holy Spirit. Ephesians 5:18 says we are commanded to "be filled with the Spirit."

Prayer and Praise:

Lord, I am amazed in the way You give anointing to the lives of Your children. I pray, Father, that You show me how I am failing to position myself for You to anoint my life. I praise You. In the mighty name of Jesus Christ, my Lord. Amen

MEETING WITH GOD
Exodus 33:7-10

Every day you are to strive to meet with God. Every day you must have a place you retreat to get alone and away from the distractions of life. Every day this must be priority, or you will grow cold, stale, and become ineffective in your life's service to God and others. You have to meet with God every day.

Moses had a special place he retreated to, to get alone with God. It was called the tabernacle of meeting. It was a tent pitched outside the camp of the children of Israel, and there Moses went to meet God. Moses's personal tent was in the center of the camp; therefore, every time he went to meet with God, he had to walk through the camp to get to it. There was one to two million people in the camp, all tribes set up like the face of a clock. Moses would have to walk a few miles just to get to the outside of the camp.

Moses had to put forth effort to get alone with God. Do you put forth effort to get alone with God? When Moses came into the tabernacle of meeting, the Scripture says, "The pillar of cloud descended and stood at the door of the tabernacle, and the Lord talked with Moses (Exodus 33:9)." How much time do you spend listening to God compared to talking and telling God all your needs and your situation? How much time do you spend praising and worshipping your Holy Heavenly Father just for who He is?

Moses listened to God's words. Do you listen to the Word of God preached? Do you read the Word of God so you can hear God speak? When Moses went to the tabernacle of meeting, others noticed; they watched Moses. Are you aware others watch you as you meet with God, or as you fail to meet with God, they take notice of both? "Everyone who sought the Lord went out to the tabernacle of meeting" (Exodus 33:7). Your influence can have great impact on others.

Prayer and Praise:

Lord, thank You for wanting me to come to You. Thank You for allowing me to enter Your presence. Let me never take You for granted. Teach me how to prepare myself to come before You. Just as Moses had to put forth effort to go outside the camp to meet with You, let me never forget our appointment each day. Teach me to listen to Your words. Teach me to be attentive to Your voice. Father, let me not miss a word You are speaking to me. In the mighty name of Jesus, my Lord. Amen.

GOATS' HAIR
Exodus 35:4-9

When I had my first job, a paper route, I made eight dollars a week. My father would have me give him eighty cents for my tithe. At the time, I did not like giving of "my" money, but my father saw the value of teaching me to tithe from my very first job. Now, some forty plus years later I cannot imagine not giving tithes and offerings to the Lord.

In these verses, Moses tells the children of Israel the command of God in regard to Sabbath regulations. Everyone who was of a willing heart is to bring an offering. A willing heart means this was not coerced, forced, or obligatory. It was a free-will offering to the Lord. They were to bring gold, silver, and bronze, all precious metals for the service of the Lord. They were to bring beautiful thread for the making of materials of all sorts of colors. They were to bring ram skins and badger skins, which would repel water. They were to bring oil for burning the lights and spices for anointing oil. They would bring the precious stones that would be set in the ephod and the breastplate of the priest.

With all the amazing gifts they were to bring and all holding such value to man, there is one item not very ornate or valuable. They were to bring goat's hair. Why would God ask for goat's hair? It has no intrinsic value or worth. It was common. You could find it along bushes where the goats had rubbed up against them. Why goat's hair?

Anyone could offer goat's hair. That is why God asked for this. You may not have the precious metals or the fine threads. You may not have the hides of animals or precious stones, but anyone could get goat's hair. All one had to do was stoop down and pick it up by the trail, or in the bush. Goat's hair was common for everyone, so everyone was without excuse in this offering. The real question is, are you willing to slow down long enough to pick it up? Will you inconvenience yourself to gather this common substance God has asked for?

When was the last time you interrupted your schedule to obey God in a simple task? You may not have what others have, but you can obey God and give freely for His kingdom advancement. All you have to do is slow down and look around, and see what it is you have to offer.

Prayer and Praise:

Lord, I thank You for goat's hair. I thank You and praise You that You ask of me what I can give. Teach me not to think my offering is too small or inconsequential. Teach me the joy of obeying You even in what seems minor things. In the mighty name of Jesus Christ, my Lord. Amen.

HOLY VESSELS
Exodus 37:17-18

The tabernacle is given about fifty chapters in the Old Testament. That should indicate to you this is an important subject. God gave specific instructions on how it was to be built and what it was to contain because the tabernacle was a foreshadowing of Jesus Christ. The tabernacle consisted of three sections: the outer court, the inner court or holy place, and the holy of holies.

One entered the tabernacle by the door, the only door, and came into the outer court. The outer court was where the sacrifices were made and the bronze cleansing basin was. The outer court had natural light. Just as one sees physically with natural light, a person comes into Christ who is the door to the kingdom of heaven, where God Himself is the light.

Progressing through the tabernacle, a person next moves to the holy place. In this area you will find the table of shew bread, the altar of incense, and the lampstand. As you progress through the tabernacle you move from natural light to Word light. That is how a Christian is to progress. You stop merely living by the natural man and you begin to live by the Word of God.

Then you arrive to the Holy of Holies. This is where the ark of the covenant rested. God comes down on the mercy seat between the two golden cherubim. This moves the believer from Word light to supernatural light—revelation that God gives as you abide in Him. It will always be in agreement with God's Word, but it moves beyond to specifics for each person in how to live. It evidences itself in a person's calling and anointing.

A child of God moves form natural light to Word light to Revelation light as he continues and goes deeper with the Father. Thanks be to God for His Word. Thanks be to God for specific revelation knowledge.

Prayer and Praise:

Lord, thank You for loving me so much that You give light. You give specific direction for me to live by. You do not leave things up to chance. You have a plan and a purpose, and I praise You for giving illumination from Your Word and by Your Holy Spirit to guide and prompt me. Let me go deeper with You. Teach me to press in and seek Your revelation knowledge. In the mighty name of Jesus, my Lord. Amen.

THE CLOUD AND THE GLORY
Exodus 40:34-38

God has promised never to leave you or forsake you. He has given you the Holy Spirit to guide and quicken your life, as well as the Word of God to direct you. You have everything you need to live a godly life for His glory.

As you read the accounts of the Old Testament, as God went before His people with the pillar of cloud by day and the fire by night, you may be tempted to think, "If only I had a pillar of fire or cloud, I could really walk with God."

Have you been cheated, shortchanged, by not having this physical and visible sign in your life? No, you have so much more as a born-again child of God. The children of Israel had the pillar of cloud and fire, but there was so much they did not have that you have. You have the indwelling Holy Spirit in your life. The Holy Spirit seals you and secures you. The Holy Spirit teaches you in truth and righteousness.

But that is not all you have. You have the Word of God in entirety. You can read it, meditate on it, memorize, and sing it every day. You are blessed beyond measure. You also live on this side of the cross. Therefore, you can know the Lord Jesus Christ that died for you, and resurrected, and ascended to the Father, and lives ever to make intercession for you.

Just because you do not have a physical sign to live by, it does not mean you were cheated. By no means have you been given less. You have been given so much more. Therefore, daily you can go to the throne of grace and obtain mercy. Daily you can receive guidance and direction. He has enabled you to have faith in Him, and daily you have the privilege to commune with God and abide in Him.

Prayer and Praise:

Lord, I exalt Your holy name. You are my God and all You ever do for me is good. You have given me the witness of Your Spirit, and I praise You. You have given me Your written Word, and I thank You. Teach me not to seek after physical signs, but enable me daily to live by faith in You. Build my faith, strengthen my faith, and allow my faith to be all You intend it to be. In the mighty name of Jesus Christ, my Lord. Amen.

FEBRUARY

THE PLACE GOD SPOKE TO HIS SERVANT
Leviticus 1:1

Most Christians realize that God is omnipresent. That simply means He is everywhere all the time. You cannot confine God to a particular location. You may not be aware of God's presence, but that does not mean He is not there. The psalmist said, "If I make my bed in hell, behold, You are there" (Psalm 139:8).

In the verse of Scripture in Leviticus 1:1, it is interesting to see the place from which God spoke to His servant Moses. It was from the tabernacle of meeting. Is that the only place God spoke from? No. As you have read through the book of Exodus, you found God speaking to Moses from the burning bush. You found God speaking to Moses while he was in Egypt. You found God speaking to Moses in the wilderness and from the mountain.

What is amazing is after Moses constructed and erected the tabernacle of meeting, God began to speak to Moses from that place. God was not confined to that place, but He chose to speak to Moses from there as He gave him instructions on how to worship, serve, and obey Him.

God still speaks today to His children. He speaks in a variety of ways. He speaks through His Word, the Bible. He speaks through His Holy Spirit as He impresses His will on your heart and mind. He speaks through your circumstances as you understand them in light of His truths. God is still speaking. Are you listening?

Do you have a place you retreat to daily to hear God speak? Do you have a place of meeting where you separate yourself from the world and the throngs of the world to communion with God? Do you go there with an expectancy to hear God speak to you?

God can speak to you anywhere He chooses. God can use any means necessary to communicate His truth to you. That does not remove the responsibility that you have for a special meeting place to get alone with God. Daily you must go to the meeting place and seek God in meditation and in prayer. You must learn to listen to God's voice before you can ever start to speak to God. What do you want to tell Him that He does not already know? Learn to listen to God. Learn to get alone with God. Have a meeting place where God can speak unhurriedly to you.

Prayer and Praise:

Lord, teach me how to meet with You every day. Teach me how to be in my place of responsibility and accountability to hear Your voice and to receive Your Word especially spoken for me. In the mighty name of Jesus Christ, my Lord. Amen.

BRINGING GUILT
Leviticus 4:1-3

Guilt is a terrible feeling. Guilt is an emotion that occurs when a person violates a moral standard he believes in. However, guilt is far greater than that definition. The person who sins against God and His Word is guilty, whether he feels anything or not. Romans 3:23 tells us, "For all have sinned and fall short of the glory of God."

When you sin (and all people sin), you are guilty. Sin brings guilt. Guilt is a tool God uses to get your attention; and the feeling of guilt closely parallels the convicting of the Holy Spirit. These are not identical. It is possible to be raised in a culture where certain acts are not wrong and, therefore, you feel no guilt. Prejudice often works this way.

If a person is taught from birth to be prejudiced against a certain color of people or race, this person may not be aware that prejudice is wrong. God is greater than a person's upbringing, and He can tear away the entire facade by His Holy Spirit and show each person his or her sin and guilt.

Guilt is a terrible feeling but a feeling God uses to get your attention so you can deal with your sin. There is true guilt that recognizes one's sin and shortcomings, and one will remain guilty until he deals with his sin. The way a person deals with sin is to bring it in honest confession to Jesus Christ. First John 1:7 and 9 say, "But if we walk in the light as He is in the light, we have fellowship with one another, and the blood of Jesus Christ His Son cleanses us from all sin ... If we confess our sins, He is faithful and just to forgive us our sins and to cleanse us from all unrighteousness."

Once sin is confessed and forsaken you have the forgiveness of God. The Devil likes to send you false guilt. He likes to remind you of your past sins and failures. This is false guilt, not true guilt.

When the Devil tries to remind you of your past, claim the assurance of sins forgiven, and then remind the Devil of his future in the horrible pit.

When you sin, God has made a way to have your sins forgiven. Are you not thankful for that? It no longer requires the blood of bulls and goats. Sin was forgiven by the precious blood of Jesus Christ. Hallelujah to the Lamb!

Prayer and Praise:

Lord, I am so thankful for the forgiveness of my sins. Thank You for disturbing my spirit with guilt when I still sin. Thank You for allowing me to come daily and know Your forgiveness and cleansing afresh as I confess and forsake my sin. In the mighty name of Jesus Christ, my Lord, Amen.

CONSECRATION
Leviticus 8:10

Coming to Jesus Christ and becoming a child of God is the greatest gift one can ever know. That is not the end; it is the starting point of the Christian life. Once a person is born again, he has become a new creation in Jesus, and he is a babe in Christ. The person is to grow, develop, and mature in his new life in Christ.

The process is called "sanctification." It means to be set apart from the world and set apart to God for purpose, to be used by the Lord. In order for a person to fulfill God's purpose, that person must be in the process of being sanctified, or consecrated to God. In the text, Moses was consecrating Aaron and his sons for service to God.

God's part is to prepare you by making you holy. God cleanses the inside at the moment of salvation and regularly as you confess and turn from your sin. God also wants to cleanse the outside of your life. He wants to wash you with His presence to make you fit for service.

Your responsibility in consecration is to separate yourself from the evils and the influences of the world that attract. You must learn to draw near to God, therefore enabling Him to draw near to you. It is while you are drawing near to God that He washes you holy and enables you for use in His kingdom work.

If you want to be prepared and equipped for service, you have to make a choice to draw near to God. Then you will be consecrated to God. God will do His part. You have to do yours. Practical holiness and the cleansing of God for service cannot be separated. God will do His part. You must submit your will to do your part.

As Aaron and his sons were consecrated, they were enabled by God to minister in His presence in the tabernacle. They daily had to do their part of separating from the world and being separated unto God.

Prayer and Praise:

Lord, You are the God who saves and Jehovah M'Kaddesh, the Lord who sanctifies. I praise You for Your saving work. I exalt You for Your work of sanctification. Continue to consecrate me unto You. Set me apart unto holiness and make me useful for Your kingdom. In the mighty name of Jesus Christ, my Lord. Amen

STRANGE FIRE
Leviticus 10:1-7

Men are often known for their successes or their failures. Babe Ruth was known for his home run hitting ability in baseball. He was also known for his strikeout record. Abraham Lincoln is known as one of America's greatest presidents, but he also had his share of failures.

Nadab and Abihu are known only for their failure. These men had every reason to succeed. They were the sons of Aaron and were privileged to be on the mountain of God with Moses and their father when God manifested Himself to them (Exodus 24). Then you see that God called them personally to be His priests (Exodus 28:1). God personally set them apart and sanctified them. Yet they failed. They failed their families. They failed themselves. They failed God.

You are told in the Scripture that they "offered profane fire before the Lord, which He had not commanded them" (Leviticus 10:1). They did something God did not tell them to do. This was an act of personal disobedience. In the act of worship they did something God did not tell them and they profaned, or made the very act of worship unholy.

When you come to worship God, are you sensitive to what God wants or do you have the idea "anything is acceptable"? It matters to God how you come before Him in worship and it matters to God how you worship Him. Your worship is to always be based on the truth of God's Word.

The book of Proverbs tells us "there is a way that seems right to a man, but its end is the way of death." You must be warned—you approach God on His terms, not your own. The sin of Nadab and Abihu was that on the first day of corporate worship with God's people, they violated worship. They disobeyed God. They could not offer God anything they wanted to and get by with it. The result—God killed them.

Learn the lesson of obedience. Learn to come before God with clean hands and a pure heart. Keep your heart sensitive to the voice of God and the Word of God. Worship God in Spirit and in truth. When God sends fire, His purifying fire, it will cleanse us and not consume us.

Prayer and Praise:

Lord, teach me to know how to worship You. Enable me to worship You in obedience to Your truth. Send the refining fire. Send the purifying fire. Send the fires of revival and renewal in my life. In the mighty name of Jesus Christ, my Lord. Amen.

THE PLAGUE IN THE HOUSE
Leviticus 14:33-34

Troubles and trials come to every believer. Sometimes they come because you make a wrong choice or bad decision. Other times they come because the Devil attacks. However, when the Devil attacks, even his attack has to be allowed into your life by Almighty God. Finally, you face troubles and trials because God sends them. How are you to understand those situations?

In the text you see God saying, "and I put the leprous plague in a house" (v. 34). Why would God put a plague in a believer's house? The Hebrew word for plague is "naiga" and it means plague or disease. It is used over one hundred times in the Bible. Here, God brought this condition. Why?

Every situation can be different. God may be teaching different things. You have the promise in Psalm 91:10, "No evil shall befall you. Nor shall any plague come near your dwelling." In order to claim this promise, you must meet the condition. The condition is found in Psalm 91:1, "He who dwells in the secret place of the Most High shall abide under the shadow of the Almighty."

The condition is to dwell in the secret place of God and to abide daily in God's presence. The sad fact is most believers do not dwell in the secret place of God. They are saved and faithful to their church, but they fail in the abiding. It is too easy to be distracted by the world and cares of life. Time is spent on trivial matters, but not with God.

God sends troubles and trials to get your attention, so you will realize He is to be preeminent in your life. Just as they had to examine the house, your life must be examined closely in light of God's Word. Just as they had to remove stones, things will have to be removed from your life. Just as they had to scrub the walls and cleanse them, your life must be scrubbed by the washing of the water of the Word of God and His Holy Spirit.

God wants you to abide in Him, and in order to accomplish that you must be clean. God desires your holiness. If the plague continued in the house after attempts to cleanse it, it was torn down. If you fail to know the cleansing only God's Word can bring as you yield ever aspect, things can get worse. Abiding is the key. Forgiveness and cleansing lead to a lifestyle that glorifies Christ; they do not lead one to a life of sin.

God sends things and allows things into your life to get you to pursue Him. His desire is always for your good and His glory.

Prayer and Praise:

Lord, I do not always understand Your ways, but teach me to trust You even when I do not understand. Enable me to dwell in the secret place, so I will be covered with Your shadow. In the mighty name of Jesus Christ, my Lord. Amen.

ENTERING GOD'S PRESENCE
Leviticus 16:1-4

The most important thing you can know, experience, and understand is the presence of God and how you enter God's presence. Many assume it means merely showing up for church service and spending time in prayer and Bible reading. Not to minimize these things, but a lost person can do all of those. There is more to entering God's presence than jumping through a set of prescribed hoops.

Hebrews 12 tells us, "and holiness without which no one will see the Lord." Before an individual can enter God's presence, he must have a holy fear of God and a reverence for God. Jeremiah 29:13, "You will seek Me and find Me, when you search for Me with all your heart." A person cannot be double-minded when seeking God.

Leviticus 16 sets forth the requirements of entering the presence of God. In verse three you are told to appropriate the blood of sacrifice. In the appropriation of the blood you are dealing with sin. It is the grace of God that enables you to apply the blood so your sin can be covered. Next, you are to put on righteousness, and you are to put on truth and honesty. You are to put on the breastplate of righteousness. You are to be girded with a sash. You are to be transparent and clean before the Lord. Finally, you are to be cleansed by washing. You are to be washed in the word of God.

The New Testament parallel passage for Leviticus 16:1-4 would be Ephesians 6:11-20. God did not meet with Aaron just anytime or anywhere. There was a right time and a right place. Sin must be dealt with. To be able to enter God's presence, you have to remain in a continued state of preparation. Preparation for what? Preparation for prayer. It is ever so important that you honor, reverence, and reflect God's character.

It is after you enter the presence of God by the blood, believing His power to forgive and cleanse that now you are able to glorify God.

Prayer and Praise:

Lord, thank You for allowing me the privilege to enter into Your presence. Thank You for making the blood of Christ available to me. Praise You and I honor You for the blood. Father, draw me close to You, so I may know Your will and Your ways. Use me as a vessel to reflect You to a lost and dying world. Be glorified in and through my life. In the mighty name of Jesus Christ, my Lord. Amen.

THE GLEANINGS
Leviticus 19:9-10

"Pick them clean." That's a phrase farmers often tell their children when it comes to harvesting the crops. They could be gathering green beans, peas or a number of other crops and the farmer wanted to be sure nothing was left behind. To leave something behind in harvest time was a waste.

In the text, you see that God commanded the children of Israel to leave the corners of the fields unharvested and not to go back over a field to gather what was dropped or missed. The dropped and missed crop was called the gleanings. Why would God want that left? The gleanings were left for the poor. This was God's welfare program for the poor and less fortunate.

If a person lacked food, he was allowed to go into the fields and gather the gleanings. He would not get rich doing this, but he would not starve either. He had to go and get it. No one was going to bring it to him. He had to go to the field, bend down to pick up the remains, and carry it home. Once he was home, he was responsible to prepare the produce for eating.

Today's society could learn much from God's welfare system. It involves work. You do not merely receive a handout. Oftentimes it is easier to give a handout than to teach someone how to work. In the book of Ruth chapter two, Boaz allowed Ruth to glean his fields. She gleaned until evening, and then she beat out what she had. This was the beginning steps of her redemption.

It is amazing how God will take a simple act, gleaning, and then let it lead to another divine encounter or intersection of one's life. You may not be gleaning food, or you may. But you can glean from many a child of God who has gone before and left something behind to help you in your walk of faith.

Prayer and Praise:

Lord, thank You for how You have a plan for my life. Thank You for allowing others to leave something behind so I may glean from them. Thank You for men of God who have gone before and left something of spiritual value for me to glean. I praise You and exalt You. In the mighty name of Jesus Christ, my Lord Amen.

PERFECT UNTO THE LORD
Leviticus 22:20-21

Have you ever been guilty of saying, "Well, nobody is perfect"? This is a true statement. Everyone on planet earth is a sinner. You are a sinner by nature and by birth. First John 1:8 says, "If we say that we have no sin, we deceive ourselves, and the truth is not in us." Romans 3:23 says, "For all have sinned and fall short of the glory of God."

The text for today is very serious. If you are to approach God in worship, you must present a sacrifice. The sacrifice you present to God is to be perfect. It must be perfect to be accepted (v. 21). How does a sinful creature offer a perfect sacrifice? You come bathed in the blood of Jesus Christ. Jesus is the perfect sacrifice. Only as you abide in Him, can you offer to God a sacrifice that will be accepted.

When you approach God to worship, are you careless and indifferent? Are you halfhearted and thoughtless? How do you prepare yourself for worship of Almighty God? Are you indifferent in your praying? Are you thoughtless in your singing God's praise? Are you careless in reading God's Word and in the hearing of the Word of God? When you seek God's presence and power, do you prepare yourself in holiness? You should strive to honor God because God deserves perfection. Perfection shuts you up entirely to Jesus Christ.

Whatever God demands, He enables, and whatever God enables, He expects. God in His infinite grace has enabled you to approach Him based only on the blood of Jesus Christ. Jesus Christ was the perfect sacrifice accepted unto God. Hallelujah!

Prayer and Praise:

Lord, I thank You for the perfect sacrifice of Jesus Christ You made for me. Teach me to abide in You so I can come before You in the righteousness of Jesus. Teach me I have no righteousness of my own. Teach me to appropriate daily the blood of Jesus. In the mighty name of Jesus Christ, my Lord, Amen.

THE SABBATICAL YEAR
Leviticus 25:1-7

When the children of Israel reached the Promised Land, there would be laws governing the land—how it was bought, sold, and used. The Israelites had to understand one clear truth: the land belonged to God. God allowed them to be stewards of the land. "The land is Mine," God told them plainly (Leviticus 25:23).

Just as God established a Sabbath rest, God also established a sabbatical rest for the land. For a year the land was to remain untilled and undisturbed. The question remained, would the people trust God to meet their needs in this sabbatical year, or would they continue to plant their crops?

In the sabbatical year, God was teaching His people to trust and depend on Him. It is easy to say this with your lips, but to live out trust with your life is completely different. The pressures of life never go away. God was saying in this sabbatical year to let the ground rest, plant no crops, trust Me and I will meet your needs.

In the sixth year, the people had to trust God for rain and good seed. They had to trust God that there would be no crop failure due to drought or insect. They had to trust God to give a tremendous harvest to last through the sabbatical year. Will you live in such a way that your life and lifestyle express and show utter dependency upon God?

So what do you do with this free time? Play games, go on trips, visit family or friends? There is nothing wrong with these things, as long as they are kept in perspective. However, the idea of a Sabbath is worship and rest. It is a time to draw near to God. It is a time to study the Word of God. It is a time to pray and to learn to pray deeper. In a sabbatical year, you are to live in the Word and in prayer.

Prayer and Praise:

Lord, I praise You for Sabbath. I praise You for rest. Teach me to learn these lessons and seek You. Teach me to trust You to meet my every need. Teach me dependency upon You and let me live out Your Word. In the mighty name of Jesus Christ, my Lord. Amen.

CAMPING BY HIS OWN STANDARD
Numbers 2:1-2

You do not have to travel very far to see a flag. Colleges and universities have them, and every country has its own flag. Businesses and corporations have flags. Clubs and societies have flags. Flags fly everywhere.

The children of Israel were made up of the twelve tribes of Jacob. Each tribe was named after its forefather, a son of Jacob. Each tribe had its own "standard," or flag. Each tribe had its identifying standard that the people camped around and that went before them as they marched from place to place. Twelve tribes and, therefore, twelve standards were symbols of their identity as tribes. The only time they put down their standards was when they went to battle or they went to worship God Almighty.

There are a lot of different churches and there are a lot of different denominations. Each denomination strives for its churches' good. Each individual church strives for its own betterment. There is nothing wrong with those things.

However, God's people must learn as the tribes of Israel, when it comes to warfare and worship, individual flags need to come down. There is nothing wrong with being a Baptist, or a Presbyterian, or a Church of God. When it comes to warfare and worship, you are to fall under the flag of Christ. United you must stand with others in order to gain victory and advancement for the kingdom of God.

When was the last time you met with a person of another church, another denomination and prayed for this country? When was the last time you went to another church's special service? There has to be a coming together, so the people of God can unite in intercession for our land. Will you take the first step?

Prayer and Praise:

Lord, show me how to initiate coming together with others to pray. Prompt my mind, stir my heart that I will seek other born-again believers who may not go to my church or be a part of my denomination but who desire You, and we will begin to pray. In the mighty name of Jesus Christ, my Lord. Amen.

THE NAZARITE VOW
Numbers 6:1-8

On a person's wedding day, vows are exchanged. When a person is preparing to testify in a court of law, he takes a vow to tell the truth. What is a vow? A vow is a solemn oath that a person is stating. It is a binding statement. When you vow on your wedding day, you promise to be faithful to your spouse in good times and in bad. When you make a vow to God, God expects you to keep your vow.

In the passage today, you are introduced to the Nazarite vow. A Nazarite vow is a vow in the Old Testament that seeks a deeper walk with God. The keeper of the vow wants to live separated unto God and live a life of holiness. He wants a closer walk with the Lord. The Nazarite wanted to be separated and totally set apart unto God. That was his passion. For some, the vow was for a set period of time, and for others it was for a lifetime. Both Samson and Samuel were set apart for this vow for life.

There were three obligations specific to the Nazarite vow. This person was to abstain from all intoxicating drink. In fact, he was to avoid anything made from grapes. He was never to cut his hair, which was the outward sign of this vow. Plus, he was never to touch or go near a dead body, not even a family member.

How does this make application for today? In order to draw close to the Lord, a believer must keep his mind clear and focused on the Lord. As for not cutting one's hair, this simply is a statement that a believer's life will bear marks of living a separated life. Seeking to live a holy life must be priority and evidenced. Finally, as a Christian you must not defile yourself with things unclean; you must not be corrupted with sin.

If your heart's desire is to live closer to God every day, these traits must be real in your life. You are to be focused, separated, and holy. The good news is as you yield daily to the Holy Spirit and live in the Word of God, you can.

Prayer and Praise:

Lord, I do desire to live closer to You every day. Help me to realize the adjustments I must make in my life and my lifestyle as not to be compromised with sin. Teach me how to pursue holiness and Your righteousness every moment of every day. In the mighty name of Jesus Christ, my Lord. Amen.

NO CARTS
Numbers 7:4-9

You have met people who carry tremendous burdens. Oftentimes they will say, "It just isn't fair." That is an understandable assessment of their situation. The fact is sometimes life is not fair. Good Christian people face tremendous difficulties and challenges. Yet, as a child of God, you are promised that God will never leave nor forsake you. First Corinthians 10:13 says, "No temptation has overtaken you except such as is common to man; but God is faithful, who will not allow you to be tempted beyond what you are able, but with the temptation, will also make the way of escape, that you may be able to bear it."

Burdens come to all of God's children. It seems at times some people bear more than their fair share. But God is faithful and He looks from an eternal perspective. If God has filtered the burden through His permissive hands and will, He has allowed it in your life for a purpose. In those times, all you can do is bear the burden for the glory of God.

The passage of Scripture before you is dealing with the tabernacle. Offerings had been brought, twelve oxen and six wagons, two oxen for each wagon. To Gershom, they received two carts and four oxen. To Merari, they received four carts and eight oxen. However, the sons of Kohath received none; they were to bear the burden on their shoulders. Does that seem fair? No. But that was God's Word and will. It is not about fairness, it is about purpose. There are some burdens in life God does not want a beast of burden to carry. God wants those who love Him and are sanctified by His glory and purpose to carry it.

The sons of Kohath were to carry the ark of the covenant. Staves were placed through the rings on the side, and they were to bear the load on their shoulders. This was their purpose in life. All their lives they carried this load.

Has God ever laid a burden on you and told you to carry it? Often that is the case. The issue is one of trust. Will you trust God even when you cannot see or understand? Will you still trust? Life is not always fair, but God is always faithful.

Prayer and Praise:

Lord, I do not always understand the load in life I have to bear. I do not always like the path I have to travel. Father, I ask You to help me to carry it without complaint and to trust You. Build my faith in You, and teach me how to trust You at all times. Let me know Your Word so my faith can move forward. In the mighty name of Jesus Christ, my Lord. Amen

COMPLAINING
Numbers 11:1

The text shows us what God thinks of His children's complaining. The children of Israel had been delivered powerfully from Egypt. They had come through the Red Sea and God had met every need that they had. He had given them water to quench their thirst and manna to feed them. The pillar of cloud and fire went before them, so that they knew exactly when to move, where to go and when to stop. They had God's divine direction, but they complained.

Why would a person with all of that complain? They complained because even being fed, satisfied with water, and having divine direction, they were not comfortable. They were not satisfied with what God was doing for and with them. They were dissatisfied with manna, and they longed for the foods they had had in Egypt.

Complaining is an evidence of lack of faith in God. To desire one's former life and lifestyle is an indicator that one is not abiding daily in the person of Christ. In the USA, this has become so epidemic that churches have embraced the idea that you can have Jesus and the ways of the world. Many professing believers still live and act like the world. They go to the world to be entertained and satisfied. Many churches give their approval of this.

The text says, "Now when the people complained, it displeased the Lord." Fire from heaven fell and consumed them. When Solomon dedicated the temple, fire from heaven fell, but this was God's response to the act of humbling themselves before Him, and God sent fire, a fire of cleansing and blessing. Here the fire was not of blessing but chastisement. The fire consumed them because of their complaining. As you read on, you find that all the complainers never made it to the Promised Land. Complaining is costly. God takes it personally when you are not following His direction in life.

If you find yourself complaining, stop it. Start counting your blessings. If people you spend a lot of time with complain, separate from them if they refuse to stop. Your relationship to Jesus Christ is the most important relationship you have and you must learn to cultivate a grateful spirit and heart. Hell is all anyone deserves, but Jesus died and rose again, and He paid the price for your sin. If He did nothing else, that is enough to be grateful for the rest of your life.

Prayer and Praise:

Lord, it is so easy to complain and whine about my situation and things I do not like. Forgive me. Let me realize quickly when I begin to complain and murmur that You hear me and You are displeased. Teach me to have a grateful heart and a thankful spirit at all times. In the mighty name of Jesus Christ, my Lord. Amen.

LEARNING TO STAND ALONE
Numbers 13:1, 25-33

If you were asked the question, "What is a man of God?" How would you answer that question? Maybe you would say a man of God is a man with a deep faith in Jesus Christ. You could say a man of God is a man who is the man of the Word of God. A man of God is a faithful man. A man of God is a man who lives out his convictions (hopefully these convictions have a biblical basis).

A man of God is a man who lives out his faith in Jesus Christ, and lives it out even when he has to stand alone. There are a lot of talkers, but what is needed is a man who will stand all by himself when the crowd goes the other way.

In the text, you have one man from each tribe chosen to represent his tribe to go into the Promised Land and spy it out. After forty days of looking it over, living in, and experiencing this land, all twelve agreed that it was a wonderful and bountiful land. However, ten of the spies said the land had giants living there and only two saw only the blessing of God. Ten said, we cannot go in, while only two said, we can go in and take this land.

The minority was right, not the majority. Caleb and Joshua were willing to stand alone, willing to go against the majority to do what was right. In the passage God never asked the spies their opinion. They merely stated it after seeing the wonderful land He had promised them. It is amazing how expressing one's opinion comes so easily, when all God wants is obedience to His Word. God is not the least bit concerned if you think it is a good idea or not, God wants obedience to His Word.

Are you influenced more by people than you are by God? Do you go along with the crowd, even when you know it is not the will of God? Even when you know it hurts your testimony? There are places Christian men and women should not go, yet it is so easy just to go along and not be different.

It is always easy to stand for God when you are in a group. God has not called us to run in a pack. He has called us to mount up with wings of eagles and soar. You never see eagles soaring in a pack. Only a few dare to climb the heights of God. To be a man of God you have to learn to stand alone, to be left out, to walk all by yourself, come hell or high water. Then you are a covenant man. You keep your covenant with God above everything else. (All of this applies to being a woman of God also.)

Prayer and Praise:

Lord, my desire is to be a man of God. Teach me how. Teach me what it means to live by the convictions of Your Word. Let me be aware of the opportunities You send so I can pass the test of a willingness to stand alone. In the mighty name of Jesus Christ, my Lord. Amen.

REBELLION
Numbers 16

The Bible tells us in Proverbs 6:16 that God hates six things. One of the things God hates is "one who sows discord among brethren" (Proverbs 6:19). Rebellion among God's people in the church is very, very serious. God hates it.

In Numbers 16, God establishes once and for all what He thinks about rebellion. In this passage you see that rebellion against legitimate spiritual authority is despised. And so it is in the church today. Nothing is more destructive than this. It always seems to be done under the pretense of righteousness.

There are several marks of rebellion in this passage. First, the agitators were influential leaders. Korah was a Levite, a member of the priestly tribe. He was in a position of influence. They formed a confederacy of at least two hundred and fifty and came together to revolt. Second, their complaint was believable. They all claimed to be "holy." They were claiming the priesthood of the believer. Third, the issue spread secretly before it went public. They shared their complaint with one another. Only after whipping the people into a frenzy did they go to Moses.

Rebellion ultimately manifested, and it was the seed bed for lies and false accusations. In Numbers 16:14, Moses was falsely accused. Strife and division dishonor God. Fourth, rebellion destroyed undiscerning people. The people were told to separate from them, but they did not listen. Judgment fell on those who refused to distance themselves from the rebels. Rebels always sway dear, sweet, kind-hearted people who lack discernment. Finally, rebellion bred more rebellion. After the first group died, you would think the others would have learned the lesson. No, in Numbers 16:42-52, fourteen thousand, seven hundred more died. Moses interceded for them, even as they were accusing him.

The priesthood of the believer is firmly established in Scripture, but it is never an excuse to attack God's ordained leadership in the church. Be very careful; learn to submit to God's ordained authority over you, be it your parents, your boss, or your pastor. Submission to God is demonstrated in submission to His established authorities.

Prayer and Praise:

Lord, thank You for establishing authorities in my life. Enable me to recognize them as just that, authorities You have established for me. Day by day let me clothe myself in humility and walk in obedience to You. In the mighty name of Jesus Christ, my Lord. Amen.

SPECIFIC INSTRUCTIONS
Numbers 19:1-9

In Numbers 19, you find the story of the "red heifer." You are told specifically how this animal was to be chosen. It could not have any blemish, it had to be red completely and no other color. It could have no defects, nor could it have ever been worked. It was to be slaughtered outside the camp, the blood sprinkled a certain way and the body, skin, and blood burned. The ashes were then collected and stored in a clean place.

Specific, detailed instructions are given for this sacrifice. Why is this offering so important? If a person has become unclean for touching a corpse, and therefore he cannot enter the tabernacle to make sacrifice for cleansing, he can take the ashes of the red heifer and when making proper application, he can be restored and clean. If he fails to do this, he is cut off from the people of God forever.

To be unclean and cut off from the people of God and the sanctuary would be the worst thing imaginable. You would no longer have access to the presence of God. No longer could you have fellowship with God or His people. No longer could you pray and have your prayers heard or answered.

Following instructions is crucial when it comes to your spiritual life. Knowing what the Bible, God's Word, says to us about confession of sin and forsaking sin is essential to your spiritual walk. It becomes easy to go through the motions of things and never truly make honest confession of sin. When this happens, your access to God is cut off and your fellowship with true believers is impacted negatively.

God has given us the ultimate sacrifice for sin in Jesus Christ. When Jesus died on the cross, He died in your place for your sin. He arose victorious over sin, death, and the grave. Jesus ever lives to make intercession for you. He is talking to the Father about you right now. Hallelujah! You must appropriate the blood of Christ daily for your sin. Do not forfeit your access to the Father. First John 1:9 says, "If we will confess our sins, He is faithful and just to forgive us our sins and to cleanse us from all unrighteousness." Thanks be to God for an ever-continuing gift of grace and mercy.

Prayer and Praise:

Lord, Thank You for providing the ultimate sacrifice for my sin in Jesus Christ. Teach me to truly make honest confession of sin to You so I may walk with You daily. Teach me the importance of keeping my sin confessed quickly and not growing calloused to You. Thank You for Your grace and mercy. In the mighty name of Jesus Christ, my Lord. Amen.

BALAAM
Numbers 22:1-5, 9-12

A donkey talking to a man? Is that not amazing? Children are instructed in the story of Balaam and his donkey at an early age. It catches their imagination and even prompts them to ask questions. Hopefully, you can answer their questions. Balaam went down in biblical history as a symbol of mixing immorality with religion. His formula is still being used today, "If you cannot curse people, corrupt them."

In the text you find that four times Balaam tried to curse Israel, but he ended up blessing them. In the New Testament there are three references to Balaam. Second Peter 2:15 talks of "the way of Balaam." Jude 11 tells of the "error of Balaam." In Revelation 2:14 we see the "doctrine of Balaam."

What is the way of Balaam? He misused his gift of prophecy for profit. Be careful you do not misuse your gifting. What is the error of Balaam? He thought Holy God would not deal in grace with sinful people. The doctrine of Balaam is that he counseled how to curse God's people. He got them to intermarry, to be unequally yoked. What Satan could not do from without, he did with success from within. The temptation has not changed in two thousand plus years. If Satan cannot curse you, he will attempt to corrupt you.

Do you need to understand this temptation? Yes, a thousand times, yes. The methods and the schemes of Satan have not changed; they just come in a different mode. Be warned and be cautious—the Devil still seeks to destroy you and the church, the people of God. But you have an advocate with the Father, Jesus Christ the Son, and He ever lives to make intercession for you. Lean on Christ and obey His Word quickly and explicitly. He will protect you. Temptation will come, but greater is He who is in you than he who is in the world (1 John 4:4).

Prayer and Praise:

Lord, keep me ever aware of the devices of the Devil. Let me know Your leading and directing, and let me be very aware of how the Devil seeks to corrupt me, getting me to compromise. Father, the cost of compromise and corruption is great. It continues to pay dividends to future generations. Oh Father, keep me close to You and clean within. In the mighty name of Jesus Christ, my Lord. Amen.

TURNING BACK GOD'S WRATH
Numbers 25:11

This is an age that worships sex. Turn on any media device and you find sex is used to sell products. It is an age of promiscuity in every form. In this passage in Numbers, the children of Israel, after forty years of wandering through the wilderness because of the past generations' sin, now commit their own sin: sexual immorality. The men of Israel begin to have sex with Moabite women. The Bible says they "committed harlotry."

The Israelites camped in the plains of Moab along the Jordan River in the area of Shittim. The men of Moab, following Balaam's advice, had the Moabite women seduce the Israelite men into having sex. They engaged in sexual immorality and then they joined the Moabites in their pagan worship. Sexual immorality and false worship are still present with us today. Be very careful.

When you play with the world, you will ultimately join the false worship of the world. The false worship of the world allows you to enjoy the immorality of the world and still be "respected," because you worship. God's judgment fell quickly on His children. He sent a plague among them and twenty-four thousand died. God judges sin. It may not be instantaneous, but God judges sin. No one gets by with anything in this life.

One man showed public affection toward a Moabite woman, as Moses and others were weeping and praying at the tabernacle because of this sin. Phinehas, the priest, interrupted prayer, took a spear and slew both of them. This act turned back God's wrath, and the plague was stopped. As a priest, he represented God before man, and he had to stand for God's holiness. Are you to take a spear and slay people today? NO, but you must stand for holiness, even when you have to stand all by yourself.

When people care nothing for the Word of God, or the holiness of God, and show blatant disrespect, it is a scary time. The generation in which you live cares nothing for God or His Word. It will seduce you if you are not a man of faith and obedience to God. It will seduce you if you do not guard your heart.

Sexual temptation has been around since the beginning. Be very careful, guard your eye, and guard your heart. No immediate pleasure is worth the wrath of God on your life.

Prayer and Praise:

Lord, help me remain clean and pure. Guard my eyes, my ears, and my heart and keep it true to You. Temptation comes to each of us. Give me sense to see the end result and not just the immediate gratification. I want to love You with a perfect heart; show me how. In the mighty name of Jesus Christ, my Lord. Amen.

A HOLY CONVOCATION
Numbers 29:1, 7

Have you ever been commanded by your employer to be in attendance to a certain meeting or training session? If you miss, it had better be an issue of life and death, because attendance is mandatory. Most people do not like these mandatory meetings, but they will comply.

The church today cannot make meetings mandatory. Why? This would infringe on the personal rights of individuals and would be frowned upon as being dictatorial. However, there are times in the life of a church that meetings should be mandatory for members. Sadly, the commentary today is the church in America is the easiest thing to join, and it requires no obligation or commitment to be a member. There is much more to it than that but this is the general impression.

In our text, the Israelites are called to have a holy convocation. Physical presence was mandatory, and no one complained. It did not interrupt their plans and activities because they lived planning around the word of God. These days were special. It was a specific time they focused more intently upon God. They did no manual labor; they gave their time and attention to God.

What would you do? Thank God for all His benefits. You acknowledge God as the Lord of your life. You adjust your schedule to Him. You learn to enjoy your salvation and you praise God for providing blood atonement, you sacrifice to the Lord. You grow in your trust, obedience, and joy. You learn to focus on God, and you practice that daily.

Do you have certain times, or does your church have certain times to help you learn to focus on the Lord? Do you make every effort to be a part of these holy convocations? Or do trivial matters take you away, such as ballgames for your child? Shopping trips? Hanging out with your peers? You may go once or twice but not to every meeting. What's wrong with this picture? You are still dictating your life and not the Lord. If Jesus is not Lord of all, He is not Lord at all.

What adjustments will you have to make to have a holy convocation with God? It is all about what you want to focus on. The temporary is appealing but it can cost you eternally.

Prayer and Praise:

Lord, help me realize the importance of having holy convocations with You. Let me realize when my church sets aside times for revival and renewal, I must be present. Let me learn to focus on You. Develop my trust, my joy, and my faith. In the mighty name of Jesus Christ, my Lord. Amen.

THE DANGER OF SETTLING DOWN
Numbers 32:1-6

It is very easy to become weary and tired while serving the Lord and making a life with your family. So many things can distract you from what is the most important issue of life. The most important issue of life is your relationship with Jesus Christ. You must be sure it is an abiding, vital and real relationship. When you start saying yes to trivial things, you end up saying no to the crucial things of life. Time is wasted easily.

In the text two tribes, Reuben and Gad wanted to settle on the wrong side of the Jordan River. They like the land. It was fertile and rich. It would be wonderful for their crops and herds. They assured Moses they would ever be ready to help and that they would continue with them until they occupied the Promised Land.

Why would someone go so far and stop when they are so close? There is always a temptation for you to settle down, settle for less than the goal, or settle for what appeals to one's flesh. When you hold your possessions tightly, your tendency will be preservation. This will cause you to want to settle for less than God's best. How you hold to the things of this world determines your attitude, passions, priorities, and obedience. Learn to hold possessions loosely.

When you settle down, you begin to rationalize God's will. This is costly. Immediately you see only good; but immediate results can be deceptive. Do not rationalize or compromise the will or the word of God. Understand your sin will find you out. Sin is often not judged immediately but it is judged. When a person is not judged instantly, it breeds an "I got by with this" mentality. Be sure your sin will find you out. Do not stop short or settle for less than God has told you.

Prayer and Praise:

Lord, You are my God and I praise You. You have promised to lead and direct my life until the end. Please, Father, do not let me settle down and rationalize Your Word or will. Enable me to press on, walking by faith and holding the things of this world loosely. In the mighty name of Jesus Christ, my Lord. Amen.

CITIES OF REFUGE
Numbers 35:10-15

You do not have to live long to understand the basic needs of life. They are food, clothing, and shelter. When these needs are met quite readily, other needs emerge. It takes just the physical and material things to sustain life, but beyond the basics there is need for meaning, purpose, and a sense of fulfillment. All of these can be known in Jesus Christ, and apart from Him you will never know abiding satisfaction in life.

God promises to meet every human need. In today's passage you are introduced to the cities of refuge. A refuge is a shelter or a protection from danger. God provided a city of protection for any person who unintentionally or accidentally killed another person. This was a place of safety the murderer could flee to until a trial could be set by the community courts. These cities were strategically located throughout the land so any Israelite or foreigner, any person, could flee for safety.

If the person was found guilty of deliberate murder, he was turned over to the avenger and executed. If he was found innocent, he was sent to a city of refuge, and he had to remain there until the high priest of that time died. The death of the high priest was a picture of blood atonement. He was protected there from the avenger. If he left the city early, the avenger could slay him.

Jesus Christ is your refuge and deliverer from the avenger of death. You must abide in Him. God not only will provide for your physical needs, but He will also provide for your spiritual needs. Jesus Christ died to save us from the condemnation of death. You must run to Him, hide yourself in Him and abide in Christ. He makes provision; will you respond?

Prayer and Praise:

Lord, thank You for being my city of refuge. You are my hiding place. You are my shield of protection and You are my deliverer. Praise You. Teach me to run to You quickly and to abide in You always. In the mighty name of Jesus Christ, my Lord. Amen.

AN ELEVEN-DAY JOURNEY
Deuteronomy 1:1-6

In the bookstore at Auschwitz, where one of the Nazi death camps was in Poland, there is a book titled, "Hope Is the Last to Die." What a powerful insight. When a person loses hope, they lose all reason to try to live.

In the text, the Israelites were on the other side of the Jordan and had not yet entered the Promised Land. They have been in the desert forty years. The first generation had died out and now the second generation was waiting anxiously to enter into the Promised Land.

Moses says, "You have dwelt long enough at this mountain" (Deuteronomy 1:6). He was saying now is the time to move into the land God promised many years ago. Today, many believers are like the Israelites. They sit anxiously waiting to enter into the provision of God. They sit anxiously waiting to move into their position of responsibility, but they sit on a mountainside and they do not move. They have sat at Horeb, which means "ruins" or "desolate," for so long they have grown to accept the desolation as normal. As exciting as the idea of moving on is, they are stuck because they have grown accustomed to the place.

They have sat for years in the same place. They have failed to grow in their faith and they have failed to grow in the word of God. Even though they sat in ruins, they were comfortable. Each person had the responsibility to move into the promises God had given him. It was time to move; they had dwelt in this place long enough.

What will it take for you to move? It takes a fresh word from God and renewed hope. When your hope is restored you can move with the Father. Moses gave a fresh word and pointing to the Promised Land. He recounted the promise made to Abraham, Isaac, and Jacob. He gave the people hope.

The children of Israel had wandered in the wilderness for forty years, while the Promised Land was only an eleven-day journey. Do not let sin prolong your stay in a wilderness. Move in obedience to God's Word. Listen once again to the promises of God. Go where God is telling you.

Prayer and Praise:

Lord, do not ever let me get satisfied living in ruins and desolation. Birth in me a fresh hunger for You and Your will. Oh Father, teach me the importance of having a listening ear to Your Word and let my hope be in You: in Your leading, directing and guiding my life. I praise Your holy name. In the mighty name of Jesus Christ, my Lord. Amen.

THE FEAR OF GOD
Deuteronomy 4:10

What is it that you are afraid of? Why are you afraid of it? People fear many things. They fear animals, crowds, even people. Fear is a result of the fall of man and sin. Fear can immobilize Christian people from moving in faith. The Bible commands you not to fear man, but to fear God.

How do you learn to fear God? In Deuteronomy 14:23-24, you are told that the fear of God is a result of tithing. In Deuteronomy 17:18-19, the fear of God is learned by reading and writing out Scripture. Do you tithe? Do you read and write out the Scriptures? As you read the Word of God, you will understand right concepts of the character of God—holy, majestic, and immense. (He is big enough to meet any need you have.) You will begin to have a pervasive sense of God's presence. When you are aware that He is with You always, it will have a controlling effect on you. Then you will understand your obligation to God. You are to love Him supremely, obey Him implicitly, and trust Him completely. It is all about your focus in life. When your focus is misplaced, it is easy for fears to creep in.

What are the benefits of fearing God? There are many. When you fear God, you are promised guidance and intimacy with God (Psalm 25:12, 14). You also are promised preservation in trials (Psalm 33:18-19) and provision (Psalm 34:9-10). You receive God's love and compassion (Psalm 103:4, 13). The book of Proverbs promises us wisdom and health (Proverbs 9:10). You have the promise of physical health (Proverbs 3:7-8) and prosperity (Proverbs 22:4). Fearing the Lord pays tremendous benefits.

What will it take for you to begin to fear God? Will you have to adjust your time? Will you have to adjust your mindset? Will you have to start reading the Bible consistently? Will you have to start writing out Scriptures? The fear of God is worth any price. It is available to every child of God.

Prayer and Praise:

Lord, thank You for giving me the ability to fear You. Teach me daily what that will look like and enable me to teach others to fear You. Let my life show forth fear of You and not a fear of man. Use me and let me walk daily in faith fearing You. In the mighty name of Jesus Christ, my Lord. Amen.

THE LORD OUR GOD
Deuteronomy 6:1-5

Is God's Word important? You can easily answer that by saying yes. However, does your life show forth that God's Word is important? How much time do you spend in the Bible every day? As you work through this devotional you will read the Bible completely through in one year. That should be the goal of every true child of God. Not just to read it in one year, but to read it through in its entirety. Once you have read it through, read it again and again and again. Read more than three chapters. You can read between forty and fifty pages of Scripture every day (depending on how many pages your Bible has, based on the font size), and you can read the Bible through in one month. Then you do it again.

The charge found in Deuteronomy six is for Moses to teach the Word of God to the children of Israel. God gave His word in the form of commandments, statutes, and judgments. They were to be taught to the people and observed. That means they were to be applied to life. As they were taught and observed the Jews would fear the Lord.

The Word of God (the Bible) is to control your life. That simply means you make decisions based on what the Word of God says. If you do not know, ask. Search the Scriptures and pray. As you read the Word, it is amazing what God shows and teaches you. But you have to be in the Word so that the Word can get in you.

It is as you are into the Word and the Word gets into you, you are then enabled to "love the Lord your God with all your heart, with all your soul, and with all your strength (Deuteronomy 6:5)." It is a privilege for the Lord God to be your God, it is not a right. You are privileged to be called a child of God. When you think it is your right is when you easily become distracted and lax.

Prayer and Praise:

Lord, You are my God. You are the only true and living God. To be Your child is a gift and a privilege. Thank You for Your Word. Let me learn it well and live it right. Let me reflect You as I live out Your Word in a world that never reads the Bible. In the mighty name of Jesus Christ, my Lord. Amen.

WHAT DOES THE LORD REQUIRE
Deuteronomy 10:12

"I just don't know what to do." Does that phrase sound familiar? From a child in school to a college student trying to make a decision on his degree, many times people express an uncertainty of knowing what to do. It is not just in school or the work world. Many Christians act and sound as if God has not left them with any instructions on what to do.

Much of the issue comes from a lack of spiritual development and maturity. God has not called us to do a bunch of activities. This is the great temptation to get busy doing things. In the doing of things, you will derive a sense of satisfaction and fulfillment. The problem is things do not ultimately satisfy, and you have to look for more things, new things.

The Christian life is impossible to live apart from an abiding relationship with Jesus Christ. An abiding relationship requires time spent with God. It requires learning to hear God speak. It does not require telling God what you want to do and then doing it as you ask for His blessing. That is why many believers express the idea, "I just don't know what to do." They have done and done. Once the newness wears off, so does the sense of fulfillment.

What does God require of you? The text tells you. Fear the Lord. Walk in His ways. Love Him and serve Him with all your heart and soul. You saw what was involved in fearing God on February 23. To walk in His ways means obedience to the Bible, and to the commands of God. Is there any area in which you are not obedient? How is stewardship of your time, talents, treasures, and the truth? When you come to God in your daily quiet time/devotions, do you spend enough time to secure God's presence? Or do you rush through just to say, "I had my quiet time." Tarrying in God's presence is crucial.

Then you are to love and serve Him with all your heart and soul. This is important. You are to love Him and serve Him and not man. Much of what is done is a man-centered love and a man-centered service.

The temptation will always be to please man. It is easy to get busy doing, yet you fail at "being" in Christ. It is only as you are "being" that God flows ministry through you. Be sure you minister to the Lord. He must be your first priority.

Prayer and Praise:

Lord, let me not get so caught up in doing that I fail to be in Christ Jesus. Teach me daily to linger in Your presence once I have secured Your presence. Wake me early as not to miss my time with You because of pressures of life. I love You. In the mighty name of Jesus Christ, my Lord. Amen.

TRUE WORSHIP
Deuteronomy 12:1-5

A common phrase that is heard today concerning church is "good worship." That is an unusual statement. Good based on whose standard? Good based on the type of music that is sung? Good based on the "relevant" message? Good based on the number of people in attendance? Good based on the response? All of these are man-centered opinions.

If you go to an area where the church is under severe persecution and you gather with worshippers in hiding, none of the above ideas will fit. In America the pervading idea is we want the convenience of feeling right without the conviction of living right. True worship, according to Jesus, is done in spirit and in truth (John 4:23). When the Holy Spirit touches your spirit as the truth of God is set forth and you yield to that, then you have worshipped. Many are like the Samaritan woman that Jesus referred to and said, "You worship what you do not know."

You do not need to look for "good worship." You need true worship. Spirit, the feeling side, and truth have to be biblically correct.

In the text, God tells His people that there is a place He has set aside for Him to be worshipped. Today it is not at the tabernacle, but at the church. You do not have substitute places of worship. God told Israel they were to destroy all the places pagan worship took place. They were to destroy the images, names, and pillars. The Lord said, "You shall utterly destroy all the places." In Scripture you are warned of high places. These were places people went to worship instead of obeying what God said. God said, "You shall seek the place where the Lord Your God chooses."

Today, there are many substitutes for "the place God chooses." God chose the church to be His place of worship—the local church. You must be very careful of anything that takes you away from the local church. You easily recognize places that tempt you to leave the church: shopping trips on Sunday or sporting activities. However, there are "Christian" things that can take you away from the local church. These can become a substitute for what God ordained. God ordained the local church.

Christian conferences on Sunday deny the local church. Christian programs that take you away on Sunday from the local church fail at what God has ordained and established. You may have a good experience, and the message may be so relevant, but it is not what God ordained and established. God called out the church to be His place of worship. Be careful you do not let a high place be established in your heart.

Prayer and Praise:

Lord, You saved me and created in me a desire to worship You. Father, let me worship in spirit and in truth. Let me meet the conditions You have set forth. In the mighty name of Jesus Christ, my Lord. Amen.

OCCULT PRACTICES
Deuteronomy 18:9-13

The occult first showed itself in the Garden of Eden when the Devil told Eve that she could "be like God," and could know good and evil. The Devil was suggesting there was a power apart from God, a secret power they could access. The occult is always independent of God, and the Devil strives to distract people from God. He is very good at what he does.

As a believer in Jesus Christ, you are called to live a life that is distinct. You are to live in such a way the world will know Holy God is real and that He can transform lives. The Word of God forbids your involvement with the occult. Do you take God's Word seriously? Or do you still dabble, reading your horoscope or allowing things into your home by means of television or Internet?

God's Word bans the occult from the lives of believers. Moses, in Deuteronomy 18, lists eight occult practices that are forbidden in the life of a child of God. Before the children of Israel entered the Promised Land, they had to understand this responsibility. The eight occult activities listed are: divination, soothsaying, the one who interprets omens, sorcery, and the use of charms, mediums, wizardry or necromancy. What these practices have in common is an effort to obtain knowledge by means of the spirit world. Also, those who practice them have a desire to control people or events.

The occult or spiritism is all about demonic activity. Demons have two main goals. First, they try to block the purpose of God. Next, they want to extend the authority of Satan. The point of the text is all of this is forbidden for a Christian. You are to have no part, nor give any place to such activities in your life or your home. This means you must guard what you allow in your home, be it a physical object or over the airwaves of television or Internet. The Bible tells you these things are an abomination to God. If a person gives himself to these things, he becomes abominable in God's sight. Abomination means an object abhorred. Can you imagine being abhorred by God?

Faith stands on the sufficiency of God's Word. You are to seek no other source of secret knowledge or power. Every day you must appropriate the armor of God to be able to stand in an evil day.

Prayer and Praise:

Lord, thank You for the sufficiency of Your Word. Daily let me be girded with the belt of truth. Daily allow me to wear the helmet of salvation to guard my mind and thoughts. Teach me to test the spirits so that there will be no connection with the occult. Give me wisdom to see what needs to be removed from my life or home. In the mighty name of Jesus Christ, my Lord. Amen.

GOING TO BATTLE
Deuteronomy 20:1

When you become a child of God, God places His fear in you (Jeremiah 32:40). It is the fear of God in you that is an enabler to obey God. As you live the Christian life, realize it is Christ living it through you as you abide daily in Him. You will face challenges, trials, enemies, and battles. You will often be outnumbered, but God says, "Do not be afraid of them; for the Lord your God is with you."

To prepare for battle your mindset has to be right. For your mindset to be right it must be filled with the truth of God's Word. Everything you are, everything you do, and everything you are to do must be as a result of hearing a word from the Lord and walking in obedience to that word. Your faith can only be based on God's Word.

Often people express a presumptuous faith. They assume on something. God has not told them anything, but they act, even say, they have a word from God. You better not presume on the Lord. He is in no way obligated to bless your efforts if He has not spoken clearly to you in the area. You can create a mess you may have to clean up later.

Do not be afraid. How do you live out "no fear" living? "He who dwells in the secret place of the Most High shall abide under the shadow of the Almighty" (Psalm 91:1). You have to learn to dwell and remain in the secret place of God. You have to learn to daily secure God's presence. That means more than going through the motions of Bible reading and prayer time. You must linger in the presence of God once it has been secured. You have to learn how to tarry with the Lord.

"He shall cover you with His feathers and under His wings you shall take refuge. His truth shall be your shield and buckler. You shall not be afraid" (Psalm 91:4-5, italics mine). As you dwell, abide, and remain in Christ, He covers you. His truth is a shield for you. Then you will not be afraid. Not being afraid is not something you have to work up in your life. It is not a determined mind. Not being afraid is a direct result of dwelling in the secret place of God. It is a result of being covered by Him. It just flows in your life. Hallelujah, what a Savior! You will face enemies and you will be in battles, but you do not have to be afraid, because the Lord is with you.

Prayer and Praise:

Lord, thank You for Your Word of promise that I do not need to be afraid. Let me ever be sensitive to the fact that when I find fear creeping in my life, I need to take refuge in You, allowing Your truth to be my shield as You cover me. Thank You. In the mighty name of Jesus Christ, my Lord. Amen.

MARCH

SPIRITUAL MARKERS
Deuteronomy 27:1-3

A spiritual marker is an experience or an event that occurs in your life that has spiritual significance. Some of these may not be initially understood as a spiritual marker, but they are. If you were blessed to be raised in a Christian home with God-fearing parents, that is a spiritual marker. You were blessed. The moment of salvation is a spiritual marker. Times you have to step out in faith are spiritual markers. Your life as a Christian should be characterized by spiritual markers.

When the children of Israel crossed over the Jordan and entered the Promised Land, the land of faith, they were told to set up stones and whitewash them with lime. This was a spiritual marker for Israel as testimony. It was for them to see, other peoples to see, and for the future generations of Israelites to see. When asked what they meant, they could explain and witness to God.

Why are spiritual markers important for you? If you will begin to remember your spiritual markers, you will see a pattern of how God has led you in the past. As you can understand how God has led you in the past, you can better understand how God will lead in the future. Past direction of God gives indication of future direction. As God sets His plan in motion and you abide in Him, He continues moving in the direction He has set.

God has every right to interrupt your life at any given time. He can interrupt us to give us a fresh word or to adjust us more closely to Him. God wants to and will direct your life whenever you seek Him with all your heart.

One way the Bible teaches that you praise the Lord is by recounting His mighty acts. When you remember, retell, and recount the acts of God in your life, you praise Him.

Prayer and Praise:

Lord, thank You for giving me spiritual markers. Thank You for how You have led me. You have opened doors and shut doors. You have spoken to me and enabled me to hear and understand Your truth. I praise You. Continue to keep me sensitive to Your leading, and let me acknowledge to others Your mighty acts. In the mighty name of Jesus Christ, my Lord. Amen.

HEART SHIFTS
Deuteronomy 30:14-17

Have you ever experienced a time in your life when you strayed from God? How did that happen? It happens the same way for each person who strays. It may not look the same on the outside, but internally it is always the same pattern.

God blesses and saves a person. That person is greatly thankful for the forgiveness Jesus Christ extended. He is grateful for the mercy and grace of God bestowed. Having his name in the Lamb's Book of Life is beyond words. Then the shift comes. It may be weeks after salvation, or it may take place years after salvation, but your heart shifts.

The lights and the glitter of the world begin to entice you. You are not drawn away to wickedness or evil, at least not at the beginning. But your heart shifts from finding its satisfaction and meaning in Christ, to wanting to experience some things the world offers. Gradually, you lose your hunger for the Word of God. Your desire to pray falls away, and you begin to just go through the motions. Yes, you pray in emergencies, but you really lack faith as you pray.

A heart shifts, and the things of God no longer are the primary concern of life. You have places to go, things to do, pleasures to experience. You come to the place that you are not hearing God as you once did. Other things now have taken priority. All the while you still go to church. You still go through the motions, but you are not as close to God as you once were. Does this sound vaguely familiar?

This is what God warned the children of Israel about in the text. Every person faces the same subtle, gradual temptation. To be forewarned is to be forearmed. The Christian life does not end when you receive Christ as your personal Savior. That is when it begins. Every day you have to make decisions. Some of the decisions can impact your walk with God in a negative fashion. You are free to make any choice you want. You are not free to avoid the harvest that decision produces.

Heart shifts are costly. Is God speaking to you? When was the last time you heard Him speak and you obeyed instantly? You adjusted your life, your lifestyle to His Word and will? If you are not hearing God, you need to examine your heart and see if a shift has taken place. If so, repent quickly.

Prayer and Praise:

Lord, I thank You for saving me. Teach me to be aware of the subtleness of Satan. Let me examine my life and know if there has been a gradual turning away. Then enable me with fresh faith to return to You quickly. In the mighty name of Jesus Christ, my Lord. Amen.

ON EAGLES' WINGS
Deuteronomy 32:11

An eagle has always been a picture of beauty, strength, and majesty. To see one in flight and hear his call is amazing. However, eagles are not born into full maturity. They have to grow and develop. Be certain, everything they need is in them to become a mature eagle, but they have to go through the lessons of life just as you do.

When eagles lay their eggs, they lay them in huge nests of branches, twigs, leaves, and feathers. When the baby eaglets hatch, they are completely dependent on the parents to care for them or they will perish.

When it comes time to teach them how to fly and for them make it on their own, the mother eagle stirs the nest. She removes the down feathers, the leaves, and the eaglet is forced to be uncomfortable. He has to spend his time standing, or he will feel the stab of a branch in his body. Standing and gripping with his talons makes the little bird develop muscle.

Then the mother eagle forces the eaglet to the side and coaxes him to fly. He is scared and refuses. Mother eagle flies while calling to him. Finally, she nudges him of the nest, as he screams and flaps his wings, right before impact the mother catches him and carries him back up to the nest. Terrified, but safe, the next day the eaglet begins flying lessons again. Slowly, the wing muscles develop and one day while falling and flapping, his own wings lift him, and he flies. His parents have released him to soar.

That is how life is for the Christian. You are completely dependent on Almighty God. He provides and cares for you. There comes a moment that you are to leave the nest and learn to fly on eagles' wings. New muscles of faith have to be developed. No matter how you protest, God created you to soar. God will do what is necessary to release you to soar. Your faith will develop if you trust and obey God by doing His will.

Prayer and Praise:

Lord, thank You for creating me to soar. Let me recognize when You are trying to develop the muscle of my faith. Even though I may protest, enable me to learn the lessons of faith. Be glorified as I take flight for You, not myself. Be honored with my life. In the mighty name of Jesus Christ, my Lord. Amen.

FACING LIFE'S RIVERS
Joshua 1:10-18, 3:14-17

It is so easy to grow accustomed to the way things have been. The constant repetitive routine of every day makes change challenging. Changing causes concern because it has never been done this way before. It is easy to grow comfortable with the known.

Imagine the Israelites; all this generation knows is wilderness wandering or Egyptian captivity. Today is a brand new start, and it is time to cross one of life's rivers and enter into their destiny. Will they obey? Will you obey?

What is involved in crossing life's rivers? To begin with, it involves making crucial decisions. Some choices in life are easy and others are not. Being a Christian does not make one immune from poor choices. You must face life's obstacles head on. To do this three things are necessary. You have to make adequate preparations, observe what is happening and has happened. Finally, you have to get your feet wet and step out in faith.

As you move forward in life, you have some things you have to leave behind. Leave behind the murmuring and complaining. Leave behind those things you have substituted for God. Keep your eyes fixed and focused and your ears tuned in to what God is saying.

Crossing life's rivers involves a disciplined life. In Ephesians 5, you are told to walk circumspectly. This means walk cautiously. It is the word picture of a cat walking along a high wall with pieces of glass sticking up. He walks ever so carefully, placing each foot down so as not to do himself harm. That is walking cautiously. You only live a disciplined life as you recognize and submit to the authority of God's Word. Many talk a good talk, but their walk is not in agreement with Scripture.

When the priest's feet hit the waters of the Jordan, the water stood up. It stood up until all were safely across. Jesus Christ is our high priest, and on the cross He died for you, so that now you can cross in victory. He will stand in that river until the last child of God has crossed over. Keep your eyes fixed on Him.

Prayer and Praise:

Lord, thank You for leading me out of the routine I so easily get accustomed to and into the land of faith. Teach me to be disciplined, making proper preparations, using my time wisely, and ultimately stepping out in faith in obedience to Your leading. The currents may rage and the winds may blow, so I ask that You keep me sensitive to Your voice and direction. In the mighty name of Jesus Christ, my Lord. Amen.

THE TRIMMING PROCESS
Joshua 5:2-8

You say the word circumcision to a man, and the mere thought of this act causes him to wince. Most men underwent this at birth and have no recollection of the pain of the ordeal. The very idea is concerning to men.

According to the text, the covenant sign of circumcision had not been practiced for forty years by the Israelite men. Before they could move forward in faith, they had to get their own lives in line with God's word. Is there any area of your life where you are out of step with God? Is there any word of God that you are not obeying right now?

You will never arrive to a place in your Christian life where your flesh will not have to be dealt with. Circumcision was a sign of the Old Testament covenant. To circumcise means to "cut back" that which you can do without. In order to receive what God has for you, you have to deal with your flesh. You cannot walk into the Promised Land, the land of faith, and possess it with your flesh out of control.

God tells you to deal with your flesh. Cut off some things; cull some things out of your life. God wants to take you deeper, but as long as these areas remain not dealt with, filth will gather there, hindering you. Once this has been addressed and dealt with, soreness will be present, but do not be afraid, that is to be expected. Tarry in the place and allow for healing, rest in the love of Christ. Trust Him, and He will lead you deeper into faith.

The children of Israel never went past Gilgal until they had aligned themselves with God's word. You can be saved and on your way to heaven, but you will never go deep with God, experiencing His ultimate provision, if you refuse to cut off things of the world and do not align yourself with God. You can be nice, respectable, and attend church regularly. You may read your Bible and pray. However, you have to be willing to remove those areas where sin can hide.

Prayer and Praise:

Lord, the very thought of cutting off things concerns me. I wonder how I will make it with these things out of my life. What will I do in my spare time for entertainment if all these areas are removed? Teach me to trust You to give my life fulfillment. Teach me to remove those things where sin so easily hides. Show me the danger of not cutting off and not culling things from my life? Father, I want to be a man of faith. Make me a man of faith. No sacrifice is too great, as long as I can walk with You. In the mighty name of Jesus, my Lord. Amen.

FAILING TO DISCERN
Joshua 9:2-15

Has there ever been a time you lacked good discernment? Have you ever made a decision and later realized you made the wrong decision? How is it you can look at all the visible evidence, hear a compelling story, and still make a poor choice, even a bad choice?

The simple answer is that things are not always as they appear to be. You have to process what you see and hear, but you have to seek the face and mind of God in every decision. The Israelites failed to make the right decision, because they did not ask the counsel of God (v. 14). Have you ever been guilty of that?

The temptation of the world is to look only at the external appearance and hear what a person has to say. Then you make your decision. You have freedom to make any decision you want but you do not have the same freedom when it comes to the consequences of a choice. You get to choose, but you do not get to choose the consequence that comes with it.

The children of Israel were lied to and deceived. They entered a covenant with this people because they did not ask counsel of God. How do you ask counsel of God? You pray. You do not do something and then ask God to bless it. You seek God's will in the matter, you adjust your life to His direction, and you listen and obey. If God is silent on a matter, you do not proceed. You learn to wait.

Discernment can keep you from much heartache later on in life. There will be things you miss, pleasures you do not get to enjoy, but discernment pays dividends, both immediate and eternal. It is sad when things are not as they appear, but you are not left to your own devices. The Holy Spirit works in a believer's life like a referee. When the peace of God is not present or if it has been disturbed, do not proceed.

After Israel made a covenant with the Gibbeonites, from then on they had the responsibility of taking care of them, providing for them, defending them, and making sure they were okay. They consumed God's people's time, energy, and resources. Be very careful to whom and what you commit yourself.

Prayer and Praise:

Lord, thank You for Your indwelling Holy Spirit. Daily keep me close as I seek to abide in You. Let me know Your warnings if I ever get tempted to make a decision that is not of You. Teach me to know Your Word as I spend time in the Bible, that I will know Your will. Bring strong conviction into my life when my prayer life is lacking. Let me choose You. In the mighty name of Jesus Christ, my Lord. Amen.

THE SUN STOOD STILL
Joshua 10:13-15

To what extent do you believe God will go in order to give you victory in your life? Victory over sin? Victory over your enemies? When Jesus died on the cross and arose from the grave, He ascended to the Father and is seated at His right hand, and victory over sin was accomplished. God went to the extreme means of letting His only Son die for your sin and the sin of the world, so that you can have victory over sin.

For victory over your enemies, you must ask yourself, "Who are my enemies?" The Bible says in Ephesians 6:12 that "we do not wrestle against flesh and blood, but against principalities, against powers, against the rulers of the darkness of this age, against spiritual host of wickedness in the heavenly places." It is easy to misidentify your enemies.

When Joshua and the Israelites were battling their enemies, Joshua asked God to let the sun stand still until they could complete the task. God heeded the voice of Joshua. God went to a great extent in order to answer Joshua's prayer and allow Israel to secure victory. Be aware, nothing God has ever done has ever caused Him to strain or stress. Every miracle and mighty act is but in accordance to His will. He is Almighty God, and nothing is too big for Him.

To what extent will God go to give victory over your enemies? You must ask yourself several things: (1) God's enemies are my enemies. Who is it you are stressing over? (2) God provides miraculously as you are doing His will. Are you actively doing the will of God? (3) When God gave provision for victory, Joshua still had to fulfil his responsibility. It was not a time to grow lax. Are you fulfilling your responsibilities to the Lord? (4) God gave victory in answer to Joshua's prayer. How is your prayer life?

As a Christian, you have to learn to walk in harmony with God and His Word. As this is done, you position yourself to call upon the Lord and to know His provision and good pleasure. Your faith is then released to experience God. Hallelujah!

Prayer and Praise:

Lord, I exalt You as my God and King. I bow before You and worship You. Father, teach me to walk in agreement with Your Word so I may know Your good pleasure. Enable me to recognize who my enemies truly are and how to seek Your provision. Let me be found faithful doing Your will as I call on You for divine help. In the mighty name of Jesus Christ, my Lord. Amen.

GIVE ME THIS MOUNTAIN
Joshua 14:6-13

Caleb was ordinary, down to earth, and common. Yet God used him mightily. When the Israelites entered the Promised Land after forty years of wandering in the wilderness and letting the disobedient generation die off, only Caleb and Joshua of that generation entered, and Caleb made the statement, "Give me this mountain." It had been promised to him forty years earlier by Moses when Caleb was forty years old. Now it was time to receive the promise. It was no ordinary mountain. Anakim lived there and they were giants. Caleb had no fear. Caleb was an overcomer.

Caleb set himself apart early in life. When the spies went into the Promised Land and brought back a negative report, only Caleb and Joshua remained faithful to God. In Numbers 14:24 it says, "But My servant Caleb, because he has a different spirit in him and has followed Me fully, I will bring him into the land where he went, and his descendants shall inherit it."

What made the difference in Caleb's life? Six times you are told that Caleb "wholly followed the Lord" (Numbers 14:24, 32:12, Deuteronomy 1:36, Joshua 14:8, 14:14). Caleb was an ordinary man, but the chief concern of his life was his relationship to his God. Caleb obeyed and followed his God without distraction or deviation. As a young man and as an old man, he followed his God. If you are strong in faith when you are young, you will not become weak in faith when you are old. As a young man he was capable and responsible. He was dominated by faith, and his life was devoid of fear. He was determined in his relationship with God. Are you?

Does your life express itself with such determination that nothing will stop you from walking with God and obeying God? How easy it is for small things to get in the way of faith. As the Song of Solomon says, "Little foxes that spoil the vines." What is your desire in life? Where your desire is, you will follow. Caleb wholly followed the Lord. What or whom do you wholly follow?

For forty years, Caleb wandered in the wilderness because of the sin of others, but he maintained his faith. The Lord "kept me" (v.10). Caleb was an overcomer. He lived a life of faith. He believed God, and God fulfilled His Word to Caleb. God will fulfill His Word to you, if you live a life of faith and wholly follow the Lord.

Prayer and Praise:

Lord, thank You for leaving us examples of faithful men. Being faithful is not merely about attendance, but also it is about faith in You and Your Word. Teach me faith. Let me hear You speak Your Word specifically to me. Enable me to have strong convictions to obey Your Word. In the mighty name of Jesus Christ, my Lord. Amen.

SHILOH
Joshua 18:1

What is at the center of your life? Is it family, work, God, pursuit of pleasures and pastimes? A person can tell what the center of his life is by what and to whom he gives his time, attention, and resources. Keeping Christ the center of your life is a daily undertaking. The way of salvation is through Jesus Christ and Christ alone. The road we are to walk is a narrow road, yet the broad road constantly beckons you to follow.

When Joshua moved the tabernacle to Shiloh, it was to establish the place of meeting God was at the center of the country. By placing the tabernacle at the center of the land, the people realized that God was to be the center of their lives. God was to be first. He was to be the focus of all they were and would be.

Genesis 49:10 says, "The scepter shall not depart from Judah, nor a lawgiver from between his feet, until Shiloh comes; and to Him shall be the obedience of the people." Shiloh is one of the names for the Messiah, Jesus Christ. Jacob predicted that Shiloh was to come through his offspring.

The word Shiloh means "rest." It can be related to the Hebrew word shalom, meaning "peace." So Shiloh is a prophecy concerning Jesus Christ. Jesus Christ is the peace giver and the rest giver. He is the Messiah, the ruler, and the obedience from nations belongs to Him.

To know true rest and true peace of mind comes only from a relationship where Jesus Christ is the center of your life. The sense of purpose, meaning, and satisfaction comes only as Christ is the center focus of your life. Other things can be important, but nothing is as important as Jesus Christ being your Lord and Savior. To be Lord means He is your Master, your controller. You must yield to Him daily. Thanks be to God for the gift of salvation and lordship.

Prayer and Praise:

Lord, thank You for allowing me to call You Lord. You are my Shiloh. You are my rest giver and my peace giver. In You I have meaning and fulfillment. Thank You. I praise You and exalt You. In the mighty name of Jesus Christ, my Lord. Amen.

THE WORD FAILED NOT
Joshua 21:43-45

Faith in Jesus Christ is based on the testimony of the Word of God. As the Holy Spirit bears witness to your spirit, you know you have been saved and are saved. The Bible is God's Word. It is holy, infallible, inerrant, and sufficient. If you fail to believe in the sufficiency of Scripture, none of the other things matter. The Word of God is sufficient to meet every need you will ever have. The Word of God is truth and the Word of God is more than capable to meet any need in your life.

Joshua gave a powerful testimony to the word of God with the words of verse forty five, "Not a word failed of any good thing which the Lord had spoken to the house of Israel. All came to pass." Is that the testimony of your life?

You live in a blessed time. Unlike the children of Israel, who had only the first five books of the Old Testament, you have the complete canon of Scripture. The word canon refers to all the books that have been inspired by the Holy Spirit as God moved on men to write; it is the completed Word of God. You have all sixty-six books. Not a word of it will fail.

The Bible promises God's Word will never fail and it will never return void. It does not promise one's life will not return void, only the Word of God. The key for you is to know the Word of God. To know the Word of God, you have to spend time in the Word of God. Daily you must read, study, memorize, and meditate on God's Word.

How will you know "it fails not" if you do not know what the Word of God says? Listen to the preaching of God's Word. Ask God to give you a specific word from Him. Learn to take the word off the page and hide it in your heart. Live by the Word of God. Never be afraid to ask questions. Ask your pastor; ask God by His Holy Spirit to illuminate Scripture for you. Seek God through His Word. The Word of God will not fail. It is precious and vital for your life.

An entire remote village in China came to faith in Jesus Christ without a missionary or a personal witness all because two men were given a portion of the gospel of Matthew. Slowly, over a period of time, two believers became three, and three became ten until finally fifteen hundred had responded to the gospel over a thirteen-year period. The Word of God fails not. Hallelujah!

Prayer and Praise:

Lord, I thank You that Your Word never fails. It does everything it says it will do. Teach me to know the sufficiency of Your Word. Speak to me personally through Your Word as I spend time reading, studying, memorizing, and meditating on Your truth. Bless Your holy name. I love You Lord. In the mighty name of Jesus Christ, my Lord. Amen.

LAST WORDS
Joshua 23:1-8

No one likes to be at the bedside of a dying loved one. Yet you want to be nowhere else but there in those last moments. You want to hold her, love her, and hear any last things she may say. Last words people say are important. You strain to hear every syllable; you do not want to miss anything. What would you say if you knew the next words you spoke would be your last?

Joshua 23 and 24 are the last words of Joshua to the leaders of Israel. He told them to remember God and all His blessings. God had fought for them. God had given them victory over their enemies. God had been faithful. They were urged to remember the blessings of God. Why? In doing this, it not only reinforced their faith but it helped their faith to increase. The same is true for you. Remember God, and do not forget any of His benefits.

Next, he tells them to be courageous; to have the quality of mind to face any difficulty or challenge without fear and stand firm in faith. You demonstrate this by carefully obeying God's Word. He told them to "keep and do all that is written" in their Bible, the Book of the Law. This is the same charge given in Joshua 1. Keep it. Keep the Word of God in your heart. Lodge it in your memories. Inscribe it on the tablet of your mind. Oh, what a strong word for today!

Finally, he says, "Do all that is written." You hear the phrase today, "Just do it." That is not always right, because the world wants you to act without praying and thinking of consequences. When it comes to God's Word, yes, do it. Do not deviate from it. Do not turn away from the Word of God.

If you choose to be courageous, keeping the Word of God and obeying it, there will be things you cannot do in this world. When you say yes to God and yes to obeying the Word of God, you automatically have to say no to other things in life. You will have to separate from things of the world. There will be places you cannot go, people you cannot hang out with, things you cannot do—if you are going to be a person of God.

Be courageous, be strong in the Lord, be careful to live a separated life, and cleave to the Lord. Hold fast to the Lord. The word cleave is used in the story of Adam and Eve, in that they cleaved to each other. They adhered to each other and were faithful. "Therefore, my beloved brethren, be steadfast, immovable, always abounding in the work of the Lord, knowing that your labor is not in vain" (1 Corinthians 15:58).

Prayer and Praise:

Lord, let me not get so caught up in life and work, family, and friends, pleasures and pastimes that I forget You. Let me seek You early every day, so that I can remain steadfast in faith. Let obedience flow naturally from my life. In the mighty name of Jesus Christ, my Lord. Amen.

A GENERATION THAT KNEW NOT THE LORD
Judges 2:10

What ensures you that the next generation will know the Lord Jesus Christ? What hope do you have that your children or grandchildren will grow up in a society or community that has a true witness for the Lord Jesus? The only hope you have is to raise your children to know God and to fear Him. The greatest thing you can leave is not a great name; it is not wealth nor is it fame. The greatest thing you can leave when you die is a son or daughter who knows Jesus Christ as his or her personal Lord and Savior.

That does not happen by casually taking your children to church at your convenience. It does not happen by your having a profession of faith with your mouth but your lifestyle has no time or room for God. If you are to leave a son or daughter who knows the Lord Jesus Christ you must make adjustments in your life to Him, to His Word, and to the body of Christ, the church. Your faith will be caught more than it is taught.

Your children must see your faith evidenced. It can be evidenced in how you live, how you give, how you extend forgiveness, and how you adjust yourself to the church. That means you put church as a priority for your life. You support your local church. You serve in and through your local church.

The children of Israel raised up a generation who did not know the Lord, nor did they know of His mighty acts. That is appalling. How could it happen? The same way it happens today. In the process of trying to make things easier for your children and trying to give them the "best" life possible, the main focus of life shifts from faith to fun, or faith to family. Or faith to whatever you want to do. Do your children know how you came to saving faith in Jesus Christ? Have they heard your personal testimony?

"Then the children of Israel did evil in the sight of the Lord and served the Baals; and they forsook the Lord" (Judges 2:11-12). When your children do not know the Lord they will also forsake Him and serve the gods of this world—gods of sports, gods of materialism, gods of pleasure, and countless others. Are you raising your children to truly know the Lord?

Prayer and Praise:

Lord, the times we live in are anti-God. People do not want to be bothered by living for Jesus. Teach me to raise my family to have a heart for You and the things You want. Enable me to stand firm in the faith, even if I am unpopular. Father, let my children and grandchildren know You in a real and personal way. Let them be a faithful testimony for their generation. In the mighty name of Jesus Christ, my Lord. Amen.

ASKING FOR A SIGN
Judges 6:36-40

In today's text, you find the story of Gideon, a man with a weak faith, but a man willing to obey God. God used him mightily. Challenged by the Midianites, Gideon and his army were outnumbered four to one. Having a word from God to go and overcome the enemy, Gideon, like many believers still, needed to have his faith deepened. So he asked God for a sign. Most every Christian has asked for a sign trying to determine God's will. It is a practice referred to as "putting out a fleece."

Is it wrong to ask God for a sign? Yes, when you already have a word from God, it is wrong. However, God loves you and meets you where you are in your faith in order to help you do His will. There are some limitations. You should never ask God for a sign concerning something you know He or His Word has already spoken against.

Gideon was facing a life-or-death situation. He would be taking men into battle, and he had better know God was leading him. He had to exemplify complete confidence in God in order for his men to follow.

Many people seek signs today; however, it is not about life and death. Often it is about convenience. Gideon lived in the Old Testament time. He did not have a personal copy of the Bible. The Holy Spirit would rest on individuals for the purpose of fulfilling God's will. The Holy Spirit did not fill a person as He did beginning at Pentecost. The danger comes when "putting out a fleece" becomes common practice. It was only mentioned this one time in the Bible. It should be a rare and infrequent act.

Today a believer lives on this side of the cross. Jesus resurrected from the grave, ascended to the right hand of the Father, and ever lives to make intercession for His people. You can have the abiding presence of God, as you walk in the Spirit. The fullness of the Holy Spirit is available. He has the completed Word of God, the Bible. You have so much more than Gideon had.

Seeking after a sign is an indicator of a weak faith. Everyone goes though times of weak faith. The answer is not in seeking a sign, but seeking God through His Word, so that your faith will be strong and not waver. As you abide in the Word of God and seek God in prayer, the peace of God, which passes all understanding, will keep you. Let God's peace be your guide. If peace comes, you have your answer.

Prayer and Praise:

Lord, I praise You. Bring me to the place spiritually that Your Word is enough. Let me be very careful about sign seeking. Let me trust Your Word. In the mighty name of Jesus Christ, my Lord. Amen.

WHEN THERE ARE TOO MANY PEOPLE
Judges 7:1-2

It is hard to imagine there can be too many people when it comes to God's work. The church always says there is room for one more. There could never be too many. When God says there are too many warriors going to the battle, you have to ask yourself why. The Israelite army was already outnumbered four to one. How could there be too many?

That should be a question you ask today. When are there too many of God's people for the task at hand? As you look to the situation taking place, with the Midianites and Israel, there were 135,000 of the enemy and 32,000 Israelites. God said, "There are too many" Israelites.

So, Gideon sent home everyone who was fearful and 22,000 went home. This left Israel with 10,000 soldiers to face 132,000 Midianites. It was easy for the fearful to hide among the faithful, and God knew you cannot win with the fearful. God separated His own people to give victory.

Next, God further removed people, and narrowed the number of Israelites to 300. God let them get tired and weary, and then allowed them to drink water from a stream. Those who cupped their hands and remained alert as they drank, God kept. The others who fell on their faces and quenched their thirst without concern for the enemy, God sent home. You cannot win with carnal-minded men—men who pursue creature comforts and fail to remain alert in times of war. Where do you fit into the story? Are you fearful or faithful? Are you pursuing what satisfies the flesh, or do you remain alert and committed? God reduced the army of Israel to make sure He received the credit for giving the victory. He reduced it to impossible odds and then everyone knew God did it.

Today, it's easy to see things accomplished for the kingdom of God, but who gets the glory? The church because it is so large and has amazing resources? The pastor because he is so "good"? The denomination because of their tremendous resources? Who gets the credit?

God often reduces the numbers to ensure He gets the credit and the glory. It is also far too easy to do things for God and attribute them to Him, when in all honesty it is the works of man. Sadly, many do not know the difference. Where do you fit into this?

Prayer and Praise:

Lord, You are my God, and You have a right to remove from my life anything that fails to bring You glory. Teach me to examine my life in light of Your Word, and see if I am among the faithful and the committed. Father, show me my life and let me make whatever adjustments that are necessary to walk in obedience to You. In the mighty name of Jesus, my Lord. Amen.

OBSCURITY
Judges 10:1-2

What does it mean to be obscure? It does not mean insignificant or unable. An obscure person is an individual who is not well known. He is a person from possibly lowly beginnings, but whom God uses mightily.

Even the church and Christians have their present day "superstars." Turn on the television or radio and see, hear, and listen to some really superb preaching and teaching. If one of these individuals' names were to be mentioned, many people will say "Oh yes, I have heard him." There is nothing wrong with having a name and being known.

Sadly, if a meeting does not offer a "big name" as one of the speakers, attendance is poor. Many a God-called and anointed man has just as strong a message and the unction of the Holy Spirit, but God has chosen to allow this person to remain in obscurity. There is nothing wrong with obscurity. Until God chooses to raise you up and bring you out, stay in obscurity.

Tola was such a man. All we know of him is from these two verses. At just the right time, God takes him from obscurity, and makes him a judge over Israel. He judged faithfully for twenty-three years. Scripture tells us "Tola arose to save Israel." Tola was a faithful man and fulfilled his responsibility.

Maybe you find yourself in a place of obscurity. You believe no one knows where you are, much less who you are. You would be wrong. God knows exactly who you are and where you are. God knows the very number of hairs on your head. You have to decide to bloom where you have been planted. If you will strive in going deep with God: deep in the Word of God, deep in your obedience and love for God, in God's time and way, He will bring you out.

That does not mean you will have a national ministry or are known all over the country. It means God will bring you out in His time to do His perfect will, and you can be satisfied doing the perfect will of God. The key is to bloom where you are planted. Are you faithful right now in your calling? Are you faithful in your giftedness? Are you faithful at work, school, home, in your thinking, to your church, to your spouse? If you are faithful in the smaller responsibilities, God promises you will be faithful in larger responsibilities.

Prayer and Praise:

Lord, You are my God and You know exactly where I am and what I am going through. There are times I feel as if You have forgotten me, but You have never forgotten me nor forsaken me. Teach me to be still and know You. Let me be faithful in the little responsibilities, and keep me from trying to advance myself to "bigger and better" situations. Oh, Father let me hear You speak and only if You give me release, let me move. In the mighty name of Jesus Christ, my Lord. Amen.

VICTORY WITH A JAWBONE
Judges 15:9-17

Has God ever intervened in your life in such a fashion that you knew it had to be God? Maybe you were driving along and found yourself in a situation that should have resulted in a wreck, yet somehow you got through it, and nothing happened other than a few tense moments. It was as if God took control of the car and you were safe.

The word for this is providence. Providence is God's purposeful foresight that guards and guides His children. It is wonderful to know when you are abiding in Christ, nothing will happen to you that is not first sifted through God and His providence.

That is what you discover in this story of Samson. The Philistines were ruling over God's people, and three thousand men of Judah went to arrest Samson in order to deliver him to the Philistines. They tied him securely with new ropes and brought him to the Philistines only after he promised not to kill them.

The judge of Israel was bound and brought to the enemy by his own people. Times must have been hard for them to do such a thing. Fear of the Philistines, their enemy, must have been great for them to do this. Samson was bound and brought to them. When the Philistines came to get him, they came shouting. Maybe they were trying to scare and intimidate Samson. Maybe they were excited that they had captured their opponent.

As they shouted, the Spirit of the Lord came upon Samson, and he broke the ropes that had him bound. He reached out and found a fresh jawbone of a donkey and he killed one thousand men. Where did the jawbone of the donkey come from? Why was it right there where Samson was when the Spirit of the Lord came on him? That was God's providence working in his life.

Perhaps a farmer had taken out this donkey going to market, and it fell, breaking a bone. He left it to die. Perhaps it was grazing, and wild animals attacked and killed it, leaving only the skeletal remains. No matter how the jawbone got there be assured of this, God planned it that way. God sent the donkey to that spot to die and leave behind a jawbone that Samson would use as a weapon against the enemies of God. Hallelujah!

God works the same for you as you walk by faith, serving Him and doing His will. He plans ahead for things you will need along the way in order to accomplish His will. Be very careful that you walk in the Spirit and seek to fulfill God's will. Know for certain nothing comes into your life that first God has not allowed.

Prayer and Praise:

Lord, I praise You and thank You that You are my God and You are in control. In the mighty name of Jesus Christ, my Lord. Amen.

THE LORD DEPARTED FROM HIM
AND HE KNEW IT NOT
Judges 16:20

Samson was called to be a judge over Israel. In order to fulfill this task, he had to have the Spirit of God working in his life. In the Old Testament, the Spirit came upon people to fulfill God's will. The Holy Spirit did not indwell them as in the New Testament after the day of Pentecost, but resided on them for the purpose of doing God's will. The Holy Spirit would come and go.

Samson, after lying in the lap of Delilah and telling her where his strength came from, lost the Spirit of God from his life. When she cut off his long hair, which was part of the Nazarite vow that he lived under, he forfeited the power and the Spirit of God. The sad comment is when he said, "He did not know that the Lord had departed from him." Do you know when you are not walking in the Spirit?

Our society does not lend itself to cultivating the presence of God in your life. In fact, it works against that. It tries very successfully to get you to be distracted from God and the will of God. If you fail to cultivate the presence of God in your life, it too can be costly. You will begin to merely go through the motions of Christianity, but it will have no meaning.

You can pursue life and making a living so diligently that you fail to realize the Holy Spirit of God is not moving in your life. You can be so caught up in things of the world that you crowd God out and you do not even know the Holy Spirit has withdrawn from you. You will realize it when a situation arises, and you need God. You will go through your religious routine, but to no avail.

Samson went out to face the enemy, just as he had done at other times, and he lost. He was taken captive and his eyes were blinded. Normally, that is when a person realizes he has drifted from God. Samson was blind and grinding in a circle. Samson had time to think and meditate on the Lord and how he got in this situation. Do you ever meditate on how you got where you are?

The good news is Samson's hair began to grow again. There is hope in repentance. God used Samson once again mightily to defeat God's enemies. The warning is clear: do not get so caught up in this world that you do not sense or know when you cease walking in the Spirit. Do not be like Samson and lose your sensitivity to God.

Prayer and Praise:

Lord, You are my God and I will praise You. Keep me so close that when I fail to walk in the Spirit, I immediately know it. Father, let me not lay my head in the lap of the world and lose Your abiding presence. In the mighty name of Jesus Christ, my Lord. Amen.

DOING WHAT IS RIGHT IN YOUR OWN EYES
Judges 21:25

Everyone is affected by learned behaviors. It is most noticeable when you enter marriage and you realize the way your family has done things is not the only way to do things. From how you fold towels (double fold or a tri-fold), to where do you squeeze the toothpaste, to how you place the toilet paper on the holder (tear it from the topside or the underside).

Those are trivial issues, but they are issues of learned behavior. Prejudice against other races and colors are learned behaviors. It's sad to say how one participates in worship can be a learned behavior. Many times people merely do what they have seen done by example and instruction. If there is no precedent for an act, many do what they feel is right, or best for them.

They follow their heart. Yet the Bible says, "The heart is deceitful above all things; and desperately wicked" (Jeremiah 17:9). They do what is right in their own eyes, and that is in violation of Scripture.

If you are not supposed to follow your heart and do what is right in your own eyes, what are you to do? You learn to walk in obedience to the Word of God. You let Holy Scripture be your rule for life. God will not tell you anything contrary to His written Word. In the book of Judges, they did not have the whole Bible. They had the Pentateuch (the first five books), the Law of God. Nor did they have the abiding presence of the Holy Spirit.

It is never enough to do merely what is right in your own eyes. You must do what is right in the eyes of God. You must adjust your life and lifestyle to Christ. This is done by first knowing for certain you are born again and saved. Then, you are active in your local church. You attend regularly, you participate in the services, the special prayer times, and the discipleship classes. It is never enough to merely attend Sunday morning and never become personally acquainted with other members of the church.

You begin to read the Bible daily. You have a set time and place you meet with God in the Word and prayer. You make yourself available to be used. Above all, you learn to listen to God's voice. You take time to meditate on Scriptures. Meditate on the sermons preached. Give serious thought to God's Word. Memorize Scripture, and recite it daily out loud, meditate on it, and in doing so, you fill your mind with God's truth.

Prayer and Praise:

Lord, keep me close, prompt me with Holy Spirit when I begin to listen to my own reasoning and what I may think is right, but You know is wrong. Let me come to the place my will is lost in Yours. In the mighty name of Jesus Christ, my Lord. Amen.

THE COST OF TURNING TO THE WORLD
Ruth 1:1-6

When a famine strikes, what do you do? First, you must be careful not to do what is right in your own eyes. You have to strive to do what is right in the eyes of God. Be warned, you will be tempted to do what you think is best. You will have ample excuses and encouragement from others to do that. That will only lead to further unpleasant circumstances.

During a time of famine in the land of Judah, among the people of God, a man from Bethlehem decided he should leave there and go to Moab to support his family. Elimelech leaves with his family, placing his trust in a pagan land to provide. He leaves the place of God, the people of God, and the provision of God, during bad times to provide for his family.

Does this happen today? Yes. People leave where God has called them and the church He has placed them in to take a better job in a pagan environment, so they can "do better" for their family. They seek a new home in a neighborhood that has the best school, and they do not consider buying a home based on an area where there is a vibrant church.

Issues arise and they are subtle at first. You do not seem to be able to find a church like the one you left. It becomes easier and easier to not go as frequently and to fill your life and time with the cares of the world. Your children grow up lacking a heart for God, for the church and the things of God. The attraction of the world is strong.

Elimelech left Bethlehem in the midst of a famine. He went to Moab for relief, and he died there. He left his wife widowed with two sons. The sons took Moabite wives, and then we read they died, also. What a tragic picture of a family, all because the father "did what was right in his own eyes."

When times are hard and circumstances are challenging, you have to be very cautious and intentional to seek the mind of God. Nowhere do you read that Elimelech prayed. Nowhere do you find he sought the will of God. He saw a bad situation and what he thought might be a way out of the situation.

God leads people in a variety of ways, but each Christian is responsible for seeking God. God may lead you in a direction that surprises you. He may lead you in a direction that pleases you. Or He may tell you to sit tight, wait it out, that this too will pass. The Lord will revisit His people. No one wants to miss that moment.

Prayer and Praise:

Lord, even in times of hardship and distress let me not forget that You will visit Your people with fresh bread. Let my mind stay fixed on You and seeking Your will. Let me not take matters into my own hands in difficult times. Let me look to You for the provisions I need and let me trust You. In the mighty name of Jesus Christ, my Lord. Amen.

A MAN CHILD
1 Samuel 1:9-11

The book of 1 Samuel describes the transition of leadership among God's people from judges to a king. All through the book of the Judges you found God judging His people for their sin, for forsaking God and going after false gods. The situation at the time of 1 Samuel was dark. According to 1 Samuel 3:1, "The word of the Lord was rare ... there was no widespread revelation."

In the middle of this dark time, God moved upon a woman named Hannah. Hannah was barren, she had no children. Hannah was broken. She lived in an atmosphere of harassment and shame. Hannah was burdened. She knew her condition was but an example of the condition of the land. Hannah prayed.

Her request was not a selfish request. She did not think merely of herself and ask for a child. She specifically asked for a man child. Why? Hannah knew it was going to take a fresh word from God to bring an end to the darkness. She knew the word of God only needed a prophet to deliver it. She prayed for a son, a man child, and she dedicated him to the Lord. She brought him to Eli the priest and left him in his care when he was but a little boy.

Hannah placed her son in a position and a place to learn the ways of God. When God called Samuel, he responded to the call. God raised him up mightily to be a deliverer of His people. Samuel was a judge and a prophet.

When you look at the condition of your society, do you ever pray that God would raise up a man filled with the Holy Spirit and faith, who could receive fresh revelation from God and proclaim God's power with unction and authority? If not, why not?

The need of the hour is men and women with the mantle of Elijah and the boldness of John the Baptist to preach the infallible word of God. In such time as this, the hour is desperate to hear from God. Not to expound a good idea, but to hear from God. Just because an idea is good does not mean it is of God. There is a difference. The good ideas of men honor man and get the results of man. However, God's Word does not return void and man is not honored; God is.

Maybe it is time you begin to ask God to raise up a new generation of prophets: men with boldness and courage, men who know how to separate from the world and get alone with the Father, and men who are not out to make a name for themselves, but only to do God's will.

Prayer and Praise:

Lord, You are still God and King even in times like these. Call out preachers of Your gospel who are not driven by numbers, but are driven by You. In the mighty name of Jesus Christ, my Lord. Amen.

RELIGIOUS ROUTINES
1 Samuel 4:1-11

The children of Israel have gone into battle with the Philistines, the enemy of God's people. God's people lost the battle and four thousand men were killed. When they returned to camp to regroup, they asked why the Lord had let them get defeated. They did not ask God, they asked each other. After further discussion, which did not include the Lord, they devised a plan. Go back into battle against the Philistines again, but this time, take the ark of the covenant with them, and it would ensure victory.

They still did not ask God in prayer, but they had a plan. They not only lost the battle, they also lost the ark of the covenant. Have you ever gone forward in attempts to get out of a situation and not sought God's guidance? Most have been guilty of this.

Notice what the Israelites did. They gathered around them their most holy object, the ark. They thought for certain if they had the ark in their possession, God would give victory. Sadly, today people find themselves in dire situations, and they begin to do all the religious things, trying to ensure deliverance and victory. People cross themselves, get baptized, even re-baptized, and they run to the church hoping God will fix their problems.

Their faith is in the religious activity. Their faith is in a deed, or thing, but their faith is not in the person of Jesus Christ. God never promises to bless faith in a religious routine. God promises to bless faith firmly planted in Jesus. What is your faith placed firmly in? Is it in Christ or a religious activity? Do you think God will bless you because you have done your "religion"?

Romans 10:17 tells us, "So then faith comes by hearing and hearing by the word of God." The way to get out of a bad situation is to receive a word from God, accept it, adjust your life to it, and obey. You must get a word from God. How do you do this? Ask God to speak a word to you, and you read the Bible regularly, completely, and hungrily. When God speaks His word, you will know it. The Holy Spirit bears witness with your spirit as a Christian to teach you and instruct you.

You can have all the religious ritual in the world and still miss God. When you have genuine faith in Jesus Christ, you will meet God.

Prayer and Praise:

Lord, You are my God and I praise You. Ever let me be aware that religious ritual does not impress You, but faith in Jesus does. Lord, let me always wrap myself in Your truth and not routines. Increase my hunger for You. Speak to me through Your word. In the mighty name of Jesus Christ, my Lord. Amen.

THE WAY OF REVIVAL
1 Samuel 7:1-6

Revival is when the presence of God moves in, shows up and demonstrates His glory, and man yields completely before God. It is not just three or four days of special meetings.

The ark of the covenant was returned to Israel by the Philistines. Now it was in Kirjath Jearim, and it remained there twenty years. It should have been in Shiloh, but they stopped short. Is not that how things go today? You tend to stop short of what God says and only go part of the way. Samuel gave instructions to the Israelites on how to get right with God and how to experience revival.

The first step to revival is personal misery over your present condition, over your sin. Samuel said, "If you return to the Lord." That means they had left the Lord, and their need was to return to the Lord. It is amazing the Christians who are unwilling to acknowledge they have left God. The church of Ephesus, in Revelation 2, "left their first love." They did not lose it, they left it. Are you miserable over your present condition? That is the first requirement for revival.

The next requirement is you must be willing to listen and heed God's message. Samuel spoke the word of God to Israel, and they listened because of their response in verse four. They listened, and then they obeyed the word of God. They put away their false gods. They put away those things that were consuming their time and attention and they served God. Have you examined your life as to what consumes your time and attention? Will you respond to God's Word and put it away?

After these things had taken place, the Israelites became involved in serving God. Look at their service. They confessed their sin, they made public acknowledgement of their sin. They drew water and sacrificed to the Lord. Their service was to God, not man. It is easy to slip into the rut of doing things for man and thinking we are serving God. You first responsibility is Godward, not man-ward. That is what often gets you into trouble, substituting services to man, as if it were serving God. There Samuel prayed for Israel and Israel fasted before the Lord. Do you fast?

Prayer and Praise:

Lord, You are God and God alone, and I praise You. You want to revive and renew my life. You want me to experience You. Thank You. Make me miserable over my sin until it drives me to my knees to seek You. Let me hear Your Word and make honest confession that I may experience You. Teach me to fast, to sacrifice before You. In the mighty name of Jesus Christ, my Lord. Amen.

STARTING OUT GOOD
1 Samuel 10:20-24

You have heard it said, "It is not how you start but how you finish." Truer words could not be more spoken. Everyone starts at a different place in life. Some people start miles ahead of others, but it matters not how you start, it is all about how you finish.

When it comes to your faith and your walk with Jesus Christ, people do not all start out the same. Some people are blessed to be raised with godly parents who instructed them in the ways of God and took them to church from birth. Others are not raised by godly parents, and were never instructed in the ways of God or the Bible. You also have those who were raised by moral parents and taken to church on occasion, but the church and the Scriptures were not priority.

People start life in different places, but what matters is not how you start but how you finish. Saul started life literally "head and shoulders" above everyone else. He was anointed by Samuel to be the first king of Israel. He had a sense of humility in that he hid from the crowds and he had proven himself responsible in his search for the lost donkeys, which seemed to be an insignificant job.

With everything going well for Saul, the end of his life was a mess. His jealousy caused him to waste time and effort trying to destroy David. Finally, he fell on his own sword, so that the enemy could not be the one who killed him. One who started out good ended in shame.

You cannot undo yesterday's mistakes, but you can learn from them and move forward in faith. You cannot change the consequences of poor decisions, but you can move forward in faith. You need to strive that your last days will be your best days. To do that, you have to confess any sin you have not forsaken and forsake it. Then you walk in obedience to the Word of God.

As you walk in obedience to the Word of God, you will experience good days and bad, exciting days and days that are not so exciting. You will know days, even months of waiting, but stay faithful to the end. There is a reward for those who are faithful to the finish. When God says, well done, enter the joy of your reward, it will be worth it all. Do you live to hear the words, "Well done?"

Prayer and Praise:

Lord, as I look at the life of Saul, it concerns me. It amazes me how a man with so many advantages blows it. It tells me that self and selfish desires can destroy a person. Teach me, Lord, to live denying myself, and let me finish the race set before me in faith. In the mighty name of Jesus Christ, my Lord. Amen.

UNSUNG HERO
1 Samuel 14:1, 6-7

It is human nature to like receiving recognition. It is taught in the workplace as a means of motivating employees to work harder and smarter. It is not that everyone likes the limelight; not everyone does. In each person there is this desire to want to know "I matter" or "I made a difference." Would you like to live your life always in the shadows and never be acknowledged? That is the role of the armor bearer.

The armor bearer has one job—be sure your leader comes back alive. The purpose for which you exist is to serve your commander. In the text, you do not know his name, where he is from, or anything about him. All you see is his absolute obedience to Jonathan. When Jonathan asked him to go over into enemy territory and face the opposition, he said, "Do all that is in your heart ... I am with you."

That is the attitude you must have in your service to Jesus Christ. It is not that He needs our protection or permission. Jesus wants you to be willing to follow Him, regardless. Jesus wants you to be so close to Him; if He whispers, you hear Him and obey. The key is the word "follow." Make sure you do not get ahead of Christ; make sure you follow behind Him, close behind Him.

As Jonathan went before the enemy, his armor bearer was right behind him. The armor bearer engaged in the conflict only after Jonathan prepared the way. Learn to wait for Jesus to prepare your way. Stay close, follow Him wherever He leads, and in His time, He will give victory.

Your name may never be known among the masses of people. You may never receive and get credit for anything you do here on earth. The end of the story is not on earth. The end of the story goes on for eternity in heaven around the throne of God. God does know your name, and He records every act, be it good or bad. God rewards the faithful.

Prayer and Praise:

Lord, I thank You that You saved me. I thank You that You have allowed me the privilege to serve You. I do not serve You for the rewards or the recognition. I serve You because You are my God, and I love You. Let me be a faithful armor bearer unto You. In the mighty name of Jesus Christ, my Lord. Amen.

FACING YOUR GIANTS
1 Samuel 17:2-4, 10-12

Everyone has his own giants that he must face. A giant is anything or anyone that opposes you from doing, being, or fulfilling God's plan for you. A giant comes at you to intimidate, to scare, and to put fear in your life if you proceed to obey God. Giants can be people or they can be issues. Everyone has to learn to face giants and overcome them. If you fail to overcome your giants, you will live your life paralyzed by the "what ifs" or the "if only" syndrome.

As Israel was camped by the Valley of Elah, the enemy was camped on the other side. Every day for forty days, the giant came and challenged Israel. Every day he got closer and closer, and Israel became more afraid.

In Joshua 11:22, you will find that all the Anakim had been driven out of the land of Israel. The Anakim were giants and instead of pursuing them, they were allowed to remain in Gaza, Gath, and Ashdod. When you allow giants to escape, they will come back to haunt you.

Saul, the king, the one who stood head and shoulders above all the other men, should have taken the lead and faced the giant, but he cowered in fear. He offered to pay someone to fight the giant for him. An unlikely young man, a teenager named David took up the task, because he could not stand for his God, the God of Israel, to be defied.

When David stepped up to face the giant, Saul tried to tell him how to go about it. There are always plenty of people who want to tell you what to do and how to do it. Saul fitted David in his own armor, but it did not fit David. David refused to go in what he had not proven, what he did not know. He removed the armor, and he took his slingshot. He took what he knew. He took what he had proven of value for himself.

In life you will face giants, and how you handle them will determine your future. You can listen to the counsel of man, or you can listen and obey the counsel of God. You will not be popular in the moment when you do not heed man's advice. You have to go with the proven. The Word of God is proven. It is your responsibility to be in the Word so that the Word is in you. You go to honor Almighty God. You take the initiative, going in faith, trusting Christ to go before You.

How are you dealing with your giants?

Prayer and Praise:

Lord, You are my rock, my fortress, and my deliverer. Let me walk in Your truth and not the "truths" that man wants to give me. Let me know Your Word, and let Your Word be proven in me. Show me how to take the initiative of faith in facing my giants. In the mighty name of Jesus Christ, my Lord. Amen.

FRIENDSHIPS
1 Samuel 20:12-17, 41-42

If you have a friend, you are a truly blessed person. Friendships often start with extended family members. Then, as school becomes a part of one's life, more friends are made. It is seemingly easy to establish friendships as a child. You learn to share and simply enjoy playing together.

As you mature, friendships change, shift and even sometimes end. Many a parent wants to protect her child from bad influences and as a result, friendships are not encouraged. Yet many a person has friends she has known all her life. What a blessing.

The older you get the more challenging friendships become, especially new friendships. Friendships take time. That is why when one is young, they develop easier; you have more time to invest. When you are married with children, and working, and faithful to your church, new friendships often end up as merely acquaintances.

David and Jonathan were friends. It was as if an instant bonding took place with them. Both were warriors, and both were seeking the advancement of Israel. With them, it was as if God knitted their hearts together. They were close, best friends.

What is a friend? For adults, a friend is someone who shares the same interests, has things in common (such as children), and they make time to be with each other. They stay connected by visiting or by phone.

When Jonathan realized his father wanted David dead, Jonathan warned David and vowed to help. That is what friends do; they help and they protect. Friendships are costly. They cost time and they can require resources, but they are worth it. David's and Jonathan's lives intersected for what seems to be a brief time, but it impacted them greatly.

When you are older, you realize you have had many acquaintances, but few friends. However, if you have had only one true friend who has lasted through the seasons of your life, you have been truly blessed. A friend you can share your heart with, pray with, and even hurt and cry with is a priceless gift. The Bible says, "A man who has friends must himself be friendly (Proverbs 18:24)."

Prayer and Praise:

Lord, thank You for making me, and everyone else, a relational person. Thank you for the greatest relationship of all, knowing You. Father, thank You for friends who share the same heart and vision as I have for You. Thank You for placing men of like faith and commitment in my life. In the mighty name of Jesus Christ, my Lord. Amen.

ESCAPING TO THE CAVE
1 Samuel 22:1

A common phrase today is "man cave." It is a place, a room, a garage, or outbuilding that men occupy. It has all their favorite things and novelties. Some of it is completely adolescent, but it is a place where a man can get away and escape the pressures of life, if only for a short while. Or so they pretend.

Saying that, let me clarify a few things. Anything can be taken to an extreme. You must be sure things, pastimes, hobbies, or even sports are not taken to extremes. They very easily can become time robbers and wasters, even idols of your heart. When a person tries to escape from the pressures of life, he is by no means to try and escape reality. If you have crossed that line, it is time to reel in things.

Life is hard and challenging, and we all need an escape occasionally. When you pour a slab of concrete, you place in the concrete "expansion joints." These joints are breaks in the concrete pour so that when there are hot or cold extreme weathers, the concrete can have room to expand without cracking.

Into one's life there is a need for godly expansion joints so you do not crack under pressure. David escaped to the cave of Adullam. He was being pursued by King Saul, who wanted him dead. He had done nothing deserving of this pursuit, so he fled. Why would he flee and not stand against Saul? Saul had been anointed king over Israel by God. Since Saul was established and anointed by God, David refused to fight, hurt, or oppose King Saul. David respected God's anointed one.

He escaped to the cave. Do you have a place where you can escape? Do you have a place that can be a retreat from life when it begins to press in on you? Is it a place you can truly recharge yourself physically? Can you rejuvenate yourself spiritually? Most of what is needed in life to maintain oneself with God is time—time, given to the reading of God's Word, studying, meditating, and memorizing; time, given to God in prayer, seeking His face, listening; time not interrupted by cellphones, emails, or television.

David escaped to a cave. You do not have to have a man cave, but you do need a place you meet with God every day to refresh your soul. Take the time. Be sure your life has expansion joints built into it.

Prayer and Praise:

Lord, You are my God and I praise You. You know everything about me. You know what lifts me to the highest and what drives me to despair. Oh Father, teach me the necessity to have a place and a time every day with You. In the mighty name of Jesus Christ, my Lord. Amen.

HEART REASONING
1 Samuel 27:1-7

Do you ever talk to yourself? Be encouraged, because many people in the Bible had conversations with themselves. However, better than talking to yourself is talking to God. The Bible warns us in the book of Jeremiah, "The heart is deceitful above all things." That means the human heart is misleading, even fraudulent. Be very careful in the conversations you have with yourself.

David had a conversation with himself: "he said in his heart"—he reasoned, instead of holding to God's revelation. When he did, it cost him. Saul pursued David relentlessly, and David was running. As he ran he thought, he "reasoned in his heart" that he would be killed by Saul. Instead of trusting in God, he fled to the land of the Philistines, the enemies of God and God's people.

In fleeing for his life, he left the Promised Land; he left the place of God and God's provision to live in the land of the enemy, the Philistines. When David did this, six hundred men went with him. His influence was great, but it was in the wrong direction.

Have you ever felt like your situation was helpless and hopeless? Have you ever "reasoned in your heart" to justify an act of disobedience and sin? Anything can be argued positively in one's heart. Anything can be justified in one's heart. You are not to "lean on your own understanding," you are to trust God. (See Proverbs 3:5.) You are to live according to God's revealed Word and that means you never side with the enemy. It may look appealing and convenient, but you never forsake God.

In your heart, you are not forsaking God. In your heart, it is your only option. In your heart, you can make this work. In your heart, it will not cost you spiritually. In your heart, you reason it out beautifully. Your heart is deceitfully wicked. It is misleading, and it will lead you in the ways of your flesh or the world if you follow your heart.

For sixteen months David lived in enemy territory. Why? Because he lacked patience and faith to wait upon God. He broke under the pressure of his situation and circumstances. Doubt and unbelief entered his mind, when he "thought in his heart." David lived all these months defeated in his faith.

Prayer and Praise:

Lord, I thank You so much for Your written revelation. I thank You for the gift of prayer. Teach me when I am tempted to follow my heart to bring it before You and surrender afresh and anew my life. Increase my faith; enable me to wait upon You. Let my life be a testimony of Your goodness and grace. In the mighty name of Jesus Christ, my Lord. Amen.

A WASTED LIFE
1 Samuel 31:1-7

It is sad to watch people waste their lives. People who start out with such promise and high hopes often end up so wrong. The old adage is right: sow a thought and reap a habit, sow a habit and reap a lifestyle. Saul started out so right, but in the end, he wasted his life.

Do you think that cannot happen to you? Do you think you are beyond the possibility of erosion and sin? No one is. If you allow sin to remain in your heart and life, it will eat at you and consume you.

Satan is in no hurry to wreck your life; he just wants to wreck it. Satan is willing to wait for wave after wave, wind after wind, for thought after thought, habit after habit, action after action, attitude after attitude. It can happen to anyone.

Saul was anointed as king of Israel. He had the anointing of God and the blessing of the prophet Samuel on his life. He started out so right, but he ended his life by committing suicide. Why? Saul refused to wait upon the Lord and His timing, and pride filled his life. His pride led him to fear of man, jealousy, anger, and rage.

What is the difference between David and Saul? Both committed terrible sins, but David knew how to repent, and Saul refused repentance. The key for you in living by faith to the glory of God is knowing how to repent and stay in fellowship with God.

Do you think it cannot happen to you? Do you think you are too slick and smooth? After all, you have gotten by with so many things so far and God has not punished you. Be sure your sin will find you out. Sometimes punishment is not paid out until the end. Are there evidences that your life is in the erosion process?

Prayer and Praise:

Lord, I am not beyond temptation and sin. Prompt me quickly when I begin to tolerate little things in my life that have the potential to erode my life away. Teach me the importance of repentance on a daily basis. Let me live for your glory and not my own. In the mighty name of Jesus Christ, my Lord. Amen.

THE UNANOINTED SHIELD
2 Samuel 1:17-27

Yesterday you saw the tragic end to the life of Saul, a man who was anointed by God, but failed. How did Saul fall? His life was marked by disobedience; he spared Agag's life. His life was marked by rebellion; he would not wait, and he offered the sacrifice before Samuel arrived. His life was marked by pride; he wanted Samuel to honor him before the people. He sought ungodly counsel and advice from a witch. Finally, he neglected to anoint his shield.

Saul fought twelve wars. Eleven times he was mostly victorious. Now, all hope was abandoned in his soul, and his shield was not anointed. The shield is most important. It is several layers of animal hides and leather; you have to keep it supple to prevent it from hardening. A hardened shield was a weak shield because arrows could now penetrate it.

You have to give attention to detail. The same is true in the Christian life. The details are important. The shield when anointed can prevent calamity. It can absorb a blow and can ward off what might have been. Have you praised God for His strength and the shield of faith He extends to you?

"Above all, taking the shield of faith with which you will be able to quench all the fiery darts of the wicked one" (Ephesians 6:16). Keep your shield strong. Keep your faith strong in the Lord. How do you do that? By hearing, listening, and living out the Word of God. "So then faith comes by hearing, and hearing by the word of God" (Romans 10:17).

Prayer and Praise:

Lord, Your Word is truth, and Your Word is how my faith will be a protector for me. Give me a deeper hunger and thirst for Your Word. Intensify my longing for truth. Your Word is truth. Let me understand how trivial things consume my time and take me away from Your Word. Let me stop the trivial pursuit and spend time in your Word. Build my faith, and let fresh anointing flow every time I face battles. Let my shield be anointed with fresh oil. In the mighty name of Jesus Christ, my Lord. Amen.

BE CAREFUL
2 Samuel 6:1-10

David had a great idea; he wanted to bring the ark of God back to Jerusalem. It had been lost to the enemy, while Eli was judge, but they returned it, not wanting to experience any more of the judgment of God. It came back into Israel, and the men of Beth Shemesh opened it and looked inside. For this act of sin, God slew fifty thousand and seventy people. The ark ended up at Kirjath Jearim, and it was there twenty years.

As David began to return the ark to Jerusalem, he placed it on a new cart pulled by oxen. David had musicians playing music, as the sons of Abinadab walked alongside. Suddenly, the oxen stumbled, and Uzzah reached out his hand to stabilize it, and God struck him and he died.

The Scripture is very clear that the ark of God was never to be moved on a cart, and this is what the Philistines had done. It was to be carried on the shoulders of Levites. David, as king, was responsible for knowing this. His advisors were to instruct him, if he forgot. The cost was serious.

You cannot do the Lord's will in man's strength. Even though something is God's will, you are still responsible for fulfilling it as God instructs. You cannot handle what is holy in an unholy fashion. When the things of God are mishandled, good intentions count for nothing. When the will of God is attempted to be fulfilled in the strength and power of man, all you get is man's results.

God is a holy God. He is good and merciful, but you have the responsibility to obey Him completely and trust Him explicitly. When you do, God gives His results and blessing. David assumed because he was involved in a good task and singing and praising God as they went, everything would be fine, and they would be blessed. Was it? No. Disobedience has consequences. No one, not even David, can manipulate God to violate His Word because they are doing a "good thing."

Be very careful. The society and culture you live in tells you just the opposite. It says, "as long as your intentions are right, it will be okay." It takes more than good intentions. Countless people are caught up in cults and false religions, but they have good intentions. Be careful, be sure you have a word from God and be sure you conform to the Word of God.

Prayer and Praise:

Lord, Your Word is truth and Your way is right. Teach me daily to take it seriously. Enable me to conform to Your Word and not merely attempt to be religiously nice. Father, a lost world is watching, so let me reflect You. In the mighty name of Jesus Christ, my Lord. Amen.

APRIL

LO-DEBAR
2 Samuel 9:1-5

Mephibosheth was the son of Jonathan, David's closest friend. He was crippled in both feet, because as a child he had been dropped (2 Samuel 4:4). Now that David was the king of Israel, he wanted to honor his covenant with his deceased friend, Jonathan (1 Samuel 20:14-15). "Is there still anyone who is left of the house of Saul, that I may show him kindness for Jonathan's sake?"

Normally, the new ruler would kill all the former royal family. Mephibosheth would have been the rightful heir to the throne, and to bring him back could be disastrous. David was a secure man and he, the king, sought to bring Mephibosheth to his palace. He found him in Lo-Debar.

Lo-Debar means "no pasture." It was a pasture-less land, a barren place to live. Many times you may find yourself living in Lo-Debar. In those times, it is good to know King Jesus comes looking for you.

When Mephibosheth arrived at the king's table, he came bearing his shameful heritage, his poor self-image, his limitations, and his uselessness. If you will get honest, you will realize that is about all you bring to the Lord's table.

It is not about what you bring to the king's table, it is about what the king brings to the table. As Mephibosheth arrived, you can only imagine all those who were sitting around the table—all the king's sons and daughters, his advisors, commanders, and warriors. They all were physically fit, strong, capable, and then comes crippled Mephibosheth, lame in his feet and useless.

It matters not how you come to the King's table. What matters is that the King (God) comes looking for you. What matters is the King sent for you, and He brought you out of Lo Debar (place of isolation).

When he got to the king's table, Mephibosheth found kindness, forgiveness, restoration, confidence, future hope, generosity, prosperity, provision, and acceptance. That is what you will find when King Jesus seeks you, if you will respond and go. Praise God for His merciful grace.

Prayer and Praise:

Lord, thank You for seeking me when I was in a dry and barren place, a lonely place and a hard place. Thank You that You did not leave me in my Lo-Debar. Thank You that when I could not come to You, You came for me. I recognize my sin, my shame, my limitations, and uselessness to You. Oh Father, I thank You that You looked beyond that and called me anyway. Your provision is bountiful and all I need. I exalt You. Teach me not to look with envy on others who appear to be more fit than I. Teach me to accept my place; any place at Your table is a wonderful place. In the mighty name of Jesus Christ, my Lord. Amen.

THE WAY BACK TO GOD
2 Samuel 11:1-2

As a youngster David was anointed by Samuel to be king. He was fearless and brave, yet humble. When he finally became king, after Saul's death, and united the country, he was held in honor. How is it he could have fallen so sharply into sin? It is the same way you find yourself in sin today.

Idleness, carelessness, and callousness are the issues that bring sin into one's life. David was on the battlefield as a young man, but not as an older man. As an old man, he was idle. He assumed the blessings of the Lord would keep coming. Do you find yourself being idle, vegetating in front of media devices?

The first look at Bathsheba may have been by chance, but not the lingering stare that followed. He was careless with his eyes. Are you careless with what you expose your eyes to? Have you grown so accustomed to the filth that is on the television, the scantily-dressed women, that you think it is normal? You even allow your sons to engage in this activity?

Callousness happens when the deceitfulness of sin so hardens your heart, you become capable of anything, of any act. David became so calloused after committing adultery with Bathsheba, he had her husband murdered. In trying to hide his sin, he committed further sin.

How did David get back to God? First, if you are truly a child of God, God will convict you of your sin. If you can sin and have no conviction, you are not saved. This denies Scripture. The Holy Spirit will convict you of sin. Next, there will be chastisement; you will receive the discipline of God (Hebrews 12:6).You can lose money, relationships, health, even death. David became physically sick. Then, there will be the confrontation. God will bring someone into your life to challenge and confront your sin. It may be a spouse, a parent, a friend, or a pastor. For David it was Nathan.

To be restored, your only response can be that of surrender. You cry out to God for mercy. You confess your sin to God, without blaming others or making excuses. You seek His cleansing. The same God who cleansed and restored David will cleanse and restore you.

Be careful what you continuously expose your eyes and mind to.

Prayer and Praise:

Lord, You are a merciful God. Teach me not to take Your mercy for granted. Convict me quickly when my eyes begin to linger in places they should not. Rebuke me to the point I turn again to You. I love You. Let me not spoil our relationship by pursuing things that only cause pain and regret. In the mighty name of Jesus Christ, my Lord. Amen.

BURNED BARLEY FIELDS
2 Samuel 14:28-33

The plot of this story is about Absalom, who had returned to Jerusalem after avenging his sister's rape and killing his half-brother. He fled and lived for three years in Geshur. David longed for Absalom to return home but once he did, David did not go to Absalom, nor did he allow him to come to him.

Absalom lived two years in Jerusalem, but he did not see his father, King David. Absalom sent for Joab on two occasions to get an audience with his father. Joab did not respond to Absalom's request. In fact, he ignored it and did nothing. Absalom had Joab's barley fields burned, and that got Joab's attention. Ultimately, Absalom got to see his father.

This is a strange story, but a strong word from God for today. If you read and listen with your spiritual ears, you will understand. Joab was a common friend of David and Absalom. Absalom, the king's son, sent a servant with a message to Joab: Come to the king's son. Joab did not come, because he was too busy with other things, and it was harvest time.

Are you deaf to God's call? In essence He is saying, "I called you and you refused, so I decided to get your attention by setting on fire the thing you love, the thing you desired more than Me." When you fail to respond to the Word of God, the call of God, God knows how to get your attention.

How do you respond when the gospel is preached, or do you respond at all? You hear the call, "Come to the King's Son." You ignore it time and time again. God will not be ignored or mocked. He can set on fire your barley fields of health or life itself.

When God set Pharaoh's "barley fields" on fire, it was with ten plagues, and finally Pharaoh called for the preachers. When the King's Son speaks to you, respond quickly and obediently. Do not ignore the voice of God, or it may cost you your barley fields.

Prayer and Praise:

Lord, keep my ear sensitive to Your voice and Word. Let me hear You when You speak and let me obey You without hesitation. Show me what things I am cherishing more than You, and let me make the necessary adjustments in my life as not to ignore You. Father, let me hunger and thirst for You and Your presence. Do not let me get preoccupied with things and not hear Your call. In the mighty name of Jesus Christ, my Lord. Amen.

A LITTLE PAST THE TOP
2 Samuel 16:1-3

David fled to the wilderness as Absalom took over the city of Jerusalem and the kingdom. His mind was racing, My own son has betrayed me. As he started up the Mount of Olives, he paused to worship (2 Samuel 15:32). Behind the Mount of Olives lies another mountain, Scopus. When David got a little past the top of this mountain, God already had someone there to help him.

When people betray you, learn to flee to the wilderness, the place of separation and isolation. In trying times, you have to learn to worship. Just as with David, during those worship times, something happens. God begins to move on your behalf and He sends someone or something to meet your need.

It seems many do not really know what they need. They think it is a physical provision, or a financial provision. It may be in certain cases, but the need you have is meeting with God and worshipping. As you worship, you can begin to get God's perspective on life. That is so needful; too often you only have man's perspective.

God heard the cry of His servant, and God sent someone ahead to minister to David. When he got just a little past the top, Ziba was there. Could Ziba fix the mess with Absalom? No. Ziba brought needed refreshment to strengthen David and his men. God had gone before and prepared a table in the wilderness for David.

All David saw as he climbed the mountain was a mountain, but on the other side, the blessing of God was waiting for him. On this side, you may only see hurt and sorrow, but just a little past the top there will be the provision of God. Hallelujah!

When you feel like you cannot go on, remember that God has promised never to leave you nor forsake you. God is already working on the other side of the mountain. On the other side of the mountain, David found rest. Donkeys were provided to carry him. He found rejoicing, and there were summer fruits. He found refreshment, juice for the journey.

Where are you? Are you climbing the mountain? Or, are you bringing the blessing?

Prayer and Praise

Lord, You are the Most High God, and You are my God. I praise You. Nothing takes You by surprise. Teach me to rest in Your sovereignty. Teach me to learn how to worship You in the midst of the difficulties of life, and keep me pressing on in faith. Father, use me for Your glory and honor. In the mighty name of Jesus Christ, my Lord. Amen.

RIZPAH
2 Samuel 21:1-14

This is a strange story, but very solemn. There had been a famine for three years, and David inquired of the Lord as to why. God told him it was because of sin. Sin has a way of doing that. Sin brings with it famine: a famine of hearing the Word of God and a famine of prayer. All too often people get used to the famine and they think it is normal.

When David inquired of the Lord, he was told it was because under Saul's reign, he slew the Gibbeonites. The Gibbeonites were not Israelites, but a covenant had been entered with them in Joshua chapter 9. Saul, in his zeal, broke the covenant and slew them. The only way the Gibbeonites would be satisfied was for seven sons of Saul to be publicly hanged.

Two of these sons were the sons of Saul's concubine, Rizpah. Rizpah displayed one of the greatest acts of love a mother has ever shown. When the dead bodies of her two sons, and the others, were hung upon the tree, she watched over them. She drove away everything that would take their decaying flesh. She protected those corpses from the beasts of prey.

She persevered until the king, David, heard of her devotion and moved on her behalf. She did not do this for a few days, but rather for weeks and months she persevered. She has left an example to follow.

Rizpah had two sons who were dead and corrupting, but she kept a watch over them. You may have loved ones living outside of Jesus Christ, and they are dead in trespasses and sin (Ephesians 2:1). They are dead and around all sorts of dangers. You are called by God to do as Rizpah did. You are to keep a constant, even sleepless watch over them spiritually.

The spiritual meaning is if you are going to watch over the souls of men and women; if you are going to pray without ceasing and labor without ceasing; if you are going to have the love of Christ for souls who are dead in sin, never give up until the shame is removed. You must face the fact that the Devil is against you. Do not stop short. What souls do you need to be praying for right now?

Prayer and Praise:

Lord, burden me for the lost. Drive me to my knees to intercede on behalf of men and women, boys and girls who are dead in their trespasses and sin. Let me see them as lost and undone, without You. Enable me to face the opposition of the Devil and not stop. In the mighty name of Jesus Christ, my Lord. Amen.

MIGHTY MEN
2 Samuel 23:8-22

Throughout David's life, he had been a warrior. As a youth he killed a lion and a bear. Then he killed Goliath, the giant. He was the commander of Israel's army. When God raises up a man to do a work, He always raises up "mighty men" to help. Mighty men are men mighty in valor, mighty in faith, anointed with the power of God. Men willing to lay their all on the altar for their king. Are you a mighty man?

The mighty men in the text show what your proper relationship with the Lord should be. Adino was a man outnumbered in battle eight hundred to one. Eleazar was a man with a sword. Shammah stood when others fled. Abishi was the man who came to the aide of the king. Beniah was a soldier like no other.

Adino was a man who refused to give up. With a spear, he defeated eight hundred men. He was a man of courage and strength. Today, this type of courage and strength comes from being yielded to Jesus Christ and filled with the Holy Spirit (Ephesians 5:18). You must yield in order to be filled.

As Eleazar fought, his sword froze in his hand. You must become one with the Word of God. Eleazar was one with the sword. The Word of God is to become part of you. Your greatest weapon is the Word of God. Read, mediate on, memorize, and utilize the Word.

Shammah stood when others fled. He risked everything for a pea patch. He was not affected by what everyone else did. The enemy was coming to rob an plunder what belonged to the king, and the king's honor was at stake. Though others fled, he was not affected by what others did. Are you?

Abishi came to the aid of the king. He was more concerned about the king than himself. What is your greatest concern?

Beniah was no ordinary soldier. He was David's personal bodyguard. He met the worst enemies in the worst places, under the worst conditions, and he won. He was loyal. How is your loyalty to Christ? How is your loyalty to His bride, the church?

All of these men stood out from the others because they had one common quality—they loved their king. It is very easy to adopt the world's philosophy that says, "It is all about me." The truth is as a disciple of Jesus Christ, a true believer, it is not about my convenience, my comfort, my time, or my whatever. It is about King Jesus.

Prayer and Praise:

Lord, You are my King, and I worship and exalt You. Teach me to bless You and honor You. Let me live so close to You that I know Your desires. Let me become one with Your Word. Make me into a mighty man. In the mighty name of Jesus Christ, my Lord. Amen.

THE PRAYER THAT MOVES GOD
1 Kings 3:5-15

What a wonderful thing to be able to pray, to interrupt God, and He responds. The concept of prayer is overwhelming. God is God of everyone and everything, not just Christians. He is the only God. He is enormous and majestic.

As a human being, you are limited, you get tired and weary. God never tires or gets weary. At the whisper of a human voice, He stops and gives attention. What a privilege it is to pray.

The Bible teaches us to ask anything in His will, and He will do it. The effectual, fervent prayer of a righteous man avails much. What a privilege to pray. A filthy, fleshly clay tongue can arrest the holiness of heaven.

God told Solomon, "Ask! What shall I give you?" (1 Kings 3:5). Could it be possible that Almighty God is right now provoking a conversation with you? This is the challenge of prayer: What am I to ask?

Solomon paused as he stumbled into the presence of prevailing prayer. He began with praise. Solomon found himself in a wonderful position of authority that he did not deserve, and he was now king. He thanked God for His mercy.

Solomon came to God as a little child and he said, I do not know what to do (v. 7). Prayer is that one fleeting opportunity to be real, to express your vulnerability. The reason God does not move on behalf of some people is they refuse to admit their need. God said, "Ask of me anything."

There are two types of prayer. There is the prayer that moves you. You start out one way, but in the process you see a higher purpose. There is the prayer that moves God. You pray to the point that God turns.

In essence, God said, "Solomon, since you did not ask for long life and riches, I am going to give you what you did not ask for, because you asked for an unselfish thing. You ask for something that is going to help you do My will. Because you sought Me first, above stuff, I will give you everything."

Do you seek God above stuff? Do you ask for that which will help you do the will of God? What you do not ask for is as important as what you do ask for.

Prayer and Praise:

Lord, teach me to know what to ask of You. Let me realize if I am praying like a lost person or merely asking to be blessed, prospered, and to have a life of ease and comfort. Oh Father, teach me to pray for Your glory and honor. Give me wisdom that I can know how to live in a society that denies You. In the mighty name of Jesus Christ, my Lord. Amen.

THE HALFWAY POINT
1 Kings 6:7-14

Solomon had not been king very long and he was only a young man. He had consolidated the power of his throne. He had stopped a rebellion by his half-brother. He had executed all the powerful and influential conspirators. Yet, as he sat on the throne, he sensed a deep inadequacy and felt helpless with the task before him.

Solomon cried out to God, and God answered him. God promised Solomon He would meet his needs. Have you cried out to God in this fashion? The task before you seems overwhelming and without God's enablement, you will not succeed. Cry out to God.

Solomon was commissioned to build the temple. David had left him all the resources he needed to build the temple. As with any project, starting is exciting. Everything ahead of you looks fresh, new, and inviting. About the halfway point, the excitement wanes. The temptation is to quit.

At the halfway point, discouragement can set in. God gave Solomon a fresh word. He told him, "If you walk in My statutes, execute My judgments, keep all My commandments, and walk in them, then I will perform My word with you" (v. 12). The fresh word was an old word. God kept bringing him back to the basics.

What are the basics? Love God, obey all God has said, and trust Him. That is as simple as it gets. That is the message from Genesis to Revelation. When you love God, you obey Him. Trust is more challenging. Obedience has boundaries; it is often "black and white." Trust has no boundaries.

You are called to trust God, no matter what the externals are saying. Trust is having strong confidence in God and in God's Word. When you know what God's Word says, trust it, do it, and rest in God.

Prayer and Praise:

Lord, so often I need a fresh word of encouragement from You. I do not need it from a man; I need to hear it from You. Let my heart and soul be in such a shape that I can hear You when You speak. Teach me the importance of listening. Let love, obedience, and trust for You flow from my life. In the mighty name of Jesus Christ, my Lord. Amen.

APRIL 9 • Bible Reading: 1 Kings 7 – 9

REGARD THE PRAYER OF YOUR SERVANT
1 Kings 8:28

Do you want God to regard and respect your prayers? Notice what Solomon did. He stood before the altar lifting up his hands and before all the people to make his request. But somewhere during the prayer, he fell to his knees, his heart broken before the Lord. He fell to his knees in humble, reverential submission.

Do you approach God in humble, reverential submission? Or are you more casual? So often, you are told that Jesus is your friend, and you treat Him as such. Jesus is a friend of sinners, but He is Almighty God, and how one comes to Him in prayer is crucial.

God is often approached rudely, flippantly and with total lack of recognition of His majesty and greatness. He is not your good buddy or grey-haired grandfather; He is the living God. Irreverence is an insult to God

Listen to what the Bible says about reverence for God:

Matthew 6:9 – "In this manner, therefore, pray: Our Father in heaven, hallowed be Your name."

Joshua 24:14 – "Now therefore, fear the Lord, serve Him in sincerity and in truth, and put away the gods which your fathers served on the other side of the river and in Egypt. Serve the Lord!"

Psalm 29:2 – "Give unto the Lord the glory due to His name; Worship the Lord in the beauty of holiness."

James 4:7-8 – "Therefore submit to God. Resist the Devil and he will flee from you. Draw near to God and He will draw near to you. Cleanse your hands, you sinners; and purify your hearts, you double-minded."

Habakkuk 2:20 – "But the Lord is in His holy temple. Let all the earth keep silence before Him."

God keeps His Word. You can trust God. He is faithful, absolutely faithful; He will keep His promises. You have to approach Him with reverence and submission. He will never fail to meet your needs.

Prayer and Praise:

Lord, let me approach You always with reverence and submission. Let me not assume on our relationship. In the mighty name of Jesus Christ, my Lord. Amen.

A HEART TURNING FROM GOD
1 Kings 11:1-3

With all that Solomon had going for him, it is quite surprising how easily his heart turned from God, or is it? The Scripture gives us the regulations for the king. The king was not to multiply horses. The king was not to multiply wives, and the king was not to multiply gold.

When Solomon began to multiply horses for himself, a shift took place in the area of his confidence. No longer was the Lord his strong confidence; now he could be confident in his horses. His horses became his defense.

How is that with you? Do you find yourself thinking you have safety and security because of your neighborhood? Because you have an alarm system or firearm protection? Where does your confidence lie, in the person of the Lord Jesus Christ or a physical thing? Always check your heart to see if it has shifted to the world.

When Solomon began to multiply wealth, another shift took place in Solomon's heart. The riches of the world and wealth that he now held began to rival the riches he enjoyed in God.

What rivals your riches that you have in Christ? Do you find your pleasure in Christ? Do you have delight in the Word of God and prayer? Or have the things of the world gotten your attention, and now you seek your pleasure from the world? Guard your heart.

Solomon multiplied wives. His heart turned because his wives brought with them their pagan gods, and Solomon was influenced by these. What a tragedy—a man brought up in the fear and admonition of God, but allowing pagan gods into his home. It is such a subtle thing, to tolerate sin just a little, yet it will shift your heart, turn your heart from God. Are there any areas in your life that you need to readjust back to the Father?

Prayer and Praise:

Lord, thank You for the warnings You give me in Your Word. Teach me to heed them quickly. Let my confidence be in You and only You. Show me any sin I am tolerating and let me lay it down and forsake it. Father, You be my delight and joy. In the mighty name of Jesus Christ, my Lord. Amen.

DISCERNING GOD'S VOICE
1 Kings 13:1-2, 8-10

This passage is a solemn warning for anyone who has a clear word from God. Obey God's Word, and do not compromise it. Here was a man of God, a prophet, given a word from God to deliver to the king, and he obeyed it completely. However, another prophet told him that God had also spoken to him, so the first prophet listened to the other prophet's word.

What can be wrong with that? They both supposedly have received a word from God. The prophet who prophesied to the king was told explicitly by God not to take anything or to return the same way you came. When tempted by the king to eat and drink, he was strong in the word of God and refused.

However, when the old other prophet said God had given him a fresh word concerning the first prophet. The first prophet listened to the old prophet and went to his home to eat and drink. As a result of disobeying the clear word that God had given him, the first prophet ultimately died. He was mauled to death by a lion.

You say, "That is not fair." Maybe so, but that is how life still is today. You live in a world where people have good intentions, but good intentions are no substitute for a word from God. If God speaks to your spirit His word, you had better obey it without compromise. It matters not who comes alongside of you to say otherwise. Your first responsibility is to the word you have received from God.

Many people have the best intentions, but many people have not heard God speaking. Nor have they heard God's word for you. The trouble that confronts the church is everyone is doing what someone else is telling them to do, but they are not hearing God speak to them personally.

Doing good deeds and acts of kindness are fine, but that does not mean you have heard from God. You can get so caught up in doing your good acts that you miss God when He speaks to you, because you are distracted by doing nice stuff.

It is imperative a person hears from God. The disciples, after Jesus Christ's crucifixion, waited ten days in hostile Jerusalem in obedience to God's command. They waited in faith, but they waited on God. When God came and spoke, they heard His voice, knew His will, and obeyed. God did more on Pentecost, saving thousands, than man could have done in a lifetime of business.

Prayer and Praise:

Lord, thank you for Your Word. Your Word is truth. Let me be so filled with Your Word that when someone tries to convince me of another way, I choose in faith Your Word. In the mighty name of Jesus Christ, my Lord. Amen.

PUBLIC SUCCESS
1 Kings 17:1-8

The story of Elijah is an amazing story. Elijah is an unheard of prophet, and he gets an audience with the king of Israel, Ahab. How he got past the palace guard and into Ahab's presence is nothing other than God's providence. God will get a man before whomever He desires, and He will do it without the aid of man.

Then, he preached God's Word to Ahab, "There shall not be dew nor rain these years, except at my word." Next, after preaching to the king of Israel, God sent Elijah to the brook Cherith to wait out the three-year drought. That does not fit the modern day mindset. Elijah should have been on the popular preacher's circuit. God's ways are not our ways.

Before you can minister publically, you must have your private ministry right. Why? You are not called to a friendly world, and your only weapon must be sharp. Your only offensive weapon is the Word of God (Scripture). The worst thing that can happen to a man of God is to succeed publically and fail privately.

God sent him to a brook, and for nearly three years Elijah went to a place of obscurity and trusted God. Who are you trusting, God or a man? For three years, God fed Elijah with a raven bringing him food daily and water from a brook in the midst of a famine. This all happened because Elijah was faithful to the word of God.

When the brook dried up, God sent Elijah another word. Be careful you do not move until God sends you His word. Things can get worse, they may get worse, but your responsibility is to wait for a word from God.

If you move without a word from God, you move in your flesh, and you will reap a harvest of the world. It is a harvest that is fleeting and deceptive. When you move in obedience to the word of God, you reap a harvest of the Spirit. This harvest gives guidance for the present and an eternal reward.

The book of Ephesians says, "Now to Him who is able to do exceedingly abundantly above all that we ask or think, according to the power that works in us, to Him be glory in the church" (Ephesians 3:20-21). Even your best idea cannot compare to what God wants to do and accomplish, and that is amazing.

Prayer and Praise:

Lord, glory and honor to Your Holy name. You are God and You have everything under control. I may not understand it or even like what I am experiencing, but You are God, and I want to trust You. You can do in five minutes more than I could accomplish in fifty years. I praise You. In the mighty name of Jesus Christ, my Lord. Amen.

UNDER THE BROOM TREE
1 Kings 19:1-8

Elijah had returned from a tremendous victory on Mount Carmel. The Lord God Almighty answered with fire from heaven, and the hundreds of pagan prophets were destroyed. Next, the rain came, and Elijah went back to the city of Jezreel. But there was no welcoming committee to greet him. How do you respond after a tremendous spiritual victory and no one congratulates you?

When Ahab arrived, he told his wife, Jezebel, what had happened and she vowed to kill Elijah. Upon hearing her threats, Elijah ran back into the desert, found a juniper, or broom tree, and prayed to die.

Have you ever been spiritually depressed? Even if you sense the power of God has been working, you still feel as if you cannot go forward. Elijah, a man of God, a prophet, prayed to die. Spiritual depression can strike anyone.

What do you do when you find yourself in this condition? Elijah slept and he ate. You have to take care of some basic issues. Get some sleep. Taking a nap can be a spiritual exercise in some situations. Eat a healthy meal. When Elijah awoke, God did not rebuke him and criticize him. God was the one who took care of him, providing him food. Also, God gave Elijah a word of direction.

It is ever so important that you take care of your physical body with nourishment and rest so that you can hear from God. Often, in the midst of a spiritual depression, your mind is filled with the voices of man. The threats of the world overwhelm you. Get alone, get plenty of rest and nutrition, and listen for God. When God gives you a word, obey it. It does not matter if you completely understand it all; you must obey the word God gives.

When you obey the word of God (specific instruction), you are positioned for the next word of God. Until you act on what you already have received, you will not receive the next word of revelation.

Prayer and Praise:

Lord, there are times I do not feel very spiritual. There are times I feel useless and defeated. In those times, I ask You to sustain me and teach me to rest. Enable me to trust You and not my feelings. Lord, I need Your word, Your revelation, and I wait for You. In the mighty name of Jesus Christ, my Lord. Amen.

EQUIPPED FOR SERVICE
2 Kings 2:1-13

The story of Elijah being taken to heaven in a chariot of fire is amazing. However, the issue has to do with Elisha being prepared for service unto God and not so much how Elijah ascended to heaven. How does God prepare a man for service?

There are no shortcuts for becoming a man of God, and there is no quick fix. You are saved by grace through faith, and it is faith from beginning to end. The road of faith is a long road, and it is a less traveled road. It is the only way you can walk, be right with God, and equipped for service.

Elijah and Elisha were at Gilgal, and God directed them to Bethel. From Bethel, they were directed to Jericho. Then, from Jericho, they were directed to the Jordan River. If you were to plot this on a map, you would find they did not go in a straight line. Rather, they crisscrossed back and forth. From Gilgal the Jordan River was about ten miles, but God led them the long way.

That is still how God leads today. It is the long road on which faith is developed. Every place God leads you, He has a purpose. There are appointed seasons of refreshing from God if you follow Him.

Gilgal was the place of remembrance of the faithfulness of God, when the Israelites came into the Promised Land. Bethel was the place of worship. There Abraham built an altar to God. Jericho was the place of conquest, victory, and sacrifice. All the spoils of the battle belonged to God. Then they moved to the Jordan, the place God had the waters to stand up, so that the Israelites could cross over into their inheritance. All of these were appointed places of refreshing.

Have you experienced places of refreshing in your own life? Be faithful, follow God closely, and the seasons of refreshing will come. Faithfulness to God in challenging and difficult times will be rewarded. Rewarded with hope, assurance, and strong confidence in God, rewarded with faithful service.

Elijah told Elisha, "If you see me when I am taken from you it shall be for you." In essence, you will get a double portion. The Hebrew translates this, "if you see what I see." In other words, if you have the same vision I have and understanding of what God has called you for, you will be blessed. What's your vision?

Prayer and Praise:

Lord, be my vision. I praise You for Your faithfulness and the seasons of refreshing You send. Father, keep my eyes fixed on You; be my vision. Help me not to focus on the negatives and the trivial; keep my eyes fixed on You. In the mighty name of Jesus Christ, my Lord. Amen.

NAAMAN THE LEPER
2 Kings 5:8-14

Naaman was a man of high position and royal favor. He was the captain of the armies of Syria. But Naaman had one drawback, he was a leper. He was a man with a handicap, but he did not use his handicap as an excuse.

He was given advice by a Hebrew slave that if he were in Israel, he could be made whole by the prophet of God, Elisha. After getting permission from his king, Naaman went to Israel in hope of being healed. When he came before the king of Israel with his request, the king got upset. He says, "Am I God? Can I fix your problem? Did you come here to cause trouble?"

When Elisha heard what was taking place, he sent word to the king, and said for him to send Naaman to him. He would show Naaman that there was a true prophet of God in Israel.

Naaman travelled to Elisha. He came with his horses, his footmen, and his chariots. He came with all the fanfare a dignitary would show. Once he arrived, Elisha ignored him. Elisha did not come out to greet him, he merely sent a servant with a word, "Go and wash in the Jordan seven times... and you shall be clean."

Naaman was insulted and his temper raged. Why had Elisha not greeted him? How could he be expected to wash in the dirty Jordan? Is that how you respond to God's word? Do you come before Almighty God with a preconceived idea of how He is going to respond to you? Do you struggle with submitting yourself to the simple command of God to "repent?" Do you struggle in your pride to seek forgiveness, or make restitution, as God's Word teaches?

Naaman had it all figured out in his mind. He would come with all his pride, and Elisha would respect that. Next, Elisha would come out to him and ask him to do something significant, so that he would be healed and still retain his pride. Is that your idea of coming to God?

You cannot do God's will man's way. Cleansing and forgiveness requires submission and obedience to the Word of God. It requires humbling yourself before others. If you want to know the cleansing and wholeness of God in your life, you must yield your attitude to God. Naaman submitted and was healed. His entire disposition changed when he did things God's way.

Prayer and Praise:

Lord, You are my King and I will praise You. You are my sustainer and healer. Teach me to come before You with submissiveness and without complaint. Show me what I need to adjust in my attitude in order to bow before You. Make me clean, holy, and useful for Your glory. In the mighty name of Jesus Christ, my Lord. Amen.

A DAY OF GOOD NEWS
2 Kings 7:1-9

Four leprous men sat at the gates of Samaria waiting to die. A famine had gone throughout the land and, compounded with that, the Syrian army surrounded the city. If they went out, they would be killed; if they stayed where they were, they would die. What do you do when neither choice is good?

How do you react and respond to difficult decisions? These four men, contaminated with leprosy, weighed out the cost of doing nothing or of seeking mercy from the Syrian army. One option was certain death and starvation. The other option offered a glimmer of hope that mercy might be extended.

In life, rarely would you find yourself in this extreme situation, but it does take place. The doctor examines your test results, and you have a disease for which little is known to combat it. You can do nothing and succumb to certain death, or you can try an exploratory treatment. The treatment may kill you, but it also may cure you. What do you do?

This is not relegating God out of the equation. You are seeking His divine intervention and healing, but you have to make a decision.

Is it possible these four men never heard the word of Elisha? After all, they were lepers and outside the city gates when he spoke. Elisha said, tomorrow, food will be in abundance. These four men either did not hear, or believe what they heard. Do you believe the word of God? Are you in a position to hear the word of God?

These four lepers chose to side with the possibility of hope. They went down to the enemy's camp only to find it deserted and food in abundance. They ate, drank, and took of the abandoned treasures. It was then they realized what they were doing was not right. "This is a day of good news and we remain silent."

You have been given the good news of Jesus Christ. You have been blessed with the mercy and grace of God. Are you silent, or do you share your faith? The sin of silence is tremendous and costly. Tell the good news. Make decisions based on faith and obedience to the Father. This is a day of good news.

Prayer and Praise:

Lord, truly You have blessed me with good news. You have blessed me with Your mercy and grace. I was contaminated with the leprosy of sin, but You intervened in my life and gave me hope. Thank You. I praise Your holy name. In the mighty name of Jesus Christ, my Lord. Amen.

RISKING FOR THE KING
2 Kings 11:1-3

Jehosheba was the daughter of Judah's King Jehoram. His mother was Athaliah and she was the daughter of Ahab and Jezebel. Athaliah was a wicked woman. Jehosheba was from a family devoted to evil and idolatry. Yet Jehosheba stands out as an example of what a God-fearing person looks like. She obeyed God even at the risk of her own life.

She was married to the high priest, Jehoiada. They lived in a dark time of Judah's history. Cruelty, immorality, and profaning the temple worship were common. The kingdom of Judah was reaping the harvest of a compromised walk with God.

When the king's mother, Athaliah, saw her son the king was dead, she rose up and began killing all the royal line. Joash, however, was saved by Jehosheba and Jehoiada. They hid him from Athaliah. In doing this, they preserved the "royal seed" from extinction. For six years, they hid the young child until he could ascend to the throne.

As you read the story of this husband and wife, several things stand out. She and her husband opposed the evil of their society. Jehoiada, as the high priest, would have sought to correct spiritual and social problems in the land. His wife was at his side.

Jehosheba was a brave woman. She took the initiative in rescuing Joash from Athaliah. She knew what needed to be done, and regardless of personal danger, she took action. Then, for the next six years, she worked, trained, and hid the future king.

Never underestimate the power of one, be it a man or a woman. One woman saw the need and acted. One woman initiated the stance to preserve the royal line of David. Even when surrounded by corruption and evil, one person can make a difference. You stand for truth and you live by faith. The example of faith is a tremendous encouragement to others.

Do you stand against the evil of your society, or do you "go along to get along?" Do you risk your own personal safety to obey God? Do you risk anything to obey God? Let your faith shine as a light in the darkness that is all around.

Prayer and Praise:

Lord, I stand amazed when I read of the courage of this one woman and her husband. I thank You that You opened a door for them to be faithful. I ask you to give me eyes to see the issues that threaten Your kingdom, and give me courage and wisdom to act in faith. I praise You. I thank You for the testimony of Jehosheba and Jehoiada. In the mighty name of Jesus Christ, my Lord. Amen.

ELISHA'S DEATHBED
2 Kings 13:14-21

Elisha asked for a double portion before Elijah was taken up to heaven in a chariot of fire. He was asking for a double anointing from God for the sake of ministry. In comparing Elijah and Elisha, Elisha performed twice as many miracles as Elijah, and he was faithful to proclaim the word of God.

Throughout his life, he watched his country and his people continue to deteriorate into sin. For decades, he faithfully proclaimed God's word, warning the people of judgment if they refused to turn back to God. Yet, his warning mostly fell on deaf ears, but until the end of his life, he continued to bear witness for his God.

On his deathbed, he still bore witness to God. He encouraged the king to have complete faith in the Lord. In this, he was demonstrating to everyone perseverance. You are never to stop on the Lord. You are never to take a break from serving Christ. You have been called, equipped, and enabled to persevere in faith.

There will be seasons of refreshing. Thank God for those. But there will also be seasons of stress and dryness. In those seasons you are to persevere. When refreshing comes from the Lord, do not waste that time. Utilize those moments and opportunities for the glory of God. Learn to linger in the presence of the Father, and go out with your faith strengthened and with determination.

Elisha never quit. He never stopped focusing on the will of God, the word of God, and the commission God had given him. Is that true of you? Do you focus on God's kingdom come and His glory? Or do you focus on the things of the world? Paul admonishes Christians to "set your mind on things above" (Colossians 3:2). When a person is not consciously doing that, he will become earthly minded. This is the constant temptation for the child of God: What will I focus my mind upon?

It requires strict discipline to "set your mind on things above." The same discipline that requires a person to get on a treadmill and exercise every day is the discipline required to "set your mind on things above." Elisha, on his deathbed, was still focused on the Lord. He was faithful to the end.

Prayer and Praise:

Lord, You are my reason for living. You have not called me to make a living, but You have called me to live for Your glory. Let me choose daily to "set my mind on things above." Show me when I am too earthly minded, consumed with stuff, others, and pleasures that I fail You. Teach me perseverance to the end. In the mighty name of Jesus Christ, my Lord. Amen.

THE DEATH OF A NATION
2 Kings 17:1-31

This is possibly one of the saddest chapters in the Old Testament. What is presented in this chapter is how a nation dies. A nation that once feared and honored the true and living God now chose to compromise. The end result was the death of a nation.

Seven things can be seen in these Scriptures that show you how it took place. In verse seven of this chapter, you see God's people acknowledging the existence of other gods. It says, "They had feared other gods."

Next, they acclimated to the lifestyle of unbelievers around them. Verse 8 says, "And had walked in the statutes of the nations (heathen, KJV) whom the Lord had cast out from before the children of Israel."

Then they attempted to keep their sin a secret. "Also the children of Israel secretly did against the Lord their God things that were not right" (v. 9). That led them to adopt the idolatrous practices of unbelievers. The text says, "They built for themselves high places." A high place was a place set aside for worship. Once the temple was completed, there was to be no other place of worship.

All of this led them to achieve the end result of their rebellion. The King James Version states it very clearly, "They followed vanity and became vain and went after the heathen that were round about them" (v. 15). They became idolaters. In verse 16 you find, they "served Baal."

Finally, they attempted a pluralistic society to appease God. In verse 27, at the command of a pagan king, they brought a priest to teach the rituals of the God of the land to try and curb the judgment of God.

The success of a nation depends on its adherence to Scripture. How is the United States of America doing? The success of a Christian does not depend on his nation. The success of a Christian depends on his personal adherence to Scripture.

How are you doing in this area? Are there things you have compromised? Are there issues you still have not dealt with? Is God's Word your goal? If not, you will compromise, and compromise is costly.

Prayer and Praise:

Lord, Your Word is true. Your Word is life giving, and life changing. I live in a land that has compromised Your Word, even denying Your Word. Oh Father, forgive me, forgive us. Forgive Your church for not standing strong on Your Word. Lord, enable me to understand Your truth and to live it daily. In the mighty name of Jesus Christ, my Lord. Amen.

SET YOUR HOUSE IN ORDER
2 Kings 20:1-6

Hezekiah was one of the good guys. He tried to do what was right and serve the Lord. Even good guys can face bad days. Even good guys get sick, sick unto death. As he was lying sick in his bed, God spoke to him through Isaiah the prophet, and said, "Set your house in order, for you shall die and not live."

How would you respond to those words if they were given to you by a true prophet of God? Would it cause you to spin in a tailspin out of control? Would it create fear inside of you? What would it drive you to do?

For most people, it does not take such a strong word to drive them to be consumed with fear and panic. Even Christian people act this way. Sadly, many live as if this is the best a believer will ever know and experience, that is, life here on planet earth. One cannot imagine not being with family and friends. That mindset affects everyone.

However, for a child of God, the best is yet to come. No, you should not have a morbid mindset, but you do not have to fear death if you are a truly born-again Christian. When the word came to Hezekiah, how did he react? He turned his face to the wall, and he prayed to God.

Look what he prayed. He asked God to remember his faithfulness and how he had walked before Him in truth and a perfect heart. Could you pray that type of prayer? Have you walked before God over the years of your life with such a faithful pattern, with the same consistence as Hezekiah expresses? He said, "I have done what was good in Your sight." Have you?

If you heard the doctor's report and it said, "I am sorry, you probably will not live," what would you do? Like Hezekiah, you would pray and you would weep. Hezekiah wept bitterly. But Hezekiah prayed an honest prayer. He recounted his faithfulness to God. He did not promise, "I will change if you spare my life." No, he merely recounted his life to God, and he was in a position to trust God. There was no one else he could go to and trust in.

God heard his prayer, and God extended the life of Hezekiah by fifteen more years. Will God do that for you if you pray? Only God knows. However, it was not only that Hezekiah prayed, but Hezekiah had a life of faith that he could recount to God. Set your house in order. What will this require of you?

Prayer and Praise:

Lord, You hold all things in Your hand. You know my beginning and my end, I praise You. Your Word tells us that death has lost its sting, Hallelujah! Let me so live for You that even the thought of death does not cause me fear. In the mighty name of Jesus Christ, my Lord. Amen.

HOW MUCH DO YOU LOVE YOUR BIBLE?
2 Kings 23:1-3

Probably in every Christian home in the United States, you will find a Bible. Actually, you might find multiple copies of the Bible. Bibles have been handed down from parent to child, worn copies of the Word of God. Bibles are given as gifts. Bibles are always the number one best seller in our land, week after week. It matters not how many copies of the Bible you have; what matters is what you do with it.

The Word of God, the Bible, is precious. Often, one does not realize how precious it is until he is unable to read it or hear it preached. It is easy to take the Holy Scriptures for granted or to try and run to the Bible in emergencies only. The Bible is to be read and reread. It is to be taken into your life daily. Just as you partake of physical food, you need a diet of spiritual food, the Word of God.

In the text, the Word of God had been found. That is a hard concept to grasp; how could they have lost it? The same way it is lost today; you fail to read it or to use it regularly. It becomes a book you carry on Sunday to church, but is ignored the rest of the week. Many churches, trying to help people, put the Scripture verses on a projected big screen, and therefore, they now sense no need to even carry a Bible.

They children of Israel found the Word of God and they read it in the hearing of all the people. Next, they made a covenant before the Lord to "follow the Lord, and to keep His commandments and His testimonies and His statutes" with all their heart and soul. They took a stand for the Bible, and they would stand on the Bible.

Have you taken such a stand? Do you meet with God every day in His Word? Do you place God's Word as vital to you as physical food? If you do not, you need to. It does require discipline to read your Bible every day. Just like getting on a treadmill for a physical workout requires discipline, so does becoming a regular student of the Word of God.

Consistent discipline in reading your Bible will lead to, over time, a desire for the Word of God, and eventually you will find your delight in the Word of God. The key is that you have to start the discipline. Set a time and place, and have your Bible with a pencil and paper ready, beginning a journey you will continue for the rest of your life.

Prayer and Praise:

Lord, I thank You and praise You for Your Word, the Bible. Let me not take it for granted and ignore it day after day. Increase my hunger for Your Word. Jesus Christ is the Word (John 1:14) and as I hunger for the Word, I am hungering for Christ. Conversely, when I am not hungering for the Word, I am not hungering for Christ. Increase my craving for Christ. In the mighty name of Jesus Christ, my Lord. Amen.

WICKED IN THE SIGHT OF THE LORD
1 Chronicles 2:3

When you read that a person is wicked in the sight of the Lord, or that he did evil in the sight of the Lord, it should cause you to pause and ask, "What did he do?" Man has his own concept of wicked and evil. A murderer, a rapist, or a child molester, all qualify as wicked. However, what man understands and what God defines as wicked are not always the same. Anything that a person does outside the revealed will of God can be considered wicked.

In the parable of the talents (Matthew 25:14-30), Jesus calls the one man a wicked and lazy servant (v. 26). Why? This man did not waste his talent in wild living. This man did not use his talent in an illegal way. In fact, he returned it to his master when asked for it. Why did Jesus call him wicked?

Wickedness can be a terrible act or deed. Also, wickedness, in the estimation of Jesus Christ, goes far beyond the surface level. This man was called wicked because of what he failed to do with what he had been given by his Lord. He detached himself from his talent, and did nothing with it for his master's service.

Do you use whatever abilities, talents, and gifting you have for your Lord's service? Have you taken the time to discover what your area of responsibility is for the Lord? Have you sought out services you can render in your church? Wickedness is terrible acts and sins, but in the eyes of Jesus it goes much deeper.

Prayer and Praise:

Lord, You see everything and You know the motivation of my heart. Speak to me about areas of wickedness that may be in my life that I am blinded to. Let me be a vessel of honor unto You. In the mighty name of Jesus Christ, my Lord. Amen.

MORE HONORABLE
1 Chronicles 4:9-10

First Chronicles contains a long list of five hundred names. When you come to the man named Jabez, in less than eighty words, God gives us a biography of him. What God tells you about a man, you can guarantee it is true. God did not just say, "Jabez was honorable." God said, "Jabez was more honorable."

Honorable means he was "worthy of respect." We are told that he was born into pain and grief. He was not born into luxury; he had no silver spoon of opportunity given him. He did not have a good start, but he was more honorable.

The difference between Jabez and all his brothers was that he knew how to call on God. Jabez knew to pray. Jabez knew the necessity and importance of prayer. Do you? Prayerlessness is a grievous sin against God. Prayerlessness is not that you just do not pray; it is also when you do not pray as much as you know God wants you to pray. Jabez prayed.

He prayed for the Lord to bless him. Outside of God's blessing, you have nothing. To say "bless me indeed" shows forth the urgency in the prayer. "God, I have to have Your blessing." That is how Jabez prayed, with urgency.

He prayed, "Lord, enlarge my territory." He was saying God, I want more territory, I want more responsibility. Do you pray for more responsibility from God or to put more burden on you? He did not pray for his load to be lightened. How do you pray?

Finally, he prayed, "Lord...that Your hand would be with me." He was praying he wanted God to control, direct, and discipline his life. He was saying, "Capture me, God, discipline me, and keep me from evil. Lord, show me what sin is in my life, and do not let me grieve You." Is that how you pray? If you are to be "more honorable" you must pray this way.

Prayer and Praise:

Lord, thank You for showing me what it means to pray through the man, Jabez. Father, make me a vessel of honor unto You, as Jabez was. Teach me how to humble myself daily and come before Your throne praying, until You say, "It is enough." In the mighty name of Jesus Christ, my Lord. Amen.

MIGHTY MEN OF VALOR
1 Chronicles 7:5

Most Christian men desire to be men of courage and faith. When the Bible says a person is a mighty man of valor, which is a strong testimony. What is involved in being a mighty man of valor?

A Christian man of valor will be able-bodied. He will be a man of spiritual alertness, energy, and stamina. Spiritual alertness comes from spending time on one's knees in prayer and learning to be sensitive to the leading of the Holy Spirit.

A man of valor will be properly equipped. He will have their shield and sword. He will take the shield of faith and the sword of the Word of God. The shield of faith will quench all the fiery darts of the wicked one. Daily, you must choose to live by faith, acting in obedience to God's Word.

Finally, men of valor will be well trained. They will take advantage of the resources available, keeping their minds sharp and focused spiritually. Again, you must feed your soul on the Word of God. You must take the written Word of God, the general principles, or the "logos," and live them. Next, you take the specific word of God, the "rhema," and adjust your life specifically to that word, given specifically to you. Then, you walk in confidence with the Father.

Prayer and Praise:

Lord, make me into a spiritual man of valor. Show me any area in my life where I am falling short. Teach me how to walk in faith every day and feed on Your Word. Show me how to take up the shield of faith. In the mighty name of Jesus Christ, my Lord. Amen.

KNOWING THE HEART OF THE KING
1 Chronicles 11:15-18

The enemy is relentless; he attacks and attacks, and often you can grow weary in the battle. David was weary after skirmishes with the enemy, and he went to the cave of Adullam for rest. Everyone needs to know how to flee to a place of rest—rest for the body, rest for the mind and rest for the soul and spirit.

David, in the place of security and rest, surrounded by his mighty men, had a longing in his heart. He desired a drink of water from the well in Bethlehem. However, the enemy was camped in Bethlehem. Nevertheless, three mighty men broke through the camp, drew water from the well of Bethlehem, and brought it to David.

What David did next is surprising and even confusing. He poured the water out on the ground; he would not drink it. How would that make you feel if you risked your life in this action, only to have the water poured out?

David did not waste the water; he poured it out to the Lord. The water was given to David by an act of great sacrifice on the part of the three mighty men. David, in turn, sacrificed to the Lord what he had been given. So often, one can forget God in moments of sacrificial blessings received, but not David. Just as these men sacrificed for him, he in turn gave their sacrifice to the highest King.

This story has more to tell. These three mighty men were so close to their king that as he uttered under his breath his heart's desire, they heard him. David did not stand and announce this desire, trying to see who would risk life and limb to retrieve the water. David, under his breath, spoke the longing of his soul. These three men heard their king when he whispered.

Do you live so close to your King, that you hear Him when He whispers? Do you know the desire of your King's heart? Are you willing to risk, in order to satisfy and please King Jesus?

Prayer and Praise:

Lord, You are my King, and my desire is to please You. Let me live so close to You that I recognize the longings of Your heart, and that I can hear You when You whisper. Let me constantly choose to live close to You. In the mighty name of Jesus Christ, my Lord. Amen.

HOW TO HANDLE WHAT IS HOLY
1 Chronicles 13:1-14

The ark of the covenant, or the ark of God, had been in Kirjath-jearam for many years. It had been away from Shiloh since it was captured in battle when Eli was the priest. Now David wants to return it to its proper place in Israel. That appears to be a worthy ambition, does it not?

The captains and leaders all agreed, and they set out to restore the ark of God back to its proper position in Israel. They called for the Levites and priests to gather in one accord to bring back the ark. The Bible tells, "The thing was right in the eyes of all the people" (v. (4). How can doing something that seems so right, turn out so wrong?

In the situation with David, he asked the captains and the leaders. He gathered the priests and the Levites. He even got the approval of the people, but he never inquired of the Lord. David failed to pray and get the mind of God. Do you ever do that?

Not only did David not pray, but David failed to fulfill part of his responsibility as king. The king of Israel was required to personally write out the book of the law (Deuteronomy 17:18-19). He was to handwrite it, and read it all the days of his life. If David had done that, he would have known there was a specified way God had already given for how the ark was to be transported.

It is not enough to want to do God's will, you must do God's will in God's way. God does not tell you to do something and leave you to come up with how to do it. God tells you His will, and He tells you how to fulfill it.

Reading the Bible, even writing out the Bible, is important. In those two ways, you will begin to learn the Scriptures and know how God wants things done in His way. It is never enough just to have a good idea or even a God-centered idea. You must hear from God, or the end result can be disastrous.

Have you heard from God lately? Are you daily reading, meditating, and even writing out His Word? Life is too short and precious to waste on good ideas, even with good intentions, and miss God. Learn to pray through every issue you face in life. Get in the Word of God and know God's will.

Prayer and Praise:

Lord, You are a revealing God. Teach me to know Your Word, and give me revelation knowledge to live daily for Your glory. Let me not seek the approval of men before I seek Your approval. In the mighty name of Jesus Christ, my Lord. Amen.

A GOOD IDEA, BUT NOT GOD'S WILL
1 Chronicles 17:1-6

David was so excited, as he should have been, because the ark of the covenant had been restored to its proper place and position. It was once again in the tabernacle. Burnt offerings and peace offerings had been made. The people blessed the Lord. Levites had been appointed to minister before the ark of the Lord, to commemorate, to thank, and to praise the Lord God of Israel. David was rejoicing.

David returned to his house, and his mind was still racing from the joyful occasion. He began to wonder aloud, "I dwell in a house of cedar; but the ark of the covenant of the Lord is under tent curtains." Have you ever begun to think good thoughts like this? Have you ever returned from an encounter with the living God, and your mind begins to think, "What can I do for God?"

David thought aloud, and expressed his thoughts to Nathan the prophet. Nathan had also experienced the rejoicing as the ark had been restored. Nathan said to David, "Do all that is in your heart, for God is with you." To David that sounded like a good idea, a wonderful idea, go for it.

It is not long before God spoke to Nathan, "Tell My servant David, you shall not build Me a house to dwell in." God said, "I have gone from tent to tent and from one tabernacle to another. I have never spoken to My judges to build me a house of cedar."

How do you know the difference between a good idea and God's will? How do you know if you are coming up with an idea that looks right and spiritual, or if you have truly heard from God? If a person does not understand this, he can spend his time and life pursuing things God is not even involved with.

When Nathan got away from the moment and in a place without distractions, or pressures of a friend, Nathan heard God say, "No." Have you ever heard God say no to a plan you wanted to pursue? It is a word from God you have to learn to process and accept, or your life will be wasted, out of God's will and blessing.

Not every good idea is God's will or plan. Be careful you seek the face of God before you seek the advice of man.

Prayer and Praise:

Lord, teach me to pray about everything. Not merely to ask Your blessing on things I want to do, but also to get Your permission if I am to be doing it. Lord, I need to train my ear to hear Your voice, especially to recognize when You say no. In the mighty name of Jesus Christ, my Lord. Amen.

OFFERING THE LORD THAT
WHICH COSTS ME NOTHING
1 Chronicles 21:24

David and Israel were under the judgment of God because David sinned. The Lord told Gad to tell David to erect an altar on the threshing floor of Ornan, to which David obeyed. When David arrived at Ornan's threshing floor, Ornan bowed down before the king of Israel.

Next, David asked Ornan if he could buy the threshing floor for full price, in order to build an altar to the Lord, so that the plague might be withdrawn from the people. Ornan wanted to give it to David. He wanted to give his king the floor, the oxen, wheat, and wood to be used for the sacrifice. Ornan was a generous man.

David refused the offer. Why? David knew the importance of sacrifice. It is no sacrifice if it does not cost a person something. David refuses the free offer and insisted he pay full price: six hundred shekels of gold. David built an altar to the Lord and made sacrifice. God was pleased. God answered from heaven with fire, consuming the offering. The plague stopped.

When you go to church on Sunday, do you prepare to worship the Lord and to offer Jesus Christ a sacrifice? Do you go to bed early enough to be rested and alert? Do you prepare to take your tithes and offerings to the Lord? Have you prepared yourself in a season of prayer? Have you dealt with your sin by honest confession and repentance?

How do you go to church—prepared or unprepared? Does it cost you anything to come before the Lord? What are you teaching your children about the worship and sacrifice to the Lord Jesus Christ? Have you taught them to pray? To tithe? To honor the Lord's Day and keep it holy? Or do you try to offer the Lord that which costs you nothing, or very little?

Prayer and Praise:

Lord, forgive me for the times I have come before You unprepared spiritually. Teach me to prepare myself daily to come before You, to bow before You and to offer You the sacrifice of my time, my treasures, my talents, and my tongue. In the mighty name of Jesus Christ, my Lord. Amen.

MAKING PREPARATIONS
1 Chronicles 22:5

David wanted to build the temple, but God said no. However, David prepared for the temple to be built by his son Solomon. How did he prepare for Solomon to build the temple of God? He put aside the materials, the iron, the brass, and the nails. He had the stones quarried and cedar lumber and logs stockpiled. David prepared his son to build the temple of the Lord.

Have you prepared your children to build the temple of the Lord Jesus Christ? Have you laid aside materials physically and spiritually to aid your children in building and living kingdom-of-God lives? What have you done to prepare your children to follow Christ wholeheartedly? What have you done to prepare your children to be witnesses of the Lord Jesus for the next generation?

The greatest thing you can leave this world is not a great name, or a lot of material wealth, but boys and girls who know how to seek the Lord: young men and young women who have a heart and a passion for Christ. Each generation will have to choose whom they will follow, but it is your responsibility to teach and to train your children in the fear and admonition of the Lord.

This is not done by force, but by example. You live it before them. You show your children the priority of your life every Sunday when you go to church to worship the living God. Or you go elsewhere for family time and entertainment.

Make preparations, live unto the glory of God, and let your life be an example of what a man or woman of God is. Just as David did, you do this before you die.

Prayer and Praise:

Lord, You have allowed me to be blessed by being a parent. Teach me that I am only the steward, not the owner of my children. Let me lead them by a godly example. Show me what I must say no to as I teach my children to pursue godliness and holiness. Thank You for Your mercy and Your grace. In the mighty name of Jesus Christ, my Lord. Amen.

OBED-EDOM
1 Chronicles 26:4-8

Obed-Edom was a loyal servant of David. Following the death of Uzzah, David left the ark of the covenant at Obed-Edom's house. It remained with Obed-Edom for three months. During those three months, he was unusually blessed by God. Later, he served as both a gatekeeper and a musician in the tabernacle in Jerusalem during David's reign.

As you read the text, you find the list of Obed-Edom's sons, and after mentioning the eighth son it says, "for God blessed him." Part of the blessing of God on Obed-Edom was his sons and how they became men of God. Is that your desire, that your children become men or women of God?

Notice the qualities they possessed. It tells in verses 6-8 they were mighty men of valor, they were strong men, and they were able men with strength for the work. Think about those qualities. They were courageous, they were persistent, and they were qualified and able for the work.

Those qualities will set men apart in any generation, but especially in service to God. Courage is an indispensable trait for a man of God— courage to stand when no one else stands with you, courage to step out in obedience to God's leading and directing. Are you a man of courage?

Strong men, or persistent, they endured and stood firm. That is a trait to be coveted when it comes to your walk with God. Are you one who stands firm and persistent in your faith and the will and the Word of God? Are you without compromise, or are you easily distracted?

Finally, he tells that they are able men, men capable to do the work of God. God not only saves individuals, he also enables them to serve and live for Him. God is not interested as much in your ability, but your availability. To whom He calls, He equips and qualifies, if you follow in absolute surrender and obedience.

Where do you find yourself in this picture of characteristics? Is there any area in which you need to make adjustments to the Word of God, as in what you give your time and attention? How long have you been a true believer in Jesus Christ, and do you see these traits emerging in your life? Oh, that to God, you would be courageous, persistent, and able men.

Prayer and Praise:

Lord, You are my King, let my life flow with loyalty to You. Make me into a man of courage to stand, even if I stand alone. Teach me to persist and never give up. Enable me by Your Holy Spirit to be competent to do Your work. In the mighty name of Jesus Christ, my Lord. Amen.

MAY

THE TEMPLE IS FOR THE LORD
1 Chronicles 29:1

David said very clearly, "The temple is not for man but for the Lord God." As you read that verse, you may think, Well, everyone knows that. Just like the commercial that says, "You can save 15 percent on car insurance." Everyone does not know what seems to be common knowledge.

Many a church exists in America not for the glory of God, but for the traditions of man. Have you noticed that truth? Often, you can find churches that are more man-centered than God-centered. You find churches that are more personality-driven rather than Word-driven, or Christ driven.

Churches have becomes athletic complexes, schools, craft organizations, even concert halls, and wedding chapels. Yet it seems to be forgotten that the temple, the church, exists for God and not man.

Smaller congregations are not exempt; they can be family-centered to the place sin can be easily excused or ignored. The point of all this is to say, the temple existed for God, not man. The church exists for God and not for man.

What is your responsibility in ensuring that your church exists for God, and not man? The above activities are not bad in and of themselves, but how do you ensure your church exists for God and not activities? How do you remain faithful to God, above all the activity-driven things that occur at church in the name of Jesus Christ?

That is a hard question, but you answer it every day with what takes priority in your life. You answer it every time you choose to ignore the Word of God just to make people happy. You answer it each time you allow an activity to take precedence over your responsibility to God and to His church.

The church exists for God, and not man. But, thanks be to God, He included you in His church.

Prayer and Praise:

Lord, thank You for Your church. I would be lost without the church, the body of Christ. Let me know my place of responsibility among Your people, and always realize that the church exists for You, not for me. In the mighty name of Jesus Christ, my Lord. Amen.

JACHIN and BOAZ
2 Chronicles 3:17

Two beautiful and towering pillars were built for the porch of the temple. They each stood about twenty-six-and-one-half feet tall, and eighteen feet in circumference. These pillars were free standing, not attached to the temple and in no way did they give support to the structure. One sat at the south corner and the other at the north corner.

The pillar at the south corner was named Jachin, which means "God establishes;" and the other pillar at the north corner was named Boaz, which means in "God is strength." These were the first things to be seen by a worshipper as he approached the temple; two massive, towering pillars symbolizing the strength and power of God.

When you come to the place of worship, your local church, do you come with an awareness of the strength and the power of Almighty God? Do you come with an awareness of the sovereignty of Almighty God? Do you come with an awareness of His omniscience, omnipotence, and His omnipresence? What is on your mind as you come to worship God?

Often, men and women come with divided minds. They are, as the book of James tells us, "double-minded." They come still thinking of the world and the things of life, but not solely focused on Jesus Christ. It takes effort to focus on Christ and Christ alone. Anything that easily distracts you should be, must be put aside.

Cell phones can be a great distraction to being single-minded. Learn to turn them off or leave them in your car; do not even afford them the opportunity to interrupt you and your Savior. Learn the importance, and teach this to your children, that nothing is worth distracting you from your living Lord.

Prayer and Praise:

Lord, I live in such a media-driven society. Help me to realize my responsibility to leave the things of the world behind when I seek to come into Your presence and worship You. Father, enable me to understand nothing is worth my attention when it compares to You. You are my strength and my strong tower. You establish me in faith and I praise Your name. In the mighty name of Jesus Christ, my Lord. Amen.

SPREADING OUT YOUR HANDS
2 Chronicles 6:12

Every person on the face of the earth has needs. God so created us that each individual has emptiness on the inside that nothing can fill or satisfy. Often, attempts are made to satisfy this emptiness with the things of the world and the pleasures of life, but it is short-lived. A person may be pacified for a time, but no one can be satisfied until Jesus Christ fills the emptiness inside.

Solomon had just completed the construction of the temple, and was leading the people in a worship service and a service of dedication to the Lord. The first act was to move the ark of God into the Most Holy Place. As the ark was set in place, the Shekinah Glory of God's presence began to fill the temple. The glory filled the temple to the point the priest had to leave that area.

As this was taking place, Solomon began to preach to the people and gave his prayer of dedication. With hands outstretched toward the heavens, he praised God for His faithfulness and for His supremacy.

It seems easier to praise and thank God when you know He is present with you. In the atmosphere taking place on that dedication day, Solomon exalted the Lord. You must remember that God is always present; in fact, he is omnipresent. Each day you must learn to live with outstretched hands to heaven, thanking Him for His grace, His mercy, His love, His joy, His peace, and His presence (whether you feel anything or not).

When you know by faith God is with you, you can live with His confidence and authority. Amidst hardships and misfortunes, you can go forward in faith, trusting the Lord Jesus Christ. When was the last time you stretched your hands out to God, other than in a corporate worship service, and exalted Him?

Prayer and Praise:

Lord, I am so blessed by Your presence. Your presence gives me strength and courage to face the challenges of life. Never let me forget that You are with me always, even to the end. Enable me not to depend merely on my feelings, but to walk by faith. In the mighty name of Jesus Christ, my Lord. Amen.

THE FIRE FALLS
2 Chronicles 7:1-3

After Solomon prayed the prayer of dedication for the temple, God answered his prayer in dramatic fashion. Fire fell from the heavens and consumed the burnt offerings and the sacrifices. Have you ever had God answer your prayers in such a visible and spectacular fashion?

When the fire fell, the priest who ministered to the Lord in the holy place could not enter the temple because the glory of God was so manifested. The brilliance of the fire and light drove the priests to their knees. In fact, everyone was driven to their knees, bowing before the splendor and glory of God. When was the last time you were compelled to your knees before the Lord Jesus Christ?

On their knees with their heads bowed to the ground (acts of humility), they worshipped God. They praised Him saying, "For He is good! For His mercy endures forever." Do you speak out loud as you worship and praise the Lord? Do you let others hear you praising God?

God answered Solomon's prayer quickly with a clear "Yes, I accept your offering." Sometimes God answers with a "No." What do you do when God says, "No," or when God says, "Wait?" Your response should be the same. You should bow in worship and praise of Almighty God. He knows what He is doing, and He is in complete control. It is an issue of trust. Do you trust Him?

Prayer and Praise:

Lord, I find myself bowing before You easily when You say, "Yes." Teach me to trust You completely when Your answer is "No," or "Not yet." Let me not live based on my feelings or emotions, but let me truly live by faith in You. Let me have strong confidence in You. The longer I serve You, the more narrow my life is to be to You. Teach me this daily. In the mighty name of Jesus Christ, my Lord. Amen.

SHIELDS OF GOLD OR SHIELDS OF BRONZE
2 Chronicles 12:9-10

When Solomon was king, he had made shields of gold to be carried and held as one entered into his throne room. It would have been an amazing sight to have seen—two long lines of soldiers holding the shields of gold as they glittered in the sun.

However, when Solomon's son, Rehoboam, became king, we are told in 2 Chronicles 12:1, he "established the kingdom, and had strengthened himself, that he forsook the law of the Lord and all Israel along with him." Even though he had an impressive army, he and Israel began a descent downward.

When Shishak, the king of Egypt came to do battle, he carried away the golden shields. Have you ever had the enemy take something from you that once stood as a glittering testimony? Rehoboam made shields of bronze to replace the shields of gold. Now, when the troops lined up with theses shields, they would still shine in the sunlight, but there was a difference. Do you know the difference between shields of gold and shields of bronze?

Gold does not have to be polished; bronze, coming from copper, has to be polished to retain its beauty and shine. That is how many try to live their faith. Because of disobedience and unbelief, a person has to "work" so that he gives the appearance as the "real" thing. He has to polish his shield to give it the appearance of purity.

The New Testament teaches that your faith is more precious than gold; gold is refined and purified. In the purification process the gold remains pure, and only the dross and impurities are removed. Gold does not tarnish. Bronze and brass come from copper, and copper will tarnish. Once it tarnishes, your energy goes into polishing it, so that it will give the appearance of purity. Your energy is now consumed with making the appearance look good, but it never lasts.

Have you examined your faith lately? Are you allowing God to refine you and remove the dross? Or are you trying to make a good appearance, polishing and buffing the external, but you never deal internally with your faith? Do not substitute bronze for gold. Get honest with God and allow Him to do His work in your life. Make adjustments of your life to the Word of God and the people of God.

Prayer and Praise:

Lord, You are my God, and I exalt You. Let my faith shine forth naturally, as I respond to You. As I walk in obedience and faith, not doubt and unbelief, let my life reflect You. Show me any area I try to polish to impress others, and let me yield that area to You. In the mighty name of Jesus Christ, my Lord. Amen.

ASA
2 Chronicles 14:1-6

Asa came to the throne after his ungodly father passed off the scene in death. Yet Asa was faithful to the Lord, and "did what was good and right in the eyes of the Lord his God." Do you find that an amazing statement? Asa was not brought up in a God-fearing home. His father and his grandfather had not walked with God, but Asa did.

That is an encouraging word. It is wonderful to have a godly heritage, but if you do not, you can still choose to walk with God. You are not bound by the sins of your father or your family. You can break the cycle and obey and serve the Lord. Is it easy? No, but it can be done.

As you are faithful to God, He gives you inner strength, courage, and power to face whatever comes. He enables you to continue. Yes, difficulties and challenges will come. Testing times will come, but even then God makes provision for you to endure. Praise His holy name.

Even though you may not have a heritage of faith from your forefathers, you can still be faithful if you so choose. Every day it is a choice you make to live by faith in Christ and His Word or to live according to your flesh. What will you choose?

Prayer and Praise:

Lord, thank You that even if I did not have a father who lived by faith, I can. Thank You that You make provisions for me to have faith and to trust You. Teach me when trials come not to shift the gaze off my life from You to the trial. Teach me not to waste times of rest indulging myself, but teach me in times of rest to be making preparations for the future. In the mighty name of Jesus Christ, my Lord. Amen.

NOT FINISHING WELL
2 Chronicles 16:1-14

Asa had a heart that was totally committed to the Lord, and for thirty-five years he was faithful. He lived a righteous life before the Lord and before Israel. He physically destroyed false centers of worship, and he commanded the people to seek the Lord only and to obey Him alone.

Later, you find him as a man of prayer. He prayed deliverance for his people from an invading army. No matter what you face, the hope of deliverance comes through prayer.

The sad fact of Asa is that he did not finish strong. He slipped away from the Lord, and he did not persevere to the end. Chapter sixteen of 2 Chronicles records this sad conclusion. You see Asa failing to turn to the Lord for help. He placed his trust in man instead of God. Asa allowed his heart to become hardened to the Lord and to the Word of the Lord.

Have you ever become indifferent to the Word of God? Do you adjust your life when God's Word challenges you? Or do you ignore it and go about doing and living as you please? That is what Asa did, until Asa reached the point he refused to seek the Lord for help. He refused to acknowledge the Lord as his ultimate sustainer of life. He even became defiant toward the Lord, rejecting the prophets' warning.

How about you? Do you walk pleasing to God, or do you do only enough to give a "Christian" appearance? It is not how you start that is important, it is how you finish. Finish well, finish in faith.

Prayer and Praise:

Lord, You are the Almighty. You know everything about me and my life. Never let me become so prideful that I put my trust in man and not in You. Move in my life with strong conviction and bring brokenness into my life when I try to make it without You. Show me when I am merely mouthing love, obedience, and trust, but it is not real inside of me. In the mighty name of Jesus Christ, my Lord. Amen.

JEHOSHAPHAT
2 Chronicles 20:1-13

It could happen to anyone: things going along smoothly, no problems to speak of, and suddenly, a crisis comes into your life. That is how it was with Jehoshaphat, king of Judah. According to chapter seventeen, he was a man who sought God, and God was with him. In spite of this, he still found himself in a circumstance beyond his control

Maybe you have experienced that. Maybe you are experiencing that right now. If so, do what Jehoshaphat did; he began to intensely seek the Lord. He proclaimed a fast and he gathered his people together to seek God and pray.

When he prayed, he began by declaring the greatness and the power of God. He recalled God's mighty acts in days past. He affirmed God was in control. He did all of this before he ever expressed his situation and crisis. Do you pray like that? Do you acknowledge the greatness and the majesty of God before you begin to make your request or need known?

Often, the temptation is to begin with the crisis, and the more you focus on the crisis, the less you acknowledge the greatness of God. Praying that way is completely self-centered, yet you are to be God-centered, especially when you come before the throne of grace.

How do you pray? Do you begin in panic mode with the problem, or do you begin bowing before the Almighty, omnipotent Father attributing to Him praise and honor? This does not come naturally, but you are not to live by your nature but by the Holy Spirit who has enabled you to have faith. Does it come easily or without difficulty? No, it comes as you daily walk in submission to the lordship of Jesus Christ and bow before Him.

Prayer and Praise:

Lord, You are God in my good days and in my not-so-good days. Teach me to come before You in humble submission, no matter what my circumstances may be. Enable me to exalt You no matter what may be transpiring in life. You are God, and nothing shakes Your control. In the mighty name of Jesus Christ, my Lord. Amen.

JEHOSHABEATH
2 Chronicles 22:10-12

When the mother of the king, Athaliah, saw that her son was dead, she began to kill all the royal line of the house of Judah. In doing so, she secured the throne for herself. She nearly succeeded. She thought she succeeded, and she would have succeeded if it had not been for the brave act of Jehoshabeath.

If Athaliah had been successful, the royal lineage would have been broken, and Jesus Christ could not have been born. The actions of Jehoshabeath made it possible for the Savior to be born through the line of Judah. Joash was the last living heir of the Davidic line, and if he had died, then David's (Judah's) lineage would have died with him. Jehoshabeath showed bravery, compassion, and faith. She is a woman to be honored.

Amazingly, she was the granddaughter of Jezebel, and wicked Athaliah was her mother. Yet Jehoshabeath was a righteous woman. Her story teaches that you do not have to allow the choices that your families make shape the type of person you become. You have the ability to choose, and by staying close to the Lord, you will have a different life than your family chose.

One person who makes good choices and follow the Lord can change the future for generations. The opposite is true as well. It only takes one person to turn away from the Lord, and generations wander in darkness until someone else chooses to break the cycle and chooses Christ.

For six years, she hid Joash in the house of God while Athaliah reigned. Do you think she ever experienced stress? Do you think she ever got tired of trying to stay a step ahead of the queen? Obedience to Christ can be costly. It can place one in a risky position. However, obedience to Christ is not an option if you are to live for Him. If Christ is your King, you have to obey, no matter what the cost.

Prayer and Praise:

Lord, You are worth everything. You are the living God. You are my Lord and Savior. I rejoice that I am allowed the privilege to serve You. Father, if it requires risking my very life to obey and serve You, enable me to have the faith and trust to do it. In the mighty name of Jesus Christ, my Lord. Amen.

UZZIAH
2 Chronicles 26:16

Uzziah is a wonderful picture of a man who started right. He did what was right in the sight of the Lord. He sought God in the days of Zechariah, the prophet. As long as he sought the Lord, the Lord caused him to prosper. Most people want to prosper in life. In this story you find the key to prosperity.

God helped Uzziah defeat his enemies, and his name and fame spread across the lands. He built towers and walls and fortified them. He had cattle and vineyards. He equipped a massive military and grew stronger and stronger. God marvelously helped him until he was strong.

The text says, "When he was strong his heart was lifted up, to his destruction, for he transgressed against the Lord his God by entering the temple of the Lord to burn incense on the altar of incense."

Does that seem like a big deal? Just burning a little incense in the temple to your God, what could be wrong with that? The offering of incense was a type of sweet smelling aroma to the nostrils of God, and it was often equated with praying. The king went into the temple, passing the brazen altar, going to the holy place just outside of the holy of holies and offered some incense and prayer—not a big deal.

Wrong, it was a major deal. Uzziah was the king, not a priest, and only priests were permitted to go and do what Uzziah did in the temple. Uzziah bypassed the order that God had established for His people. Do you ever try and bypass or supersede the order God has placed and established in His church? Do you think the pastor is just another man, that his words carry no more weight than anyone else? Do you think you can do anything you want at church?

If so, your heart has been lifted up against you as it is full of pride. Pride is the most basic sin that man struggles with. Pride says, "Not Your will and way, God, but mine." Pride can damn a soul to hell or cause a Christian to miss God in the present and face His chastisement. All the while, you try and justify your deeds, "I am only seeking God." You are to seek the Lord the way He establishes, not just doing what is right in your own eyes.

Prayer and Praise:

Lord, You are God and King, and I must submit to You. Your way is right and can only be found as I seek You and adjust my life to your Word. You have an established order in the church; teach me to submit to Your order. Teach me to respect Your pastor and Your established authority. In the mighty name of Jesus Christ, my Lord. Amen.

OPENING THE DOORS
2 Chronicles 29:3

The first thing Hezekiah did when he became king was to open the doors of the house of the Lord. Amazing! Before he passed any acts of reform, before he reviewed past policy, and before he began any construction that he may have as a legacy, he opened the doors to the house of the Lord.

The obvious question is how did the doors to the house of the Lord become shut? To understand this, you have to go back a few generations in Hezekiah's lineage. Uzziah, his great-grandfather, tried to burn incense on the altar, and had to be physically removed from the temple. Only the priest was allowed to perform this act. Once he was removed from the temple, he basically got mad and did not go back to the temple. He quit going to "church" so to speak.

Uzziah's son, Jotham, did not go to the temple, just like his dad. His son, and Hezekiah's father, shut the doors of the temple (2 Chronicles 28:24), and destroyed many of the articles of the house of God. Do you see the progression?

Does this sound like it could happen in our places of worship? One man got his feelings hurt at church and quit going. It did not matter that he was the one in the wrong. His son did not go to church, but seemed to be a good man. His grandson, full of himself, shut the doors of the church, so that no one could go to the house of the Lord. All because Granddad got his feelings hurt.

Be careful that you do not forget that the church is for the Lord and not for you. Yes, you can be blessed there, but the church exists for the glory of God and not man.

Praise the Lord for Hezekiah, the great-grandson of Uzziah. Even though his daddy shut the doors, Hezekiah opened the doors of the house of the Lord. He broke the cycle. He gave hope that things do not have to continue as they were. Will you be one that breaks the cycle of sin and once again opens the doors for others to come into the Lord's house?

Prayer and Praise:

Lord, thank You that You do not hold me accountable for the sins of my forefathers. Thank You that you allow every man to choose for himself whom and what he will worship. As for me and my house, I will serve the Lord. Hallelujah! In the mighty name of Jesus Christ, my Lord. Amen.

IN AFFLICTION
2 Chronicles 33:12

It is amazing how one could have such a godly father and turn ever so quickly to ungodliness. This is the case with Hezekiah's son, Manasseh. Manasseh was one of the most evil kings Judah ever had, and his reign was fifty-five years, the longest reign of any king in Judah.

Even the prophets charged him with committing more evil than the nations whom the Lord had destroyed (2 Chronicles 33:9). As you read the first ten verses of chapter thirty-three, you can see twelve perversions Manasseh committed.

He lived a wicked life, committing evil in the sight of the Lord (v. 2). He followed the practice of unbelievers (v. 2). He rebuilt the high places of false worship (v. 3). He constructed altars to the false god, Baal and the goddess, Asherah (v. 3). Next, he introduced to the nation the Assyrian worship of the sun, moon, and stars (v. 3). He built altars to the heavenly bodies and placed them in the temple of the Lord (v. 4-5). He carried out human sacrifice (v. 6). He lived in the world of the occult, practicing sorcery and witchcraft (v. 6). He placed a carved pole for the goddess, Asherah, in the temple (v. 7). He completely disregarded God's law and commandments (v. 8). He led the people astray and became a stumbling block to the nation (v. 9). Finally, he refused to listen to God's Word (v. 10).

This is a sad list. Do you see our country following any of these same sins? Are you following any of these sins?

As a judgment upon Manasseh for his evil, God allowed Assyria to invade the land, to capture Manasseh, and take him to Babylon. They put a hook in his nose, bound him with shackles, and exiled him to Babylon.

Sometime later, in deep pain, humiliation, distress, and affliction, Manasseh cried out to God. God's mercy flowed and saved him. Do you know someone so hardened to the gospel, so wicked, that you think is beyond hope? If God saved Manasseh, no person is beyond hope. Affliction is one of God's best tools to get one's attention, making him or her desperate for the Lord.

Sadly, Manasseh's conversion could not undo all the evil he had performed. The people still followed the false gods, and his own son was not impacted by his father's conversion. Do not waste your life thinking you can make it right before the end.

Prayer and Praise:

Lord, You are truly a God of mercy and grace. I am just as Manasseh, undeserving, but thank You for saving me. In the mighty name of Jesus Christ, my Lord. Amen.

SEEKING GOD WHILE YOU ARE YOUNG
2 Chronicles 34:1-3

Josiah was an amazing young man. While he was but a boy, he began to seek the Lord. The time line of Josiah's life is powerful. He reigned thirty-one years, and despite the lack of a godly upbringing, he chose to do what was right in the sight of the Lord.

At the age of eight, he became king. When he was sixteen, he began to seek the Lord. Four years later, when he was twenty, he began to rid the land of idols and idol worship. Finally, at twenty-six years of age, after he had purged the land and the temple, he found the book of the law, and reestablished it in Israel.

The question that comes to mind is, "How do the people of God lose their Bible?" The sad truth is, Israel lost the Word of God, and they did not even know it was missing. How about you? Can you go for days or weeks and not even realize you have failed to be reading, studying, and meditating on the Word of God, the Bible? How many days can you go without digesting God's Word before you realize it is missing from your life?

People go from Sunday to Sunday and never pick up their copy of the Bible. They come to church services and wonder why things do not happen. They show up unprepared to meet God, ill-equipped to hear from God, and they wonder what is wrong with the preacher. They still like the music, it is so uplifting and stirring, but the preaching of the Word of God never seems to connect. Why? Their consciences have been seared with a hot iron, and now they have become indifferent, hardened to God's Word because of lack of use.

Josiah, as a boy, set his life in a direction to please God, and when he rediscovered the Word of God, it further propelled him to walk with God. He adjusted his life and the lifestyle of the nation to the Lord. When was the last time you adjusted your life to the Word of God? Or do you merely try to fit the Word of God into your schedule?

Josiah's life proves that God can use a person of any age. God's Word is relevant, sufficient, and precious to all people of all ages. However, only you can keep from losing the Word of God for your life.

Prayer and Praise:

Lord, thank You for Your Word. Thank you for the testimony of a boy who set his heart to seek You. Teach me the importance of daily adjusting my life to You, and not merely trying to fit You into my schedule. Continue to grow my hunger for Your Word. In the mighty name of Jesus Christ, my Lord. Amen.

CYRUS'S DECREE
Ezra 1:1-5

As you begin reading Ezra, realize God's people have been in captivity in the land of Babylon for seventy years. Finally, Cyrus, the king of Persia who conquered Babylon, sets the captive Israelites free with his decree in the first few verses of Ezra.

It is difficult to imagine being a slave and being held captive in a foreign land. You find this situation happening twice to Israel, the people of God. They were first captives in Egypt and then hundreds of years later, they were taken captive by Babylon.

Why were they in captivity a second time? In 2 Chronicles 36:21, you are told the reason. Israel had not allowed the land to rest, as God had commanded. God commanded a Sabbatical rest every seven years for the land. God allowed Israel to be in captivity the amount of time for the land to experience her Sabbatical rest. This took seventy years. Do you get the idea that God is serious about his word being kept?

When Cyrus released the people, only seven percent went back to Israel, about fifty thousand people. Why did so many stay in Babylon? The same reason many believers today live in bondage to sin and this world—because they have grown comfortable in captivity. Is there any area of your life that you know is outside of God's will, but you are comfortable with? Is there any sin you refuse to confess and forsake? It is costly to become comfortable with disobedience.

When the decree was made, only a small number of priests returned. What a sad commentary to a life supposedly dedicated to the service of God. These were ones who had been entrusted to teach the Law of God, to instruct in the Word of God. Sin tempts every person to take the way of ease and comfort. When a person surrenders to the comfortable path of the world, the next generation pays a terrible price for their forefathers' disobedience. They pay the price of ignorance of the Word of God.

Is there any area where you choose to remain in the comfort of the world at the expense of obedience to God and His Word? The danger is that you lose the sting of conviction over so long a time, and you are not even bothered by your sin. Your heart has grown calloused to your disobedience. For example, if you miss mid-week prayer service, or Bible study, you may feel bad, but if you miss it the next week, you do not feel as bad. Now you have not been to mid-week service for so long, it does not even bother you.

Prayer and Praise:

Lord, You are a liberating God. Teach me day by day to walk in Your liberty and teach me not to take Your liberties for granted. Let me repent and walk with You daily, as I adjust my life to You. In the mighty name of Jesus Christ, my Lord. Amen.

Discernment
Ezra 4:1-5

Can you imagine having a large and difficult task and out of seemingly nowhere people show up and offer to help? It could change everything. The task could be completed so much quicker, the hours of manpower saved, so that other endeavors can be attempted. How could this be a bad thing? How could you know whether it would a blessing or a curse? The key is spiritual discernment.

Do you have spiritual discernment? Most people want to think they are discerning. However, many people show their lack of discernment by the way they approach everyday issues of life. Discernment is the ability to perceive or recognize something based on the senses. Things just do not look right or "feel" right. However, when it comes to spiritual discernment, this has nothing to do with your physical senses, but it has everything to do with your spiritual understanding.

Spiritual understanding comes from the Word of God received into your life and lived by, and the Holy Spirit filling and controlling your life. If you do not live by faith, filled with the Holy Spirit and actively adjusting your life to the Word of God, you will lack spiritual discernment. When you lack spiritual discernment everything that is "nice" will appear okay. Yet, everything that appears "nice" and "good" is not always okay.

When the Israelites returned to Jerusalem to rebuild the temple, why did they refuse help from the people of the land? Because they were not God's people, and God's people are not to be in relationship with the people of the world. How far has the church drifted from that principle today?

God's work is to be carried out by God's people without the aid of the world. The enemy is not to be given any credit for the accomplishment of the purposes of God. When a believer or a church looks to the world for support, the outcome is compromised. God's will is crucial, but it must be carried out in God's way. The people of God are never to be obligated to the world.

The church must recognize the areas where the world wants to join hands, as if to support the work of God. The church must practice spiritual discernment in all things. When the people of God refused the help of the world, those same people turned on them and became adversarial to them.

The purity of the work requires purity of faith.

Prayer and Praise:

Lord, teach me to yield daily to Your Holy Spirit and to constantly be adjusting my life to You. Show me areas of compromise, and let me by faith surrender afresh to You. Give me spiritual discernment so I may live unto Your glory. In the mighty name of Jesus Christ, my Lord. Amen.

PREPARE YOUR HEART
Ezra 7:8-10

Almost six decades have passed before Ezra arrives in Jerusalem. He was a priest and a scribe, a descendant of Aaron. His purpose for going to Jerusalem was to "to seek the Law of the Lord and do it, and to teach the statutes and ordinances to Israel."

Jerusalem needed the law of God, as do every people group and nation. In Jerusalem, they were being threatened and opposed by non-Jews, and Jews could not care less for the things of God. Do you live in a time and place where people are careless and disregard the things of Almighty God? Do you know the truths of God sufficiently to stand in faith when this opposition comes? Ezra was greatly needed for a time such as this.

The text tells that he "prepared his heart to seek the Law of the Lord." What do you do in preparation for your quiet time, devotional, or study time? Do you spend time in prayer getting your own life right with God? Do you make necessary adjustments in order to be in a place with no distractions? Do you turn off your cell phone? Do you enter His courts with "thanksgiving in your heart?" Do you sit silent before the Lord, waiting on Him to commune with you?

So many people want to rush into the presence of God, and they never "secure the presence" of God. They read their Bible and say short prayers for blessing, but they never wait long enough to meet with God. They go through a religious exercise, but they fail to meet God. How about you? What is it going to take to slow you down and make seeking God and preparing your heart a priority?

Prayer and Praise:

Lord, teach me to come before You willing to wait upon You. Forgive me for trying to dictate my schedule to You. In the mighty name of Jesus Christ, my Lord. Amen.

NEHEMIAH PRAYS
Nehemiah 1:5-10

What is the greatest need that America faces right now? The answer depends on whom you ask. Some will say health care, others employment, and others will say education. However, the greatest need America has is for God to move with a sweeping revival. The results of true revival will be repentance, restitution, restored homes, and transformed lives.

So when does true revival come? J. Edwin Orr said, "You can expect God to move in revival when God's people get right with Him about their sin."

In the book of Nehemiah, Nehemiah was greatly concerned over his homeland, Jerusalem. Jerusalem was lying in ruins. God was laying a burden for His people on the heart of one man. Because of this burden, Nehemiah began to pray. One man prayed, and the end result was amazing revival among God's people.

Throughout this book, you find Nehemiah praying nine times. He begins with prayer, and he prays throughout the entire book. It all began with Nehemiah's seeing the need. Do you see the need of your city? Are you driven to your knees because of the spiritual condition of your community?

How did Nehemiah pray? He began by getting the right perspective. He acknowledged the greatness of God. His heart was filled with reverential fear for God. Next he made confession of sin. Then Nehemiah recalled the covenant, the basis of his relationship with the Father. In verses 8-10, he prayed specifically, he prayed the "word that You commanded." He prayed Scripture. This was the pattern of successful praying.

How has your prayer life been this week? Are you burdened over the condition of your church? Are you concerned and burdened over the condition of your family? Will you be an agent of revival? Will you begin to pray and not to faint? Time is running out, do not wait.

Prayer and Praise:

Lord, burden my heart with what burdens You. Drive me to my knees to seek You. Teach me how to approach Your throne of grace. Use me as an agent of revival for my church, my community, and my family. In the mighty name of Jesus Christ, my Lord. Amen.

OPPOSITION WILL HAPPEN
Nehemiah 4:1-6

Movement always generates friction. This is true in the physical realm, and it is true in the spiritual realm. The Christian life is about change. When a person comes to Christ and is born again, he is changed. He does not change himself, but rather, God changes him into a new creation. The Christian life is a life of constantly being changed into the image of Christ. It does not stop with salvation. Salvation is only the beginning.

When you commit to do God's work, God's way, there will be friction created with others. Why? It is because your life touches and impacts others. Obstacles and barriers begin to emerge, and opposition will take place.

The city of Jerusalem lay in ruins. The walls of the city were torn down, and there were no lines of demarcation. There was no distinction from the city of God and the world. Nehemiah appeared on the scene, and they begin to rebuild the walls of Jerusalem, and the world did not like it. The enemies of God's people rose to oppose the work.

When you commit to do God's work in God's way, expect opposition. The enemy came on the scene and they began to ridicule, and they began to mock the workers of God. Rumors began to fly. The quickest way to spread a rumor is to feed it to people with fear.

The results of the opposition opposing the work of God and the people of God were tremendous. The people became fatigued, their strength was gone. They were frustrated, all looked hopeless, and they became afraid the enemy would attack. The enemy has two goals: hinder God's Word and stop God's work.

How do you respond to opposition? You pray, you turn the matter over to the Lord. You continue diligently in your efforts. Do not stop working the work of God. Learn to pray through opposition.

Prayer and Praise:

Lord, why do I get surprised when opposition comes? I should expect it as Your Word plainly shows. Teach me to pray through problems and opposition. They attempt to distract me from the work. Thank You for showing me this truth. In the mighty name of Jesus Christ, my Lord. Amen.

PREACH THE WORD
Nehemiah 8:1-6

This is a dramatic moment. For the first time in a hundred years or more, Israel was safe behind the walls of the city, with a completed temple and a functioning priesthood. It all happened in the seventh month, a month devoted to worship of the Lord. The Word of God would be preached.

The tragedy of all of this is that the people of God had heard the message of God from Jeremiah and Isaiah, but they rebelled against the Word. They did not allow the Word to penetrate their hearts and affect their lives. The result was personal and collective captivity.

Now, over one hundred years later, the people were hungry for the Word of God. What is your attitude toward the Bible? Is the Bible central in your thinking and decision making? As the Word of God was preached for six hours, the people stood. When was the last time you stood for the preaching of God's Word? You were so hungry for the Word, you stood for six hours?

Notice the response of the people to the preached Word of God. They showed up, even with no music playing. They were attentive. There was respect given, they stood. They said amen. This Hebrew word means "truth." They were in agreement with the Word being preached. They lifted their hands to God. They bowed their heads as they worshipped God.

How do you respond when you hear the Word of God preached? Do you respond, and do you adjust your life to the Word of God? Do you obey? There is no acceptance of the Word of God if there is no obedience to the Word of God.

You are told in verse 12 that they rejoiced greatly; they celebrated. Why did they celebrate? They understood the Word of God delivered to them. Do you understand that the Bible is God's Word? It is not the word of a man. God reveals Himself and His ways to you through His Word. That is a cause to celebrate.

Prayer and Praise:

Lord, Your Word is truth. Teach me truth. Show me how to make application of Your Word to my life in a practical way. Show me the areas where I need to adjust my life to Your Word if I am to continue walking in fellowship and communion with You. In the mighty name of Jesus Christ, my Lord. Amen.

PRAISE
Nehemiah 12:27-47

In Nehemiah 12, you see the people of God gathered in corporate worship just to praise the Lord. They have come together as the temple has been completed, now the walls around Jerusalem are finished, and there is a functioning priesthood. God's people united together to thank the Lord.

Praise and thanksgiving is to be the norm for every child of God and church. As God blesses, your heart and your mouth should be filled with praise. Think for a moment all God has done for you this week. He has allowed you to breathe, to have life. He has allowed you the ability to process thoughts. He has kept you safe. He has loved you and extended grace and mercy to you. Praise His name.

In the text, you see the preparation for praise. The people were prepared by Scripture. They took the Word of God seriously. They were following the commands of David. Next, they sought out the Levites, and were led in singing and the playing of instruments. This was loud, not to draw attention to themselves, but to let the world know they were exalting God.

They were prepared by sanctification (v. 30). Before the praise took place, they had to be pure and clean. Often, this is the point of departure by many. They fail to be clean before God, and they merely go through the motions of praise. To have a joyful heart you must have a clean heart. Sin is what keeps one silent. When you know you are clean and pure, praise flows.

As the people of God were prepared, the praise began to burst forth. They sang loudly and enthusiastically. They were united; all the people were a part of the procession of praise. They offered great sacrifice and rejoiced. When was the last time you praised God in this fashion?

Prayer and Praise:

Lord, I exalt You. You are my God and King. Praise Your Holy Name. Teach me daily to be filled with praise and thanksgiving. Let me ever be aware that having life is a gift from You. Let me not take things for granted, but always recognize Your blessedness in and on my life. I adore You, Lord. I bow before You in worship. Glory be to Your Holy Name. In the mighty name of Jesus Christ, my Lord. Amen.

VASHTI
Esther 1:9-19

The book of Esther is a unique book. It is one of only two books in the Bible named after a woman. Also, in this book, the name of the Lord is not mentioned. The Lord's name may not be mentioned, but His presence is obvious because you can see the traces of God are all over it. The word prayer is not mentioned, but it is obvious that prayer is involved.

The book gives an overview of the large number of Jews who stayed in captivity, even after they had been allowed to return to Jerusalem. This book is, therefore, referred to as a postexilic book.

As the story goes, Vashti, the queen, fell out of favor with the king. Basically, the king threw a big party, got drunk, and he called for Vashti to come before the people and show her beauty. She refused. She disobeyed her king's command and she was dethroned.

King Ahasuerus represents the world view of life, while Vashti represents the God view. Today, you still have tension between the world's view and God's view. You must answer the question, "Which view do you embrace?"

The world view shows several things: a lust for power, a weakness for strong drink, moral deficiency, and self-seeking. No one knows exactly what the king asked Vashti to do, but she refused, knowing it would cost her the kingdom. He may have asked her to simply say hello. Why would she refuse this? It is more likely he asked her to show more than her pretty face to a room full of drunken men. The world view was clear: you are to do what I want.

Vashti, who represents God's view, was a good wife. She supported her husband. She entertained the women while her husband handled the men. She took a stand on her convictions, even when it cost her the kingdom. Do you have convictions? Do you stand firm on your convictions?

Finally, you see that she was used in the providence of God. Knowing what would happen to her, she stood for her convictions. Ultimately, she set in motion the rescue of thousands of Jewish lives.

When you take a stand on God's Word, though the immediate circumstances may seem bleak, you can stand and trust the providence of God. The problem appears to be too much world view and not enough God view.

Prayer and Praise:

Lord, let me always seek Your face and Your mind. Give me strong convictions based on Your Word. Let me stand for You and Your truth, regardless of the cost. In the mighty name of Jesus Christ, my Lord. Amen.

FOR SUCH A TIME AS THIS
Esther 4:14

It was a crisis hour, and in a crisis hour God looks for intercessors, and sometimes He looks in vain. The enemy was about to move in upon the people of God and destroy them. Such was not the case with Esther; she would go in before the king and make supplication unto him. She would stand in the gap for God's people.

Are you aware of the movement of the enemy against the people of God today? Are you concerned over the attacks against Christianity and the Bible? Or do you even give it a thought? Can you go about the normal routine of life and never be challenged because you are a Christian? If that be the case, you are not a very good Christian.

Can God count on you to intercede, to pray? Look around, and listen to the politicians and the news. The United States of America is in a desperate situation. Can God count on you? Do you show up for prayer meeting at your church? Do you pray?

Esther could have held her peace, and she may have been fine. However, she would not be silent. She could not be silent, because these were her people who would die. Often, God allows opportunities for His children to stand—to stand when everyone else is silent, or to choose the wrong. Will you stand? Do you recognize those moments when they come. Or will you remain silent, seeking to preserve self?

Are you glad Jesus did not remain silent for you? Are you not thankful that Christ stood in the gap for you?

Your prayers can make a difference. Not those superficial, hurried, pre-rehearsed prayers, but true intercession. It is those times you get still before the throne of God and you pour out your heart. Your soul groans to the Father because you are so burdened over the condition of your land, your church, and your family. You linger in His presence, silent before God, surrendered to Him. Have you ever been that burdened? If not, why not? Open your eyes and see the waves of destruction upon us. Realize that maybe God has you here for such a time as this.

Prayer and Praise:

Lord, I listen to the politicians, and they concern me. Our country has gone the way of tolerance and heathenism. Burden my heart for this country. Burden my heart for the church. Father, stir in me a spirit of intercession, and let me stand in the gap. In the mighty name of Jesus Christ, my Lord. Amen.

TAKE THE WORD
Esther 8:10

When wicked Haman's evil plot was exposed, the king had a decree written that would enable the Jews to protect themselves and their property from the coming slaughter. He instructed them to send this message throughout the land. He specifically told them to send "couriers on horseback, riding on royal horses bred from swift steeds."

Unlike today, where cellphones, text, email, and fax machines exist, horseback was the fastest way to send a message or to sound the alarm. The king was saying "HURRY! Do not wait. Get the message out." Why? Because it was a matter of life and death.

Do you sense the urgency to get the message of Christ out to a lost and dying world? Do you realize it is a matter of life and death? Do you take the gospel of Jesus Christ seriously enough to share it with your friends, coworkers, and associates? Or do you waste time, acting as if there is plenty of time?

Read your local newspaper, and you will be surprised to find the number of young adults and middle-aged adults that have passed into eternity this very week. Did you know any of these names? Have you shared with anyone the message of Christ this week? Mount the horse, get the swiftest steed, time is running out. People's lives hang in the balance. Tell the good news of Christ.

Prayer and Praise:

Lord, thank You for Your saving work. Burden my heart for lost people, and make me aware of the opportunities You place before me every day. Use me as a witness for Your grace and mercy. Let me sense the urgency of the hour. In the mighty name of Jesus Christ, my Lord. Amen.

SATAN'S PLAN
Job 1:6-12

Scripture gives insight into suffering, but the final answer is not completely given. There are some things you will not know until you get to heaven. In the first two chapters, you see suffering is penitence. Satan is behind it and he is the ultimate cause. Job says suffering is a puzzle. He cannot know the reason. You can know some truth, but not all.

Job's friends, miserable comforters, say suffering is penal—the only reason one suffers is because of sin. Suffering is also seen as purification. It has an educational purpose behind it. Finally, suffering is providential. Sovereign God has a purpose behind suffering. It is designed for the blessing of the person involved, but often it is too complicated for the finite mind to grasp. You must trust that God knows what He is doing.

Job was written before the Law was given, before the whole revelation of Scripture was completed. This tells you Job had a limited concept of God. You have a better understanding of suffering than Job, because you have the complete revelation of God in the sixty-six books of the Bible.

There is something behind the scene you must understand. Something has happened in the heavenlies that is far bigger, or greater, than mere mortal men. Often one is so self-absorbed and self-centered. Are you? You look inward at your problems, failing to realize this is bigger than you.

In our passage, God has already cast Satan out of heaven, along with a third of the angels. Satan has come back into God's presence saying, "God, You are not fair." This is the only time this happens. Satan says, in essence, "God, You present Yourself as fair and just. The way I see it, no one could love You just because You are You. There has to be an ulterior motive. I am the only one really honest. I said it, I want my own way." Satan has appealed his case, and God allowed it.

The main thing God was doing with Job was showing that He created man to prove to the angels (man who is lower than the angels and inferior to them), that man can choose to love God, no matter what. This problem is a trial case.

What was happening to Job was bigger than Job. God designed it, and if Job was to fit into God's plan, no matter what, he must trust God. God then proved that Job was not serving Him for what he could get, for the benefits.

Prayer and Praise:

Lord, I am nothing, I am lower than nothing, yet You saw fit to save me. Enable me day after day to trust You. In the good days and the bad, let my faith, my trust be evidenced to those around me. In the mighty name of Jesus Christ, my Lord. Amen.

HOLD MY TONGUE
Job 6:24

"Teach me and I will hold my tongue." Have you ever said that prayer? Do you need to say that prayer? One's tongue or one's voice can be used to bless, or it can be used to curse. It can spread the Word of God, or it can spread slander and gossip. Be cautious how you use your tongue.

Job had been accused by his friends of having sin in his life; therefore, that was why he was suffering as he was. Yet Job denied that he had willful, unconfessed, or unforsaken sin. As he tried to present his case, he realized how easy it would be to sin with his mouth while trying to defend himself.

Do you realize that temptation? Have you ever tried to justify yourself to someone who thinks you have done wrong when you have not? It can be a very frustrating time. Guard your tongue at all times.

Prayer and Praise:

Lord, teach me to guard my tongue, my mouth, my voice. Let me so trust You that You are my defender. In the mighty name of Jesus Christ, my Lord. Amen.

CHARACTERISTICS OF A GODLESS MAN
Job 8:13

As you read through the book of Job, you can put together characteristics of a godless man. A godless individual is a person who has no time for God. He may be wicked, or may be nice, but he has no time for God. He does not adjust his life to creator and redeemed God. He lives for self, and is self-satisfied.

The characteristics of a godless man are as follows: (1) he forgets God (Job 8:13); 2) he places his hope in things that perish (Job 8:13); (3) he cannot come into God's presence (Job 13:16); (4) his religion is barren (Job 15:34); 5) he appalls the innocent and upright (Job 17:8); (6) his joy or exhortation is short-lived (Job 20:5); (7) he has no hope (Job 27:8); (8) when disciplined by God, he stores up anger and does not cry out to Him (Job 36:13); (9) he gnashes his teeth at the righteous (Psalm 37:12). (10) he destroys his neighbor with his mouth (Proverbs 11:9).

Do you give God your time? Do you schedule Him into your daily activities? Or do you merely give Him the leftovers, if there are any, of the day? Is God placed before your favorite television show?

Do you display the characteristics of godlessness with your life, but try and deny them with your talk?

Prayer and Praise:

Lord, show me if I am godless. Show me to what I truly give my time and attention. Bring great conviction to my heart, if I merely am a church attender and nothing more. In the mighty name of Jesus Christ, my Lord. Amen.

A WEARY SOUL
Job 10:1-2

"My soul is weary of life." Have you ever felt that way? Job had gone through the most excruciating season of life, and he was still in it. His friends who have come to comfort him are miserable comforters. They are accusers. Be careful when you attempt to comfort others that you indeed comfort and not accuse.

There will be times in life when every person faces hardship and difficulty. There will be times in life when even the best Christian will have questions. John the Baptist, in a prison cell, sent word asking of Christ, "Are you the Coming One, or do we look for another (Matthew 11:2-3)?" John was the forerunner of Christ. He had baptized Jesus in the Jordan River when the Holy Spirit descended like a dove upon Christ, and God spoke. Now, in a prison cell, John expressed doubt.

Difficult times can bring weariness to one's soul. Difficult times can cause questions and bring confusion. In difficult times and situations, do not be afraid to express your concerns to God. That is what Job did in the next verse. He asked God not to condemn him, but to tell him why he was facing such difficulties. Do not be afraid to ask God questions.

Job asked God why, but he did not receive an answer right away. Not until the end of the book does God speak to Job. When a person comes before God with a question, he or she should ask the question without being accusative. Learn to speak to God in a respectful voice. Learn to wait and to listen. Examine your life to see if there is anything you have done to bring such difficulty upon yourself. Get honest.

In Malachi 3:9, you are told, "You are cursed with a curse," if you do not tithe. Do you believe that? Is it true? It is the Word of God. This was not Job's issue. First Corinthians 11:29-30, tells that if you partake of the Lord's Supper unworthily, not examining your life, you may die prematurely or become sick. Do you believe that? It is still God's Word. This was not the case for Job. Job suffered because God was using Job as a testimony of how a righteous man suffers. Does God want to use your situation as a testimony for others?

Prayer and Praise:

Lord, teach me daily to examine my life for any sin. Enable me to endure suffering, in order to be a testimony for others of Your greatness. In the mighty name of Jesus Christ, my Lord. Amen.

THOUGH HE SLAY ME
Job 13:15

Job had been reproved by his friends for justifying himself. His friends defended their bad theology, not God. Job is weary with their accusations. In this context Job said, "Though He slay me, yet I will trust in Him." Do you understand that statement? Could you make that statement?

Job was seeking God. He wanted God to justify him to his friends. He wanted God to allow him to come before Him and make his plea. Now in those times, to barge into the presence of the king, when not called for, could mean death. Job expressed that he had little hope he would come out of this alive. Have you ever been in a situation you felt you may not make it out alive? Another translation for this phrase is, "Behold, He will slay me, I have no hope."

The words do not end there. Job goes on to say in the next verse, "He [God] also shall be my salvation." Job had strong confidence in God. Do you have such confidence in God? Is your relationship with Jesus Christ so real that even in the pain of life, you have strong confidence in your God?

This is key to living the Christian life to the fullest—strong confidence in your Savior, Jesus Christ. How does a person get such confidence? It starts before the trial arrives. Job was a man of faith before the troubles and trials came into his life. Job was a man who knew his God before he lost everything in this ordeal.

The question comes to you: do you cultivate a relationship with Jesus in the good days of life, when things are going well? Or do you waste your time pursuing the things of the world, not preparing for difficulties that are ahead? Your relationship with Christ must be cultivated.

How do you cultivate your relationship with Christ? Look at Job, Job was "blameless and upright, and one who feared God and shunned evil." The Bible also says that Job "sanctified" his children to the Lord, and offered burnt offerings according to their number. Do you take such detailed care for your life and the life of your children? Prepare your life spiritually before the trial comes.

Prayer and Praise:

Lord, You are my God. Teach me to not waste time in the blessed days, so that I am not prepared spiritually for difficult challenges. In the mighty name of Jesus Christ, my Lord. Amen.

MISERABLE COMFORTERS
Job 16:2

Job's friends had good intentions, but they failed to comfort Job. They started out okay. They came and sat with Job, no words were spoken. They wept, cried, and grieved with Job. They even listened as Job began to speak his heart. If they had left it there, they would have been comforters to Job, but they did not let it alone.

After seven days of this, they made the fatal mistake of talking, or rather, telling Job why he was experiencing all he was experiencing. Interesting is the fact that Job did not ask them for their assessment of his situation. They offered that freely and ignorantly. All three of Job's friends believed Job was guilty of sin, or else he would not have experienced such devastation.

Job probably believed basically the same thing his friends believed before he was afflicted. The difference now was Job's experience. Job asked for understanding and compassion, but he failed to receive it from his friends.

It is easy to fall into the role of a "miserable comforter." Someone you know is sick, facing difficulties or losses. It is easy to assume this person has sinned, and brought it upon himself. Be warned, such is not always the case. You must learn to sit in silence with a grieving and broken brother. You weep and grieve with him, but be hesitant to offer an explanation for his pain. God may be using him as a testimony. If there is hidden sin, let God reveal it.

If they ask your ideas, be sure to proceed with grace. Job's three friends could not accept that the righteous suffer. You have the complete Bible, and it teaches that very principle. First Peter 3:14, "If you should suffer for righteousness' sake, you are blessed." Oftentimes, the greatest comfort is simply your presence without words.

Prayer and Praise:

Lord, You are the greatest comforter. Teach me how to comfort those who are hurting without passing judgment on them. Let me be refreshment to their souls. In the mighty name of Jesus Christ, my Lord. Amen.

MY REDEEMER LIVES!
Job 19:25-27

Job has lost his family, his flocks, his finances, and his health, but he made such a powerful confession in these verses. "I know that my Redeemer lives." What certainty Job spoke with, and what confidence he had. Even in all his pain, there were some things that he knew beyond a doubt. Even in your pain there are some things you can "know" as well.

Job states that he knows there is a Redeemer. What is a redeemer? It is one who purchases or delivers another by paying a ransom. Job is saying, "I know my Redeemer." Job has a personal relationship with his Redeemer. This is not speculation, but truth uttered from a heart of assurance and firm conviction. Do you have that same assurance? Do you know personally your Redeemer?

Job also expresses his confidence that he would see God. Job says, "Whom I shall see for myself, and my eyes shall behold." Job was certain he would see His God. The apostle John writes, "Beloved, now we are children of God; and it has not yet been revealed what we shall be, but we know that when He is revealed, we shall be like Him, for we shall see Him as He is (1 John 3:2)." You can have certainty, as a child of God, that you will behold Him in all His glory. What formerly you have believed by faith will one day be seen by sight. Hallelujah!

Job made an exclamation of his intense desire for this to happen. He said, "My heart yearns within me!" I am overwhelmed with the thought of seeing my Redeemer. Can you testify of this same desire? Or have you allowed things of the world to so consume you the thought of eternity with Christ has been pushed away for a later time? Is there any desire in you for the presence of Christ?

Prayer and Praise:

Lord, You are my Redeemer and I exalt You. I long for Your presence. When trials and troubles come, they serve to increase my longing for You. Thank You for saving me and giving me true assurance of my salvation. I can say with Job, "I know my Redeemer." In the mighty name of Jesus Christ, my Lord. Amen.

WHERE I MIGHT FIND HIM
Job 23:3

Have you ever listened for God and all you hear is silence? Has the silence of God ever been deafening to you? Have you ever wanted or needed to find God, but all your attempts seem to fail? This is how Job felt. He could not seem to get God's attention. He couldn't seem to get God to acknowledge him, and he was weary in the search.

You must learn this lesson. When you seek for God and He seems far away, it is not because He does not care. It is because He is trying to teach you faith and trust, when you seem to have no reason to have faith and trust.

You grow weary in prayer as you pray and you see or sense no change in the situation. Be assured, God is still in control. When you do not see any activity, be of strong faith; your heavenly Father knows everything that is taking place. Your faith cannot rest on the visible or the outward. You have to learn to walk in the Spirit, even in the dark.

Are you experiencing a trial, a testing, or a season of silence from God? Do not stop praying. Persevering prayer requires pure faith. Pure faith comes from living daily yielded to the Father and walking in the Holy Spirit. It comes as obedience flows from one's life. It comes as the Word of God is taken off the pages of the Bible and buried in your heart. "Faith comes by hearing, and hearing by the Word of God (Romans 10:17)."

Job, weary from the trial and tired from the constant badgering of his friends, had to wait upon the Lord. Maybe that is what God is calling you to do—wait upon Him. Will you? As you wait, will you maintain your submission and surrender to Him? Will you be faithful as you wait in silence to feed on the Word of God? Will you trust God when there is no visible evidence to continue?

Prayer and Praise:

Lord, teach me to wait in the position of surrender. Teach me to trust You, even when my flesh, friends, or family tell me it is ridiculous. Father, let me glorify You in the trials of life and in the seasons of silence. In the mighty name of Jesus Christ, my Lord. Amen.

JUNE

June 1...............Job 25:4, Being Justified with God
June 2...............Job 28:12, In the Place of Understanding
June 3...............Job 31:1, A Covenant with My Eyes
June 4...............Job 34:1-12, Man's Explanation for Suffering
June 5...............Job 38:1-4, The Lord Answers
June 6...............Job 42:3, I Uttered What I Did Not Understand
June 7...............Psalm 1:1-6, The Blessed Man
June 8...............Psalm 9:1, 9-11, I Will Praise God
June 9...............Psalm 15:1, I Will Abide
June 10.............Psalm 23:1-6, The Lord Is My Shepherd
June 11.............Psalm 32:3-8, Pitfalls
June 12.............Psalm 40:1-3, Waiting on the Lord
June 13.............Psalm 47:1, Clap Your Hands
June 14.............Psalm 51:1-3, Have Mercy Upon Me
June 15.............Psalm 63:1-3, Thirsty for God
June 16.............Psalm 68:19, The Benefits of God
June 17.............Psalm 71:8, Let My Mouth Be Filled With Praise
June 18.............Psalm 78:1, Listen to God's Word
June 19.............Psalm 91:1, The Secret Place
June 20.............Psalm 94:17, When God is Silent
June 21.............Psalm 105:1, Give Thanks to the Lord
June 22.............Psalm 108:1, A Steadfast Heart
June 23.............Psalm 116:1, Why I Love the Lord
June 24.............Psalm 119:1-5, Reasons to Read the Word of God
June 25.............Psalm 121:1, Lift Up Your Eyes
June 26.............Psalm 128:1, To Fear the Lord
June 27.............Psalm 137:1-3, Hanging Our Harps
June 28.............Psalm 150:1, Praise the Lord
June 29.............Proverbs 1:24, Called and Refused
June 30.............Proverbs 4:5, Get Wisdom

BEING JUSTIFIED WITH GOD
Job 25:4

Bildad, one of Job's miserable comforters, asked the question, "How can a man be righteous before God?" That is a most important question that still must be answered today. Are you righteous and justified with the living God? Do you know for certain things are right between you and God?

The word justified has been defined as "just as if I never sinned." How does a person get justified? The Bible tells us, "Abraham believed God, and it was accounted to him for righteousness. Now to him who works, the wages are not counted as grace but as debt. But to him who does not work but believes on Him who justifies the ungodly, his faith is accounted for righteousness" (Romans 4:3-5).

A person is justified with God by believing God. It did not say by believing in God. Many people today believe in God just like they believe Abraham Lincoln was the sixteenth president of the United States. They believe in God with intellectual assent. However, that is not the same as believing God. To be justified with God, you must believe God.

You do not believe in the mere existence of God, you believe all God has revealed to you in the Bible. You believe all Jesus Christ did on the cross, dying for your sin. You believe the tomb is empty, and Jesus is seated at the right hand of the Father ever making intercession for you. You believe and God accounts it for righteousness. To believe is an act of faith in God and His finished work.

Believing, as an act of faith, changes you. God no longer looks upon your sin, but rather, when God looks upon you, He sees the righteousness of Jesus Christ covering your life. God sees you justified because you are in Jesus Christ.

Being justified with God is so much more than saying a prayer. It is Christ becoming real in your life, as you believe. The moment you truly believe, the Holy Spirit comes into your life to live and reign. The Holy Spirit teaches, directs, and convicts of both righteousness and sin. God, in the person of the Holy Spirit, now lives within your life. Has this ever happened to you? Do you know you are justified with God? Do you know this without some man having to tell you? If you do not know this with certainty, you can. You can come before the Father and believe God.

Prayer and Praise:

Lord, thank You for justifying me. It is not by works I have done, but by my believing You. In the mighty name of Jesus Christ, my Lord. Amen.

IN THE PLACE OF UNDERSTANDING
Job 28:12

Three times Job has been referred to as a man that fears God (1:1, 8; 2:3). Job was a wise man. Yet as wise as Job was, he could not comprehend God's ways. He could not understand why he was facing all he was facing. He asked, "Where is the place of understanding?"

He answered the question in the last verse of the chapter, "Behold, the fear of the Lord, that is wisdom; and to depart from evil is understanding."

Listen to David, "When I thought how to understand this, it was too painful for me. Until I went into the sanctuary of God; then I understood (Psalm 73:16-17)." When David went into the place of God, the sanctuary, he stopped complaining and whining, and God gave him understanding.

What made the difference? David got in the sanctuary and he got the right perspective. Often that is how it is still. If you can get your eyes to perceive from God's viewpoint, it will make all the difference in the world. From what viewpoint are you looking at your situation? Do you need to come into the sanctuary of God and allow Him to give you His divine perspective?

Life brings many difficult challenges. The only way to have true understanding is to begin seeking God's point of view. It is to come into God's sanctuary and allow Him to let your eyes see the spiritual, as well as the physical. Only you can make the choice to enter into God's sanctuary.

Prayer and Praise:

Lord, when I do not understand why things happen as they happen, teach me to see life from Your vantage point. Let me draw near to You in faith and allow You to give me Your perspective. Enable me to understand Your perspective is always right and best. In the mighty name of Jesus Christ, my Lord. Amen.

A Covenant With My Eyes
Job 31:1

Throughout Job's life he sought to please God. He had his priorities right; and God was preeminent in everything. Many people today who profess to be Christians cannot come close to Job's faithfulness. Ask someone if he or she is a born-again Christian, and you will receive a variety of responses, such as "I have been a good person;" "I go to church;" "I like helping people;" "I believe in God."

None of these claims will save you. You read two days ago what it means to be justified with God. Lost people can go to church, give to the needy, believe in God, and are good people (in their own eyes). The only thing that makes one acceptable to God is the righteousness of Christ and His death on the cross, applied by faith in his or her life personally.

Job lived long before Jesus Christ, yet Job was saved by faith. Jesus Christ is the Lamb of God slain from the foundation of the world (Revelation 13:8). The way any person in the Old Testament was made right with God is the same way you and I are made right with God: by faith in God. Job confessed his Redeemer lives.

Job addresses his friends in an attempt to persuade them of his innocence of the claims they are making. In this chapter, he states eleven sins he was not guilty of: (1) Job was not guilty of sexual lust (v. 1-4); (2) Job was not guilty of dishonesty nor of deceiving people (v. 5-6); (3) Job was not guilty of covetousness (v. 7-9); (4) Job was not guilty of adultery (v. 9-12); (5) Job was not guilty of injustice (v. 13-15); (6) Job was not guilty of neglecting the needy or helpless (v.16-23); (7) Job was not guilty of putting his trust in money or false gods (v.24-28); (8) Job was not guilty of hating an enemy (v. 29-30); (9) Job was not guilty of being inhospitable (v. 31-32); (10) Job was not guilty of hypocrisy (v. 33-37); and (11) Job was not guilty of greed (v. 38-40).

Job understood sin well. The desire of Job's heart was to live pleasing to God. He took the necessary measures to ensure that was completed. Have you? Is the desire of your heart to please God or is it to have the best and happiest life possible right now? Have you taken the necessary steps in order to please God and glorify Him?

Prayer and Praise:

Lord, let my life be lived to please You above everyone else. In the mighty name of Jesus Christ my Lord, Amen.

MAN'S EXPLANATION FOR SUFFERING
Job 34:1-12

If you were asked to name someone not walking close to the Lord, could you? Most believers know others, family and friends, living in sin. Some even profess to be saved. Do you have a responsibility to these people? Yes, according to the Word of God, you do. How you do this is crucial. When confronting someone about his lifestyle, you must approach him in the right spirit and, you must be sure it is needed.

In the passage of Scripture you read, Elihu is going to try and correct Job. He believed Job was guilty of sin. He was going to ask Job to repent of the sin he had committed and get right with God. The problem was Elihu was mistaken. Elihu was acting in his flesh and not with the leading of the Holy Spirit.

Elihu accused Job of claiming God to be unfair (v.5-6). He accused Job with being arrogant (v.7). He said Job was seeking the companionship of the wicked (v.8). Finally, he accused Job of denying God's love and goodness (v. 9). Everything Elihu accuses against Job were based on Elihu's misunderstanding of the situation.

The Bible teaches that you are to confront sin. Some sin is easily recognized. Willful disobedience to God's Word is sin; you can make a list of them. There are sins of omission and commission. However, when you are dealing with a fellow believer with no action of sin, no deliberate deed of sin, you must be very cautious. Elihu was assuming Job had committed some sin because of the situation he was in. It never crossed his mind, or the other friends, they could be wrong. Just because a believer is facing challenges and trials does not mean he or she has committed sin. Be careful you do not judge a person because of his or her situation. Oftentimes in this type of setting, silence and prayer are the best approach.

Prayer and Praise:

Lord, teach me to be ever so sensitive to Your leading. Teach me to keep my mouth shut when all I have is assumptions. Let me be a vessel of encouragement to those who are suffering, not a discouragement. In the mighty name of Jesus Christ, my Lord. Amen.

THE LORD ANSWERS
Job 38:1-4

In today's text, Job finally heard from God. He heard from the One he had been seeking, from the One to whom he had been praying. The Almighty God who he had said was silent and ignoring him spoke to Job. When God spoke to Job, Job knew that it was God speaking. That is important. When God speaks to you, you will know it is God. If you have concerns with who it is that is speaking, it probably is not God. Why? John tells you, "The sheep hear His voice, and He calls His own sheep by name and leads them out ... and the sheep follow Him; for they know His voice ... I am the Good Shepherd, and I know My sheep, and am known by My own" (John 10:3, 4, 14).

God's Word tells you, if you are a child of God, you will recognize and know God's voice. It also tells that you will follow Him. This means you will respond positively to God. That is to say you will obey His voice, His Word.

Job heard God speak; out of a whirlwind God answered Job. God asked Job several questions. God did not speak to Job answering all his questions. God did not offer to Job an explanation of what had taken place. God called Job on the carpet and asked him who he thought he was asking for counsel without understanding.

That is often how it is with God. He speaks to you by asking you questions, by challenging your understanding. He asked Job, "Where were you when I laid the foundations of the earth?" He was teaching Job his own inadequacy of understanding. He was teaching Job life did not revolve around him.

That is the issue everyone has to come to grips with: Life does not revolve around you. You are saved by God's grace. The purpose for which you were saved is not to have the most meaningful life possible. It is not to enjoy all the things you can enjoy. You were saved for one reason—for God's glory (Ephesians 1:4-6).

Many of the issues you face in life are because your perspective is wrong. You were saved for God's glory. You were saved for holiness, not personal happiness. When you come to terms with holiness, the only thing that makes you happy is glorifying Christ Jesus. God still speaks. Are you ready to hear His answer?

Prayer and Praise:

Lord, You are my Lord and Savior. Thank You for speaking to me. Give me sense to understand life is about You being glorified in me. In the mighty name of Jesus Christ, my Lord. Amen.

I UTTERED WHAT I DID NOT UNDERSTAND
Job 42:3

Have you ever said something and wished you could have taken it back and never said it? Have you thought something and when you find out the truth, you are ashamed you even let your mind go in the previous direction? Understanding is essential to proper perspective.

Job had had a difficult time with life in the recent weeks and months. He had lost everything he held dear on the earth. Yet he refused to deny his faith. Job refused to allow his friends to sway him to a false confession just to appease them. However, when God spoke to Job and challenged his questions, Job replied, "I uttered what I did not understand, things too wonderful for me, which I did not know."

What does Job mean by that statement? He means when he finally got into the presence of God, the very thing he had been seeking after, he realized even his questioning and doubts were not worthy. He realized God's presence was the only thing that really mattered. As the psalmist says, "In thy presence is fullness of joy" (Psalm 16:11).

When God manifested Himself to Job, Job's questions were insignificant; all the issues were resolved merely by being aware of the presence of God. That is difficult to comprehend, but Scripture does not lie. In the manifest presence of God, issues are resolved. For some that will be comforting and cause them to seek God more intently. For others, where the pain they have experienced is equal to Job's, they may still struggle with this truth.

Whatever the case, understanding comes from God's perspective. God's perspective is eternal and above everything. Psalm 91 teaches that those who know God's name, He sets them on high. That means He gives you His perspective. Hallelujah to the Lamb of God! Whose perspective do you have today?

Prayer and Praise:

Lord, thank You for being in control and never being shaken. You are God. Enable me, especially in the difficult times of life, to seek and to know Your perspective. In the mighty name of Jesus Christ, my Lord. Amen.

THE BLESSED MAN
Psalm 1:1-6

Most people desire to be blessed. The problem many have is a misunderstanding of true blessedness. If you ask the average Christian what does it mean to be blessed, the common answer is going to be material blessing or physical blessing. Health and wealth always lead the pack in people's minds.

If you study the Scriptures, you will realize true blessedness is not about health and wealth, but it is about your fellowship with Christ. Fellowship is not hanging out and having fun. Fellowship with Christ is about abiding in Christ day after day.

A blessed man is a man who lives a separated life. He does not walk in the counsel of the ungodly, nor stand in the way of sinners, nor sit in the seat of the scornful. He takes conscientious steps not to be influenced by people who have no time for God. Do you? Or are your closest friends people who have no time for God? They do not go to church regularly, they do not read their Bibles daily, nor do they pray on a daily, consistent basis. Blessed-by-God people live separated from the world.

Blessed people live saturated in the Word of God. They delight in the Word. They meditate and give thought to the Word all day long. Do you read your Bible daily? Do you think about the Scriptures throughout the day? Every time a Scripture comes to your mind, God is speaking to you. That is exciting. You should be thankful. Hallelujah!

Blessed people live situated by the river of life, and they bring forth fruit in season. Your life will prosper. Prosper how? In the things of God.

Prayer and Praise:

Lord, thank You for the promise of blessing me in You. Teach me to understand what true blessing is. In the mighty name of Jesus Christ, my Lord. Amen.

I WILL PRAISE GOD
Psalm 9:1, 9-11

Learning to trust comes naturally to most individuals. Being raised in a home where unconditional love is extended and provision made, make it easier for trust to develop. Knowing and experiencing the love of an earthly father is a great enablement for one to learn to trust his heavenly Father. Sadly, many never have that opportunity, but one can still learn to trust God.

You have been promised the God of all creation will come initiating a relationship with you. You must "simply" respond. The key to your relationship with God is to continue responding to the Father. As you do this, you begin to know God in an intimate, personal way. It is more than facts; it is a deep personal relationship with Him, as a result of seeking Him in the midst of your personal pain and discovering Him and trusting Him.

God will be your refuge in times of trouble. However, you must choose to run to Him. In times of trouble God is your refuge, but you are responsible for seeking God. Do you seek God? Do you intentionally adjust your life, lifestyle, and your decisions to Scripture?

As you seek Him, trust will begin to develop and grow instinctively. Praise will spring forth. Praise is internal; it springs from within. It is external; it is evidenced outwardly. Praise is eternal; it continues beyond this life. It is supernal; it is coming from on high. Praise the Lord!

Prayer and Praise:

Lord, You are my God and King, and I will praise You. I will lift You up, exalting You with my words and my life. Bless Your holy name. Let trust show forth in my life. Let trust be normal in my life to You. In the mighty name of Jesus Christ, my Lord. Amen.

I WILL ABIDE
Psalm 15:1

David begins this psalm by asking the question, "Who shall abide in thy tabernacle? Who shall dwell in thy holy hill?" Have you ever stopped to consider these questions? Do you abide in Christ? Do you dwell in Christ? Abiding is not just having a good experience in the Lord every now and then. Abiding means to dwell, or to remain on a continuing basis in Christ. It is not being on one day and off the next. Do you qualify?

After David asked the questions, he answered himself. He tells the three things it requires to abide in Christ. Abiding in Christ is determined by your walk with the Lord, the works you have with the Lord, and finally, the words you speak and how you speak them.

David says you must walk uprightly. He means you live doing what is right in the sight of God. Your behavior is a reflection of how Jesus behaved and lived while in the flesh. He lived righteously.

David next says you work righteousness. Righteousness has to do with rightness. It is about the holiness and purity of Christ being lived out in your life. As that takes place, the works that flow from you are works of righteousness. They do not necessarily have to be specific deeds or actions, but works flow from who you are in Christ.

David finally says he speaks the truth in his heart. Truth is crucial. Without truth, you have no basis of abiding in Christ. God's Word is truth. You are to speak truth not only with your lips, but the truth you have buried in your heart. The truth of Almighty God has become the vital part of your life. You cannot live without God's truth. God's truth is God's Word.

Prayer and Praise:

Lord, I long to dwell in Your presence. My desire is not just to experience You occasionally. I long to abide daily. Teach me to secure Your presence daily. Show me what things I pursue more than You. Move on my spirit with strong conviction until I turn from them. In the mighty name of Jesus Christ, my Lord. Amen.

THE LORD IS MY SHEPHERD
Psalm 23:1-6

This is probably one of the most beloved psalms in the entire Bible. Yet it is not always applied as the Scripture sets it forth: "The Lord is my Shepherd." To make this Psalm applicable in one's life, the Lord must truly be Lord of one's life. For Christ to be Lord of your life means He is the controller of your life. Can you say Christ is the controller of your life? Is your life adjusted to the Word of God? Lordship is crucial.

Only when Christ is Lord, is He your Shepherd. Only when Christ is Lord can you experience true satisfaction in life. When Christ is Lord of your life, He gives you rest and refreshment. The psalmist is expressing what takes place in a life that is surrendered to the Father's will and way.

Three things must be in a sheep's life before he will know this rest. First, he must be in sight of his shepherd. If he cannot see his shepherd, he will grow weary from exhaustion and fear. Next, he must know the safety of the flock. If he is alone, he will wander and as he wanders alone, he is exposed to many dangers. Finally, he needs to be free of predators. If lions or wolves are in the area, he will not lie down. Anxious sheep do not rest.

Do you know this kind of rest and satisfaction in your life? If you do not, you can. You must settle the issue of lordship. Who is, or what is, the Lord of your life? What consumes your time, attention, and resources? Is the Word of God priority every day? Is it merely about reading a devotional? Or is it really meditating on what God's Word says and how to apply it daily to your life?

Do you have a set place and time when you come before the Father to pray and intercede on behalf of others? Or is your practice to simply say "buckshot" prayers throughout the day, without ever coming in a season of prayer at some point in the day?

Prayer and Praise:

Lord, You are my Lord. If there is any area of my life not yielded to Your lordship, please show me. If my time, my finances, my talents are not surrendered completely to You, move with great conviction upon my life. Nothing is more important than knowing You. Nothing is more important than You. In the mighty name of Jesus Christ, my Lord. Amen.

PITFALLS
Psalm 32:3-8

No matter how hard you try; no matter how committed you may be, every believer faces pitfalls. A pitfall is a concealed trap designed to get you to fall. The Devil desires to trip and trap you so you will quit your walk of faith. Thanks be to God, He gives you instructions on how to overcome.

David is acknowledging and praising God for the forgiveness and cleansing of his sin. He is thanking God that He is his hiding place, his refuge. He says, "You shall preserve me from trouble; You shall surround me with songs of deliverance." Next, David tells that God "will instruct you and teach you in the way you should go."

It is a wonderful blessing to know God will instruct and teach you. However, there are pitfalls even in guidance. How can that be? When instruction is given, that is the beginning. Instruction must be followed.

Here is a list of pitfalls in guidance: (1) you have an unwillingness to think; (2) you are unwilling to think ahead; (3) you are unwilling to take advice; (4) you are unwilling to suspect yourself of any sin or wrong; (5) you are unwilling to discount personal desires or attractions; (6) you are unwilling to wait.

Any or all of these things will hinder and prevent one from receiving the instruction God gives. Next you are told not to be like a horse or a mule. A horse wants to run ahead and does not wait to hear from God. The mule lags behind; he will not step out to go when he knows the will of his owner.

Pitfalls are all throughout life. Be very careful. God has a plan for your life, and He will communicate that plan to you. When He speaks, obey quickly.

Prayer and Praise:

Lord, teach me to recognize the traps of the Devil. Enable me to wait upon You, but when You speak, help me obey You quickly. In the mighty name of Jesus Christ, my Lord. Amen.

WAITING ON THE LORD
Psalm 40:1-3

Oftentimes life is like a revolving door—it goes in circles. However, there is something about a revolving door---you control it. You can decide when you want to step out of it. What these verses represent is David stepping out of sin and returning to God. David had willfully allowed sin into his life. Have you? Now David was getting right with God.

Getting right with God requires a few things. "David waited patiently for the Lord." The word "patiently" means that David had done all he could do in this process, and now he was waiting on God. What had David done? He had turned to God in honest confession of his sin to God with genuine repentance. That is all anyone can do and then one must wait.

What was David waiting on? He was not waiting on forgiveness or cleansing that came with the honest confession and repentance. He was waiting on God's peace and assurance to be restored. Peace and assurance do not come instantaneously. Joy and peace are fruits of the Spirit, and fruit does not appear in an instant; it takes some time.

Have you ever experience this? You have brought honest confession and forsaking of sin, you have genuinely repented, and now all you can do is wait upon the Lord. In time, fruit will develop and come forth. The fruit of joy and peace will flood your soul. You have to learn to wait upon the Lord.

What do you do while you are waiting? You trust God. You stay close to God in His Word and in prayer. Consistency must be evidenced in your life over time, but you wait with full faith, having done all you can do.

Finally, it says, "God heard my cry." Hallelujah! Praise the Lord! Your God hears and responds. God cares for you. He sets you on the "rock." He stabilizes your feet, so you can walk in His will. God is so good.

Prayer and Praise:

Lord, thank You for hearing my cries. Teach me to wait patiently on You. In the mighty name of Jesus Christ, my Lord. Amen.

CLAP YOUR HANDS
Psalm 47:1

How often do you clap and cheer? At a ball game when your team wins the game on a buzzer beater shot? When your child is able to do something for the first time like ride a bicycle without training wheels? Or are you in a concert after a tremendous performance has brought the house down? Do you ever clap to the Lord?

Psalm 47:1 is the only reference to clapping hands in the Bible during worship. Is that surprising to you? It is done in conjunction with shouting to God in loud songs of joy. In worship to the Lord Jesus Christ, clap and shout praises to Him. Do you do that?

What is the difference between clapping and applauding? Applause is clapping of approval, but it is done to a person. God does not need your approval, God wants your praise. You must be very careful whom you clap for and why you clap in a worship service. You are not there to applaud a person. You are there because the Lord Jesus Christ has saved you and forgiven all your sin. He has written your name in the Lamb's book of life. He alone is worthy to be praised. You are to clap and shout for joy because of Christ.

Often, applause in the church is nothing more than the influence of the world coming in, if we are applauding a person. The Bible teaches Christians are to say "amen" (1 Corinthians 14:16). When people are applauded in church, children and others are being taught something that is not what God intended.

Yes, "clap to the Lord," but leave applause with the world. Be sure you are praising the Father and the Son. Shout for joy. Learn to say "amen" loudly. Christ is worthy, is He not? He alone is worthy of praise and honor.

Prayer and Praise:

Lord, teach me daily how to exalt You. Teach me the difference between applause and clapping to You. Let me be ever so careful all my praise goes to You. In the mighty name of Jesus Christ, my Lord. Amen.

HAVE MERCY UPON ME
Psalm 51:1-3

This is the prayer of a king, David. David was a man seeking the heart of God. However, David had sinned and got away from God. This psalm reveals David's returning in repentance to the Lord. He is on the road back to God. When you sin, you too must take this road back to God. Every person must walk this road at one time or another, because everyone sins.

David had let sin accumulate and build up over time. Have you ever let your sin accumulate? Have you ever failed to deal with sin quickly? If so, you are in the right chapter of the Bible. How do you get back to God? What must a person do?

The road back to God consists of an awareness and admission of sin in your life. If you will not admit it to yourself, you will never admit it to God. David calls it sin, iniquity, and transgression. David was naming his sin. He was bringing acknowledgment and confession to the Father. In this action he was turning it over to God. He was saying, "God, I cannot atone for my sin, I cannot make it right. I give it to You."

From the beginning of this prayer there is the recognition of the necessity of truth in wholehearted sincerity as David approached God. In order to know forgiveness and experience restoration, this is the path of approach to God. David used the words purge, wash me, blot out, and create me anew. He was desperate to be right with God. Have you ever experienced that type of desperation?

David was utterly casting himself upon the mercy of God. He was seeking his relationship with the Father to be restored. God heard his prayer. The result was David began to praise the Lord (v. 15). When was the last time you began to praise the Lord for the forgiveness and cleansing He has brought in your life?

Prayer and Praise:

Lord, be merciful to me. I have sinned. Wash me, cleanse, me and restore me. In the mighty name of Jesus Christ, my Lord. Amen.

THIRSTY FOR GOD
Psalm 63:1-3

Have you ever stopped and considered what it is that makes you thirsty? Hard physical work and exercise are obvious. The sun beating down on you creates thirst. Not having something to drink over a period of time makes you aware of being thirsty. Eating salty foods makes you thirsty.

If you purchase popcorn while attending a movie, have you noticed how salty it is? That is done for a reason—to get you to purchase a drink. Are you aware that Jesus said those who are His followers are the salt of the earth (Matthew 5:13)? Combine that with Jesus's being the living water (John 4:10-11). Do you see the connection? A Christian is to live such a life for God, others around him will experience the salt of his life, and it will create a thirst in them that only the "living water"—Jesus—can satisfy. Do you live a salted life?

The question of the passage is, "Are you thirsty for God?" Can you say as the psalmist, "My soul thirsts for You, my soul longs for You"? What are you thirsty for? Sadly, many people get thirsty, but they try to satisfy their thirst with an artificial substitute. A can of sugary soda does not satisfy an intense thirst. Water is the only thing that will satisfy. Even sports drinks cannot satisfy your longings for water.

The psalmist said, "Early will I seek You." Do you seek God early in your day, or do you wait for a more convenient time? There will be some days emergencies happen, and your time seeking God may have to be postponed. If that is every day, you have a problem. You have to have a set time and place to seek God. Consistency is essential. If you do not, you will never be the man or woman of God. God intends you to be.

Seek God early, cry out to Him with a longing to experience Him. To know Him in His power and glory, that is your desire. Are you thirsty for God?

Prayer and Praise:

Lord, like the psalmist, my soul longs for You in a dry and thirsty land. There are so many artificial substitutes, teach me to know the difference. I long for You. Let Your power and glory be real in my life. In the mighty name of Jesus Christ, my Lord. Amen.

THE BENEFITS OF GOD
Psalm 68:19

"Blessed be the Lord, who daily loads us with benefits." Is that a great verse or what? There is an old song named "Count Your Blessings." Are you old enough to remember the first line? "Count your many blessings, name them one by one." A blessing is a benefit from God.

Two of the things a Christian is to be characterized by are thankfulness and gratefulness. In order to be thankful, you have to slow down long enough to recognize what you have been blessed with and how God has benefited your life recently. When was the last time you paused long enough to count your blessings?

If you are a Christian, you are blessed. You have been benefited with God's marvelous salvation. You are a child of God. Your sins have been forgiven and your name written in the Lamb's Book of Life. Hallelujah! Please, do not take that for granted. Without salvation, you have no starting point or foundation for present or future blessings from God.

God has blessed you by allowing you to be born in a free country where you can go to church without fear of arrest. God has blessed you with the ability to think and process thoughts. God has blessed you by giving you the person of the Holy Spirit to convict you of sin and wrong. The Holy Spirit is God in you. He teaches you truth. The Holy Spirit leads you in righteousness. You are blessed.

You are benefited by having your own personal copy of the Bible, the Word of God. You are benefited by being able to have Christian books and devotions to encourage you in your journey of faith. You are benefited by the church, the people of God with whom you worship and are accountable to. You are a blessed person. Do you recognize how blessed you are? Do you give thanks for your blessings?

The temptation is to focus on your hardships and difficulties and not the benefits of God. Is this true about you? Do you spend more time whining and complaining about your situation, or things you do not have, than praising God for His saving you, sealing you with the Holy Spirit and securing you eternally? Count your blessings and do it daily.

Prayer and Praise:

Lord, You have blessed me greatly. Let me stay focused on Your benefits, and not my felt needs or lacks. Teach me to be thankful. In the mighty name of Jesus, my Lord. Amen.

LET MY MOUTH BE FILLED WITH PRAISE
Psalm 71:8

"Let my mouth be filled with Your praise"—is that your heart's desire? How do you get your mouth filled with praise? Is it by simply saying praise words such as "Hallelujah, Amen, Glory?" No, you understand that words can be meaningless and empty, if they are merely words.

In order for your mouth to be filled with praise, true praise to the Father, your heart must be filled with praise. How do you get your heart filled with praise? It all starts by having a personal relationship with Jesus Christ. You must be born again. Once you know for certain you are saved, you remember the great forgiveness God has given you. You remember the mighty acts God has done on your behalf. You recall the faithfulness of God in your life. You understand that God so loved you, He gave His only Son, Jesus Christ, to die for your sin.

When these memories come to your mind, you have to praise the Lord. You have to release the joy and the thankfulness welling up inside of you. So you shout hallelujah to the Lamb of God. You express glory to the Lamb slain. You are thankful. To praise the Lord, you have to stop focusing on what you do not have, and you begin to focus on all Christ has done for you. For true praise to fill your mouth, your motive must be pure.

Your motive is not to impress God or try and secure some benefit from the Father. Your motive is not to impress other people. Your motive is only to praise Him, because He is worthy to be praised. Amen. Your motive is all about the worth of Christ and not about you.

Let your mouth be filled with praise. Let your life be filled with thanksgiving and joy. Let praise be the norm of your life.

Prayer and Praise:

Lord, I will praise You because You are my God. You are my Savior and Lord. You alone are worthy to be praised. Father, be glorified in my life and let praise be continually on my lips. If my praise is not pure, show me. Let my praise not be simply words to be heard by men, but let it be to You alone. In the mighty name of Jesus Christ, my Lord. Amen.

LISTEN TO GOD'S WORD
Psalm 78:1

The story is told of President Franklin D. Roosevelt and how he greatly disliked all the formal protocol he had to participate in while being president. He wearied of the social events that took place at the White House, the receptions and the formal parties. One day he decided to see if anyone really was paying attention when he received them in the greeting line. As each individual came forward and shook his hand with greetings, he would lean in toward them and say, "This morning I murdered your grandmother."

Instead of people being shocked, they simply replied, "That is so wonderful," or, "How nice." Only one diplomat heard what President Roosevelt said and he replied, "She probably had it coming." You read that and you smile.

How well do you listen to God speaking? Can you hear Him when he whispers, or does He have to thunder from the heavens? God still speaks. The issue is do you hear Him? Are you truly listening? Often, people are so consumed with what they want to say, that they fail to hear. Is that true of you? Do you want to talk to God about your situation, but you do not listen for God to speak to you?

God instructs us in this psalm to listen, to incline our ears to His words. What does "incline your ears" bring to mind? It is a picture of someone leaning forward to hear and not miss a single word or syllable that is spoken. Is that how you listen for God to speak to you, inclining to hear? If it is not, it should be.

Hearing God speak is wonderful. Comprehending that the Creator of all existence is speaking personally to you is overwhelming. You should strive not to miss what He is saying. Cultivate a listening ear. Learn to recognize the voice of God when He whispers or when he thunders from the heaven (2 Samuel 22:14).

Prayer and Praise:

Lord, You are the God who speaks. You are the only God. You are my God. Teach me to incline my ears to Your words. Teach me to be still and know You are God. Let me realize Your Word is all that matters. In the mighty name of Jesus Christ, my Lord. Amen.

THE SECRET PLACE
Psalm 91:1

The New Testament companion to Psalm 91 is John 15. As you know, John 15 is about abiding in Christ, remaining, staying put in Christ. It seems as if some Christians have a difficult time staying put in Christ. It appears they like to dabble with the world and the things of the world. In so doing, they do not abide as the Word of God instructs.

Psalm 91 is a tremendous psalm of promise for those in difficulties and distresses. You should commit this entire psalm to memory. "He who dwells in the secret place of the Most High shall abide under the shadow of the Almighty."

What is the secret place? It is in the presence of God, through the person of the Holy Spirit, as you are yielded to Him daily, moment by moment. It is not some level you reach; it is a place you remain. That is the challenge. In the secret place God promises to cover you, to shield you. You are promised divine protection and covering from the Father. Hallelujah!

The human factor of it all is this: you have to choose daily if you will dwell in the secret place. No one else can do this for you; it is your responsibility. Do you dwell, do you abide in Christ all the day long? Or do you sort of hit and miss? Only as one dwells in the secret place does one have the promise of God's covering. God's covering is wonderful.

What are some things that would tempt you to keep from dwelling in the secret place? Time restraints to read the Bible and pray is one often mentioned. The answer is to look for time wasters and make the necessary adjustments. How much time do you spend watching TV, Facebook, or Internet? You do the things that are important to you. The question is, is dwelling in the secret place important to you? What do you let keep you from church on the Lord's Day? Sporting activities, races, reunions? What is more important than worship of King Jesus to you?

You determine and control the human factor. It starts by surrendering to the Lord and then filling your mind with His truth, His Word. It is only as you renew your mind that you will not conform to the world.

Prayer and Praise:

Lord, You are the Most High God, and I exalt You. Teach me daily to secure Your presence and walk therein. Let me daily renew my mind with Your truth. Give me a hunger for You that Your Word increasingly satisfies. In the mighty name of Jesus Christ, my Lord. Amen.

WHEN GOD IS SILENT
Psalm 94:17

What do you do when you pray and God does not answer? Do you quit praying? Has this ever happened to you? Does it concern you? Why is God silent at times when you pray? These are questions that are faced daily by men and women who love the Lord Jesus Christ with all their heart and soul. These are questions men and women faithful to God and His Word deal with every day. What do you do when God is silent?

When God is silent in your life, the best thing you can do is examine your life. "Examine yourselves as to whether you are in the faith; test yourselves" (2 Corinthians 13:5). No person is beyond sin. Sin that has not been dealt with by honest confession and repentance oftentimes causes God not to speak to you. Ask yourself if God has told you by His Word or through the Holy Spirit something you are to do, and you have not done it yet. Examine your life for any sin of omission or commission or any disobedience.

If you cannot find any known unconfessed sin, or undone deed, wait upon the Lord. Many times the silence of God is a test to see if you will remain faithful amidst the silence. Job waited and waited, and God ultimately did speak. Do not get in a hurry and act or move without knowing God's will. In the waiting, you continue doing the last thing God told you to do or be about. You continue to be in the Word, reading, studying, and memorizing Scripture. You continue to praise and give thanks to the Father. You continue faithfully in the stewardship of your time, talents, and treasures.

In God's time, not man's time, God will speak His word and His will to you. Do you recall when Elijah was sent to the brook of Cherith to wait? He was fed by the ravens daily and he drank from the brook. Nowhere in the story are you told once he arrived in Cherith that God spoke to him, but Elijah was faithful as he waited. After three years of waiting, "the word of the Lord came to Elijah." Wait upon the Lord. He will speak in His time His Word into your heart.

Prayer and Praise:

Lord, in times of silence teach me to trust You. Teach me to examine my own life for any unconfessed sin. Teach me to wait, doing the last thing You told me to do. But Lord, let me anticipate You speaking to me every day. In the mighty name of Jesus Christ, my Lord. Amen.

GIVE THANKS TO THE LORD
Psalm 105:1

How are you at giving thanks to the Lord? " When was the last time you paused to count all the blessings God has poured out on you? It will amaze you when you begin to think in this fashion and to number all the blessings God has bestowed upon you.

There are so many things that are taken for granted, often not even acknowledged as a blessing. You are able to read this book, and in doing so, you are processing thoughts. Have you ever thanked God for allowing you the brain power to process thoughts? You do not have to look very far to realize not everyone seems to have this blessing. You can think; thank God for Him allowing you this ability.

Have you walked through a hospital or a nursing home lately? The operative word is walked. Many people do not have the mobility that you have. Wheelchairs, walkers, or crutches are a common sight. Have you thanked God for your health and your ability to move about freely?

Are you breathing fresh air right now? Have you thanked God for that? This is an easy one to take for granted; it is done without thinking. No one has to tell you to breathe, you do it naturally. Have you thanked God for breath? It is easy to take things for granted. Learn to be thankful and express that thanksgiving to the Lord.

Thankfulness is an act of submission to God. It is recognizing that He is the one who has and is blessing your life. Yes, there will be difficult days and trying times, but regardless of the situation you are to give thanks to God in everything. That is an act of faith. It is an acknowledgment that God is your source and resource. You will trust Him, no matter what.

Job said, "The Lord gave and the Lord has taken away, blessed be the name of the Lord" (Job 1:21). Even amidst the pain of loss, Job was yielded to God and submitted. Did he feel like giving thanks? Probably not, but he responded in faith to God. You have to learn to respond in faith to God in all things, even giving thanks.

Prayer and Praise:

Lord, You are my God and worthy to be praised. You have blessed me beyond measure by saving me, and I thank You. Teach me to count my blessings regularly and to thank You from my heart and soul. In the mighty name of Jesus Christ, my Lord. Amen.

A STEADFAST HEART
Psalm 108:1

The word steadfast means, "established, prepared, made ready, fixed, certain, or right." All of these words seem to overlap by definition. When something is fixed it is firmly implanted, or made stable. When the psalmist says, "O God, my heart is steadfast." He is stating the permanency of his heart to God and for God. Is your heart fixed in that manner?

How do you get a heart that is steadfast? It begins with an act of your will. You have to determine in your mind to be steadfast to the Lord before it will be determined in your heart. Often we consider the heart as the seat of emotions. You have to choose with your will before your emotions will experience such steadfastness.

How does a steadfast heart evidence itself? When a heart is steadfast to the Lord, the results will be a life that sings and gives praise to the Father. This psalm was written after the Babylonian captivity of seventy years. These were a redeemed people, and they were rejoicing. All redeemed people should be characterized by rejoicing. Are you?

A heart not fixed on Christ sees fears and frustrations. These are hindrances to a steadfast heart. When fears and failures consume your mind, you will not sing and give praise to the Lord. When fears and frustrations press hard upon your mind, this is the time to focus intently upon the Lord. To focus requires faith and trust. As you do this daily, it becomes fixed in your heart. And praising the Lord anyway helps the feelings to catch up.

Prayer and Praise:

Lord, let my heart ever be steadfast toward You. Teach me when fears and frustrations come, these are but reminders to focus on You with praise and rejoicing. In the mighty name of Jesus Christ, my Lord. Amen.

WHY I LOVE THE LORD
Psalm 116:1

Most people know the obvious reason they love the Lord Jesus Christ; it is because He first loved them. Nothing is greater than knowing you are loved by Christ. Nothing is more assuring than knowing your sins have been forgiven and that you have peace with God.

Have you ever considered the other reasons that you love the Lord? In this psalm, several reasons are set forth for why one loves the Lord. In verse two, you see that God inclines His ear to you. This simply means God listens. That is a wonderful blessing to know God listens to His children. The Lord not only listens, He also hears and responds to the cries of His children (v. 3-4). God cares about you. Hallelujah!

The Lord listens, He hears and He delivers you (v. 4). As you look at these verses, you realize all of this is progressive. God listens, God hears, and God delivers. The point is that God meets your needs. These are all the more reasons to love the Lord.

How do you show your love for God? To begin, you should be in a position for Him to bless you (v. 12). Are you in a position for God to bless you? Are your sins confessed and forsaken? Are you abiding daily in Christ Jesus?

Another way you show your love for God is by spending time with God (v. 13). As you spend time with the Lord, you also keep your promises to God (v. 14). You pay your vows. Finally, you show your love to God by offering the sacrifice of thanksgiving (v. 17). Are you thankful to the Lord? Do you express your thankfulness in the presence of others?

Do not merely say you love the Lord, show it with a lifestyle lived for His glory.

Prayer and Praise:

Lord, You are my Savior and King. I bow before You and worship You. Let my life be an expression of love for You and let it show to others. Thank You for hearing my prayers. Thank You for Your abiding presence. In the mighty name of Jesus Christ, my Lord. Amen.

REASONS TO READ THE WORD OF GOD
Psalm 119:1-5

For the past six months you have been reading your Bible every day. The more you read it consistently, the more you will want to read God's Word. God's Word is nourishment to your soul. It is the means by which God imparts His will to your life. God's Word is your shield and defender. Praise the Lord for this unspeakable gift of the Word of God.

Psalm 119 is the longest chapter in the entire Bible. It has 176 verses. The theme of this psalm is the Word of God. As you read this psalm, there are at least twenty-two reasons given why to read God's Word.

1. God's Word establishes your ways (vv. 1-5).

2. God's Word purifies your heart (vv. 9-11, 15, 18).

3. God's Word gives counsel (v. 24).

4. God's Word exposes and removes everything false in you (v. 29).

5. God's Word produces reverence for God (vv. 37-38).

6. God's Word increases your courage (vv. 45-46).

7. God's Word gives comfort (v. 50).

8. God's Word guards you from panic (vv. 61-62).

9. God's Word teaches discernment and knowledge (v. 66).

10. God's Word makes you resourceful (v. 79).

11. God's Word cultivates patience (v. 87).

12. God's Word keeps you spiritually recharged (v. 93).

13. God's Word accelerates your understanding (vv. 98-99).

14. God's Word creates a joyful heart (v. 111).

15. God's Word sustains you when you feel helpless (v. 116).

16. God's Word enables you to honor right and to hate wrong (vv. 127-128).

17. God's Word causes you to walk in truth (v. 133).

18. God's Word surrounds you with delight in spite of difficulties (v. 143).

19. God's Word develops the discipline of prayer (v. 147).

20. God's Word rescues you when you are defenseless (vv. 153- 154).

21. God's Word fills you with peace (vv. 164-165).

22. God's Word draws you back when you stray (v. 176).

Prayer and Praise:

Lord, Your Word is a source of strength and hope. I thank You for such a wonderful gift. Teach me to cherish Your Word. Greater still, teach me to live Your Word daily. In the mighty name of Jesus Christ, my Lord. Amen.

LIFT UP YOUR EYES
Psalm 121:1

What things do you look at in daily life? You watch the weather. You watch your children. You look at the traffic around you. You give your eyes to media and social activities. How purposely do you lift your eyes to the Lord? Once you do this, how intently do you focus on the Lord?

The psalmist says, "I will lift up my eyes to the hills—from whence comes my help? My help comes from the Lord." Do you recognize where your help, your hope, your strength come from? A person has to consciously look to the Lord every day before he will know the help of Almighty God. Do you have a set time every day to get alone with the Father? Do you have a set time you go to the Lord in prayer and the reading, meditating, and memorizing of the Word of God? That is how to lift your eyes to the Lord.

The constant temptation is to drift with the world. The world tells you, "You are okay. You can get along just fine by being a 'good' person." The world is a liar. You cannot get by on your own goodness. You desperately need the direction of Almighty God, and that only comes when you slow down and lift your eyes to the Lord.

Prayer and Praise:

Lord, teach me to set the gaze of my life on You. Teach me to daily look to You and not the world for direction, guidance, and to seek Your permission. Lord, You are my strong tower and refuge. In You I will trust. In the mighty name of Jesus Christ, my Lord. Amen.

TO FEAR THE LORD
Psalm 128:1

(This devotion is similar to February 23, but it is a very important teaching.)

What are you afraid of? People fear animals, individuals, traffic, even showing their emotions. Fear is the place the Devil wants you to live. He desires to create circumstances where you are afraid. Fear has the ability to paralyze a person. People fear many things, but blessed is the person who fears the Lord.

What does it mean to fear the Lord? To fear God means you have right concepts of God's character. You view Him correctly. He is almighty, He is majesty: grandeur, nobility, and dignity. He is glorious, He is holy, He is immense. God is sovereign, He is in control. To fear God, you must grasp His character.

Next, you must become aware of the pervasive sense of His presence. God is omnipresent. He is everywhere, and you must become aware of this fact, regardless if you feel anything. This awareness has a controlling effect on your life.

Then, you must have a constant awareness of your obligation to the Lord. You are to love Him supremely, obey Him implicitly, and trust Him completely. Obedience has boundaries; you know when you have obeyed. Trust has no boundaries; it is developed as you know a person more and more intimately. This is what it means to fear the Lord.

What are the marks of a lack of fear of God? You have an over-attachment to the things of the world, and you have an under-attachment to the things of God. You pursue the physical and material at the expense of the heavenly and spiritual.

Prayer and Praise:

Lord, teach me the necessity of fearing You daily. Show me if my life is wrapped up in this world's things. Enable me to make whatever adjustment is necessary to truly fear You. In the might name of Jesus Christ, my Lord. Amen.

HANGING OUR HARPS
Psalm 137:1-3

As you read this psalm, you need to understand God's people are in captivity and long for home. You understand what it means to be captive to something. You are so involved, engrossed in something, you do not seem able to get away from it. On a small scale, you may be watching your favorite television show and the phone rings, or there's a knock at the door, and you ignore those because you cannot bear the thought of missing this moment on TV. You have spent all season watching; now you have to see the ending.

Maybe you know captivity on a greater scale. You have a habit of tobacco, and you cannot imagine a day without it. Possibly, you or a loved one is in captivity to drugs or alcohol, and you know the pain this has brought.

In this psalm, God's people are in captivity to Babylon. They have been taken captive. For seventy years this was their existence. When they remembered Zion, they wept and hung their harps upon the willows. The joy, the song had gone out of their lives. Has the song gone out of your life?

There are three indicators that the music has stopped in one's life. The first is when discouragement becomes greater than faith. This is why it is crucial to maintain your faith in God. "Faith comes by hearing and hearing by the Word of God" (Romans10:17). The Word of God must be taken in daily in order to not lose faith.

Another indicator is when your life starts functioning out of the external circumstances. Do you live based upon what you see? Or do you live by faith in Christ Jesus and His Word? Finally, when you find yourself drifting toward mediocrity, you are showing that the music has stopped in your life. Drifting is so easy. Do nothing to fortify your faith and hope in Christ and you will drift with the world.

How do you stop this if you see it is happening to you? Show up for worship. Meet God in private and corporately with the body of Christ, the church. Next, look up. Take your eyes off your situation and circumstance and look up to the Father. Finally, grow up. Cultivate an attitude of trust and obedience to the Lord, no matter what. Let your faith develop. Grow up in the Lord.

Prayer and Praise:

Lord, often I feel as if I have hung my harp in the willows and the music has stopped in my life. The world tries to pull me away and drifting is so easy. Forgive me. Enable me to look to You, to worship You privately and corporately. Let me not put other things before You. In the mighty name of Jesus Christ, my Lord. Amen.

PRAISE THE LORD
Psalm 150:1

If you are a child of God, born again through the blood of Jesus Christ, you are commanded to praise the Lord your God. What does that mean? How do you go about that? Praise is as natural to a true believer as eating is to a hungry human being.

To praise God is to exalt Him as God, to recognize His holiness and majesty, to honor His righteousness and rightness in all things. To praise God is a by-product of yielding to the Holy Spirit. It is not about you. Rather, it is about God. He created you for His good pleasure, and praise brings God pleasure.

When you praise the Lord, your motivation is everything. Praise is not merely parroting biblical phrases such as, "Praise the Lord," "Hallelujah," or "Thank You, Lord Jesus." These words must spring from a heart that truly desires to honor and please God. Merely to say a phrase without thinking is not true praise.

Praise springs from a heart that is wholly devoted to the Lord and His will. That is why you are told in the book of James, as you endure temptation, you praise God. Leviticus teaches that praise is an offering you give to the Lord.

Praising God is an act of faith, because you praise Him in good times and not-so-good of times. You praise Him while healthy, and you praise Him when health is not so good. In every situation of life you are to praise the Lord. This requires one being yielded and submitted to God at all times.

Prayer and Praise:

Lord, You are God, and You are worthy to be praised. Let me praise You with all my heart and soul. As long as I have breath let my mouth set forth praise and my life show forth praise to You. In the mighty name of Jesus Christ, my Lord. Amen.

CALLED AND REFUSED
Proverbs 1:24

As you read the first chapter of Proverbs, the call for wisdom is evident. However, by the time you get to verses twenty-four to the end of the chapter, you need to slow down and read these very carefully. They have a promise and a warning from God that is very startling. You cannot afford to miss it.

Basically it says, "Because you refused the call of God, you ignored God counsel and did not regard His truth, calamity will come to you and God is going to mock you in your terror. In the midst of your calamity, you will call out to God, but He will refuse to hear you. He will not answer you. Because you hated knowledge and you do not fear God, you will eat the fruit of your choices." That is scary.

With such a warning, do you not think it would be wise to completely listen to and obey the Lord? Do you not think it wise to do everything God instructs you to do in His Word? The last verse is the hope. It says, "But whoever listens to me will dwell safely, and will be secure without fear of evil." It pays significantly to listen and obey the Lord. Peace of mind is amazing as God instills it in you.

The warning is to be very careful to seek God, obey God, and honor God with your life. If you refuse and think you know what is best for your life, disregarding the counsel of God, get ready for God to mock you.

Prayer and Praise:

Lord, Your Word is so strong, teach me to treasure it; but greater still, instill in me the need to obey Your counsel quickly. Let me know Your provision and let my life reflect You. In the mighty name of Jesus Christ, my Lord. Amen.

GET WISDOM
Proverbs 4:5

There are many types of wisdom. There is the wisdom of the world, the wisdom of man, and the wisdom of God. You must be careful which you seek after. Each person will seek one of these. The Devil will do all he can to keep you from the wisdom of God.

The world's wisdom is simply that—it is seeking the world. Do you seek the world's treasures? Do you seek the world's pleasures? How do you spend your time, money, and resources? Is your time spent on the cares of the world?

The wisdom of man is very similar. It tempts you to pursue what impresses other men, things such as fortune, fame, and power. It constantly rings in your mind, "This is what it means to be successful." The wisdom of man is foolishness compared to the wisdom of God.

The wisdom of God is the ability by the Holy Spirit within a child of God to see things from God's perspective; to see and understand the futility of temporal pleasures and the pursuit of things. Learning to see life from God's point of view is priceless, and it pays eternal benefits.

How do you get God's perspective? You receive God's perspective by yielding to the Word of God in obedience and by daily asking and seeking the infilling of the Holy Spirit. As this becomes real in you, you will be able to recognize the leading and the directing of God in your life. Only as your life makes major adjustments to God and His perfect Word, will you receive the wisdom of God.

If you refuse to submit, receive, or adjust to God's truth, you will never know God's wisdom. You will ever be second-guessing what you are about, and never knowing the peace of God that passes all understanding. Seek God's wisdom. "If any of you lacks wisdom, let him ask of God, who gives to all liberally and without reproach, and it will be given to him" (James 1:5).

Prayer and Praise:

Lord, I need Your wisdom. I ask You to give me Your mind, Your truth and wisdom, so I may live fully to Your glory. In the mighty name of Jesus Christ, my Lord. Amen.

JULY

FLATTERY
Proverbs 7:21

The word flattery is defined as, "to seek to please by complimentary speech or attentions. To compliment or praise insincerely." Most everyone enjoys receiving flattery. It does something to your mind; it is as if pleasure hormones are released mentally. Flattery feels nice; but be warned, flattery can led you to destruction.

The warning of this text is especially directed to men. It starts in chapter two with a warning to flee sexual temptation and to preserve you from the immoral woman. Sexual immorality is a perilous sin. It hooks you, and you are unable to extricate the hook alone.

In Proverbs 5:1-3, you are given the marks of a seductive woman. This is how you will recognize her. Her mouth drips honey and her words are smoother than oil. She is a flatterer. She knows how to talk and woo you.

When you arrive in Proverbs 7, you see the picture of the young man who has not been instructed, or failed to heed the advice; he is referred to as a "simple" one. He is captured by her dress; she has the attire of a harlot. It is provocative and immodest. She grabs him, kisses him, and pursues after him. She flatters him, and he falls for her trap. She tells him no one will find out, and that there will be no consequences to this sin.

Finally, she moves in for the kill, and her enticing speech has caused him to yield. Destruction soon follows. Proverbs 6:32 says, "He who does so destroys his own soul." Proverbs 5:11 says, "Your flesh and your body are consumed." Proverbs 2:18-19 says, "For her house leads down to death … none who go to her return."

These are promises, albeit scary promises, of God's Word. It all begins with the idea, "I can handle it." Then you cannot excoriate the hook. Guard your heart and your mind.

Prayer and Praise:

Lord, teach me to guard my heart, my mind, and my eyes. Burn in me the consequences of receiving this type of flattery. Let me live a holy life in mind and action. In the mighty name of Jesus Christ, my Lord. Amen.

GOD'S WISDOM FOR THE TONGUE
Proverbs 10:31-32

The most addressed issue in Proverbs concerns the tongue. That should not surprise you since yesterday's topic on flattery. Your words come from your heart. They are not accidental slippages of speech. You speak what you truly are.

In Proverbs you find seven negative tongue sins. They are listed below with their Scripture reference:

1. Lying, Proverbs 6:16-19

2. Flattery, Proverbs 26:28

3. Gossip, Proverbs 11:9, 16:27

4. Boasting, Proverbs 6:17, 25:14

5. Verbosity (you rattle on and on, you speak too much), Proverbs 10:19

6. Quick speech, Proverbs 29:20

7. Harsh speech, Proverbs 15:1

When the Bible calls something sin, you are not left to merely quit doing that. You are to put off and to put on. You are to mortify those sins—put off. You are to replace them (put on) with the commanded virtues and graces by the Holy Spirit.

A true believer is to use his tongue in several positive ways. You are to disperse knowledge, Proverbs 10:30-32. You are to deliver loving rebukes, Proverbs 25:12, 27:5-6. You are to encourage, Proverbs 12:18.

As a believer, you need to be known as a person who guards his tongue, Proverbs 13:3, 21:23. You have been given a tongue so you can be blessing to God with praise and adoration and to encourage others.

Prayer and Praise:

Lord, my tongue is such a small instrument, yet it wields so much power for good or evil. Teach me to guard my tongue daily. Enable me to use it for only what glorifies and honors You. In the mighty name of Jesus Christ, my Lord. Amen.

THE BACKSLIDER
Proverbs 14:14

When you hear the word backslide, or backslider, probably a number of things come to your mind. It means, "Once you were here, but now you have gone backwards." A lost person having never experienced God's grace has nothing to fall back from. Therefore, the term applies to the Christian.

A backslidden person can be one who goes into overt sin. Backsliding can be an outward activity. However, a great amount of backsliding is done by Christian people who never leave the church. The text says, "a backslider in heart." Backsliding can be, and is, most often, expressed inwardly.

A person can be backslidden, out of fellowship with God, and never get out of church. He can go to Sunday school, worship services, he can hear the Word of God preached, be consistent in giving, and still be backslidden. When a person becomes filled with his own ways, backsliding is present.

How do you know if you are backslidden? A backslider is unhappy in service to the Lord Jesus Christ and the church. You evidence backsliding when you are unbroken toward sin. A major indicator of backsliding is when one has an unforgiving spirit. When these are in a person's life, that individual has no concern for the lost.

The book of Hebrews warns against drifting. When a person drifts, he moves with the world. The important point is you can stop drifting when you choose to yield to the Lord Jesus Christ and His Word. Respond to the Lord.

Prayer and Praise:

Lord, let me be aware if I have drifted with the world and am backslidden. Open my eyes to see what it is I am living for. Show me if I am filled with my own ways. Lord, let me return to You in honest confession of my sin and genuine repentance. In the mighty name of Jesus Christ, my Lord. Amen.

THE WAY THAT SEEMS RIGHT
Proverbs 16:25

Have you ever felt like you were doing what was right and yet in the end, it was wrong. That is a confusing place to be. It is a very common place where many people live. How does such a thing happen?

The world tells you that you are good, you are acceptable, and your best efforts are enough. The world, the flesh, and the Devil will seduce you into believing the lie. The lie is that God winks at your sin, and in the end everyone will be alright.

If you believe the lie, you will live your life being respectful to those whom you think deserve respect. You will try to make it to the end of your life with your good deeds outnumbering your bad deeds.

The point of error is in the idea that you believe you have the mental capacity to determine what is right. This is why it is so important to be in a Bible-believing church where the Word of God is preached without compromise. It takes the Holy Spirit to illuminate one's eyes and mind to truth. The Bible says in 2 Corinthians 4:4, "Whose minds the god of this age has blinded, who do not believe." However, for those who have been born again by God's grace, the promise of Philippians 2:5 is theirs, "Let this mind be in you which was also in Christ Jesus."

You do not have to follow your gut instinct. You do not have to spend your life doing the best you know how. You can know the true way to live as you yield to Jesus Christ and the Word of God every day. If you commit your works to the Lord, He will establish your thoughts (Proverbs 16:3). What a tremendous promise!

The key to not wasting your life is to know without a doubt you are genuinely born again and to obey the Word of God. To obey the Word of God, you have to read and know the Word of God. Then you make adjustment of your life to God's Word. If you fail to adjust to the Word of God, all is wasted.

Prayer and Praise:

Lord, let me realize in my own strength and intellect all I can do is wrong. Teach me daily to yield to Your Word. Give me a hunger for Your truth. In the mighty name of Jesus Christ, my Lord. Amen.

WINE IS A MOCKER
Proverbs 20:1

Why would the Bible say "wine is a mocker"? Because it deceives people into believing when they drink alcohol and it will not affect them or impact them negatively. About 40 percent of adult Americans have a direct family experience with alcohol abuse and alcoholism. Alcohol is a drug. It may be socially acceptable, but alcohol is a drug.

Many believe the answer is drinking alcohol in moderation. Drinking in moderation is not a solution, but rather it leads to abuse. According to the Word of God, Proverbs 20:1, wine and strong drink have the tendency to "lead one astray." Astray from what? You are led astray from the path of wisdom.

The wine of today compared with the wine of Bible days is not the same. Bible-day wine was naturally fermented. Wine of today is not only fermented as much as possible, but alcohol has been added in the process. In the Biblical day, wine was actually mixed with water. Three or four parts water mixed with one part wine.

The problem today is the alcohol content. Though fermented wine was drunk in Bible times, and though the Bible approves of wine drinking, one needs to remember that the alcohol content of ancient wine was much less than that of wine today. What is consumed today is not the wine of the New Testament. Due to the alcohol content, all wine, beers, liquors, and wine coolers are actually considered "strong drink" according to alcohol content. Strong drink is forbidden in Scripture.

Alcohol is just one of the many substitutes for the joy of Christ. The Word of God tells you, "And do not be drunk with wine, in which is dissipation, but be filled with the Spirit" (Ephesians 5:18). There is no need for a bottle if you know the Lord Jesus. Be encouraged to Christ.

Prayer and Praise:

Lord, teach me to seek my joy from You and not an artificial substitute. A substitute can be in the form of a bottle, a pill, or even a hobby. Fill me with Your joy as You fill me with Your Holy Spirit daily. In the mighty name of Jesus Christ, my Lord. Amen.

TRAIN UP A CHILD
Proverbs 22:6

This is a verse that is quoted often. Many times a person quotes this verse without confidence in what it really is teaching. This verse does not mean, or say, if you drop your children off at the church, or if you take your children to church, they will be all right in the end. Many people will quote this verse with having done the minimal of exposing their children to the gospel.

This verse teaches parental responsibility in the spiritual training and development of a child. The Christian school cannot do it for you; the Sunday school or youth program cannot do it for you. They can reinforce the teaching of Bible truth you give, but they cannot do it for you. You are personally responsible for this instruction.

The phrase, "in the way he should go," means based on your child's particular bent. People are bent different ways. Some are bent toward athletics, while others are bent toward art or music. You are not to force your bent on your child. Every person is unique; God created each person for a purpose. You train a child with the understanding of his unique bent.

When a parent does this, then he or she has a tremendous promise. When the child is old, he will not depart from the faith. It does express the idea that he will backslide and return. No, he will not depart even as he grows older and older.

Is Sunday school, youth group, or Christian school wrong? Absolutely not! If they are strong bible based, they will reinforce your instruction. If you expect them to do what God called you to do in the training of your children, then you have missed the reason you have had children.

Prayer and Praise:

Lord, teach me to understand my personal responsibility in training my children. It is not enough to teach them to throw a ball or cook a meal. I must train them in the Word of God. Therefore, I must live before them in such a way as to be reinforced by Scripture. In the mighty name of Jesus Christ, my Lord. Amen.

IRON SHARPENS IRON
Proverbs 27:17

"As iron sharpens iron, so a man sharpens the countenance of his friends." Your friends are important to you. You can learn from them, and they can hold you to a higher accountability. The key issue is whom do you choose to be your friends? Do they hold to the same standards of Scripture as you?

In life you will associate with all sorts of people. There are those who love and serve the Lord, and there are those who have never grown up. Some may be family, others coworkers and some will be friends of many years. It is important that you carefully choose to whom it is you give the majority of your time and attention. You need people of faith, deep faith in your life, to help sharpen you into the person God wants you to be.

This is why "iron sharpens iron." No one can afford to give her time to people who pull her down spiritually. Sometimes you have no option, but in those times you have to maintain your integrity to Christ and His Word.

Sometimes old friends, childhood friends, have never come to Christ, and they live only for the moment. In these situations, you must be very careful; they drain your faith. You need to consciously seek to spend time with people who know and love the Lord with all their hearts; people who hunger for the Word of God, seek God in prayer, and people with whom you can pray.

You make the ultimate decision of where you spend your time and with whom. Iron does sharpen iron. Ask God to reveal to you those people who build you up in faith and those who bring you down. Your best friends should be strong, committed Christians.

Prayer and Praise:

Lord, teach me to be an iron sharpener. Let me have people in my life regularly who sharpen my life. Teach me to spend my time wisely. Place in my life those I need to boost my faith. In the mighty name of Jesus Christ, my Lord. Amen.

CONFESSION AND FORSAKING SIN
Proverbs 28:13

Sin is a terrible thing. It separates a man from God. It causes hurt, loss of hope, and difficulty. For a season it appears to be fun and enjoyable. That season soon passes and the season of pain begins. It is as a hog being led by a food trail to the slaughter. It continues blindly enjoying the moment and suddenly judgment falls.

The good news is that there is a remedy for sin. The blood of Jesus Christ cleanses us from sin. You have to apply the blood personally to your life. You cannot do it for someone else. You can train and encourage, but every person must apply the blood of Christ for themselves.

The text tells that if a person tries to hide his sin, he will not prosper. He will not experience prosperity. Externally it often appears the wicked prosper. However, real prosperity is the result of a work of God in the life of one who seeks God with all his heart. The wicked are merely acting as the hog being led by a food trail. It will not last.

Also, you see confession of sin. Confession means to acknowledge your sin. If a person will not acknowledge his sin to himself, he will never acknowledge sin to God. You must admit sin.

Next, you must forsake sin. The result of honest confession of sin is the forsaking of sin. To forsake means to depart or to abandon. You abandon sin, and you replace it with the righteousness of Christ. You put off and put on. If you merely put off and do not replace it, it will come back to you worse than it was the first time.

The means by which you receive the mercy of God is by confession of sin and the forsaking of sin. Without both, confession is merely words expressed, but not followed.

Prayer and Praise:

Lord, teach me to acknowledge my sin. Show it to me if I have tried to cover it. Expose it. Enable me by the Holy Spirit and Your Word to forsake it. Fill me fresh with Your presence and enable me to walk in righteousness. In the mighty name of Jesus Christ, my Lord. Amen.

THE PRAYER OF AGUR
Proverbs 30:7-9

Agur is only mentioned one time in the Bible. His name means, "to gather" or "to harvest." He speaks to God saying, "Deprive me not before I die." He is an old man hoping to see the harvest of his life. Having walked many roads and taken many paths he offers wisdom to those who listen.

He requests two things from the Lord. The first is to remove what is false. In this prayer, you do not find success built on shifting sand or deception. He may have walked in this for a time, but now he desires to be free from it. Remove—drive away falsehood—that which is vain and useless. He is encouraging you to guard your mind and mouth from falsehood that comes knocking at your heart.

There is falsehood of the mind, falsehood of motive, and falsehood of the mouth. Remove these and release what is true. Releasing the purity of God to shield, protect, and provide, letting the Word of God become real in your life.

Next, he asks for the Lord to neither give him poverty nor riches. That sounds so un-American. The idea is, if I become poor, I may steal and profane the name of God. I resolve to serve the Lord with what I have. Let your life know contentment. This prayer is not self-motivated.

Do not give me riches. In America the trend is to super-size everything. Agur realized the subtle temptation riches bring. First Timothy 6:9 warns that, "Those who desire to be rich fall into temptation and a snare." Jesus warned it was hard for a rich man to enter into heaven. Agur does not want to deny his Lord. Do you have that same desire?

He asked for humble contentment to live a balanced life: contentment to learn of God and contentment in leaning upon God. Are you content with what God has given you? Are you content with God? Is God enough for you?

Prayer and Praise:

Lord, teach me to be content with You. Let me be a seeker of You. Enable me to understand having a balanced life. Show me when I am being tempted with money or the things of this world, and let me run to You, my refuge. In the mighty name of Jesus Christ, my Lord. Amen.

VANITY
Ecclesiastes 1:1-3

The book of Ecclesiastes is the quest for reality on the part of a man looking for happiness and satisfaction. He searches all the normal avenues of life, and it all appears to be a dead-end street. Are you looking for satisfaction, happiness, and meaning to life? Have you found that the things of this world do not produce lasting results?

The word vanity is used thirty-seven times in this book. It means emptiness or futility. This book should be a warning to anyone who thinks he can find satisfaction in the things of this world. It is easy to get swept up in this world. Those with children know the constant pressures added to life, as you try and guide your children in the ways of the Lord, and yet the world consumes them in all directions.

The writer summarizes the futility in verse nine of chapter one. He says in essence, "Life is just the same old thing repeated over and over, it is monotonous." Then in verse eleven he states, then you die and no one will ever know you were here. Simon and Garfunkel summarized it perfectly on a line from one of their songs, "Like a rat in a maze, the path before me lies. And the pattern never alters, until the rat dies."1 That is how Solomon the writer felt.

Someone made the statement that three things make life worth living: (1) a self-fit to live with, (2) a faith fit to live by and (3) a purpose fit to live for. All of these will only be found real as you have an abiding relationship with Jesus Christ that begins with salvation and continues daily in a life lived for His glory.

Life is too precious and too brief to be spent in trivial pursuit. Life does not have to be meaningless and full of vanity. Life is meant, for a child of God, to be abundant and joyful, full of meaning and purpose.

Prayer and Praise:

Lord, teach me not to live my life playing out trivial pursuit. Fill me with Your abundant life and allow me the privilege of living a life of fullness and meaning. Lord, speak Your truth into my being and continually change me. In the mighty name of Jesus Christ, my Lord. Amen.

1. Simon and Garfunkel, Album, "Parsley, Sage, Rosemary and Thyme," Columbia Records, 1966.

DRAW NEAR TO HEAR
Ecclesiastes 5:1

Why would you be commanded to draw near to hear when you go to worship the Lord? Because many people go to church for wrong reasons. The most important thing for a child of God is to hear God speaking. Jesus said, "My sheep hear My voice, and I know them and they follow Me" (John 10:27). The issue is not whether or not God is speaking, because He is. The issue is whether or not you are listening for God's voice. Do you know how to recognize the voice of God?

Many voices clamor for your attention today: the voice of man, the voice of the world, as well as the voice of the Devil. The Devil speaks not with a demonic quality, but rather, the Devil speaks as an angel of light. The Devil will tell you partial truth in order to get you to stray away from the whole truth.

How do you prepare yourself to hear God speak? First, you must examine your life to see if there are any barriers that have been erected that would keep you from hearing God. Barriers block a person from hearing, such as willful sin and disobedience, barriers of not reading, studying, and memorizing Scripture, and barriers of a wrong attitude. If your attitude is wrong toward others because of an unforgiving spirit, you are not in a position to hear. If you have an unteachable spirit, you will not hear God.

When was the last time you heard God speak specifically to you? What did he say? Do you come to church intentionally expecting God, the Almighty God of eternity, to speak to you? If not, why not? Draw near to hear, not to go through the motions of worship and sacrifice, but come prepared and expecting God to speak. When God speaks, obey Him immediately.

When you pray, do you take time to listen for God to speak? Do you relate what is going on in your life with your prayers? A mark of a true child of God is he or she knows the voice of the Lord and acts on what He says. Do you act on what God says? Do you adjust your life and lifestyle so that you can walk in obedience to the Father? If you do not make adjustments, you will soon fail to recognize the voice of God.

Prayer and Praise:

Lord, I thank You that You love me so much and that You still want to speak to me. Teach me to be clean before You so that I can hear You clearly. Enable me to recognize the voice of the Devil when he tries to seduce me away. Let me always be willing to make adjustments of my life to Your Word. In the mighty name of Jesus Christ, my Lord. Amen.

THE HOUSE OF MOURNING
Ecclesiastes 7:2

As you read this verse, you are probably asking yourself, Is this really true? Why would anyone want to go to the house of mourning, the house where death has occurred, above going to a house of feasting, a place of celebration? The previous verse gives a clue. "A good name is better than precious ointment; and the day of death than the day of one's birth" (Ecclesiastes 7:1).

The entire focus of Ecclesiastes is on life and understanding life's true meaning. All through this book the meaning of life is in relationship to God. If a person has no true relationship with God, a relationship that is vital and daily active, this person will exist through life, but never experience true life. Much of what is taking place in the United States is not true abundant life, as the Scriptures teaches, but merely existence on a lower plane than ever intended.

The day of one's birth is a day when family and friends rejoice, but it is also a day of much uncertainty as to what is in store for the newborn. There will be days of great joy and great sadness; but much will be determined by the choices made by the individual. The moment you are born, you begin to die. This life is not forever. Choices and decisions you make in this life will follow you to the next life, be it in heaven or hell.

For a person to live his life for the glory and honor of God, as all are supposed to, the day of mourning is also the day of rejoicing eternally in the presence of the Lord Jesus Christ. It is life well lived unto the Lord that will carry on with the Lord. You have to get beyond looking at life through physical eyes and see into eternity.

All through Ecclesiastes, you are encouraged to understand the vanity of this life. Only those who realize this will understand how to live and prepare for the next life. Which life are you living for? How are you making preparations for the next life? What treasures are you laying up in heaven?

Prayer and Praise:

Lord, please teach me how to live for eternity while I am living on planet earth. Show me how to make decisions, not for the moment, but for everlasting life. Enable me to see the broader picture. Life is so deceptive; it makes you think you are missing things if you do not pursue the world. Give me sense to recognize this deception and pursue You. In the mighty name of Jesus Christ, my Lord. Amen.

DEAD FLIES IN THE OINTMENT
Ecclesiastes 10:1

If you were to walk the halls of Solomon's great complex in the city of Jerusalem, you would find the place the perfumer worked; a place where perfume was made for the king. The man who worked there would carefully add oil to oil, in just the right amounts, mixing these chemicals together to produce a fragrance fit for the king.

He was a professional, and he always brought the elements together in proper fashion. Picture this: just as it was nearly ready to present to the king, a fly comes into the room. Drawn in by the aroma, in one unguarded moment, the perfume is ruined. "Dead flies make a perfumer's oil stink" (Ecclesiastes 10:1, NAS).

How much time have you put into your life and family, being ever so careful as not to hurt or destroy all you have worked for? But in one unguarded moment, all you have worked for and accomplished can be ruined. What was once fragrant and sweet now stinks.

Guard your life, guard your eyes, guard your mind, and guard your time. It only takes one unguarded moment to ruin everything.

Prayer and Praise:

Lord, let my life be lived for Your glory. Let me not be so busy doing what is right that I miss You. Protect me from the attacks of the Devil, and enable me to keep my guard always on alert. In the mighty name of Jesus Christ, my Lord. Amen.

THE ROSE OF SHARON
Solomon 2:1

The message of the book of Solomon is what God wants you to know of the purity of marriage and the sanctity of sex inside of marriage. In the first chapter, Solomon has some property in the North and he visits his land dressed as a shepherd. Once there, he sees a woman and falls in love.

He expresses his love for her, and then he disappears, leaving her lovesick. When he returns, he returns dressed as the king, and this woman is not interested, because she is in love with a shepherd. However, when she realizes the king is her shepherd, they are then married.

Shulam, which is the reference to the woman, means "peace." The word Solomon means Shulam. What you find is a play on words. Shulam is the feminine for Solomon. All through the book, she is called the Shulamite. The story is how the two meet and find peace in each other.

Jesus Christ is referred to as the Rose of Sharon; it is in Christ that you are to find your deepest love and true peace. He is your Rose of Sharon and the Lily of the Valley. Christ is everything you have ever needed, wanted, and more than you can comprehend. His desire is for you to love Him with an ever-increasing love.

Prayer and Praise:

Lord, You are the Lily of the Valley, and I praise You. You are fairer than any other, for there is none to compare You to. I praise You. I adore You. In the mighty name of Jesus Christ, my Lord. Amen.

RESPOND TO THE LORD
Solomon 5:2-6

As you read this passage in the Word of God, you are challenged with the understanding that every time God knocks on your heart's door and speaks to you, He expects a response. The Shulamite woman had made herself ready for bed, and she felt like she should not be disturbed or bothered. Her beloved came and knocked on the door of the chamber, yet she hesitated and did not open to him.

Has God ever spoken to you and you hesitated? You pause and think of the trouble it will take to respond. It is such a foolish thing to hesitate when God speaks. When the Shulamite did go to the door, it was too late, her beloved had left. In a brief moment you can miss the Lord if you fail to respond.

Responding to Christ is not a onetime thing that happens at salvation and then you are set for the rest of your life. No, you are to respond to God after salvation every time He quickens your heart and speaks to you. If you want to "think about it" for a time, you will miss God. When you miss God, you have missed an opportunity to draw closer to your Lord. You miss intimacy with the Father. It is costly to miss God.

Sadly, many believers have neglected the voice of God for so long they are now indifferent to His voice. Yet, they think they are just fine because they jump through their spiritual hoops every day. They say their prayers and they read their Bible, but they do not respond to the very words they read.

When God knocks on your heart respond to Him. He will not linger if you hesitate to obey. Respond to the Lord quickly. Say as Samuel was instructed to say, "Speak, Lord, for our servant hears."

Prayer and Praise:

Lord, You are the living, eternal God. You are my Savior and Master. When you speak to me let me respond quickly to Your voice, Your Word, Your Holy Spirit's prompting. Father, let me always make time and room for You. In the mighty name of Jesus Christ, my Lord. Amen.

WHEN WORSHIP IS HYPOCRISY
Isaiah 1:13

Isaiah 1 is the picture of a court trial. God is the judge and His people are the defendants. God calls heaven and earth to bring charges against His own chosen people. Why would God have to do such a thing? Because His people are guilty of rebellion and have become evil and corrupt. They have forsaken God, turning their backs on Him. They were being judged. Their only hope was to hear and heed the Word of God (Isaiah 1:10).

Today, how many people do you know who have turned away from God and God's Word? How many people do you know who may still go to church but have turned away from the Word of God? They come and are entertained by the music and the choir; the preacher has become a master storyteller, even jokester. They walk away remembering the stories, but what did God say? Did God speak at all in the service? If a person can leave a worship service of the Almighty God and go to live how he or she pleases, to do his or her own thing, something is terribly wrong. That is rebellion against God. You may never shake your fist in His direction, but to walk away and live life how you want and not adjust to God and His Word is rebellion.

This is the indictment of Isaiah 1:11-20. In verse 13, He says, "I cannot endure iniquity and the sacred meeting." Their worship was insincere. Is yours? As soon as they left the worship service, they returned to their immoral and selfish ways. False worship is unacceptable.

Yet God still seeks His people, and He makes them an amazing offer. The people could be spiritually cleansed from their sin if they would do three things. They must first repent (v. 16-17). They must turn from their evil and do right. Next, they must come to the Lord and reason with Him (v. 18). They must come and admit their sin and guilt. Finally, they must come to the Lord for forgiveness (vv. 19-20). If they were willing to turn from their sin and obey God, they would be rewarded. God would make them white as snow.

If they continued, they would be destroyed. Judgment would fall on those who refused God and His Word. How is your worship? Is it God-centered or man-centered?

Prayer and Praise:

Lord, You are my God and King. Teach me to worship You and not the music and the man. Teach me to come seeking to hear You speak to my heart and soul. In the mighty name of Jesus Christ, my Lord. Amen.

MY BELOVED'S VINEYARD
Isaiah 5:1-6

The Lord planted a very special vineyard—Israel. He went to the extreme, making sure Israel, the vineyard, had every opportunity to produce the highest quality of fruit. He planted it on a fruitful hill; a hill was the most difficult place, but it was a place of favor, it was fertile. Then the Lord cultivated and removed all the stones so nothing could obstruct the growth. The implication is with these stones He built a wall around the vineyard.

Next He planted choice vines, not seeds, in His vineyard. Finally, He built a watchtower and a winepress. He built a winepress. God expected His vineyard to produce the finest grapes for the finest wine. It takes four years for grape vines to harvest. God did everything possible for His vineyard to be fruitful. The harvest was wild grapes.

God pronounced judgment against the vineyard. He removed the wall and the hedge of protection. It would soon be destroyed, trampled by others. Since it produced wild grapes, there was no need for God to cultivate it anymore. It would become altogether unproductive.

God does the same thing in your life. God builds a tower to protect His field. God's presence is what protects you. He cultivates the heart, and He removes the stones. The Lord builds a wall, a hedge, a watchtower. He plants only the best vine in you. God gives time for the vine to grow, develop, and mature, but God expects a harvest from you. Do you bear good fruit?

Far too many believers still engage in sinful behavior, and God warns against producing a harvest of sin. How does it take place? The people forget God, and they have no sensitivity to God's Word. They become like the world. Are you like the world?

✱ "Do not be deceived, God is not mocked; for whatever a man sows, that he will also reap. For he who sows to his flesh will of the flesh reap corruption, but he who sows to the Spirit will of the Spirit reap everlasting life" (Galatians 6:7-8).

Prayer and Praise:

Lord, You have cultivated my life. You have built a wall, a hedge, and set a watchtower in me. Let me bring forth fruit for Your glory. Keep me ever sensitive to You and Your Word. Enable me not to bring forth a harvest of sin. In the mighty name of Jesus Christ, my Lord. Amen.

THE NAMES OF CHRIST
Isaiah 9:6

How much thought do you give to Christ's coming? Does it excite you? Do you realize the implications?

When Jesus Christ came, He came as the God-man. He was fully man and yet fully God. Matthew Henry says, "Christ's being born and given to us is the great foundation of our hopes, and fountain of our joys, in times of greatest grief and fear." Christ comes to rule. He will rule and execute perfect righteousness and justice among His people.

There are four descriptive names given to Christ. He is the Wonderful Counselor. He can direct, guide, and comfort your life. He is the Mighty God. He is divine and this means He is omnipotent (all powerful), omniscient (all knowing), and omnipresent (everywhere present). He is able because He is Mighty God. He is able to deliver, to save, to heal, to give hope.

He is Everlasting Father. He will love His people with a perfect love as a father loves a child. He will care for, nurture, and nourish. He will comfort and assure. He will provide and protect. He is the Prince of Peace. Peace will reign externally and internally. Peace to the human heart will be the norm. Jesus Christ is the Prince of Peace. Hallelujah!

Prayer and Praise:

Lord, You are my Prince of Peace. You are my Everlasting Father. You are my Mighty God. You are my Wonderful Counselor. I praise and exalt Your name. In the mighty name of Jesus Christ, my Lord. Amen.

THE SPIRIT OF THE LORD
Isaiah 11:1-2

As Isaiah continues his prophetic writing of Christ, the Messiah, he began to explain how the Spirit of the Lord would manifest and work in Him. Colossians 1:19 tells us, "For it pleased the Father that in Him all the fullness should dwell." In Colossians 2:9 it says, "For in Him dwells all the fullness of the Godhead bodily." Jesus Christ was and is able to fulfill all the work of God with the complete power of God because the Spirit of God rests on Christ.

Isaiah 11:2, "The Spirit of the Lord shall rest upon him." It then shows six other gifts rested upon Christ. Isaiah paired them in twos, and refers to them as "the Spirit of." These are not additional spirits, but gifts of the Spirit that was on Christ. What are these six gifts?

Strong's Exhaustive Concordance of the Bible defines these. There is the gift of wisdom, which means to be skillful, to have good sense, and to act wisely. It is practical wisdom for knowing what and how to do things correctly. There is the gift of understanding. This is the ability to grasp knowledge or facts that lead to understanding. There is the gift of counsel, which means advice, purpose, or plan. Jesus Christ could see into a situation and know exactly how to react, respond, and deal with every situation.

There is the gift of might or power, which means to be strong and prevail. Jesus Christ was victorious over every obstacle, opposition, and enemy. The gift of knowledge is the ability to know and fully understand or have full comprehension. Jesus understood everything past, present, and future.

Finally, the gift of the fear of the Lord, which is a reverential awe for the Father. Christ walked with the Father, yielding moment by moment to the Father's will. Oh, that you would know such reverential fear of the Lord.

All that the Father enabled and gifted to Christ, He offers to you. Will you walk with the Lord that these gifts are realized in your life? Once you are saved, the Holy Spirit comes to live within your life. The Holy Spirit is your teacher and your guide. He warns and directs you as you yield to Him. He comforts and brings conviction of sin. He is God with you. Thank the Father for His ever present Holy Spirit.

Prayer and Praise:

Lord, You are so wonderful, filled with the fullness of the Godhead, and You are my Savior. I praise You and I thank You. In the mighty name of Jesus Christ, my Lord. Amen.

6 gifts:
Wisdom and understanding
Counsel and might
Knowledge and Fear of the Lord

LUCIFER'S FALL
Isaiah 14:12-15

Tucked into this section of Scripture is the fall of Lucifer from heaven. Lucifer means "light bearer." He is known by the names Satan, the adversary, and the Devil. He was an angel created by God for the purpose of bringing God glory. In fact, he may have been the highest angel in rank, but he has fallen into the pit of hell. How could this happen?

Lucifer was created with a purpose: he was to protect the glory of God. However, he said in his heart that he would ascend and exalt his throne above God, and he would be like the Most High. In that instance he lost his position and his place.

It is a dangerous and a scary thing to think you can exalt yourself above God. Surely man would not do things like that today. Anytime a person chooses to ignore God, or God's plan, that person is exalting himself above the Most High.

Angels are created beings, as is man. Angels have a free will to choose, as does man. One third of the angelic host chose to side with Lucifer, and they also were cast out of heaven and committed to the pit. The constant temptation everyone faces is to do one's own will and not God's.

Be careful; be very careful you live your life for God's glory and not your own. In an age and a society where man's will and way is most important to many, choose to live humbly with your God and King. Do not exalt yourself with your own pride. God resists the proud, but He gives grace to the humble.

Prayer and Praise:

Lord, it saddens me to think of all those Lucifer has led astray. Teach me to walk daily with You. Enable me to clothe myself with humility moment by moment, and let me live for Your glory and not my own. In the mighty name of Jesus Christ, my Lord. Amen.

FORGETTING YOUR GOD
Isaiah 17:10

The phrase "because you have forgotten the God of your salvation," is a disturbing thought. How can a person forget God, the God of their salvation? How could a people forget their God? Can a church forget the God of their salvation? Yes, if it is possible for an individual to forget, then a group of individuals could forget; therefore a church could forget.

How does this happen? You do not have to look very far to find it. Professing Christians regularly seem to forget their God. They forget it is Sunday, a holy day, not a holiday. They forget that going to church, being a part of the church, and giving worship to God is essential. But many forget that this is the Lord's Day.

Many forget their God when it comes to stewardship. Do you tithe? Do you set aside at least ten percent of your income to give to the Lord through the local church? Do you tithe your time? Do you spend more time in the Bible than you do on social media? Are you a proper steward of your talents? Do you serve the Lord with your gifts and abilities?

So many seem to "forget" that service to Christ is first and foremost and that being a steward is natural for a Christian who does not forget his God. Many add God into their schedule, if they have time or nothing else to do. Forgetting does not mean you do not remember. Forgetting means you choose not to do what God asks you to do. It means you are the lord of your life and Jesus Christ is not.

If you read the next verse, the result of forgetting your God is that you will reap ruins. Everything you do sow is either to the Lord, or to the world and the flesh. If you do not sow to the Lord, you will reap ruins. The only way you will not reap ruins is by not forgetting your God.

Do not forget your God, the God of your salvation. Be a true Christian steward of your time, your talents, your treasures, and of the truth. Do not put the world before the church. Sunday is the Lord's Day, be faithful and consistent every week to be in church to corporately worship the God of your salvation.

Prayer and Praise:

Lord, thank You for reminding me of my responsibility. Show me regularly the areas in which I am tempted to forget You. Continue to stir in me fresh desire to live for You. In the mighty name of Jesus Christ, my Lord. Amen.

NAKED AND BAREFOOT
Isaiah 20:2

This passage is awkward to say the least. Isaiah, the prophet of God, is told to remove his clothes and walk barefooted for three years as a sign and wonder against Egypt and Ethiopia. It was a picture of what was going to happen to these countries. They would be shamed.

It still is a difficult passage to understand. It brings to mind a question of obedience. If God told you to do this, would you? You can make all the excuses you want of society, culture, and logic, but the question remains, what would you do if God told you to walk naked as He did Isaiah?

What would you do if God told you to dance, as He did David in 2 Samuel 6? David wore only a linen ephod (apron type garment) and he danced as the ark of the covenant was restored to Jerusalem.

You can search the Scriptures, and you will notice on occasion that God asked His faithful servants to do strange things. Isaiah walked naked, David danced, Ezekiel lay on his side for 390 days, and Simon Peter was told to catch a fish and pay their taxes with the money in the fish's mouth.

The issue is not how strange the request may appear; the issue is, are you willing to humble yourself before the Lord and obey Him explicitly? No, I do not think God will ask you to walk around naked, but He may require of you to dance before Him and to trust Him for financial resources that only He can supply.

The issue is do you hear God when He speaks, and do you obey quickly what He says? Have you cultivated an intimate walk with the Lord so you do recognize His voice? Do you struggle with humility? Then expect God to work in these areas so you can learn to clothe yourself daily in humility.

Prayer and Praise:

Lord, You are my God and I want to obey whatever You say. Teach me that my obedience has more than one purpose. It is about obedience, but it is also about testifying to the world that You are my God, and I will submit to You regardless. In the mighty name of Jesus Christ, my Lord. Amen.

JUDGMENT
Isaiah 24:1-3

Judgment is not an idea that is pleasant to talk about or to write about. However, judgment is coming, and in some places judgment has already come. Holy God will judge every person and nation. As you think on this, it should be comforting to know that true Christians will not face a terrifying judgment as a lost person will. A true child of God has been saved and his sins forgiven by the blood of Christ.

Isaiah's proclamation that God's word of judgment to people and nations that reject Almighty God applies to His people today. The United States of America has a wonderful Christian heritage, but now, this country appears to be like a flower cut from her stalk and wilting. A child of God faces ramifications because you live in a sin-fallen world and society, plus you still have the capacity and capability to sin.

The key for you as an individual is to live your life with a passion for Christ. Live your life consumed with the Word of God. Is there anything in your life you are more passionate about than Christ? Are you daily adjusting your life to the Word of God? If not, you may be wilting right along with the country.

Every person will face ramifications for the society and of the country in which he or she lives. Yet, as child of God, God will sustain you and give you grace to face every situation so you can glorify Him more. The key is understanding you are to glorify Christ, and not your children or yourself. Yes, there will be difficult days, challenging days, and even dark and agonizing days, but amidst them all you live for God's glory.

How do you live for God's glory in hard times? You stay faithful to Christ, His Church, and His Word, regardless of what pain you may be in. You learn to spend large quantities of time in prayer. You learn to abide in Christ. You know you are abiding in Christ when your passion is Christ. Ask God to help you.

Prayer and Praise:

Lord, I read Your Word, and I see judgment and hardship on people and nations. Teach me how to remain faithful amidst pain. Teach me and release in me a fresh passion for You. Find me faithful. In the mighty name of Jesus Christ, my Lord. Amen.

EXALTING GOD
Isaiah 25:1

What does it mean to exalt God? The word exalt is a word used in worship, and it means to lift up. To exalt God is to "lift Him up." Obviously this is done metaphorically in this verse, for it is not possible for one to pick up God.

How do you exalt God? You exalt God by recognizing He is already higher than anything in the universe (all creation) in terms of greatness and glory. Then, in light of the reality of God's inherent exaltedness, you use words to praise Him. You proclaim what is true about Him.

The verse shows that God is to be personal. Isaiah says, "You are my God. I will exalt You." Based on a personal relationship, you praise Him. You praise His name. Are you aware of the many names God has? He is El Shaddai, God Almighty, the pourer forth of blessings. He is El Olam, the everlasting God. He is El Elyon the Most High, sovereign over all. He is El Gibbor, prevailing and conquering God. Do you know Him?

You praise His acts because He has done many wonderful things. Can you stop and recount some of the wonderful things He has done for you? You are breathing right this moment. You have been blessed with ability to process thoughts. You are having time right now focusing on the Lord. There are countless wonderful things God has done in your life.

You are to declare His faithfulness and truth. Just as Isaiah praised God's faithfulness, you can trust and declare His faithfulness. The Lord is faithful, and He will keep His Word. "God is faithful, by whom you were called into the fellowship of His Son, Jesus Christ our Lord" (1 Corinthians 1:9).

Prayer and Praise:

Lord, I exalt You. You are King of kings and Lord of lords. Your majesty exceeds my imagination. Your glory is beyond my wildest dreams. Your authority is supreme. I lift You up in praise, and I bow before You as my God and King. In the mighty name of Jesus Christ, my Lord. Amen.

DRAWING NEAR WITH YOUR MOUTH
Isaiah 29:13

The old saying, "words are cheap," is correct. What that means is, they are easy to say but more difficult to do. When it comes to your relationship to Jesus Christ, do your words match your lifestyle? It is easy to give lip service to God, but does your life flow with obedience?

As Isaiah addressed God's people, God was charging Israel with just that. He said, "They honor Me with their lips, but their heart is far from me." Then He proceeds to tell how this happened. God says, "Their fear toward Me is taught by the commandment of men." Instead of having a genuine fear of God that was initiated by the Holy Spirit, these people were merely going through the motions of "faith in God," based on what man had told them.

The issue is that these people were simply doing what they were told by man. They may have been instructed all their lives on how to "walk with God." The problem was it was all external to them; it did not involve their hearts. In fact, their hearts were far removed from God.

Is that an easy practice to slide into today? Yes, it is so easy to relegate your Christian life down to a few deeds, as if your keeping all His deeds means you are walking with God. NO! The motivation with which you do these deeds determines the genuineness of your faith. You are not to do things merely by rote or habit.

You are commanded to draw near to God (James 4:8). You do not do this by simply doing external acts. The motivation of your heart has to be that of one hungering and thirsting after God. Do you long for God's presence? Andrew Murray coined the phrase, "securing God's presence." Do you understand that?

To secure God's presence means when you seek God in prayer and Bible study, you stay in prayer and the Word of God long enough to know you have met God. You do not read one or two chapters of your Bible and say a quick sixty-second prayer and secure God's presence. You must learn to stay, to linger and dig deeper. Then you will want to linger in the presence of God as long as possible.

Prayer and Praise:

Lord, teach me to secure Your presence. Show me if I only draw near to You with my lips and not my heart. In the mighty name of Jesus Christ, my Lord. Amen.

WHOM DO YOU RELY ON?
Isaiah 31:1

Where do you go for help? As life spins faster and faster, there is a great possibility it will fly off the track. When it does, where do you go for help? Isaiah is giving a warning to those who look to and go to the world for help.

What does it look like to go to the world for help? It says, "...and rely on horses, who trust in chariots because they are many." The idea is on whom or what do you rely? Your employer employs you, and you make an income, but do you rely on him to provide for you, or do you rely on God, knowing He is the one who has blessed you with the ability to work and He is the One who has allowed you your employment?

Do you honor God by tithing your income to the local church? Do you acknowledge God by being faithful at your workplace to be a witness for Him? Do you strive to live a life of obedience? Are you in church on Sundays to worship and exalt your Lord? Those who are about these things are showing whom they rely on.

Or do you spend your tithe on paying bills and eating out? While at work, you do not witness for the Lord. You live as your coworkers live and act, and your life does not evidence a relationship with Jesus Christ. You go to church only if there is nothing better to do; family activities and hobbies take first place. These things demonstrate a life that relies on the world.

To rely on the Lord, you must seek the Lord. Seeking the Lord requires time and attention. To seek the Lord does not come naturally, it is an intentional action. To seek the Lord, your life and lifestyle must be that of constantly adjusting to God and His Word.

The world is very appealing. It never stops seducing you to join her. The cost is too great to rely on the world and not Almighty God. Only you get to make the choice. If you realize you have failed, repent and start now. Make the Lord your refuge, rely on Him.

Prayer and Praise:

Lord, it is so easy to follow the world and drift. Teach me to walk close to You. Show me the areas of my life where I need to adjust and readjust to You. Let my wife and my children recognize a difference in me. In the mighty name of Jesus Christ, my Lord. Amen.

A HIGHWAY OF HOLINESS
Isaiah 35:8

When you hear the phrase "highway of holiness," what comes to your mind? Is it a straight and narrow road? Is it a way of righteousness? Is it the coming of the Lord? Is it the path upon which true believers walk? It is a narrow road, and it is a life of righteousness that longs for the coming of the Lord.

God is holy, and He expects you to be holy. However, He does not leave it up to your humanity; He enables you by the Holy Spirit. Your responsibility is to learn to yield to the Holy Spirit. John the Baptist came preaching the kingdom of God and to prepare the way. That is what you are to still be about, preparing the way of the Lord and building the highway of holiness.

To be holy means to be dedicated or consecrated to God. It is to be set apart for God's service and glory. Do you live a life of service to the Lord? Is your life being set apart for Christ's glory? How do you determine this? By what you give yourself to. By what you spend your time and money on. When you examine the passions of your heart, you will see what you live for. Is Christ what you live for, and do you arrange your life around Him?

When you set your life on the highway of holiness, you will not go astray. The psalmist said, "Your Word is a lamp to my feet and a light to my path" (Psalm 119:105). The only way to get off of this road is to ignore the light. Do not ignore the light of God's Word.

This life is only the beginning. There is all eternity to look forward to. If you choose to ignore the Word of God and the highway of holiness, it will impact your eternity. Live holy unto God and if you fall, get up and start over with honest confession of your sin. Live for God's glory.

Prayer and Praise:

Lord, holiness is not a word I am comfortable describing myself as, but it is what You have called and enabled me to be. I praise You, let me live for Your glory and not my own. Let holiness characterize my life. Let the Holy Spirit direct my thoughts and steps. In the mighty name of Jesus, my Lord. Amen.

GOING TO THE HOUSE OF THE LORD
Isaiah 37:1

How do you respond to bad news, devastating news? Do you remember where you were on 9/11? Do you remember what you thought and felt as you watched those planes crash on purpose into the towers? Do you remember the feelings you had as you saw the cloud of dust so thick with people stumbling out with their clothes torn and bodies bruised and bleeding? Devastating news causes shock and brings despair.

Hezekiah had just heard devastating news. Assyria was going to attack them, and they planned to pillage and plunder until nothing was left. Hezekiah, the king, was trying to appear strong for his kingdom, but his insides were churning. What did he do? He tore his clothes and put ashes on his body; he went into mourning. That is how one feels when the news is devastating.

Not only did he mourn, Hezekiah also went to the house of the Lord. Why? He knew that God was a tremendous comforter. He went to the place where he believed he could hear a word from the Lord. Do you do that?

In times of difficulty and despair, do you mourn? If that is all you do, you will miss the relief. In times of distress you have go to the house of the Lord; go to church. Go to the place of worship, and pour your heart and soul out before your king, King Jesus.

Hezekiah was a man who walked regularly with the Lord. After he mourned and after he went to the house of the Lord, he received a word from God. Isaiah the prophet proclaimed to him, "Thus says the Lord, do not be afraid." Is that not the same words you seek to hear from God. Do not be afraid. God was saying, I have this under My control. Do not be afraid, trust Me.

If you want to hear God's word, you must assume the position of humility and place yourself in the place of worship, and be still and wait upon the Lord. When He speaks, receive His word by faith. Will it make the problem go away? Probably not, but God will comfort, and He will allow you to know He is in control, and your responsibility is to trust Him. Do you walk regularly with the Lord? You cannot play catch-up after the problem arises.

Prayer and Praise:

Lord, You are my God. Let me walk with You in good times, so I will be ready when the not-so-good times come. Teach me how to run to You clothed in humility. Enable me to recognize and receive Your Word. Let my trust in You be evidenced in my life. In the mighty name of Jesus Christ, my Lord. Amen.

WAITING UPON THE LORD
Isaiah 40:31

Isaiah forty is a favorite chapter of many people. It is about the people of God being comforted. In verse eleven you read, "He will feed His flock like a shepherd; He will gather the lambs with His arm, and carry them in His bosom, and gently lead those who are with young." He feeds you His Word. You rest in His everlasting arms and He disciples you gently. Hallelujah, what a Savior!

When you come to the end of the chapter, you see such assurance. "Have you not known? Have you not heard? The everlasting God, the LORD, the Creator of the ends of the earth, neither faints nor is weary. His understanding is unsearchable. He gives power to the weak and to those who have no might He increases strength" (Isaiah 40:28-29). Thank You, Lord.

Then we see the promise to those who wait upon the Lord: renewed strength, soaring as eagles, running, and finally walking and not fainting. The key is waiting. How good are you at waiting? What are some things you have to wait for? You wait to see the doctor or dentist. You wait in line to check out your purchases. You wait for your spouse to come to the car. You wait to pick up your children after school. That type of waiting compares nothing to waiting on God.

God often requires you to wait, and as you wait, all others options begin to vanish. Will you still wait on the Lord, or will you take matters into your own hands? How do you wait on the Lord? You wait on the Lord with faith. Faith comes by hearing the Word of God (Romans 10:17).

How is your faith? As your faith is, so your waiting ability will be. Faith is stable confidence in the will of God. You trust God, and your life is an expression of that trust. Evidence of true faith is a life pattern of obedience to God.

Prayer and Praise:

Lord, You ask me to wait in order for my strength to be renewed; teach me daily how to wait in faith. Let my lifestyle be that of walking in obedience and rhythm with You. There will be days I will soar and run, but most of my life will be a walk; let me walk in faith. In the mighty name of Jesus Christ, my Lord. Amen.

FEAR NOT
Isaiah 43:1

One of the greatest obstacles you face is fear. Fear is that overwhelming emotion that causes you to hesitate, to stop, to turn and flee. It comes from a variety of sources, but the main culprit is the Devil. The Devil knows if he can get you afraid, then he will render you useless.

The command you have from God is "fear not." Why would God say that? God commands this because he has redeemed you and He has called you. When you became a child of God, God came into your life in the person of the Holy Spirit. Therefore, you have no reason to be afraid.

The key is for you to continue to abide daily in Christ. As this is real in you, the Holy Spirit is free to move, direct, comfort, and fill your life. When fear is filling your life, at that moment you are quenching the Holy Spirit. Do you have a fear-filled life?

"For God has not given us a spirit of fear, but of power and of love and of a sound mind" (2 Timothy 1:7). To walk in fear is to fail to walk in the Holy Spirit and abide in Christ. Isaiah continued his prophecy, saying of God, "When you pass though the waters, I will be with you ...When you walk through the fire, you shall not be burned." He was telling you this is going to happen; do not be surprised. You will face difficulties and challenges, but God says, "Fear not, for I am with you." (Isaiah 43:5).

The presence of God in your life will make all the difference in the world. Do you know God's presence in your life? Is God a living reality in you or merely a concept? His presence is real. His provision is available, but you are required to trust Him explicitly and obey Him completely.

Fear not, God is with you. When life begins to overwhelm you, readjust your eyes to the Father. Look to Him and not to your problems. Face your fears in faith and God will sustain you and see you through.

Prayer and Praise:

Lord, You are my God, and I will trust You. Let my eyes look to You and not the situations and circumstances that can so easily consume me. I praise You, ever-present Father. In the mighty name of Jesus Christ, my Lord. Amen.

YOUR REDEEMER
Isaiah 48:17

What a promise! God your Redeemer will lead you in the way you should go. The promise of leading and directing throughout your life is tremendous. The issue is always the same—will you follow? The Lord promises to lead, but will you follow?

How does God lead you today? This is speaking to believers, those who have been truly saved by the blood of Jesus Christ. He leads His children. Jesus said, "I am the good shepherd; and I know My sheep, and am known by My own" (John 10:14). Then He tells you, "My sheep hear My voice, and I know them, and they follow Me" (John 10:27).

As a Christian, you have been given the tremendous ability to recognize and hear the voice of God. This should not be taken lightly; this is a privilege beyond imagination. This is the reason your lost family and friends often do not understand why you do what you do as a child of God. However, once Jesus speaks to you, you are responsible to adjust your life and obey His Words.

You have the promise that God will lead you in the way you should go. He leads by His voice. God still speaks and He uses whole sentences. God leads you through the Bible. It is the Word of God. God leads you with the Holy Spirit who lives inside of every Christian. God leads. Are you willing to follow?

God does not lead you always in an easy direction. Life is not about your comfort. It is about you living to glorify the Lord. The way one glorifies the Lord is by being faithful, even in difficulties. You glorify the Lord by becoming Christlike. If you are to be Christlike, you will face suffering and persecution.

"That I may know Him and the power of His resurrection, and the fellowship of His sufferings, being conformed to His death" (Philippians 3:10). If you think you can follow Christ and not suffer, you either have not read your Bible, or you read it with American eyes. God will lead in the way you should go. Follow Him no matter where it may be.

Prayer and Praise:

Lord, let me follow wherever You lead. Let me trust You completely. In the mighty name of Jesus Christ, my Lord. Amen.

AUGUST

August 1...........Isaiah 49:1, Listen
August 2...........Isaiah 52:1, Awake, Awake!
August 3...........Isaiah 55:1, Everyone Who Thirsts, Come
August 4...........Isaiah 59:1, The Lord's Hand Is Not Short
August 5...........Isaiah 61:1, The Spirit of the Lord Is upon Me
August 6...........Isaiah 64:1, Rend the Heavens
August 7...........Jeremiah 1:10, The Challenge
August 8...........Jeremiah 5:22-23, Boundaries
August 9...........Jeremiah 7:11, A Den of Thieves
August 10.........Jeremiah 12:5, Wearied
August 11.........Jeremiah 13:9, Pride
August 12.........Jeremiah 18:2-4, The Potter
August 13.........Jeremiah 19:1-2, The Potsherd Heap
August 14.........Jeremiah 23:1, Woe to the Shepherds
August 15.........Jeremiah 25:5-7, Repent
August 16.........Jeremiah 29:11, God's Plans
August 17.........Jeremiah 33:3, Call to the Lord
August 18.........Jeremiah 35:2, Rechabites
August 19.........Jeremiah 38:7-11, Ebed-Melech
August 20.........Jeremiah 42:2, Let Our Petition Be Acceptable
August 21.........Jeremiah 45:3, Grief to My Sorrow
August 22.........Jeremiah 48:10, Doing the Lord's Work Deceitfully
August 23.........Jeremiah 50:6, Worthless Shepherds
August 24.........Lamentations 3:23, Great Is Your Faithfulness
August 25.........Lamentations 4:20, Under His Shadow
August 26.........Ezekiel 1:1, Among the Captives
August 27.........Ezekiel 6:8, The Remnant
August 28.........Ezekiel 8:4, The Glory of the Lord
August 29.........Ezekiel 10:18, The Glory Departed
August 30.........Ezekiel 14:3, Setting Up Idols in Your Heart
August 31.........Ezekiel 16:49-50, The Sin of Sodom

LISTEN
Isaiah 49:1

How are you when it comes to listening to God? Many genuine believers seem to struggle in this area. They begin to go through life doing the same thing every day, hoping it is pleasing to God. They are living their life by rote, but not really hearing God. They have their "quiet time" and they are off to face the world. But they are not sensitive to God when He speaks. They know how to talk to God and tell Him their needs, concerns, and woes, but they do not know how to listen to the Lord.

How do you listen to God? You hear what you are used to hearing. Have you trained your spiritual ears to pick up on God's voice when He speaks? How do you train your spiritual ears? You have been given a helper, the Holy Spirit, to guide and teach you. The main factor is that you must yield to the direction of the Holy Spirit. If you choose to ignore His leading, the voice of God will grow fainter in your hearing.

A good place to begin the process of hearing God speak, and listening, is to ask the Lord to show you any sin in your life; past or present. Any things you are to be about that you have not done? Anyone you need to forgive or ask forgiveness from? How is the stewardship of your time, your money, and your talents? If you will not deal with sin, you will be greatly limited in hearing God speak.

Once sin is dealt with by honest confession and the adjustments in your life, you are now in a position to hear God. As you read the Word of God and you take time to pray, ask God to speak and then wait in silence before Him. Wait upon the Lord. Ask Him to speak to you throughout the day. When He speaks, respond in obedience.

Often God speaks subtly. Do you realize every time the thought passes your mind to read your Bible that is God speaking to you? In your flesh, these ideas will not come; it is the prompting of the Holy Spirit. The issue is, do you read your Bible, or do you ignore the voice of God? If you ignore God's voice, over time your ability to hear God is marred.

Prayer and Praise:

Lord, thank You for speaking to me. Let me obey Your voice quickly when I hear You speak. Train my ear to be sensitive to You. In the mighty name of Jesus Christ, my Lord. Amen.

AWAKE, AWAKE!
Isaiah 52:1

Have you ever known a person who has a difficult time waking up in the mornings? He sleeps through the alarm clock, or hits the snooze bar over and over. He answers his wake-up call only to go right back to sleep. You go to his room and he assures you, "I am awake." But he rolls over just as you leave. Do you know someone like that? Maybe you are like that.

The message of Isaiah in the text is a message to God's people to wake up. Let's apply this to the church. Many do not realize they are asleep. They see the building kept up nicely and the pews are filled every Sunday; how can she be asleep? The church is busy with children's events, youth activities, choir specials, and senior citizen trips. How can she be asleep?

These activities are nice, sweet, and exciting, but they are not the purpose of the church. What is the purpose of the church? Some say the great commission, to evangelize the lost. This is a biblical purpose. Many churches need to be awakened to this.

Jesus also said, "My house shall be called a house of prayer." How much praying does your church do? On a Sunday morning you may have the pastoral prayer, the offertory prayer, a prayer before the sermon, and the benediction. How much time do these take? Four to five minutes for all. Does that constitute a house of prayer? More time is taken for the announcements in many churches.

Most churches need to quickly wake up to their purpose of being a house of prayer. All other true ministries are held together by and through prayer. Your church will fall into one of three categories. You will be crisis-praying church, and you only pray in times of need. You will have a prayer ministry, where prayer is a program. Or you will be a praying church, and prayer is the ministry.

It starts with you. Will you be a man or woman of prayer? Will you put forth the time and effort?

Prayer and Praise:

Lord, wake us up to Your purpose that we are to be a house of prayer. Wake me up to my responsibility to be a man of prayer. In the mighty name of Jesus Christ, my Lord. Amen.

EVERYONE WHO THIRSTS, COME
Isaiah 55:1

Have you ever been thirsty and you could not get water? The description Isaiah gives is of a person thirsty, desperate for water, and it is offered. Why would you not accept it? Why would you turn it away?

He continues to ask, "Why would you spend money for what is not bread and your wages for what does not satisfy?" As it was in Isaiah's time, so it is today. People spend their lives looking for happiness and fulfillment in things that are not lasting. They have been so blinded by the glitter of the world that they do not recognize what will bring true satisfaction.

How about you? Do you look to the world to satisfy your need for excitement? Do you allow the world to pacify you from the boredom you may experience in life? Or do you know how to go to Christ and let His Word and truth fill you and sustain you?

These are lessons you must learn and pass on to others, especially your children. Only Christ can satisfy. Only the living water He offers is lasting. The world offers sugary substitutes, but they leave you feeling empty and lifeless. With these substitutes, you constantly have to be looking for more to pacify you. This is a tremendous lesson to learn. Blessed is the man who learns it early in life. Jesus Christ offers abundant life; He satisfies your life as you abide in Him.

Isaiah says, "Come," do not waste your time and resources on what will not satisfy." Later in the same chapter he tells you, "Seek the Lord while He may be found, call upon Him while He is near" (v. 6). The message is clear: do not wait too late to seek Christ Jesus. When he stirs in your heart, respond to Him quickly, for He may not always be available. You can wait until it is too late. While He is calling, come, let Him satisfy you and fill you.

Prayer and Praise:

Lord, forgive me for seeking to be satisfied with the world and the things of the world. Let me recognize that only You can satisfy and fill me with contentment. You are my God and King. In the mighty name of Jesus Christ, my Lord. Amen.

THE LORD'S HAND IS NOT SHORT
Isaiah 59:1

Sin is a terrible thing. It separates. It separates husbands from their wives and children. It separates children from their parents. It separates wives from their families. Sin separates friends, family, and coworkers. Sin is a terrible thing. Above all, sin separates people from the Lord.

God is a holy God, and He will in no way tolerate or condone sin. He sent Jesus Christ to pay the penalty and price to cover your sin. Christ bore the sin of the world on the cross. He bore your sin. When Jesus arose from the grave and ascended to the Father in heaven, He sat down at the right hand of Almighty God. Has sin been paid for and dealt with? Yes. Yes, a resounding yes! If the sin debt had not been paid in full by Jesus Christ, He could not have entered back into the presence of the Father.

By entering into the presence of God, God showed the sin debt was paid. Now, a man or woman comes to Holy God by grace through faith, based on the death and resurrection of Jesus Christ. Salvation is free to man, based on the death of Jesus Christ. However, each person must come to Christ. Once you have been saved, fellowship and communion with the Lord is costly, but it is worth it all.

When the Scripture says, "Behold, the Lord's hand is not shortened that it cannot save; nor His ear heavy that it cannot hear. But your iniquities have separated you from your God; and your sins have hidden His face from you, so that He will not hear." That word should concern you. It affects how you pray.

It simply is saying, if as a Christian you have not dealt with sin in your life; when sin is unacknowledged, unconfessed, and sin unforsaken, your prayers are not heard by God. The price has been paid and forgiveness offered. Do not let sin separate you from your God. Is there any sin you need to deal with right now?

Prayer and Praise:

Lord, You are a forgiving Father. Jesus paid the ultimate price for my sin. Show me any sin that I have failed to bring to You in honest confession. Show me any sin I am justifying and have not forsaken. In the mighty name of Jesus Christ, my Lord. Amen

THE SPIRIT OF THE LORD IS UPON ME
Isaiah 61:1

Have you ever experienced the Spirit of the Lord being upon you? This is not necessarily the same as being full or filled with the Holy Spirit. This is a time of anointing and unction from God, released on your life for a time of effective ministry.

The Spirit of the Lord is ever present to lead and guide through life. He will teach all things. Your responsibility is not to grieve or quench the Holy Spirit. There may be times that the Holy Spirit is upon you in a powerful fashion for the purpose of proclaiming His truth to those around you who are lost without hope, without Christ.

In order to know the anointing of the Spirit of God, you must walk in the Spirit of God. You must yield to the Spirit. You must be in agreement with the Word of God in your life. Is there any area you are not yielded to the Word of God?

When you walk in the Spirit, there will be opportunities that arise that God has ordained for you to share your testimony or to share the truth of the gospel. It is in those moments when the unction of the Spirit comes upon a person. The unction, or anointing, is when God takes human words and seasons them by His Spirit, and they now penetrate a human heart for the gospel.

The blinders of the Devil are removed, and the message is shared under the anointing of the Spirit, and God gives the increase. Amen.

You can share Scripture almost anywhere, but it takes God's Spirit to make it alive to a lost and hopeless soul. One of the most common ways the Holy Spirit is quenched is through fear. The Bible says, "For God has not given us a spirit of fear, but of power and of love and of a sound mind" (2 Timothy 1:7). Walk in the Spirit, yield to the Spirit, and be very careful not to grieve or quench the Spirit.

There is an anointing that is available. It is what brings forth effective ministry.

Prayer and Praise:

Lord, I am so grateful for Your Holy Spirit. Show me any area of my life that I am quenching or grieving Your Spirit. Let me, by faith, yield it to You. Use me for Your glory, and let me know Your anointing. In the mighty name of Jesus Christ, my Lord. Amen.

REND THE HEAVENS
Isaiah 64:1

"Oh, that You would rend the heavens and come down." Oh, that God would move among your church. Oh, that God would demonstrate His glory and power. Oh, that God would manifest in a tangible way. Do you have that desire?

A rent heaven is an open heaven. When Jesus was baptized, the Scriptures tell that the heavens opened, and the Spirit descended like a dove, alighting upon Christ. And God spoke audibly from heaven. "This is My beloved Son, in whom I am well pleased" (Matthew 3:16-17). Luke 3:21 tells that as Jesus was baptized, and while He was praying, the heavens opened, the Spirit descended, and the voice of God spoke. In order to experience an open heaven, prayer was involved.

In Revelation 1, John was in the presence of the living Lord; he was caught up in worship of Christ. When you come to chapter four, you find an open door into heaven and an angel saying, "Come up and I will show you things."

To have an open heaven or a rent heaven is a wonderful experience for a child of God who is walking in agreement with the Lord. In Isaiah 64, when the heavens rend, mountains flow down at the presence of God. Obstacles are taken away. Fire brings about change, water boils. There is a transformation power that comes from the presence of the Father coming down.

Nations will tremble at His presence. Have you ever trembled before the presence of God? Has God's Word and Spirit ever so gripped you that all you can do is tremble? If not, why do you think you have not? There are many references in Scripture of trembling in God's presence. Search them out. James 2:19 says, "You believe that there is one God. You do well. Even the demons believe---and tremble!"

"And when they had prayed, the place where they were assembled together was shaken; and they were all filled with the Holy Spirit and they spoke the word of God with boldness" (Acts 4:31). The place shook, they were filled afresh with the Holy Spirit, and they proclaimed the Word of God boldly in a hostile society.

When the heavens are rent, God moves and displays Himself with power. Is that what you long for? Are you willing to pay the price of prayer to know this? Not sweet, nice prayers but rather seasons of praying and seeking God?

Prayer and Praise

Lord, You are what I desire. Oh Father, rend the heavens and come down. Move among Your church and shake me, shake us. I surrender all to You. In the mighty name of Jesus Christ, my Lord. Amen.

THE CHALLENGE
Jeremiah 1:10

Jeremiah is relating his call by God to preach. He makes the same excuses Moses made, as well as many others. He says in essence, I cannot speak, I am too young. But God does not change His call. He even tells Jeremiah to, go where I send you, speak what I say speak and do not be afraid of the faces, for I am with you.

Everything depends on knowing God has sent you and that God is with you. As long as you know that, you go in faith. If you do not know that God has sent you, or that He is with you, then you will fear man.

To obey the Lord, you have to live by faith. Faith is the bedrock conviction that God is God and His Word is true. When God gives you a specific word, you obey regardless. Often the word God gives you to share will not be popular. In fact, it will be a difficult word. The Lord told Jeremiah "to root out and to pull down, to destroy and to throw down, to build and to plant."

Two-thirds of the message is negative. You can only proclaim the positive after the negative has been preached. Today, we want to only hear the positive. That is impossible, because sin must be dealt with, and sin is a negative.

In order to construct a house, the first thing that must happen is the ground must be cleared and leveled. This is disruptive but essential. Next, you have to dig the footer, again a destructive act, but both of these are necessary in order to be constructive. It is only after the negative that the positive can flow forth.

Prayer and Praise:

Lord, doing Your will is not always easy, nor is it popular. Teach me to be submissive to Your Word, regardless of the challenge. Teach me that obedience is absolutely essential. Give me courage to do Your will when it is not popular or pleasing to men. Be glorified in my life. In the mighty name of Jesus Christ, my Lord. Amen.

BOUNDARIES
Jeremiah 5:22-23

Are you familiar with boundaries? You recognize them in athletic events, knowing you cannot step out of bounds. If you do, you are disqualified. Boundaries are established for children and youth. You can go here, but you cannot go beyond this point. Do not cross the street. Do not stay out past eleven o'clock. Do not go in a car with this person because she drives too recklessly.

Boundaries come in all phases of life. As an adult, there are still more. There are boundaries of speed limits, rights of way, topics of discussion with the opposite sex, etc. Boundaries face everyone.

In the text, Judah is trying to go out of bounds, and God is showing that she must observe the limitations He has established.

Do you stay within the boundaries God has set for you, or do you act as a spoiled child demanding your own way? What are some boundaries God has established? Worship only Him. He demands your time, attention, and praise. Seek only Him, do not seek the approval of others. Live His Word, abide in Him.

Every boundary a parent establishes for a child is for a positive or protective reason. So it is with God. He establishes boundaries for your benefit. You must stay within the bounds to walk with God and to know His good pleasure.

Why are boundaries difficult to obey? Human nature likes us to live risky lives and see what all we can get by with. Human beings think they know what they can handle and deal with. The sin nature never goes away. It must be constantly held in a crucified position before the Lord. Humans do not know better than God.

When you revolt against God, you will not win. God loves you; therefore, He sets boundaries for that reason. Yield to the Father.

Prayer and Praise:

Lord, there are times I do not understand why You tell me no or why You have set restrictions in my life, but I trust You to know what is best, and I yield to You. When I try to press against the boundaries, show me quickly and sternly. Teach me to yield day by day to Your plan. In the mighty name of Jesus Christ, my Lord. Amen.

A DEN OF THIEVES
Jeremiah 7:11

As Jeremiah continues his prophetic book, he makes reference to the house of God becoming a den of thieves. This can be somewhat confusing if you do not understand the situation taking place among the people of God.

God's people were to be holy and set apart to the Lord. Here, God's people had compromised with the world. They lived like the world, but they would go to the temple and go through the motions of worship. Does that still take place today?

They would go to "church" and think they were safe and everything was going to be alright. It did not matter how they lived in sin and rebellion. As long as they went to the temple, the house of the Lord, everything would be fine.

Jeremiah challenged them. He said they had turned the house of the Lord into a den of thieves. A den of thieves was a hideout where a thief thought he was safe. He could return to the den and count his money, plan his next robbery, and hang out with other thieves, because he was secure in his den. That is what Jeremiah said of the people of God.

You come to the house of the Lord just like a thief goes to his den. You feel safe and secure, but you are not safe and secure. You can think what you want, even do anything you want, and believe anything you want, but you are not secure. It takes more than going to the house of the Lord to know God's security. It requires coming before the Lord in yieldedness and surrender, forsaking yourself and sin, and obeying the Lord (adjusting your lifestyle to Him) to know His security.

In the American church, many have turned it into a den of thieves. The idea is, "I went to church today, now I have paid my dues and everything will be alright." Following Christ is so much more than attending a meeting. It is so much more than showing up and giving an hour of time. It is coming before the Lord to worship and honor Him.

Have you ever been tempted to make the house of the Lord into a den of thieves?

Prayer and Praise:

Lord, teach me not to seek security in a building. Teach me to seek security in You and a life yielded to Your will and word. In the mighty name of Jesus Christ, my Lord. Amen.

WEARIED
Jeremiah 12:5

Have you ever gotten weary? Have you ever gotten weary spiritually? Most believers will answer that question with a strong yes. Have you ever stopped to think about what it is that causes weariness to come upon you?

In the text you are warned that if you cannot contend with the footmen, how will you make it when the horses arrive? It is very important for you to understand weariness and why it comes. One of the primary causes is physical exhaustion, and the cure is physical rest. Spiritual weariness can come from many things. Sin, disobedience, enemy opposition, and even judgment bring weariness. The cure is fourfold: rest, remember, return, and receive.

Rest, slow down, and catch your breath spiritually. Remember who your God is. He is the sovereign, almighty, creator, giver, and sustainer of life. Rehearse His names, and once again, see His character. Return, if you have sin or disobedience in your life; deal with it by honest confession and repentance. Make yourself accountable to someone in these areas. Finally, receive. Receive the forgiveness God extends; receive the rest, the refreshment that He offers. Receive His Word into your life. Receive His perspective and remain in Him.

Most everyone experiences seasons of weariness, but not everyone stays weary in his or her faith. It depends on your responding to the Father. A good beginning place is His Word. Read it and pray it back to Him. Memorize Scripture, and share with others what you are feeling so they can agree in prayer with you.

When you are weary, learn to seek the Lord for renewed strength.

Prayer and Praise:

Lord, I get weary and struggle; teach me by the prompting of Your Holy Spirit to run to You. Teach me to cast my burdens upon You and not to try and carry them alone. Teach me to rest in You and not to try and find rest in a recliner in front of a television. Send seasons of refreshing to my soul. In the mighty name of Jesus Christ, my Lord. Amen.

PRIDE
Jeremiah 13:9

Pride is a subject everyone understands. In America, the idea of having pride is seen as a good thing. However, God is very clear—pride and being proud is not a good thing. The Scriptures teach, "God resists the proud" (James 4:6). To resist means to stand against, to oppose. Do you want Almighty God opposing you?

In today's society, you hear people expressing pride in numerous ways. You hear phrases like, "I am proud of my children. I am proud of my job. I am proud of my church. I am proud of my family and friends. I am proud of my car." Yet every time you express such pride, God resists you. The better phrase would be, "I am thankful for my family." Thankfulness is not the same as being prideful.

Pride is the absence of wisdom; when pride comes in, wisdom leaves. Wisdom is seeing life from God's perspective. Wisdom is the presence of God's mind in you. The Bible teaches that God loves to give wisdom to those who ask for it (James 1).

The book of James also tells that there are two kinds of wisdom. There is earthly wisdom; it is unspiritual and devilish (James 3:15). It is the wisdom of boasting. The other wisdom is from above, the wisdom of Jesus Christ. When you desire the acceptance of man, or the opinions of man matter more to you than God's favor, you forfeit the true wisdom of God.

There are consequences to the forfeiture of God's wisdom. You will not know God's ways or direction. You will be left, as the world, to do the best you can, which is far short of what God requires. Man's best is but filthy rags (Isaiah 64:6).

Seek God's wisdom, ask for God's wisdom and mind. The test will, and you will, prove which wisdom you possess—when you have to stand against the opinions of man and the plans of man that sound so good, obey God.

Prayer and Praise:

Lord, I need wisdom from above—Your wisdom. I ask for Your mind, Your wisdom. In the mighty name of Jesus Christ, my Lord. Amen.

THE POTTER
Jeremiah 18:2-4

Jeremiah is sent to an ordinary place to hear a word from God. He is not sent to the school of the prophets, nor is he sent to the temple. He is sent to the potter's house. Oftentimes, God will speak to you in the ordinariness of life. That means you should always be sensitive to the voice of God.

Many talk about God speaking in a still, small voice, and He does. Scripture also teaches that God thunders from the heavens. The psalmist tells us that, "The voice of the Lord is over the waters; the God of glory thunders. The Lord is over many waters. The voice of the Lord is powerful. The voice of the Lord is full of majesty" (Psalm 29:3-4).

God does sometimes speak in a still, small voice, but sometimes His voice thunders from the heavens. The key is to be able to recognize the voice of God. Jeremiah went to a common and ordinary place, and he heard God speak.

God is like the earthly potter in one way and one way only. He has the right to touch our lives any way He wants. He is God, and you are a creature of His creation.

You are like the clay in one way and one way only. You are to respond to the touch of the potter. God expects you to respond submissively to His touch. Do you respond to the hand of God? Or do you push back the hand of God and say, "Do not touch me there"? God is the potter and you are the clay, and the clay yields to the potter.

God so wanted the clay to yield to His touch, He sent his only Son to become clay and die on a cross for your sins. That is how much God wants you to yield to Him.

Prayer and Praise:

Lord, let me recognize every day that You have a right to touch my life any way You see fit, and You are not required to give me an explanation. In the mighty name of Jesus Christ, my Lord. Amen.

THE POTSHERD HEAP
Jeremiah 19:1-2

It is a natural progression to move from the potter's house to the potsherd heap. The text says the Potsherd Gate, but it means the same. Every piece of pottery leaves the potter's house either through the front door, a vessel unto service and usefulness, or it leaves through the back door to the potsherd heap, a vessel that was marred in the potter's hand.

A marred vessel is a vessel that refused to yield to the potter's touch. The rough spot resisted and remained in the clay, therefore, making the piece useless. A useless piece was thrown into the potsherd heap, the potsherd heap of garbage pottery pieces. Every piece of pottery there had a rough spot that resisted the potter's touch.

Do you resist the potter's touch, the potter's hand? When God touches your life, do you pull back and say, "Do not touch me there," or, do you yield to His touch? How do you know if you have yielded to the Father's hand? You make adjustments of your life to Him. The stewardship of your life lines in agreement with Scripture. Your time, talents, and your finances all are in positive agreement with God.

How else can you know you have yielded to the Lord? You daily put off the old man and you put on the new man in Christ Jesus. Constantly you examine your lifestyle, your behavior, and your attitudes to see if they are conforming to Christ or the world. Do you live based on what you feel like doing, or do you live based on the principles of Scripture?

Many times you will not feel like going to church. Many times you will not feel like reading the Word of God. Many times you will not feel like praying, witnessing, or serving. If you follow your feelings, you will ultimately be cast to the potsherd heap. Surrender daily to the lordship of Jesus Christ.

Prayer and Praise:

Lord, let me daily examine my life and make necessary adjustments to You and Your Word. Make me into a vessel of usefulness and honor for Your glory. In the mighty name of Jesus Christ, my Lord. Amen.

WOE TO THE SHEPHERDS
Jeremiah 23:1

This seems like an unusual verse—a warning to men who shepherd the flock of God. Why would such a warning be necessary? Shepherds can get distracted just as others get distracted from their walk with the Lord. However, when a shepherd of the flock of God gets distracted, the costs and ramifications can be tremendously bad.

When a shepherd gets distracted from his responsibility to the flock, the flock can scatter. When a flock scatters, they become open targets for wolves, coyotes, and other dangerous predators. The warning, set in the wording of "woe," is a serious warning.

The responsibility of a shepherd is to feed the flock of God by leading them to green pastures and still waters. The responsibility is to protect them from danger. Doctrinal error and being busy for the sake of being busy are two areas of danger. The truth of God's Word must not be compromised. Also, the flock need not be busy with activities that drain their energy and are not ordained by God.

This latter aspect is a very serious issue facing the church today. Churches find themselves being activity-driven instead of Word-driven. There is a time to work and labor, but you are to have a walk with God, not a work-for-God relationship. Learning to walk by faith is crucial.

Shepherds attend to the flock of God by offering fresh food. Not stale or yesterday's leftovers. Feed the flock of God. Minister living water and satisfy their thirst. Keep the flock free from insects and pests. Tend to the flock.

You may be thinking, I am not a pastor, so this does not apply. Are you a parent? Do you have people to whom you are responsible? If so, in whatever walk of life, guide them with a shepherd's heart and teach them God's Word.

Prayer and Praise:

Lord, thank You for Your Word. Your Word is truth; enable me to understand and live by it. Let me use every opportunity to share it with others. In the mighty name of Jesus Christ, my Lord. Amen.

REPENT
Jeremiah 25:5-7

How much time do you spend thinking about repentance? It is one of those words the world never wants to hear, much less practice. You can understand this word by seeing how it is used in the Roman army. As the troops marched forward, the commander would yell, "Repent!" and instantly, the soldiers would turn on 180 degrees and go in the opposite direction.

The term used today is "about face," which means "turn around." That is repentance. It is a life going in the wrong direction, and the Holy Spirit of God speaks to your soul and says to repent. You, at that moment, will obey God, or you will continue going in the wrong direction.

Repentance is a part of salvation. When a person turns to Christ by faith, he is repenting of his sin. You cannot turn to Christ in faith and still hang onto your sin. It is as if repentance and faith are opposite sides of the same coin.

Once you are saved, you still practice biblical repentance daily, in order to walk with God. Repentance is not a onetime action, and you are good the rest of your day. As the Holy Spirit brings conviction to your soul and mind, obey, and repent. Genuine repentance is how a true believer lives.

Repentance is a gift from God. Apart from the Holy Spirit working in your life, you cannot repent. God enables us to repent. It affects your will, your mindset, and your emotions. Living with a repentant spirit is how you walk with God every day. Just as grace is a gift to you, so is repentance. Repentance releases more grace.

Think about a soldier who hears his commander shout, "Repent!" If he refuses repentance, he is walking in territory without the provision of his commander. How costly would that be?

Prayer and Praise:

Lord, let me daily live with a spirit of repentance. Let me know the convicting of Your Holy Spirit, so I can repent quickly. Teach me daily to realize the gift of repentance. In the mighty name of Jesus Christ, my Lord. Amen.

GOD'S PLANS
Jeremiah 29:11

Often this verse is read and the background is missed. God is thinking about His people, and He has a plan for His people. However, when this prophecy was given, God's people were in distress and bondage due to their disobedience. Yet God still thinks about them and has a plan.

It is so wonderful to know God is thinking about you. It is amazing, with all the people on the earth, to realize God thinks about individuals, and has a plan for each person. Your responsibility is to understand God's plan.

God's will is not like an Easter egg hidden in tall grass. No, God's plan and will is knowable and doable. God wants you to know His plan, and that is why Jesus came and died, and the reason you have the Bible.

God's thoughts, or plans, means He is offering you hope. Maybe you are in bondage or going through a difficult time; you must remember God still has you in His thoughts. The true strength of the passage is not in the plan, but it is knowing God's thoughts.

The literal word for thoughts or plans means to weave as fabric. Trials of life weave life into a plan. When you look at individual hardships, it is difficult to see. However, taken together with all of life, the plan begins to emerge.

It is much like baking a cake. You have flour, sugar, vanilla, butter, and a pinch of salt. Each ingredient by itself is not very tasty. In fact, many of the ingredients alone are terrible to try and eat. When you add the ingredients together, mixing them properly and placing them in the oven to bake, the end result is wonderful.

As a Christian, are you in a difficult season of life? Do not forget God has you in His thoughts, and He has a plan for you. All things work together for good as you yield to the Lord.

Prayer and Praise:

Lord, thank You for the assurance of Your Word. It is so comforting to know You have a plan for my life. In the mighty name of Jesus Christ, my Lord. Amen.

CALL TO THE LORD
Jeremiah 33:3

Many people have learned this verse as a child in Sunday school. It was commonly referred to as God's phone number, Jeremiah 33:3. Calling on the Lord is basic to prayer. It is the simplest form of praying.

Call and God will answer. Cry out and the Lord will show you great and mighty things. The Lord will show you things you do not even know. Jeremiah was shut up in a prison when this word from God came to him, encouraging him to pray.

Why do you need encouragement to pray? Often, you can get so wrapped up in your circumstances, or prison, that you forget. You get distracted from the Lord, and you fail to pray. Distraction creates distance, and distance from the Lord is not healthy.

How wonderful it is to know that in times of distress, distraction, and even doom, God initiates and comes to prompt you to pray. When you sense the need to pray, realize God is the one who shows you the need to pray. God is the one who initiates prayer.

Prayer and Praise:

Lord, thank You for initiating me to pray. Let me realize to pray to You is not my idea or a good idea. The very thought of prayer to You is You prompting me to pray. I praise You. In the mighty name of Jesus Christ, my Lord. Amen.

RECHABITES
Jeremiah 35:2

The Rechabites were a tribe of people that sought refuge from Nebuchadnezzar in Jerusalem. They had distinguished themselves as a people of strong convictions and commitment. God told Jeremiah to take them to the temple and give them wine to drink, which they refused. This was done to show the contrast between Judah and the Rechabites.

The point of contrast was between consistency and inconsistency, faithfulness and unfaithfulness, obeying and disobeying God, and honoring God and dishonoring God. Even though they were compelled to drink wine, they stood firm and refused.

They went on to explain the loyalty of their commitment in verses 6 and 7. They were to drink no wine. They were not to live in houses. They were not to farm. They were to live in tents and be nomads. For two hundred years they had been faithful to this commitment. The only reason they were in Jerusalem at this time was because of the Babylonian invasion.

The consistency of the Rechabites is an example of what is needed even today among the people of God. Judah had violated and broke this commitment in many ways and was inconsistent. Are you consistent with your commitment to the Lord Jesus Christ? Are you faithful in the stewardship of your life to Christ?

Consistency in one's walk with the Lord is essential to living victoriously. To live as an overcomer, you must be faithful in your life to the Lord. The Rechabites lived separated from sin. They strove to live away from the corruption and immorality of the world. They resisted being influenced by the world. Do you?

If you read verses 18 to 19, God gave them a wonderful promise because of their faithfulness: God promised they would always have godly descendants. What a blessed promise. God demands you to obey His Word and live righteously.

Prayer and Praise:

Lord, these examples of righteousness in hard times are encouraging. Hard decisions must be made every day. Teach me to make them based on Your Word and will. Let me know the promise of godly descendants. In the mighty name of Jesus Christ, my Lord. Amen.

EBED-MELECH
Jeremiah 38:7-11

Have you ever felt like you were in a pit? Most people have. Pits come in a variety of styles. A pit can come because of relationships with others. People you love let you down and you cannot fix them. A pit can be from a bad decision you have made, and you have suffered the consequences. There are financial pits, emotional pits, even spiritual pits.

Jeremiah was in a pit because he was faithful to proclaim the word of God. He was in the pit because people did not like the message he gave forth, and they put him in a muddy cistern. Have you ever been in a pit for obeying God?

When Jeremiah was about to be overcome, God raised up Ebed-Melech. Ebed-Melech means "the king's slave." You do not even have his real name. This slave saw the situation Jeremiah was in and he went before the king, petitioning him for Jeremiah's release. The king granted his release.

Have you gone before King Jesus this week on behalf of someone else who is in a pit because of his or her faith? Have you been willing to be courageous enough to plead before the throne of grace on behalf of another who is struggling?

Ebed-Melech, along with thirty other men, took old rags for Jeremiah to place under his arms and sent down a rope to pull Jeremiah out. He was going to pull Jeremiah out, but Jeremiah had to do his part. He had to put the rags in place, and he had to receive and hang on to the rope.

In the New Testament, the lame man had his four friends who were stretcher bearers. Paul was let down in a basket when men sought to kill him by rope holders. Ebed-Melech was a king petitioner and a rag extender—all for the purpose of lifting a man of God in need.

Are you willing to be a stretcher bearer? A rope holder? A king petitioner? Are you willing to help those who cannot help themselves?

Prayer and Praise:

Lord, let me be willing to petition the King on behalf of others in need. For those who suffer for the gospel's sake, let me be sensitive to them. Teach me how to bear the load. Enable me to just hold the rope. In the mighty name of Jesus Christ, my Lord. Amen.

LET OUR PETITION BE ACCEPTABLE
Jeremiah 42:2

Does it ever concern you that you may be praying prayers that are not acceptable to God? Do you believe all prayers and petitions to God are valid and right? When was the last time you examined your prayer request?

This is the question in the text. The remaining leaders came to Jeremiah and asked him to accept their petition and pray for them so they would know God's direction. These people, at this moment, wanted to obey the Lord and know what they should be doing. Is that your heart's desire?

The key issue is the acceptable petition. People often approach the throne of grace with petitions that are not acceptable to God. People offer prayer requests and they have not the slightest idea of God's will or plan. Then they proceed to pray their own will to the Father. Most everyone has done this at some point.

Someone may be sick, hospitalized, and professes to be a Christian. Some other person makes a prayer request that she will be healed, or have a successful surgery. The unknown factor may be that she is where she is because she has unrepentant sin in her life. She has never confessed and forsaken her sin. God is using the sickness to get her attention, but you offer prayer for her healing. Is that an acceptable prayer?

Not every sickness or need is due to sin, but some are. You have a responsibility to seek God's mind on how to pray for people. Just because a prayer request is offered does not mean it is God's will. God's will is for men and women, boys and girls to love Him with all their heart, soul, mind, and strength. Willful sin in a believer's life creates a spiritual blocker wherein they are stuck until they deal with their sin.

Seek God's mind. Ask Him to show you how to pray. If possible, ask the person if there are any spiritual blockers that would prevent God from answering her prayer. Some common spiritual blockers are bitterness, unforgiveness, unbelief, unrepentant spirit, willful acts of sin, or compromised lifestyle.

Nothing is more important than knowing the way in which God would have you go and doing the things God would have you do.

Prayer and Praise:

Lord, teach me not to be quick to pray about matters of which I have not sought Your mind. Enable me the boldness and faith to ask hard questions. Teach me not to assume on Your will. In the mighty name of Jesus Christ, my Lord. Amen.

GRIEF TO MY SORROW
Jeremiah 45:3

Grief and sorrow are not welcomed emotions, but everyone will experience them in life. The reasons why you experience them may vary, but you will experience them. Jeremiah was a faithful prophet of God and preached during a time when the king of Judah was evil. Jeremiah warned the people of the judgment of God that was coming. Yet the people were influenced more by the king than Jeremiah.

Who are you more influenced by: the Word of God and the preacher or the economy and the government? What, or who, influences you is crucial to your lifestyle. Jeremiah was not a popular preacher, and because of this, he suffered much persecution, as did his associate Baruch. The result was grief and sorrow.

Have you ever experienced grief and sorrow for being obedient to Jesus Christ? These two words are very similar in meaning. In fact, often they are used interchangeably. The word meaning in Hebrew gives a better understanding. Sorrow means sorrow with the sense of affliction. Grief means mental anguish.

You are not only hurting with affliction, but you may also have mental stresses to add to the pain. That is a hard situation to be in. However, the lesson to be learned is simple: do not base your hope in this world; your hope is in Jesus Christ. This world seduces you with recognition, positions, and honor. It tries to make you think it can give you peace and acceptance. Nothing in this world will last. Eternity is forever. You must make sure your motivation is not the temporal things of this world, but that you are living in light of eternity.

Prayer and Praise:

Lord, help me every day not to get so attached to this world that I would be limited in the next world. Let me live amidst persecution and rejection for Your glory. Teach me to examine the influencers of my life daily. In the mighty name of Jesus Christ, my Lord. Amen.

DOING THE LORD'S WORK DECEITFULLY
Jeremiah 48:10

That is a difficult phrase to process, "doing the Lord's work deceitfully." You may ask how that is possible. No one would dare do such a thing. Oh, but it happens all the time.

If you remember, in the New Testament after Jesus's baptism He was led by the Spirit into the wilderness. For forty days, Jesus fasted and communed with His Father. It was at the end of the fast that Satan came and tempted Jesus. It was at a time of physical weakness, Satan attacked the Lord.

The temptation was three-fold. Jesus was hungry and the temptation was to turn stones to bread. Satan's attack appealed to His physical needs. That is still how he tempts today. He tempted Jesus with the kingdoms of this world. Satan's attack appealed to His ambition. He still tempts with power and success. He tempted Jesus to dazzle the people with the spectacular, "Jump off the pinnacle, and angels will catch you." He still tempts today with amazing feats.

The moment Jesus publically yielded to God's will, He met the Devil head on. The Devil tempted Jesus to be another type of Messiah—just do not go to the cross. Be a bread Messiah, give the people what they want. Be a spectacular Messiah, dazzle them with tricks. Be a compromising Messiah, yield to Satan. Be the Messiah; just do not go to the cross.

Today, a person can do the Lord's work deceitfully by compromising the message of truth; by compromising the Word of God and still "serving the Lord." Are you compromising any areas of Scripture? Are you like Martha, so busy serving, doing deeds, but you fail to sit at the feet of Christ and worship, adore, and learn of Him?

Prayer and Praise:

Lord, it is so easy to go through the motions of serving and my motives not be pure. Show me any area I am compromising Your Word, and let me yield immediately to You. Let my service be acceptable to You. In the mighty name of Jesus Christ, my Lord. Amen.

WORTHLESS SHEPHERDS
Jeremiah 50:6

In this passage, God's judgment has fallen on Babylon. Babylon has always represented the world's system that man builds which is opposed to God. It began in Genesis with the tower of Babel (later called Babylon). In this process of judgment, God promised to set His people free.

Freedom is a wonderful thing. Freedom in Christ is way more wonderful than physical freedom. As God's people were promised freedom, they needed to remember what caused their captivity. Sin is what always causes captivity. "My people have been lost sheep." God pictures His people as sheep and their leaders as shepherds. They were called lost sheep because their shepherds had led them astray.

Is that not a sad commentary on the shepherd? How does a shepherd lead the sheep astray? This is how a shepherd becomes worthless. When a shepherd fails to stand on the holy, infallible, and inerrant Word of God, he is leading the flock away. When a shepherd fears man and not God, he leads the flock away. When a shepherd fails to feed and protect the sheep, he is leading the flock away.

The most important thing a shepherd does is feed his flock the truths of God's Word. Well-fed sheep are healthy sheep. A worthless shepherd fails to feed the flock the Word of God. He substitutes pop psychology, man-exalting messages, and cute stories or jokes. He speaks to make man feel good about himself because he fears man and not God.

Worthless shepherds. Be warned of this type of shepherd, and flee from him to a true shepherd of God.

Prayer and Praise:

Lord, give me the wisdom to recognize a true shepherd from a worthless shepherd. Let Your Word always be the test of truth. In the mighty name of Jesus Christ, my Lord. Amen.

GREAT IS YOUR FAITHFULNESS
Lamentations 3:23

Do you question the faithfulness of God? In times of distress and pain, do you ever wonder where God is in all of this? Questions come to every child of God at some time in his or her life. It is part of life. You may handle personal issues well and never flinch, but when it happens to your child or loved one, that is the moment the mind begins to race with questions.

I have heard the expression more than once: "In the midst of all the difficulty, God has been faithful." Amen, God is always faithful. The real issue is, are you faithful to God in every circumstance of life? How is your faithfulness?

Jeremiah wrote the book of Lamentations as a lament, an expression of mourning over the judgment that had fallen on God's people and Jerusalem. The people were taken into captivity, and the city lay in ruins. However, in the midst of what appeared to be the worst thing possible, Jeremiah states God is faithful.

Seeing and knowing the faithfulness of God amidst the mess of one's life is amazing, but it is possible. You are never promised a life of ease and comfort. You are promised, as a child of God that you never have to face life alone. As you abide in Christ, He will see you through. Abiding day in and day out is the key.

Many of God's people in Jerusalem in that day were not abiding. It was their sin that brought about the destruction and captivity. Still, God is faithful. God is on the throne and in control of everything. When life gets messy, are you faithful to your God? He is always faithful. His Word is always true, and His mercies are new every morning.

Faithfulness is seen in a life that flows with obedience and passion for the Lord. Are you obedient in the little things? Are you passionate about the Lord Jesus Christ, or are you more passionate about social media?

God is faithful. Hallelujah!

Prayer and Praise:

Lord, You are my God and King. Thank You for Your faithfulness, even when I struggle to be faithful to You, You are always faithful. I praise You. In the mighty name of Jesus Christ, my Lord. Amen.

UNDER HIS SHADOW
Lamentations 4:20

Does the thought of being under the shadow of God excite you? Does it cause you to realize the closeness of relationship it requires to be under the shadow of God?

"He who dwells in the secret place of the Most High shall abide under the shadow of the Almighty" (Psalm 91:1). The secret to being under the cover of Almighty God is abiding. When you cultivate a life of dependency on Christ's life within you, then that is abiding.

The life of dependency is deepened by growth in prayer and saturation in the Word of God. That is the "human" factor. That is your responsibility. If you fail in the responsibility, you forfeit the covering that comes with close abiding.

Under the shadow of God is the place of security. It is the place of protection. Under the shadow of God is a place of submission and rest. Under the shadow of God is abiding in Him, but you must choose this place daily.

Under His shadow is not a place you arrive at in a worship service. It is a place of daily remaining in Him. You must first have this conviction that you cannot live the Christian life successfully in any other way. When His shadow covers you, you know Him and you rest in Him.

Prayer and Praise:

Lord, I praise You that You allow me to come into Your presence and dwell with You. Thank You for the covering You give to me. Let me live daily, dwelling in You. In the mighty name of Jesus Christ, my Lord. Amen.

AMONG THE CAPTIVES
Ezekiel 1:1

Ezekiel had a glorious vision of God and the end result was remarkable. Most people would like to have this experience, but they do not understand what is required of them. What was it that preceded this vision with Ezekiel? Ezekiel had to get honest about where he was and the condition he was in. Where was he? He was among the captives of God's people.

Many times you want God to move in your life, but you have not gotten honest about your situation. You have not gotten honest about what it is that holds you captive. Many people are captive to drugs and alcohol; those are easily identified. Others are in captivity to relationships, to people, and the fear of man fills their lives. Others are captivated by material things and modern technology. The question is, to what are you in captivity? What is it that controls and consumes your life?

Until a person answers that question, he will go no further with God. Ezekiel got honest. What will it take for you to get honest with yourself and also with the Lord? Once Ezekiel got honest, he had a vision, and God's Word came to Ezekiel (v. 3). Do you want to hear God speak? If so you must get honest. Honesty positions a person to be able to hear God.

Ezekiel not only heard God speak, but also, the hand of the Lord was upon him (v. 3). What does that mean? Ezekiel was captured by the Lord. Do you desire to be captured by the Lord? It all begins with becoming honest with God.

Ezekiel encountered God and he had a vision. Do you want to encounter God? Ezekiel heard God speak; he knew expressly the word of the Lord for himself. That is how faith comes—by the word of the Lord. Ezekiel's faith increased. Do you want your faith to increase? Ezekiel was captured by the Lord; the hand of God was upon him. When the hand of the Lord is upon a person, great things happen. God's will is accomplished. Do you desire God's will to flow through your life unhindered? Where does it all begin? Get honest with God about your condition, your hang-ups and your sin.

When you read the last verse of this chapter, you see Ezekiel heard the voice of God. Is that not a blessing? What a powerful encourager, hearing God speak time and time again. It all starts with admitting where you are.

Prayer and Praise:

Lord, You are awesome. Let me always be honest with You, myself, and others. In the mighty name of Jesus Christ, my Lord. Amen.

THE REMNANT
Ezekiel 6:8

If you know the Lord and have a meaningful relationship with Him based on submission and obedience, you are well aware that the church is living in difficult days. Of course, days have always been difficult for the body of Christ. Jesus told and warned of persecution, opposition, and suffering for His sake. In the United States these things tend to take the church by surprise.

Even when things are hard, God always has a remnant of true believers. Testing and trials prove the genuineness of one's faith or the lack of true faith. The point is God always has a remnant.

A remnant can imply many things. You can have a remnant of cloth, just a little bit left over from making a quilt. You can have a remnant of food left over from a meal. You can have a remnant of supplies, that which has not been sold or used. The remnant is that small amount that is left. God always has His remnant, the small number of true believers who will be faithful regardless of the cost. Are you part of God's remnant?

No matter how bleak things may appear, God is still on His throne, and He still has His people. Churches may compromise the Word of God and the message; God still has His faithful ones. The remnant will remain. They will endure and they will be loyal to Christ. Are you remaining loyal to the lordship of Jesus Christ, or does your loyalty fluctuate?

God has promised a remnant in Ezekiel 6. What can a remnant do? They offer the present generation and the future generation a true witness of Jesus Christ. The remnant works as an influencing agent toward others for the kingdom of God. Praise God for the remnant.

Prayer and Praise:

Lord, make me a part of Your remnant. Let me be faithful amidst difficulties and opposition. Let me be an influencing agent for Your kingdom, for this generation and the next. In the mighty name of Jesus Christ, my Lord. Amen.

THE GLORY OF THE LORD
Ezekiel 8:4

The situation in Jerusalem was bleak. The people of God were committing great abominations against the Lord, yet the Lord's glory still lingered. Why? Why would God still stay close to a people caught up in idolatry and sin? Because these were His people and He had great love for them. However, even God's patience wears thin.

Do you realize how dependent you are on God? As a Christian, your very life is to flow from the leading of the Holy Spirit. You are to abide daily, and walk in agreement with Christ. He is to be your passion. When that is real in you, you have great assurance.

Does this mean you will not face difficulties or challenges? No. Ezekiel was faithful to the Lord, and he lived in the midst of a people who were unfaithful. You will face difficulties sometimes because of the sin of others who resist the Lord. Many people fail to realize willful sin is a barrier to God's glory.

God's glory is His essence; it is the weightiness of God. Only those who live unto His honor and majesty are able to bear this weight. When sin abounds in a believer or a church, the very thing you desire, the glory of God manifested, is withdrawn.

Ezekiel, once again captured by the Lord, is allowed to see the condition of the people, and God tells him the consequences of their sin. It must have been a sad day to realize people he knew and associated with had so pushed back the hand of God that they would not know God's glory.

The same principle holds true today. You cannot control your fellow man or church member, but you do determine your own course of life. You decide whether you will be faithful to God, even when others are not. You determine by your passion for and obedience to God your usefulness and the acceptableness of your worship. Be faithful; God is worthy.

Prayer and Praise:

Lord, teach me the importance of being faithful, even when others are not. Show me Your glory and empower me for service. Capture me for You. In the mighty name of Jesus Christ, my Lord. Amen.

THE GLORY DEPARTED
Ezekiel 10:18

The words, "then the glory of the Lord departed," may be some of the saddest words in the Bible. Yet many people seem to live, act, and think this could not happen today with the church, but they are wrong.

There were four distinct stages of the glory of God's departing. In Ezekiel 10:4, the glory went up and paused over the threshold of the temple. In Ezekiel 10:18, the glory departed from the threshold and stood over the cherubim. Ezekiel 10:19, the cherubim, with the glory overhead, went up and stood by the door. Ezekiel 11:23, the glory left the city and to the mountain on the east side, the glory of God departed, and only Ezekiel recognized this.

The Revelation chapter 2 tells the story of the church of Ephesus. This was a seemingly good church, a really good church. They were a church that was doctrinally correct, were hard working, and they refused to tolerate false teachers or teachings.

The charge that Christ brought against them was they had left their first love. They had not lost their first love, they left it. They were told if they did not repent and do the first works, loving Christ first and foremost, God would remove their lampstand from their midst.

A lampstand gives light, or illumination, for direction and guidance. A lampstand can give off warmth to those closes by. This lampstand is what makes a church a church; it is the presence of Almighty God in their midst.

To have your lampstand removed is the same as the glory departing. You can still meet, sing, pray, and preach, but if God is not in your midst, all is vain. Ezekiel saw the glory, and he knew the glory was lingering even as Judah was forsaking God. Finally, God withdrew Himself, and the glory began to depart from the people of God and the place of God.

Whatever it requires of you, seek God's glory. Whatever it requires of you, do not be guilty of allowing the glory to depart while you are capable of obeying the Lord. Guard your life. Make sure you are not drifting with the world. God's glory is crucial.

Prayer and Praise:

Lord, I long for Your glory to be manifest and real in me and in my church. Show me how to protect the glory. In the mighty name of Jesus Christ, my Lord. Amen.

SETTING UP IDOLS IN YOUR HEART
Ezekiel 14:3

Do you know what an idol is? Often, an idol is thought of as an inanimate object of stone, wood, or metal that a person sets up, and they act as if that is God. You have read the stories of the Bible and remember the golden calf in Exodus. You remember Dagon in the book of Judges and possibly other false idols.

How do you set up an idol in your heart, and what are the consequences of such an act? An idol in your heart is anything you cherish more than Jesus Christ. It could be your spouse or your children. Countless people make their children their god. They serve their children, they do everything to make their children happy, and their children completely consume their lives; therefore, God is pushed aside.

Yes, you are to love your children and provide for them, but you are not to worship them, nor are you to compromise Scripture because of them. Idols can come in many forms and fashions. It is about what you give your heart to, and whom you give your heart to. It is about what you pursue or whom you pursue. Idolatry is a terrible, grievous sin.

Have you set up any idols in your heart? Ezekiel tells you your idols are what cause you to stumble into iniquity. Iniquity is sin and carries the idea of being perverse, crooked, or twisted. It is a breaking away from authority.

The consequence of having set up an idol in your heart is that God will not speak to you. He will answer you according to the multitude of your idols. In other words, "Let your idols answer you." That is a scary place to be.

What is God's solution for idols of the heart? Repent and turn your face away from your abomination. An abomination is something detestable to God. God is saying repent or ruin; it is your choice. The best way is to never set up idols in your heart. Stay close and clean before the Lord Jesus Christ, and let nothing rival your loyalty, alliance, and love for Him.

Prayer and Praise:

Lord, show me any idols in my heart. Expose to me anything in my life that is close to becoming an idol that competes with You, and let me repent. In the mighty name of Jesus Christ, my Lord. Amen.

THE SIN OF SODOM
Ezekiel 16:49-50

When one hears the word Sodom, he might automatically think about Sodom from the book of Genesis. You may remember two angels of God who came to warn Lot and his family to flee the wicked city. Next, you remember God destroyed those cities with fire and brimstone. As Lot's wife fled from there, she longingly looked back, and instantly the judgment of God fell on her, turning her into a pillar of salt.

The conversation Abraham had with the Lord in Genesis 18 had warned of the destruction, because of the wickedness of Sodom. What was the wickedness? Ezekiel tells exactly what their sin was. Knowing the result of such sin should compel you to strive to walk in holiness.

The sin of Sodom was six fold. They had the sin of: (1) pride, (2) fullness of bread, which means they had plenty of food and provisions, (3) idle time, or time wasted, (4) failure to help the poor and needy, (5) haughty, or arrogant, and (6) morally repulsive; they committed abominations, a reference to the blatant homosexuality.

Does this list concern you as you look at the United States of America? It should. It should disturb any Christian as he compares the United States and Sodom. Someone once said, "If God does not judge the USA, He will have to apologize to Sodom." Be aware that God will never owe anyone an apology.

Prayer and Praise:

Lord, You are my God, and I exalt You. Teach me to come before You in true intercession for my country, just as Abraham did for Sodom. Teach me to flee if You say flee. In the mighty name of Jesus Christ, my Lord. Amen.

SEPTEMBER

WHEN A NATION TURNS FROM GOD
Ezekiel 20

This is a sad chapter, but after seeing the sin of Sodom in the previous chapter, it is a necessary chapter. A person, a church, a community, or a country cannot sin and get away with it. Once the full measure of sin has been reached, God will send judgment.

How does judgment come on a people? There are several characteristics, but Ezekiel 20 gives seven consequences when a nation turns from God.

1. The Sabbath is desecrated and secularized. This is seen in verses 16, 21 and 24.

2. The commands of God are rejected. This is seen in verses 13, 21, and 24.

3. The nation's children are sacrificed for gain or greed. This is seen in verse 26.

4. The remaining generation questions God's authority. This is seen in verses 3 and 8.

5. The people become materialistic and full of unbelief. This is seen in verse 32.

6. The Lord's name is disgraced and profaned. This is seen in verses 9, 14, 22, 39.

7. The people suffer psychological disorders. This is seen in verses 31 and 43.

Are there any of those you do not see taking place in the United States right this minute? Do you know people who suffer psychologically? How many children are aborted daily? What happened to no one shopping on Sundays?

This country is right in the middle of the consequences of their sin, as you read this. What should you do? Cry out to God for mercy. Witness to your lost friends and family and tell them the time is short. Stay faithful to the Lord.

Prayer and Praise:

Lord, this land, my country, is experiencing every consequence listed in Ezekiel 20. Father, show me daily how to intercede for this land. Show me daily to whom I should witness and share. Let me not get so distracted with this world that I fail to warn them. In the mighty name of Jesus Christ, my Lord. Amen.

STAND IN THE GAP
Ezekiel 22:30

Standing in the gap—what does that mean? Ezekiel is repeating the words that God spoke trying to convey the seriousness of the time. The people of God had strayed, and they knew they had gone astray. The land and the people were not clean.

There was a conspiracy among the prophets (Ezekiel 22:25), and the priest had violated God's law and profaned the holy things. They were making no difference between the clean and the unclean (Ezekiel 22:26). The leaders were like wolves and destroying the people (Ezekiel 22:27), and the people were oppressing and mistreating others (Ezekiel 22:29).

In the midst of this mess, a call was issued for a man to stand in the gap and build up the wall. He was asking for a person to come and put a stop to the open access of sin that was taking place, but he found no one to respond.

How about you? Will you stand in the gap and build up the wall? Will you intercede on behalf of your community and country for the flow of sin to stop? Sin flowing from the prophet to the priest to the prince of the land; will you stand in the gap?

How much time do you spend in prayer for your community? How much time do you spend in prayer for the United States? Do you call out to the Lord on behalf of your county or city mayor? Do you pray for the president? Do you intercede for senators and congressmen? How often do you pray for the Supreme Court judges?

Standing in the gap is a lonely place, but someone has to do this. Will you be the man or woman, or will God still find no one?

Prayer and Praise:

Lord, teach me to stand in the gap for my land and people. Burden my heart to obey You in prayer. In the mighty name of Jesus Christ, my Lord. Amen.

I AM AGAINST YOU
Ezekiel 26:3

Have you ever considered what it would be like if God was against you? In the text, God says to the people of Tyre, "I am against you." Then He pronounced judgment and doom upon her. It is a frightening thing to live in such a fashion for God to set Himself against you. The consequences are devastating.

How does a person or a country come to the place where God is against them? It happens because of pride. You saw in Ezekiel 16 that one of the sins of Sodom was her pride. Pride is still alive and well. The New Testament book of James 4:6 tells you, "God resists the proud but gives grace to the humble."

Are you a proud person? The United States is a proud nation. As you saw in Ezekiel 20, it is a consequence of a nation turning from God. God opposes the proud. God stands against the proud. However, God gives grace to the humble. That is comforting.

How do you go from being proud to humble? You submit to God. In submitting to God, you get your life in line or agreement with His Word. Do you make adjustments of your life to Scripture? When did you last do this? What did you do?

Are you adjusted to God in your consistent attendance to church, tithing, reading the Bible, and witnessing? Is your attitude adjusted to God, or do you hold bitterness toward another? Do not cause the Lord to turn against you; humble yourself before Him. If a life does not flow with obedience to God, then the appearance of humility is false.

Prayer and Praise:

Lord, You are the only God, and I submit myself to You. I seek You and ask You to lift me up for Your glory. Teach me to walk in humility day by day. In the mighty name of Jesus Christ, my Lord. Amen.

THE ANOINTED CHERUB
Ezekiel 28:14

It is hard to grasp that Satan was the anointed cherub who protected the glory of God. It is difficult to imagine how an angelic being could allow his heart to be lifted up with pride and want the glory of God for himself. That is exactly what you find in this section of Scripture.

Satan was positioned higher than the other angels, but he fell to the lowest pit. How? Iniquity—sin was found in him. Angels are created beings that have the seal of perfection, but angels have a free will just as you do, and they are capable of sin. Satan allowed his heart to be lifted with pride. His wisdom was corrupted and God cast him to the ground.

Angels have no hope of redemption. Unlike man, angels reside in the presence of the Father in heaven and are ministering spirits He sends forth to help believers. Since creation, they have ministered to God's people, never drawing attention to themselves.

Satan, as all the angels, was created in a perfect environment, not having a sin nature as man does, but he deliberately allowed sin to enter in. This should cause every believer to take notice of the seriousness of pride.

When Satan sinned, a third of the angelic host sinned with him. Demons are fallen angels who desire your destruction. The New Testament tells that demons come as angels of light to deceive. Be warned, everything that appears as light is not the true light of God.

You need not fear the demonic, as long as you abide in the secret place of the Most High, as long as you are covered by His shadow. This means you stay very close to God and always realize the potential corruption pride brings.

Prayer and Praise:

Lord, I have never known perfection as an angel, but I do know Your righteousness, and I ask You to keep me close and clean. Show me any area of pride that has attached to me so I can repent of this terrible sin. In the mighty name of Jesus Christ, my Lord. Amen.

WATCHMAN ON THE WALL
Ezekiel 33:6

Do you understand what is meant when you are called a watchman on the wall? A watchman was a guard that stood his post and gave warning of anything suspicious or of an enemy attack. He was to be in his position of responsibility and fulfilling this role. If he failed, it could mean devastation for the people.

If the watchman failed to sound the alarm and warn the people of the city, the watchman was responsible for the lives lost. If the watchman warned the people and the people ignored the warning, the watchman was not responsible for lost lives.

Is warning people fun? Some will say yes, but it is a difficult assignment to be the bearer of impending doom and judgment. As difficult as it is, it must be done. You do not take the responsibility because it is fun; you have been given this responsibility because it is necessary and crucially important.

The context of this passage is warning the people of God of attacks of the enemy and warning lost people of dying without a true relationship with God. A Christian brother shared the story of being in another country and trying to get a deathly sick man to the hospital before he died. They got the man there, left him for the night, and returned the next day only to find that the man died a few hours after arriving. The man said all he could think about was that he failed to witness and share Christ with a dying man, and time ran out.

Do you enjoy when your pastor preaches warnings of God's judgment? Most do not. They say he is being too negative. The truth is he is being the watchman on the wall, trying to save souls and protect the saints. It can be a thankless task, but it still has to be done.

You are a watchman. Are you in your position of responsibility? Are you in your place of accountability? Are you interceding consistently for those under your watch? Be warned; to fail here places their blood on you. Show up, stand up, and speak up for the truth of God.

Prayer and Praise:

Lord, You have called me to the responsibility of watchman. Keep me awake while I am on the wall, and give me clear vision of everything taking place. Let me not fail in my responsibility. In the mighty name of Jesus Christ, my Lord. Amen.

I WILL PUT MY SPIRIT WITHIN YOU
Ezekiel 36:26

This promise is incredible. God so wants you to live for His glory and honor, He promises to give you the Holy Spirit, so you will be enabled to do so. He promises to remove the hard, indifferent heart and place His Spirit inside of you. Hallelujah!

Do you not find that exciting? Does that not stir you to want to live and please God? The great love God has for you, for His people are beyond earthly words to express. He not only saves, but also He seals and secures you. He sanctifies you and cleanses you. He puts His Spirit inside of you, so that you are never alone, never without the resources of God. Amen!

Your responsibility is to live and walk in agreement with the Holy Spirit. You are not to grieve, quench, or resist His Spirit's working or leading. As you walk in the Spirit, you will not fulfill the lust of the flesh. You can overcome anything.

Prayer and Praise:

Lord, thank You for the promise of the Holy Spirit. The Holy Spirit is the gift that enables me to live for Your glory and not my own. Keep me sensitive to the Holy Spirit, and let me yield to the Spirit's leading. In the mighty name of Jesus Christ, my Lord. Amen.

VALLEY OF DRY BONES
Ezekiel 37:1-3

Have you been faithful to what God has called you to do? Have you been faithful to share His Word even when it is not popular? Have you been faithful to perform every act God has told you to? Ezekiel was such a man.

God had put Ezekiel through a variety of tests, all for the purpose of proving Ezekiel would be faithful, even if he stood alone. Ezekiel passed the test. Now, God took Ezekiel to another strange place. He took him to a valley of death, a valley of dry, sun-bleached bones. It was in this place of death that God asked Ezekiel a question.

God was not asking because He did not know the answer. God was asking this question to see Ezekiel's response. Would it be a response of faith or doubt? It is amazing throughout this book that God spoke to Ezekiel countless times, and Ezekiel only spoke one time to God. The time he spoke is in this chapter.

That should teach you that listening to God is far more important than telling Him things. What possibly could you say to God that He does not already know? Prayer is a two-way communication between man and God. In those times when you speak to God, it should be in expressions of praise, dependency, and seeking direction. However, God knows everything and He does not need a person telling Him how to handle the affairs of this life.

"Can these bones live?" What would you say? Today, many people live in the valley of death and decay, and God wants to hear their reply. How you reply tells your faith or your faithlessness. Ezekiel replied, "Lord God, You know." That was a safe answer.

God told Ezekiel to preach to dry bones. You know the rest of the story. God sent life. Do you want to minister life, resurrection life, to dead lives? If you do, you have to rub shoulders with dead people. Are you willing to do that, or do you want to be in a "lively" situation?

Be faithful to the call, be faithful to the Word of God, be faithful to the Lord, and preach life to people who are spiritually dead.

Prayer and Praise:

Lord, You are my God, and I exalt You. Teach me to daily be listening to Your voice and following You. Show me the words to speak that will minister life. In the mighty name of Jesus Christ, my Lord. Amen.

INTO THE SANCTUARY
Ezekiel 41:1

The context of this verse begins in chapter forty, when God once again places His hand on Ezekiel and captures him. His hand is upon Ezekiel, and He takes Ezekiel back to the holy city and to the temple. Then He brings Ezekiel into the sanctuary, the holy place of the temple. Do you realize that the holy place, the sanctuary of God, cannot be reached by human efforts or strength?

Every child of God needs someone to take them there. Yes, you can seek God and be yielded to the Lord, but to get to the holy place, the sanctuary of God, is beyond human ability to attain. You need the Holy Spirit to capture you and bring you into the place of God.

Have you been captured by the Lord? Has God so gripped your life that all you desire is to walk in obedience to Him and please Him? Have you adjusted the stewardship of your life to the Word of God? Or does the world still consume you? Do you spend wasted hours, or just minutes on social media ignoring the working and moving of the Holy Spirit?

In order to be captured, you must surrender. Have you surrendered your all to Christ? Is His will and Word your passion? If not, cry out to the Father now and surrender, and ask Him to capture you for His glory.

This is not an emotional appeal or a way to manipulate God to do certain things for you. This is an appeal to bow before the lordship of Christ and surrender all, saying, "Your will be done."

Why does God bring you to the holy place, the sanctuary? So you can worship Him. So you can lie before Him, prostrate on the floor and know Him in your submission. The Lord knows when you go back into the world, you will need supernatural strength to maintain such surrender. It is in the sanctuary that God supernaturally empowers you, the Holy Spirit consumes you.

Prayer and Praise:

Lord, capture me for Your glory. Teach me how to surrender day by day. Show me any strongholds of resistance that keep me from absolute surrender. In the mighty name of Jesus Christ, my Lord. Amen.

THE GLORY RETURNED
Ezekiel 43:1-5

You saw the glory depart in Ezekiel 11. Here you see the glory return. It returned after the people of God were restored in chapter 37. That is a wonderful word from God. Even now, though times get bleak and the church seems to struggle, even losing the glory of the Father, there is still a promise that God's glory will return. Hallelujah!

Are times difficult in your life? Are oppositions mounting? Do you feel as if you are the only one at your workplace that strives to live for the Lord? Do not despair. God may remove His conscious presence for a time, but the glory can return.

Oftentimes in life you will be tested. Your faith will be tested. Your obedience will be tested. Your steadfastness and perseverance will be tested. It is part of the Christian experience. Will you pass the test? Will you continue in faith, even when you have no feelings or excitement? Do not quit, help is on the way. God will move in your life if you hold on to Him in faith.

Everything Ezekiel went through had been to bring him and the people of God, to the place where God's glory was manifested among them again. This is good news. God's glory returns when the conditions are met. Praise His name.

Prayer and Praise:

Lord, You are the living God, and I magnify Your name. Teach me to be faithful in times I do not sense You. Enable me to trust You day in and day out. Let Your glory return among Your people. In the mighty name of Jesus Christ, my Lord. Amen.

THE WATER FLOWS
Ezekiel 47:1-8

As you read this section of Scripture, you see water flowing—holy water flowing from the house of the Lord. As the water flowed, it was measured ankle-deep and then knee-deep. Then the water came to his waist, and finally, it became a river one could swim in.

There is a deepening work of God. Is this depth real in your life? Do you see, realize and experience the deepening work of God? There is nothing more important than for a child of God to experience the seasons of refreshing that God wants to pour out.

As you continue reading this chapter, you see the place the river flows is a place of growth. You find fish in abundance, fruit trees, and health. Do you know this in your spiritual life? Is God so flowing through you that you are spiritually healthy? Are you equipped and prepared for service? Is your life bearing fruit?

To know this deepening work of God, you must be positioned by the river of life and your roots run deep into the soil, drawing your resource from the Father.

Prayer and Praise:

Lord, take me into the deep waters where my feet cannot touch the bottom. Teach me to swim in Your river of grace and hope. In the mighty name of Jesus Christ, my Lord. Amen.

STANDING ALONE
Daniel 1:8-9

Have you ever considered the stress and pain Daniel was enduring at this time? He was a mere teenager forcibly removed from everyone he knew, loved, and cared for. He was taken to a strange city which held different values and standards than he did. Daniel was alone in a city of pagan idolatry.

There were other Hebrew young men present, but Daniel was alone because his family support system was gone. Now he would make choices and decisions for which he would assume full responsibility. Have you realized that each person faces that moment in life? It may not be as radical as Daniel's moment, but each person will face this time.

How do you stand when it comes to standing by yourself? Standing with no parents or family to rely on, or to whom to give an account? Will you stand for Christ when you are all alone and no one is there to support your decision, or to tell your family what you have done?

It is simpler to be Christian when others are encouraging you, and you have accountability to them. When no one knows or cares about you and your faith, what will you do then? When you cannot do it in a group, what will you do?

This land desperately needs young men and women to learn to stand for Christ, especially when alone, and it is not popular. This land needs older adults to stand for Christ and live by faith in the Son of God and the Word of God, especially when others refuse.

The key to doing this is found in verse eight, "Daniel purposed in his heart that he would not defile himself with the king's delicacies"—with the world's things. Have you made that commitment? Have you chosen consciously not to defile yourself with the ways and cares of the world? Until you do, you will never stand for Christ when you are alone.

When Daniel made this decision, the other three Hebrew boys were enabled in their faith to make the same decision. Your obedience encourages others to obey. You learn to stand alone by being faithful and obedient in the little things. For Daniel, he refused to eat food not permissible for a Jew to eat. Once you are faithful in the little things, your faith increases so you can be faithful in bigger issues of life.

Prayer and Praise:

Lord, thank You for allowing little things to test me before the major issues of life challenge me. Let me be faithful in little, so that I can be faithful in much. Show me the bigger picture of my faith and obedience. In the mighty name of Jesus Christ, my Lord. Amen.

THE LION'S DEN
Daniel 6:10-23

This is one of the favorite stories you learn in church and Sunday school as a child. It has all the excitement and intrigue of a modern-day movie. Have you ever stopped to consider the fact that this type of betrayal still takes place today? Many faithful Christians have been betrayed by friends, even family, because of their stance on the Bible and for Jesus Christ.

No, it may not be a literal lion's den, but many have been faced with lions trying to devour and destroy them. The Devil is referred to in Scripture as a "roaring lion" (1 Peter 5:8). In Psalm 91, as you dwell in the secret place with God, you are promised the enabling of Almighty God to "tread upon the lion and the cobra." You can overcome. Hallelujah!

Daniel was in the lion's den but the lions could do him no harm. Why? Daniel was a man of faith, prayer, and obedience. He would not compromise his walk with the Lord to please a man. Do you live to please men, or do you live to please the Lord?

When lions are roaming, your one responsibility is to look up to the Lord Jesus Christ. If you watch the lions, they will consume you. They will consume your thoughts, your attention, and your strength, all of which makes you more vulnerable to them. Your eyes must stay on Christ. It is an act of faith to focus on Christ while lions are on the prowl.

Prayer and Praise:

Lord, lions seem to be abounding. They are coming from the most unexpected places, but they are roaming. Teach me to focus on You and not the lions. Enable me to look up every day. In the mighty name of Jesus Christ, my Lord. Amen.

SETTING MY FACE TO PRAY
Daniel 9:3-5

Have you ever been reading the Bible and God shows you something you have never seen before? He shows you something you have never understood before? It is an amazing experience when God speaks personally to you with His Word. The Lord gives you revelation knowledge. That is exciting!

That is what happened with Daniel in this text. Daniel was reading (the prophet Jeremiah) and he said, "I understood by books the number of the years." He understood through Jeremiah's scroll that the people of God would be in Babylonian captivity for seventy years. Because Daniel now understood, it impacted his prayer life.

Do you realize that whenever God speaks to you it will inevitably impact your prayer life? When Daniel understood the Word of God, he set his face to pray. He began further seeking God in prayer, with fasting and in brokenness (sackcloth and ashes).

What did he pray? He made honest confession of the greatness and awesomeness of God. He confessed his sin and the sin of the people. He used the pronoun "we," thus identifying himself with the people. He was taking responsibility for sin. Do you take responsibility for the sin of God's people?

He confessed that they had failed to listen and heed the words of the prophets. Do you take heed to the preached word that you hear every week? He acknowledged that was why the children of Israel experienced confusion. Have you made that connection in your life or the life of your church?

Daniel prays, "...our God, hear the prayer of Your servant, and his supplications, and for the Lord's sake cause Your face to shine on Your sanctuary, which is desolate..." It was for God's glory he prayed, but it started when he set his face to pray. Do you need to set your face to pray?

Prayer and Praise:

Lord, let me set my face to pray. Teach me how to pray. I know how to say my prayers, but teach me how to pray. In the mighty name of Jesus Christ, my Lord. Amen.

PRAYING THROUGH
Daniel 10:1-3, 12

Are you familiar with the phrase "praying through?" The phrase means to continue praying until you have prayed through to the answer. You do not stop until the prayer burden is lifted and you have the answer, whether it is evidenced physically or confirmed in your spirit that you have received it, even before it has happened.

Praying through is a type of spiritual discipline which true intercessors understand. John Wesley said, "God does nothing but in answer to prayer." Daniel prayed through. He prayed and fasted for three weeks, and the answer came. Do you combine fasting with your prayers?

The Scripture tells that Daniel's prayer was heard the first day he began the intercession. Immediately, God dispatched a messenger (angel) with the answer. However, the heavenly messenger was interrupted by an evil spirit (the ruler of Persia). The struggle ensued for twenty-one days.

In those twenty-one days, if Daniel had grown weary and stopped praying, stopped the intercession, he would have missed the answer. You must be persistent in prayer. Persistence is not needed to persuade God, but to overcome the opposition. Are you persistent in prayer?

Can you recall a time you were praying about a matter and you never got an answer? Did you detract with other "good" things and fail to pray through? Did you fast as you prayed? Have you ever recognized the enemy trying to keep God's answer from you?

Praying through is not a sweet and nice little prayer experience. It is a time you continue to press in to the Father, even when you have prayed for days, weeks, or months and you still have no answer, but the burden has not been lifted. Do not stop and miss God's answer or God's blessing. Persist in prayer.

Prayer and Praise:

Lord, thank You for the privilege of prayer. Thank You for allowing me to share Your prayer burden. Father, teach me to pray and not to quit. Show me when I am to fast for specific needs. Enable me to continue until I pray through. In the mighty name of Jesus Christ, my Lord. Amen.

GOMER
Hosea 1:1-3

Hosea was a prophet of God who received a difficult command from God. God told the prophet, this man of God, to marry a lady named Gomer. The difficulty was that Gomer was a prostitute. How do you marry the clean with the unclean? How do you bring together the holy and the unholy? How can a man of God marry such a woman? The answer is simple: because God said so.

Why would God command such a thing? God was going to use this marriage as a living illustration and example of how Holy God and Israel have been wed. This was to show how Israel had committed spiritual adultery against the Lord, and the Lord still loved her.

When a spouse is not faithful to his or her mate, great pain is the result. When God's people forsake Him and go after other things to fill their lives, God is hurt, He is grieved. Hosea was grieved and hurt because his bride, Gomer, continued in prostitution after they were married. Hosea loved Gomer, just as God loved Israel and loves you.

Hosea went to an auction block, and he paid the price for his own wife to be brought back to him. Does that sound like the Lord's love He has demonstrated toward you? He came down to where you live, He saw the sin you lived in, and He still loved you enough to purchase you. Hallelujah!

What love God has for His children! He had so much love that He paid the ultimate price with Jesus dying on Calvary to pay your sin debt. Even when you willfully stray away from God, He still loves you and seeks to bring you back. What a Savior!

God told Hosea to do something that did not make sense—marry a prostitute. He may tell you something that does not make human sense. You are to live by God's revelation and not human logic. If God does tell you to do something that does not make human sense, be aware it is for a greater purpose than your comfort.

Prayer and Praise:

Lord, whatever You want me to do is what I want to do. Teach me to live by divine revelation and not human reason. In the mighty name of Jesus Christ, my Lord. Amen.

LACK OF KNOWLEDGE
Hosea 4:6

Most people are aware of areas of their lives where they lack knowledge. You may not have the knowledge to work on a broken car, fix faulty plumbing, or build a house. However, when Hosea tells you that "people are destroyed for the lack of knowledge," he is not referring to worldly knowledge. In fact, he goes on to say they "rejected knowledge."

They made a conscious decision to reject the knowledge that would give them life, hope, and a future. What did they reject? They rejected the word of God. Have you received the Word of God in your life? Have you made adjustments to your life based on the Word of God? Are you daily adjusting your life to Christ, the living Word?

In Jeremiah 3:14-15, you find these words, "Return, O backsliding children, says the Lord; for I am married to you ... and I will bring you to Zion. And I will give you shepherds according to My heart, who will feed you with knowledge and understanding."

What a promise. God will feed you knowledge and understanding by His shepherds. Your pastor is an important part of your life. He has a responsibility to feed you the truth of God. That is his main responsibility. Sadly, many a pastor is sidetracked and distracted with trivial concerns.

In Exodus18:19-20, the main responsibility of spiritual leadership is told: prayer and intercession and teaching and preaching God's truth. In Acts 6:4, the apostles stated they would give themselves to prayer and the ministry of the Word of God. That is the main two-fold responsibility of the pastor.

If the pastor is so consumed with other things, and prayer and ministry of the Word is pushed back and not the primary ministry, everyone suffers. Lack of knowledge is a direct result of pastors failing to feed the people knowledge and understanding.

How are the other responsibilities and tasks to be accomplished? By godly lay men and women who understand the Word of God and take up the mantle of service.

Do you want to be fed knowledge? Do you want to understand? Undergird your pastor, pray for him for fresh revelation and anointing. Make yourself available to serve.

Prayer and Praise:

Lord, teach me Your truth. Feed me Your Word and give me knowledge and understanding. Be with my pastor and give him a fresh release of Your Spirit as he studies and proclaims Your Word. In the mighty name of Jesus Christ, my Lord. Amen.

SOWING THE WIND
Hosea 8:7

Sowing to the wind is a phrase you do not hear very often; you may have never heard it. To sow to the wind means to sow nothing. When people depend upon a harvest to sustain their life, they must first plant the seed. If they plant nothing, they are sowing to the wind, and they will not survive.

What are you sowing? Are you sowing seeds of righteousness and obedience to the Lord? Are you sowing merely good intentions, but you never seem to get around to obedience? In the New Testament you find the following words, "Do not be deceived, God is not mocked; for whatever a man sows, that he will also reap. For he who sows to his flesh will of the flesh reap corruption, but he who sows to the Spirit will of the Spirit reap everlasting life" (Galatians 6:7-8).

The law of sowing is a basic principle of life. You sow and you reap. Whatever you sow, you normally reap more than you sowed. If you sow a life of complacency and apathy that will be what you reap. If you sow indifference to the things of God, that is what you will reap. If you sow nothing but the wind you will reap emptiness, want, and lack.

You can sow to the glory of God. You can sow faith and truth. You can sow obedience and love. You can sow a heart of worship and praise. You can sow hunger for the things of God. In order to sow to the glory of God, you have to intentionally seek the things of God. Good intentions are of no value. There must be follow-through.

Prayer and Praise:

Lord, teach me not to sow to the wind. Teach me to realize daily that I will reap what I sow. Let me sow to Your glory. In the mighty name of Jesus Christ, my Lord. Amen.

BREAKING UP FALLOW GROUND
Hosea 10:12

This is one of the strongest verses in the Bible. It is a command to the people of God. To the church God is saying, "Get ready! You have a part to play, a responsibility to fulfill so that God to move in power on your life and church."

Yesterday, you saw the warning of sowing to the wind. Today, you have the command of sowing righteousness. Righteousness is related to rightness. In this context, it is the rightness of God to be displayed in our lives. The righteousness of Jesus Christ has been afforded to the Christian at salvation. His righteousness became the Christian's righteousness. You are responsible to put it on daily. Paul wrote under the inspiration of the Holy Spirit to "put on the breastplate of righteousness" (Ephesians 6:14b).

Break up fallow ground. Do you know what fallow ground is? It is ground that was once productive and bore fruit, but has been left unattended and now is overgrown with weeds and vines. The ground has become hardened by lack of cultivation.

You are challenged to break up this soil, the soil of your heart. Place the plow in the dirt and begin the process of plowing the ground so it can receive the seed of the Word of God as it brings forth fruit.

When the plow hits a root or a rock, what will you do? Leave it and walk away, or remove it? It is easy to say, "Lord, use me." When the plow of the Word hits a hard place, what will you do then? You have to respond; you have to remove the hard place. That happens only as genuine biblical repentance comes forth from your life. Along with repentance must come restitution.

Then, as you have sought the Lord, He can come and rain righteousness on you. God will move on your behalf. Many people want God to move on their behalf without breaking up the fallow ground. According to Scripture, you must break up the fallow ground.

Prayer and Praise:

Lord, put the plow of Your Word deep in my life. Anything it strikes, let me remove it by faith and repentance. Rain your righteousness on me. In the mighty name of Jesus Christ, my Lord. Amen.

HEALING BACKSLIDING
Hosea 14:4

When you think about the word backsliding, probably a variety of thoughts come to your mind. Some think it means to lose one's salvation; it does not. Others believe it is to commit a serious sin. Still others will tell you it is to get out of God's will.

To be backslidden mean you once were here, but now you have gone backwards. A lost person has nothing to go back from, or they have nothing to relapse into, because they have always maintained the same lost condition. The most common concept of backsliding is when a Christian falls into some overt immorality. Such was the case with David and his adultery with Bathsheba. Truly this is backsliding, but it is not the only way to backslide.

A great amount of backsliding is done by Christian people who are not caught up in overt immorality, and they never leave the church. Proverbs 14:14, says, "The backslider in heart will be filled with his own ways...." The key is the phrase "in heart." Backsliding can be experienced by an outward activity, but most of the time it is expressed inwardly, where only the individual and God know about it.

Therefore, you can be backslidden and out of fellowship with God and only you and God know about it. You do not have to leave the church, stop going to Sunday school, stop giving regularly, and stop attending worship, but you can still be backslidden.

When a child of God becomes filled with his own ways and derives satisfaction from a certain type of behavior, his priorities are not right, and he is backslidden on God and needs to repent.

How is it with you? Are you filled with your own ways, or the ways of God? What is your heart's desire?

Prayer and Praise:

Lord, show me with what my life is filled? Show me what I derive my satisfaction from, and if it is not of You, enable me to turn from it. Let me find my satisfaction, joy, and purpose in You. In the mighty name of Jesus Christ, my Lord. Amen.

WEEPING PRIEST
Joel 2:17

What is it that makes you weep? Not cry, but weep. The difference in crying and weeping is travail of your heart. People cry out of joy, out of happiness, and yes, in sadness and grief. Weeping is this uncontrollable expression of emotion that comes because your heart and soul is so heavy with the burden. Why is it that you weep?

In this text, God has told His people to turn back to Him with all their hearts, to turn back to Him with fasting, weeping, and mourning. They were to rend their hearts and not their garments. They were to deal with the internal condition of their lives, not just go through the external motions.

Finally, He says, "Let the priests... weep between the porch and the altar." The spiritual leaders were to be so broken over the condition and need of the people that it should have broken their hearts with weeping before they got to the altar to offer sacrifice. The spiritual leaders should have been carrying such a burden, one that drove them to weeping.

When was the last time you were in a church service and your pastor wept? When was the last time you were in a church service and you wept? Has your pastor ever wept publically? Have you ever wept publically over the condition of the church?

This land, this country, needs men of God who know how to weep over the condition of the church. Your church needs men of God who are unconcerned about what others may think of them, and they weep over the condition of their church.

When was the last time your soul was that heavy? When was the last time you received the burden of the Lord, and you were broken to the point of weeping and wailing? If you have never wept as such, would now not be a good time to ask God to burden you in this fashion until you did weep?

Prayer and Praise:

Lord, I need a heaviness of soul over the condition of the church, Your church. I need brokenness in my life so I can weep and wail before You. Please, Father, let me weep before Your throne on behalf of Your people and do not let me stop until You restore us. In the mighty name of Jesus Christ, my Lord. Amen.

GOD REVEALS SECRETS
Amos 3:7

This verse of Scripture is a tremendous promise of comfort. It says, God will reveal His secrets to His servants, the prophets. God reveals His secrets. Hallelujah! That is exciting. God reveals. God gives revelation. Do you fully grasp what that means?

God's plan and His will are not like a green-striped Easter egg hidden in tall green grass. God reveals His will and plan. God shares His secrets. To whom does He share? God openly shares with His servants, the prophets. God shares with those who are men and women of God. Do you want God to reveal His truth, His Word to you? Do you want revelation knowledge? You must be a man of God.

Today, people listen to politicians. People pay attention to Wall Street and investors, but very few people seek truth. Christians tend to listen to the world more than to the Word of God. Yet God promises He will reveal His secrets. What are you listening to, who are you listening to? Knowing that God promises to reveal His secrets to men of God should cause you to listen to true men of God with intensity.

Prayer and Praise:

Lord, You give such a wonderful promise of the willingness You have to reveal Your secrets to men of God. You give such a rich word of hope; thank You. In the mighty name of Jesus Christ, my Lord. Amen.

AT EASE IN ZION
Amos 6:1

Being at ease is a wonderful thing; you have calm, peace, even serenity. It is easy to get comfortable and to settle down and slow down. Yet, in this text it is not a commendable quality. In this context, it is a sign of apathy, indifference, and ultimately, sin. How can a child of God be at ease while away from God? How is it possible for a Christian to be at peace and have calmness when the judgment of God has been foretold or is falling on individuals? "Being at ease in Zion" is in the context of a "woe." The word woe means something that causes sorrow or distress. Synonyms of woe are misery, sorrow, distress, heartache, regret, or gloom.

The Lord is saying, "Distress to you who are at ease in Zion," or the homeland of God's people. Just because you are in a certain place or location geographically doesn't mean you are spiritually right with God. If you are not walking in rhythm with the Lord, you are in a position of woe.

The question you must ask yourself is this. "Am I at ease, but am not walking in agreement with God?" Are you comfortable with life, but your life is not glorifying to God? The warning is clear; do not settle down on the Lord until He brings you to the place and season of refreshing. Stop resting in the world, and learn to rest in the Lord.

Prayer and Praise:

Lord, show me clearly if I am at ease in Zion. Prompt my mind and spirit with strong conviction about my spiritual need, and let me run to You. In the mighty name of Jesus Christ, my Lord. Amen.

FAMINE OF THE WORD
Amos 8:11

It is difficult to imagine a famine of food when cupboards, freezers, and grocery stores overflow with products. It is challenging even to say the Lord's Prayer, when it says, "Give us this day our daily bread." It is hard to pray in faith for food when you have money in your pocket and can purchase food, and you have a stockpile of food in your home. However, not everyone is so blessed.

When you think of a famine, you think of a food shortage. The Bible tells of another type of famine. Amos introduced a famine of the spoken word of God. To be contextually correct, he did not warn of a famine or shortage of the spoken word of God, but of hearing the spoken word of God.

One aspect of God's judgment on a people, even His own people, is they will not hear God's Word, the Bible. The Word will be preached, taught, read, and expounded upon, but people will not hear it. If you cannot hear the Word of God, you are in serious trouble. As a Christian, your entire life hinges on hearing God speak.

Jesus said, "My sheep hear My voice (John 10:27)." Do you hear the voice of God speaking in your life? Or has there been a famine of hearing taking place, and you have been unaware of it? The Word of God is going forth into the world by media, Internet, and pulpit as it never has before. Missionaries are taking God's Word to the uttermost parts of the world. Is there a famine of hearing?

As you look at cities and towns across this land and you see the ungodliness and moral depravity, you say "Yes, there is a famine of hearing the Word of God." It is evidenced in cities, states, and nations that there is a famine of the truth of God's Word being heard, not heralded.

How is it in your life? When was the last time God spoke to you? What did He say specifically to you? How did you respond? If you fail to respond personally to the Word of God, you will experience a famine of hearing God's Word, though it is proclaimed every week in your presence. The Word of God will do more than stir your emotions; it will change your life as you respond positively to it.

Prayer and Praise:

Lord, Your Word is truth; it is life-giving, life-sustaining and precious. Let me quickly recognize when I have grown comfortable and complacent, and have failed to respond to it. Lord, let there be no famine of hearing Your Word in my life. In the mighty name of Jesus Christ, my Lord. Amen.

PRIDE DECEIVES
Obadiah 1:3

Have you ever been deceived? If you have, it was not a pleasant feeling. When did you realize you were being deceived or that you had been deceived? You always realize this after it has happened. If you knew the deception beforehand, you would not have been deceived. So it is after the deception has occurred that you learn the truth. Sadly, many never learn the truth, even when it is told to them.

Satan is a liar, he is the accuser of the brethren, and he is the deceiver of many. He deceives people into believing lies. Sometimes he does not even have to tell you a specific lie. He merely has to let your life become filled with pride.

To the world pride is a good thing. It is a feeling of satisfaction derived from one's own efforts or achievement. In America, you are instructed that pride is a good thing, or that there is a "good" pride—pride in your accomplishments, your job, your family, where you live, the car you drive, even pride in your church.

The Bible is clear God hates pride (Proverbs 8:13). What you must learn to express is thankfulness. Thankfulness is directed toward the Lord, pride is directed toward self. It is in that subtle distinction that one gets deceived by pride.

"The pride of your heart deceives you." Your heart is the issue. It has been allowed to think, express, act in ways that feed pride and not humility to the Lord. Think for a moment; what are some things you take pride in? What are some things you are prideful of? Realize it is a deception of the Devil, and he is attempting to lead you away from God and His great will.

You cannot hold onto pride in any form or fashion and walk in rhythm with God. Ask God to forgive you of your specific areas of pride and to clothe you with humility day by day, moment by moment.

Prayer and Praise:

Lord, show me any area of pride I have in my life. Show me where pride has hidden and created a stronghold and by faith, let me confess and forsake it. Cleanse me for Your purpose and glory. In the mighty name of Jesus Christ, my Lord. Amen.

FLEEING FROM THE LORD
Jonah 1:1-3

This is a Bible story most people have heard since they were children. Jonah, the prophet of God, was swallowed by an enormous fish. If that was not bad enough, he was later vomited out onto dry ground. How would you like to have experienced three days in the muck, slime, heat, odor, and darkness of a fish's stomach only to be regurgitated a few days later?

Jonah described it as being in hell. He was fully conscious and miserable. Many people today exist in a living hell. They breathe and move about, but they have no true life. They go from one stimulus to another, just trying to get through another day. What started out as "fun" has captured them and destroyed them.

Sadder still, some Christians experience that type of existence. Jonah did. Why does this take place in many lives? For the same reason it did for Jonah; he fled from the presence of God. He heard God speak specifically to him. He knew God's will and he did the opposite; he ran from God. Have you ever run from the Lord?

Why do Christians run from the Lord? Why do Christians believe God's will is not right and best for them? Why do Christians ignore the Word of God? Some refuse God's will because of fear, but the New Testament teaches that you have not been given a spirit of fear, but of power, love and a sound mind (2 Timothy 1:7). The main reason Christians run from God is the lack of surrender. Many who profess Christ as Savior have never surrendered to Him as Lord, or Master, of their lives.

Is Christ the Lord and Master of your life? Does your life flow with obedience as you walk in rhythm with God? Do you know what it means to be yoked to the Father? Every day is a brand new day, and it requires a fresh surrender. Have you surrendered your life today to Christ?

It was only when Jonah adjusted his life to the Word and will of God that he knew and understood satisfaction of life. Yes, in the last chapter he was complaining again, and that was because he once again sought his will instead of God's. What will you do?

Prayer and Praise:

Lord, teach me daily to surrender all to You. When I hear Your voice, let me respond in instant obedience. I only ask that You enable me to recognize Your voice. In the mighty name of Jesus Christ, my Lord. Amen.

DO NOT PRATTLE
Micah 2:6

Micah prophesied in a time when the people of God, Israel, were in deep trouble. These were God's people, but they were not godly people. Do you know what constitutes a person who is godly? He has time for God; an ungodly person has no time for God. If a person has no time for God, or limited time, such as going to church for an hour on Sunday, they would easily fall into the practices of the world.

Micah preached to a people who were ungodly and away from God. However, Micah's hope was not in these people or in himself. Micah's hope was in the Lord. Where is your hope today? Have you placed it in a person or people, or is it truly in the Lord Jesus Christ? Do you have time for Him daily?

This book is a series of prophecies, judgments and the message of hope. Israel loved false prophets. They loved for these false prophets to tell them how good they were and how blessed they were going to be. Many in the church are no different today. They come to church to be stroked and bragged on and told how good they are. False prophets do not carry a sign that says "false prophets." You recognize them by the message they preach with no scriptural base.

The word prattle is a word you do not hear very often. It means to talk at length in a foolish or inconsequential way. That is what false prophets do, they prattle on and deceive many a person into thinking everything is alright. Do you go to the doctor for him to only tell you good news? If you had cancer, would you not want him to tell you the truth? Would you not want the honest truth and for the doctor to tell you what you need to do to overcome this?

Sadly, many do not want to hear the truth about their spiritual condition. Living for the moment is more important to them than eternity. Think about that statement. Do you live for the immediate or for eternity? The only thing that gives people hope is truth, not prattling. Preach the truth and live the truth. There is hope, but it is only in Jesus Christ and He is Truth.

Prayer and Praise:

Lord, please do not let me be a prattler or fall in love with prattle. Give me a hunger for Your truth, and let me be convinced hope is only in Your Truth. In the mighty name of Jesus Christ, my Lord. Amen.

WHAT THE LORD REQUIRES
Micah 6:6-8

There are many Christian people who struggle with the question, "What does God want from me?" They approach God's will like trying to find a needle in a haystack Such is not the case with God's will. God tells clearly and explicitly what He wants from His children.

Micah expresses it so clearly in the text. God is not seeking offerings of calves, rams, or rivers of oil. God has showed what He requires, and it is three things. You are to do justly, love mercy and walk humbly with your God.

How do you do justly? You do that which is right and just. In all of life you do right. As rightness flows from your life, the righteousness of Christ is manifested in you. You love mercy. I do not want justice from God, I want His mercy. If I received justice I would burn in hell, but I thank God for His mercy and that He withholds what I deserve and extends to me His grace and favor.

Finally, you are to walk humbly with the Lord. How do you do that? You adjust your life radically to the Word of God. One way you put on humility is to totally forgive others of wrongs done to you. Forgiveness of others is tied to humility. Forgiveness keeps one from being puffed up, and it is done daily, not merely one time.

Do you do justly every day? Do you love mercy, or do you take it for granted? Do you walk humbly with your God?

Prayer and Praise:

Lord, You are my God, and I will exalt You. Fill my heart, soul, and mind with the desire to do justly, to love mercy, and to walk humbly with You. In the mighty name of Jesus Christ, my Lord. Amen.

THE LORD IS SLOW TO ANGER
Nahum 1:3

The book of Nahum and the book of Jonah were both addressed to the city of Nineveh. Jonah preached, "Forty days and Nineveh will be overthrown." The judgment of God would fall unless they repented. Nineveh repented and God withheld his judgment.

Nahum wrote one hundred years after Jonah's message, and he wrote that Nineveh would be destroyed in thirty to forty years. God had shown mercy to Nineveh for nearly two hundred years because of their repentance. Now, God raised up Nahum to bring His Word of judgment once again.

Why would you read in verse three that God is slow to anger if He is going to bring judgment? Because God is slow to anger, but He does not ignore continual sin. Being slow to anger means God is a God of great mercy and patience. God demonstrated His patience with Nineveh and He honored their repentance. Every breath you breathe proves God is slow to anger.

Even as God is slow to anger, you must not presume on God's patience. When He gives a warning, you had better respond. Jonah warned them, and they repented. Nahum warned them, and they were destroyed. God will not acquit the wicked. You do not get away with sin. We see that "the Lord has His way in the whirlwind and in the storm" (v. 3).

The good news is God is slow to anger. The warning is God is not mocked. Do not try to take advantage of God. Do not try to become too familiar and at ease with the Lord. In the book of Revelation, the saved are bowing and casting their crowns at the feet of the Father. No one is hugging the Lord.

"The Lord is good. A stronghold in the day of trouble; and He knows those who trust in Him" (Nahum 1:7). What a good word. Are you not glad the Lord is good? He is a stronghold and a shelter. He knows those who truly trust in Him. Do you trust Him?

Prayer and Praise:

Lord, You are my stronghold and I run to You. Show me any area my trust in You is lacking. Thank You for being slow to anger. In the mighty name of Jesus Christ, my Lord. Amen.

TAKE YOUR PROBLEMS TO THE LORD
Habakkuk 1:1-3

Habakkuk was a prophet with a problem, a personal problem. A problem he could not solve himself. It was a problem a committee could not handle. The only place Habakkuk could take his problem was to the Lord. Have you ever had such a problem as this?

When God gave the answer, Habakkuk did not like it. The answer God gave only caused him further questions, and again, he appealed to the Lord. Habakkuk always went to the Lord with his problems. Do you? It is so easy to seek the counsel of man, but man's advice, counsel, and opinions are faulty. God's counsel is never faulty.

This book breaks down into three simple chapter headings: "Faith Tested," "Faith Taught," "Faith Triumphant." When faith is tested, the key is to take the problem to the Lord, without suggestions of how He should handle this. The answer may not be what you want to hear, but this is how God tests your faith.

Habakkuk felt God was being indifferent to His children and had forgotten them. Do you ever think God has forgotten you? He said, in essence, "Lord, I have prayed and You do not care. You do not seem to care about the suffering of the innocent." You must remember what Timothy said, "All who desire to live godly in Christ Jesus will suffer persecution" (2 Timothy 3:12).

When you take your problems to the Lord, if you stick around, He will answer. Habakkuk 1:3 tells you that God is in control and He is doing a work. That is good news. Often things will get worse before they get better (v. 6). Never forget, God is in control.

Dr. Martin Lloyd Jones gave four steps in the proper procedure to help know how to deal with problems: (1) pause to think; get God's light on the situation: (2) restate the principle. Do not begin with the problem, remind yourself of the character of God; (3) apply the principle to the problem. The principle of all you know about God and His Word: (4) yield the problem to God in faith.1 God is building His kingdom, not the United States of America or your kingdom. God is everlasting, holy and faithful. He is in control.

Prayer and Praise:

Lord, let me never forget You are in control, and my one responsibility is to trust You. Teach me daily to run to You with my problems and to trust Your answer. Enable me to reflect on Your character and not the problem. In the mighty name of Jesus Christ, my Lord. Amen.

1. Lloyd-Jones, Martyn, "Spiritual Depression," Eerdmans Publishing, Grand Rapids, Michigan, 1965, pg. 5ff.

SETTLED IN COMPLACENCY
Zephaniah 1:12

This book was written when Josiah, a godly king, was ruling over the people of God. When he came of age, he began to repair the temple of God and in the process, rediscovered the Word of God. Josiah led the nation back to God. The result was a time of revival among God's people.

In this time, God raised up Zephaniah the prophet; his message was instrumental in the revival. The message was for a people who were experiencing God's blessing. One would think it was a message of comfort, but strangely enough, it was a message of judgment. In a time when the people were burning their idols, you would think the message would be, "Keep up the good work." No, the message came, "You are not cutting it."

Is this message applicable for today? Yes, then as now, the people listened to the Word of God. The holiness and presence of God was being manifested. They sensed God in their meetings. The tragedy was that it was only external reform and change, and God was telling them they needed an internal change.

It is easy to become settled in complacency, especially when things are going well. It is easy to go to church on Sunday and do your spiritual thing, and there be no true change of heart. What really takes place in your heart when you come to worship? Is there a hunger and thirst for righteousness? Or is it only a ritual?

The message of Zephaniah is: God wants to bless His people but His people must be in line with His Word and His will or there will be no blessing.

Prayer and Praise:

Lord, let me not just go through the external motions of worship, but let me come before You hungering and thirsting after You. Teach me the difference between external religious actions and true internal faith. In the mighty name of Jesus Christ, my Lord. Amen.

OCTOBER

THE TIME HAS NOT YET COME
Haggai 1:1-2

Time is the most important thing a person has, and every person has the same amount of time. Time cannot be saved or put back for future use. If you waste your time, you waste your life. If you use your time wisely, it will bless and benefit you and others.

Haggai was preaching to God's people, and the people had said, it is not time yet to build the house of the Lord. What do you think about that statement? Do you think it is time to do the Lord's work, or do you still have many things you want to do for yourself? Is your priority the kingdom of God or your personal kingdom?

It is easy to fall into the idea that you have all the time in the world to do the Lord's work. It is easy to put off today what you should be doing for the kingdom and think you can do it when you have more time. When will you have more time? When the kids are grown and you come to retirement? You are not promised another day. The Bible tells you that life is but a vapor, it is here a little while and then it is gone (James 4:14).

In the text, the people of God had grown tired of building the temple of God, and work had come to a stop. It had been stopped for fifteen years. Haggai challenged them to get back to the task of the kingdom of God. Nothing is more important than living in close intimacy with God. Nothing is more important than His will being done. Be careful to whom you listen to because time is short.

Next, God spoke through Haggai and He said, "Consider your ways." He went on to say that you work and earn a wage, but you cannot make ends meet at the end of the week. It is as if your pockets have a hole in them and you lose what you have worked for. How frustrating. Does that speak to you? Is your life one frustration after the other? Consider your ways.

The time is now to be about the Lord's work and building, expanding God's kingdom. Whose kingdom are you serving?

Prayer and Praise:

Lord, help me to consider my ways and to examine my life in light of whose kingdom I am seeking to build. Do I have time for service to You, or am I serving my own kingdom? Teach me to know the difference. In the mighty name of Jesus Christ, my Lord. Amen.

A WALL OF FIRE
Zechariah 2:5

When you think of fire, various thoughts come to your mind. You think of heat and destruction. As you consider further, you may also realize warmth, food preparation, and even protection. Fire is a multi-purpose agent. It can be deemed good or bad, leaving either a positive or a negative effect.

In the text, God promised to be a wall of fire for Jerusalem, the holy city of God. In a time when anything is acceptable and the church is being seduced and absorbed by the world, how do you stay pure in a worsening society? How do you maintain holiness in the midst of such corruption?

Not one thing that happens to you catches God by surprise. The Bible teaches that things will get worse until the end of time and the return of Jesus Christ. When the enemy comes like a flood, God will raise up a barrier against it. God will give shelter. The church must rest in that promise.

As a believer, you must rest in that promise as you pursue the Lord.

This age is an age that has lost the dread of sin. Many in the church have no dread of sin. This is a man-centered age and not a Christ-centered age. You are still responsible to live differently than the world. You are to live separate and holy lives unto God. If there is willful sin in your life, there will be no fire and no power from God.

The promise is that if you will get away from the influencers of this age and the spirit of this age and live abandoned to the Father, then God will be a wall of fire around you. God will keep His church. God will keep His people, and God will keep His servants. God will keep His Word to you, but you have responsibilities to keep as well.

In a time of promiscuity and corruption, you must stand against the spirit of this age and allow God to be your protector and defender.

Prayer and Praise:

Lord, thank You that You are my protector and defender. Show me any area I am compromising with the world, and let me turn from it. Be a wall of fire about me. In the mighty name of Jesus Christ, my Lord. Amen.

NOT BY MIGHT...BUT BY MY SPIRIT
Zechariah 4:6

The most wonderful thing Almighty God does for a person who comes to Him in repentance and faith for salvation is to forgive the person of her sins and give her the indwelling gift of the Holy Spirit.

Because of this, a person receives the witness of the Spirit. God's Spirit bears witness with your spirit that you are truly His child and have been saved. Do you know anything of this? Or are you trusting in a pastor's telling you that because you have said a prayer, you are now saved?

Salvation is a work of God in a person's life, and the witness of the Spirit is what gives one the assurance to know that she is indeed saved. No words of man can fulfill only what the witness of the Spirit of God gives.

The Holy Spirit comes into your life to teach you, to direct you in truth, to continually convict of sin and righteousness. The Holy Spirit is the umpire in your life to let you know what to do or not do in making decisions. The Holy Spirit is always in agreement with the Word of God, the Bible.

When God spoke these words in Zechariah, "Not by might... but by My Spirit," He was once again reinforcing the fact He was in control, and He would fulfill His will. God does not need man, but He uses men who are dependent upon Him and the Holy Spirit.

You are to be cultivated and to assist in the cultivation process, but God gives the increase. You are always dependent upon the Father and not yourself. You are to hoe the garden, but never forget God will give the increase. It is by His Spirit and not human works, though works will be present. You cannot do God's part and He will not do your part.

Do you know how to trust His Spirit to work? You adjust your life to Scripture. You pray without ceasing, and you are a witness as you go about your daily life.

Prayer and Praise:

Lord, it is by Your Spirit and not my works or good deeds that enables me to be faithful. Teach me to trust You to work. In the mighty name of Jesus Christ, my Lord. Amen.

GOD KEEPS HIS WORD
Zechariah 8:14-23

The last part of verse fifteen reads, "Do not fear." How can you keep from fear? It is because God keeps His Word. Hallelujah! Just as God punished Israel's forefathers, sending them into Babylonian captivity for judgment, God's Word promises blessing to His children. What a wonderful promise.

God keeps His Word, but what is your responsibility? You are to speak the truth. You live in a generation that constantly is tempted to lie, to seek honor from man, and not God. You are to speak the truth (v. 16). You are also to guard your heart. Do not devise evil in your heart against others (v. 17). Finally, be very careful what you listen to. Do not love a false oath (v. 17).

God keeps His Word. Do you spend time in the Word daily? Do you know the Word of God enough to know truth from error? Do you have a plan for memorizing Scripture? God keeps His Word, but can you tell the difference between God's Word and man's?

Counterfeit money has always been a problem. Today there are machines that use an ultraviolet light to help a person recognize the genuine from the false. However, federal agents can recognize the genuine from the false by looking at the bill with their eyes. How do they do that? They never study a counterfeit bill; they only study the true bill. They are so familiar with the true bill that when they see a counterfeit, they immediately recognize it.

Are you so familiar with the truth of God's Word that when you hear error you recognize it? Are you so acquainted with God's truth that error sticks out like a sore thumb? You are the only one who can choose to spend time with God's Word for yourself. No one can do it for you. God keeps His Word. Amen. You are responsible to know God's Word.

Prayer and Praise:

Lord, thank You for keeping Your Word. Thank You for allowing me to have a copy of Your Word, the Bible. Let me be so acquainted with Your truth that I recognize error immediately. In the mighty name of Jesus Christ, my Lord. Amen.

FALSE SHEPHERDS
Zechariah 11:4-8

As you have journeyed through the Scriptures, you have seen the warnings of false shepherds. Today, a false shepherd would be a pastor of a local church whose primary concern is personal gain. There is nothing wrong with being compensated as a pastor, but your primary motivation cannot be money. This is the difference between being a hireling, hired by the church, and being called by God and a local church to be the pastor.

The false shepherds are hirelings. They are leading for personal gain, and they are not truly concerned about the sheep. They may say the right words and sound good, but they are driven by material gain, and they do not possess godliness.

Why does the Lord judge the people if it is the shepherd who is leading them? Who is at fault? The people have chosen to follow the hireling instead of the Word of God. Their responsibility is to discern if the shepherd is a spiritual man of God or not.

There are several marks of a spiritual man. First, he has truly been born again. He is a saved man. Next, he is indwelt daily by the Holy Spirit. His life is filled with praise, joy, thanksgiving, love, and submissiveness to God. The fruit of the Spirit is evidenced in his life. Also, he is filled with the Word of God. He knows the Bible, and he applies the Bible to his own life. Finally, he will be discerning. He understands spiritual truth and is able to teach and preach this truth. He recognizes the true from the false and will stand for truth.

As sheep, you have the responsibility to follow God's truth and to follow God's shepherd. As a true shepherd leads the flock, he guides them to green pastures, he feeds them the Word of God. This feeding of God's Word creates hunger in the sheep for the Word of God. Are you hungry for the Word of God?

Prayer and Praise:

Lord, I praise You for placing true shepherds in the flock. Teach me to know the difference between the true and the false. Create in me a greater hunger for You, Your Word, Your truth. In the mighty name of Jesus Christ, my Lord. Amen.

THE DAY OF THE LORD IS COMING
Zechariah 14:1

The phrase, "the day of the Lord," is used twenty-six times in the Scriptures. When you think about the day of the Lord coming, does that make you excited, scared, nervous, or all the above? Most Christians think of going to heaven and being with Christ, and that is a blessed thought.

What is it that makes heaven so wonderful? Is it streets of gold? Is it no more sorrow or tears? Is it being reunited with loved ones who knew Christ as their personal Savior? All of these things are good, but they are not what make heaven, heaven. Heaven is heaven because Jesus Christ, the Lamb of God, is on the throne. You can worship Him for all eternity.

The day of the Lord is a glorious day. However, for a person not born again, it is a painful and sorrowful day. All they have to look forward to is an eternity separated from God in a place called hell, a place created for the Devil and his demons.

The longer the Lord delays His return, lost people will still have a chance to respond to the gospel and be saved. Saved people have the opportunity to lead one more soul to Christ and expand the kingdom of God. When was the last time you witnessed to a lost person?

Prayer and Praise:

Lord, I thank You for the promise of heaven. I praise You for making salvation possible. Use me for Your glory to reach someone for Your kingdom. In the mighty name of Jesus Christ, my Lord. Amen.

WHO CAN ENDURE
Malachi 3:1-2

Most every believer would say they would love to experience a fresh touch from Almighty God. They would love to meet with God in true revival. However, revival is not a three- or four-day meeting where you have church services every evening (though that is what it has been deemed, especially in the southern United States). Revival is when God moves in on a life or a church and pours forth new refreshment and life.

Revival can be messy. Everyone will not be jumping on the band wagon and getting excited. No, when God moves in a life or a church, He comes bringing great conviction of sin. The sin that has separated and rendered one ineffective must be dealt with in honest confession and repentance. Not everyone is going to be excited about repentance, brokenness, and surrender.

God comes as a fuller's soap to wash and cleanse. Cleansing can hurt. God comes as a refiner's fire to purify. Fire burns and a burn is painful. Revival is a season when God moves in mightily in order to make His people fit for His presence.

Malachi asks, "Who can endure the day of His coming?" Yes, the end result of revival is amazing, but the process is very painful; however, it is worth it. Seek God for revival. Allow Him to wash and purify you, regardless of the cost.

Prayer and Praise:

Lord, I do desire to see and experience true revival, no matter the cost. Cleanse me and purify me so I can endure Your coming. In the mighty name of Jesus Christ, my Lord. Amen.

THE OBEDIENCE OF THE FATHERS
Matthew 2:14

Joseph was not the father of Jesus Christ. Jesus is the Son of God, and therefore, God is His Father. Joseph was his earthly father in the sense that Jesus was raised in the household of Joseph and Mary. Jesus was fully God and fully man, and He came to save the world from its sin.

Joseph, being the earthly father of Jesus, made decisions that impacted Jesus's life, as well as Mary's. After Jesus had been born and the wise men had come offering their gifts, God spoke to Joseph in a dream warning him to flee to Egypt, because Herod was seeking to kill Jesus.

Joseph obeyed what God said. By the obedience of the father, the mother and the child were saved. Have you ever considered that your obedience to God has ramifications for the lives of others?

How has your obedience, or lack thereof, affected others? Have you been faithful to church attendance every week? Or have you taught your children to forsake the church for "fun" family activities? Do your family and coworkers ever see and hear you pray before you eat a meal? Or do you just blend in without any expression of thankfulness? Does your copy of God's Word show evidence of use?

The obedience of the fathers saves the family. It can save the family from needless decisions of what you will do on Sunday; you will be in church. It can save the family from not knowing whom you bow before; it is Almighty God. It can save your family not knowing which book you receive your directions from—the Bible or the newspaper—and that you live the Word of God.

The obedience of the fathers can determine if young lives will be shaped by the gospel of Jesus Christ or become indifferent to the gospel message of Jesus Christ. Are you an obedient father?

Prayer and Praise:

Lord, show me clearly any area I am withholding from You. Make me into an obedient father with a passion for You. Speak to me by Your Holy Spirit and through Your Word so I can yield to You. In the mighty name of Jesus Christ, my Lord. Amen.

WORRY FREE
Matthew 6:25

Worry seems to be a common activity even with Christian people. Why is that? Jesus teaches that the cares of this world will choke out the Word of God, not the Devil, but the little worries. Whenever you put other things first, there will be confusion, and where there is confusion there is worry.

What causes worry? When you think like the world and crave the things of the world, you will worry like the world. Contentment comes from seeking the things of Christ. What is the cure for worry? Seek God's kingdom first. Seek God's righteousness. Learn to live one day at a time.

What are the results of worry? You forget who your heavenly Father is; He is Almighty God. You erase the promises of God from your mind, and you act like an unbeliever.

To overcome worry, your relationship to God has to be your first priority. Is it? Do you spend time daily in the Word of God reading, studying, and memorizing Scripture? Talk is cheap. Do you have a regular place you go to pray every day? Do you seek the face of God, or do you only seek His hand? As your life becomes increasingly consumed with your Lord, your worries diminish and your faith is increased.

Everybody worries on occasion. However, worry is not to be the common theme of your life. A phone call is all it requires to cause panic in your life, but as soon as you realize what is happening, you begin to pray and seek God. As your custom of seeking God is increased, the more natural it will become to seek God in trying times.

It is so wonderful to have a heavenly Father whom you can call on any time. It is such a blessing to be able to pray. As you learn to pray in the good days and the blessed times, you also learn to pray through the difficulties of life. It is not that you will have a worry-free existence, but you will have a Father to whom you can go in times of need. Hallelujah!

Prayer and Praise:

Lord, worries can come from many directions. However, You are always on Your throne. Teach me to seek You first. Teach me not to waste the good days, but to seek You especially when days are good, so that I will be able to seek You when days are not so good. In the mighty name of Jesus Christ, my Lord. Amen.

ASK
Matthew 7:7

Have you ever considered why some people have a difficult time asking for help? They will tell you that they do not want to be a bother or that there are more pressing needs for help. Why would a person hesitate? It may have to do more with one's independent mindset than the aforementioned reasons.

Many people have been brought up with the idea of "pulling himself up by his own bootstraps." The idea of being self-sufficient and independent gives the impression that you do not want to bother or be indebted to anyone. This attitude smacks of self, because everyone is going to need help at some time or another. You should not abuse others in the process of asking for help, but the mentality that you will not ask for help will ultimately isolate you from God.

Every person needs the Lord. Jesus Christ came to seek and to save sinners. Sinners cannot save themselves. They cannot be good enough, nor can they do enough good works for their good to outweigh their bad. The key to salvation is coming to Jesus Christ in biblical repentance and asking.

Once a person has been saved, that is the beginning of the journey, not the end. Daily, you must come to the Lord and ask for forgiveness of sin where you have failed and messed up. Daily, you must come to the Lord and ask for His mind and direction on how to make decisions and live in His righteousness. At times, you will have to ask others to intercede on your behalf because of burdens you feel you cannot bear alone.

What does asking accomplish? It places you in a position of dependency upon the Lord. You have to humble yourself and admit you cannot do it. You have to submit yourself to the rule of Almighty God and His Word. Asking takes away your pride as nothing else can, because you are admitting you are not self-sufficient, you cannot live independent of God or others.

"Ask, and it will be given to you; seek, and you will find; knock, and it will be opened to you." Whom do you ask? God is the one. Why do you ask? You cannot do it on your own. When you learn to live in dependency on God, it is amazing what He does on your behalf.

Prayer and Praise:

Lord, thank You that You want me to ask of You. Teach me this position of humility so I can walk and live in harmony with You. Teach me dependency upon You. In the mighty name of Jesus Christ, my Lord. Amen.

YOKED TO CHRIST
Matthew 11:28-30

Many people today have never been around a farm or farm animals. They see them on television or as they drive down lonely roads with pastureland beside them. Jesus lived in an agrarian culture and used this terminology in teaching how His disciples were to live. He took the normal things of life and used them to teach.

When Jesus used the word "yoke," He was referring to a wooden crosspiece with two bow-shaped pieces beneath, one at each end, each bow enclosing the head of an animal. To be yoked together is to be joined together.

When you are told to "take My yoke upon you, and learn of Me," Jesus is instructing you to submit to Him, and you do this by submitting to His Word. A yoke prevents one from wandering aimlessly, and the necessary work gets accomplished. When you try to get ahead of Christ, or lag behind, the yoke will pinch and rub against you. When this occurs, you realize your need to fall into pace with Jesus. Has His yoke ever pinched you? How did you then respond?

Walking in harmony and rhythm with the Lord is crucial to your spiritual life and development. You are not left to go your own way or chart your own path. You have been equipped by the yoke to abide in the presence of Christ. If you refuse, the yoke can and will rub you raw and bring much discomfort.

The only way to know the strength of Christ is by submitting to the yoke of Christ and learning of Him. The Word of God tells you, "For the joy of the Lord is your strength" (Nehemiah 8:10). If you refuse the yoke of Christ, you will not know the joy or strength of Christ.

Take Christ's yoke upon you and learn of Him. You will find rest for your soul—rest for your weariness and rest for your stresses. God is so wonderful.

Prayer and Praise:

Lord, teach me how to submit to Your yoke, and let me know Your rest. In the mighty name of Jesus Christ, my Lord. Amen.

LITTLE FAITH
Matthew 14:31

In this passage, Peter had just done the humanly impossible; he had walked on water in obedience to Jesus's invitation. None of the other disciples even got out of the boat. Why did Jesus give a mild rebuke to Peter saying, "O you of little faith, why did you doubt?" Everything that was over Peter's head was under Jesus's feet.

Has God ever rebuked you? Has God ever spoken to you, challenging you on how you acted, responded, or failed to act at all? Why did Jesus not rebuke the ones who never got out of the boat? Scripture does not tell the reason, but maybe it was because Peter started walking on the water by faith, and he got distracted by the waves. Jesus was trying to teach him an important principle; it is not enough to start by faith; you also have to finish by faith.

How easy is it for you to take your eyes off of Christ and onto the storms of the world? How easy is it for you to start out excited and obedient, but to finish well seems to elude you? How easy is it to talk the talk, but walking the walk is another story?

Jesus gives a stinging rebuke, "O you of little faith...." How do you get your faith to increase? Faith is like a muscle; the more you exercise it, the stronger it becomes. Faith is exercised by taking in the Word of God. "Faith comes by hearing and hearing by the word of God" (Romans 10:17). There will come a point where you have to act in obedience to the Word of God. You will have to stand on the doctrinal truths of Scripture and stand alone.

When you stand alone, you may cast your eyes to the winds and the waves; in doing so you may begin to sink. Even then, you can still cry out to Jesus. He may mildly rebuke you, but you at least got out of the comfort of the boat; and next time, you may go further without being distracted. Do not stop; continue seeking God and allowing Him to build your faith.

Prayer and Praise:

Lord, thank You for faith. As I feed on Your Word, teach me how to walk by faith every day. Even when You have to rebuke me, let me not stop, but rather learn from it. In the mighty name of Jesus Christ, my Lord. Amen.

DENY SELF
Matthew 16:24-25

In today's society denying self is not a popular topic. In fact, everything you see and hear on media is the opposite of self-denial. You are told, "It's all about you." If you are not happy, and your needs are not being met, and your feelings are not feeling positive, then you should pout and leave, looking elsewhere for fulfillment.

The sad thing is that it is so contradictory to the Bible. If you seek your own life, you will lose it. No vote, no debate, not up for discussion, and that is one reason the world does not readily embrace Christianity. The Bible teaches self must decrease and Christ must increase.

As a Christian seeking to walk with Christ daily, how do you practice self-denial? Do you deny yourself anything? Do you deny yourself food? Do you deny yourself entertainment so you can spend more time in prayer and Bible study? Do you deny yourself friendships, because they are not healthy and pull you down spiritually? Do you deny yourself financially so you can give obediently to God's kingdom? How do you deny yourself?

The reason for self-denial is not because God does not wish for you to have a good time, but that He wants You to know and experience His best. It is to teach you to seek Him, your God, above all things. It is to grow and develop you in Christlikeness. It is to equip you to face the future in faith with the joy of the Lord.

Prayer and Praise:

Lord, self-denial is one of my greatest challenges; teach me daily to deny myself for Your glory. Enable me daily to trust You to guide me in this area. Let me seek You with all my heart, soul, and strength. In the mighty name of Jesus Christ, my Lord. Amen.

A HOUSE OF PRAYER
Matthew 21:13

The context of the passage is when Jesus entered the temple and cleansed it of the moneychangers. What started as a good thing had spiraled down to greed. People traveling from far distances could purchase their sacrificial animals upon arriving in Jerusalem, if they so desired. Over time this practice had become a money-making scheme. Overpriced animals and greedy men ruined what once was helpful.

Jesus entered the temple and began to overturn the tables and drive out the moneychangers. Jesus cleansed the temple of this sin. After the temple has been cleansed, He then stated, "My house shall be called a house of prayer."

Jesus never said His house should be a house of preaching, though there is nothing wrong with preaching. Jesus never said His house should be a house of praise, though there is nothing wrong with praise. He said, "My house shall be called a house of prayer." Once the temple was cleansed and purity was established, the Lord's house was ready to be a house of prayer.

Cleansing is essential in your personal life and the corporate life of your church, if you are to be a person of prayer and your church a house of prayer. When was the last time you sought the Lord for cleansing in your life? When was the last time your church sought corporate cleansing?

Once the cleansing came and prayer had been reestablished, the power of God began to move. The next verse says, "The blind and the lame came to Him in the temple and He healed them." Hallelujah to the Lamb of God! A house of purity becomes a house of prayer. A house of prayer becomes a house of power. Finally, a house of power becomes a house filled with praise. The following verse tells us the children cried out, "Hosanna to the Son of David."

Do you strive to be a person of prayer? How much time do you spend in prayer daily? Where do you pray? Do you have a prayer sheet with names, issues, and needs that you pray over daily? What countries do you pray for? Do you pray for the president and senators that lead this land? Does your church have a designated time to pray together, other than a few prayers offered throughout the service? God's will for every believer and church is to be a house of prayer.

Prayer and Praise:

Lord, thank You for the privilege of prayer. Continue to teach me to pray. Enable me to encourage my church to pray. In the mighty name of Jesus Christ, my Lord. Amen.

THE DAYS OF NOAH
Matthew 24:37

The return of Jesus Christ is closer than it has ever been. You have heard this statement all your life, and it is a true statement. Jesus Christ is coming again for His church, His bride, and you had better be ready.

Even though you know Jesus is coming again, you do not know the exact time. However, He tells us what the conditions will be like when He does return. It will be like the days of Noah. What were the days of Noah like? They were much like today; therefore, you had better be prepared for Jesus's soon return.

In the days of Noah, people were consumed with eating and drinking. Do you see that pattern happening today? In the days of Noah, people were busy marrying and giving in marriage. That is still a common factor today. In the days of Noah, people were buying and selling, going here and there, busy with the normal routines of life. They were so busy they did not take time to consider God seriously.

That is the generation you live in. People are caught up in life and making a living, but they have no time or concern about God. People are caught up in the things of this world, but they fail to recognize Almighty God. People are godless.

What does it mean to be godless? It means people have no time for God. Yes, it can show itself with terrible and evil activities, but it is seen mainly by a person not having time or consideration for God in her life. Do you take time for God in your life? Do you schedule the activities of your life around the Father, or do you merely try and fit Him in when it is convenient for you?

The Lord is coming back, and you are the only one who can prepare yourself for His soon return. Be very careful that you do not get so caught up in life that you fail to be ready. His return will be glorious, only if you are prepared, expecting, and watching.

Prayer and Praise:

Lord, I praise You that You are coming again. I thank You for that promise. Teach me to be ever watching and expecting. Teach me to daily make time for You and not to slide into the condition of being godless. In the mighty name of Jesus Christ, my Lord. Amen.

THE COMMISSION
Matthew 28:19-20

This is probably two of the best known verses of Scripture in the Bible. It is called the Great Commission. These verses are the marching orders for the church and the individual Christian. It is the call to evangelize and disciple others. It is the assurance that Christ is with you. Having said all that, how are you doing in fulfilling the Great Commission?

In order to fulfill this commission, several things have to be understood. First, you must acknowledge the lordship of Christ in your life. In verse seventeen, it is said of the disciples that they worshipped Christ. They acknowledged Him as God and Lord. Yet some doubted. There are still doubters. Have you surrendered to the lordship of Christ?

Next you must obey what Christ commands. Obedience is the test of your love for Christ. The commands are to "go." As you are going about life, you teach the truths of Christ. As you are going about life, you proclaim the Word of God. You teach obedience and submission to Jesus Christ. Once this has become a pattern of your life and you are making disciples, you will also be involved in the baptism of these new believers. You may not personally or physically baptize a person, but they are responding in obedience to Christ partly because of your witness and teaching.

Evangelism that does not follow through with discipleship is not complete evangelism. You are to make disciples, not merely see converts.

The reason you can go and make disciples is because you know that you have the assurance of Christ's presence with you. You go in His authority, and you have assurance of His presence. He will not leave you. He is with you always.

Finally, you persevere to the end. You do not stop, you do not quit, and you do not give up. You persevere. You continue. You keep going in good days and bad. You remain faithful in days of plenty and days of little. You're going, teaching, and making disciples is not dependent on what you see; it is an act of obedience, as you have surrendered to the lordship of Jesus Christ.

How is your perseverance? Perseverance is a proof of true salvation. Perseverance is assurance of salvation. Thank God He enables you to persevere.

Prayer and Praise:

Lord, let me live the Great Commission daily. Let me persevere to the end. Let me know, by faith, Your presence. In the mighty name of Jesus Christ, my Lord. Amen.

THE CYCLE OF DISCIPLESHIP
Mark 3:13-15

When Jesus called the twelve apostles, they responded to His invitation. The same should be true of you. Jesus initiates a call to you to come to Him, be it for salvation or a specific task, your responsibility is to respond in obedience. Everybody will respond some with obedience, and others will ignore the call, therefore, will be disobedient. It is a dangerous thing to ignore the call of God, the Word of God, or a command from the Father. It could cost you your eternal soul.

Jesus called the twelve, and they responded to His call. The call was to a three-fold task. They were first called to be with Christ (v. 13). Their next responsibility was to preach God's Word (v. 14) and finally, they were called to minister in their giftedness: they were to heal the sick and cast out the demonic.

If you fail in the first area, being with Jesus, spending time with Jesus, growing in intimacy with Jesus, you will be ineffective in the other areas. You must take the primary calling seriously. You must adjust your schedule around Christ.

In Luke 9, you find what is to happen after these first three assignments are completed. Jesus sent out the twelve, and in verse ten, they reported back to Christ. They went to a desert place to rest. That is the next calling of God that you must learn to rest in Christ.

They told Jesus all the success they had experienced, and they rested. Why tell Jesus what has happened? They told Him so He could evaluate and give further direction or guidance. They started all over again seeking the presence of Christ, seeking intimacy with Christ, before they went to engage in future ministry of the Word and their giftedness.

The cycle of discipleship is: respond to Christ by spending time with Christ; preach the message of Christ; minister in your giftedness, and then return to the presence of Christ for rest and refreshment. You cannot serve God effectively out of your own resources. You must rely on Christ by spending time with Him in the Word of God and prayer.

Prayer and Praise:

Lord, thank You for calling me. Thank You for equipping me. Thank You for allowing me to spend quantity time with You, so I can fulfill Your will. Teach me to regularly seek You for seasons of refreshing. In the mighty name of Jesus Christ, my Lord. Amen.

DELIVERANCE
Mark 5:8-9

Have you ever considered what a person is worth? Satan wants to destroy the person. Society wants to dispense with the person. The Savior wants to deliver the person. What a wonderful Savior is Jesus Christ!

As you read this story, it is amazing that the village people were more concerned about their pigs than the man being set free and delivered. They were more concerned about their jobs than this man's life. It is very easy to get preoccupied with the world and forget about those around us in bondage to sin and Satan.

When Jesus delivers a person, it impacts the individual, the family of the individual, and the entire community. This person whom Jesus delivers now can be a productive citizen, a provider for his family, and a vital part of the local church. You could listen to this person's testimony over and over, never getting tired of hearing how a life ruined with sin is now alive to serve the Savior. Hallelujah!

You may not have been delivered from such depths of sin as the man in the Scripture passage, but if you are truly saved, you have been delivered and set free from your sin. It is just as life-changing as this man's. Now you have an eternal purpose to live for—the kingdom of God and His glory. Now you have the power from God to fulfill it.

Prayer and Praise:

Lord, I may not have been delivered from demonic oppression as this man was, but You delivered me from my sin and shame, and I praise Your holy name. Use me for Your kingdom and glory. In the mighty name of Jesus Christ, my Lord. Amen.

MAKING THE WORD OF GOD OF NO EFFECT
Mark 7:13

The Word of God is powerful, sharper than any two-edged sword. The Word of God is living and life-giving. The Word of God is the source of one's strength and hope. It is difficult to comprehend that you can make the Word of God of no effect. How could a person make it of no effect? By living life based on the traditions of man and not based on the Word of God.

Religious traditions such as rituals, regulations, procedures, and form can render the person empty of God's Word. When good things, such as prayer, church attendance, Bible reading, and devotions become form without substance, you render the Word of God of no effect.

To make no effect means to make void, annulled, or deprived of authority and power. Jesus was addressing the religious establishment. The Jewish leaders were more concerned about this world and their religious practice than the truth Christ Jesus gave.

Even in Christian churches today, traditions can choke out the Word of God. One man said, "Tradition is the living faith of the dead. Traditionalism is the dead faith of the living." You must be very careful your Christianity and faith are not mere tradition from the past. If you find yourself clinging to things of the past while ignoring God's Word for the present, you find yourself in a "dead faith" condition.

Let the Word of God be alive, powerful, and sharp. Apply it daily to your life. Live by the Word of God. Live by faith, and do not merely live religiously.

Prayer and Praise:

Lord, teach me to know the difference between Your living Word and traditions of my past. A tradition may be good, but never let it come before Your life-giving Word. In the mighty name of Jesus Christ, my Lord. Amen.

WHAT MUST I DO TO INHERIT ETERNAL LIFE?
Mark 10:17

Eternal life is the greatest gift a person can receive, but it can only be received in the person of Jesus Christ. John 17:3 tells that, "This is eternal life, that they may know You, the only true God, and Jesus Christ whom You have sent." Eternal life means personally and intimately knowing God.

In the text, a man asked, "What shall I do to inherit eternal life?" That is a question most people want answered; they just may not like the answer. Jesus told him to obey the commandment, obey the Word of God. The man replied that he did obey, or keep, all the commands. To which Jesus answered and said, "You lack one thing." How many people do you know that lack this one thing? How many people do you know who allow one thing to keep them from coming to Jesus Christ as their Lord and Savior?

Jesus said, sell everything you have, give it to the poor, take up your cross and follow Me. Do you think Jesus still requires that today? Do you think Jesus asked this man something unfair? Do you think Jesus meant what He said?

Jesus still requires people to put aside anything between them and God. You must turn from anything that competes with God. It could be your possessions. It could be a relationship. Jesus did not ask this man to do anything unfair. Jesus still asks you to do the same thing. Christ must be first without any competition in your life, or you cannot receive Him. Jesus meant what He said. If you fail to take up your cross, you will miss Christ in this life and for all eternity.

What must a man do to inherit eternal life? Separate from anything that you place before Jesus. No price is too great to pay to be able to come to Christ. Take up your cross and follow Christ.

Prayer and Praise:

Lord, no price is too great to be able to come to You and follow You. Teach me daily how to carry my cross for Your glory. In the mighty name of Jesus Christ, my Lord. Amen.

BROKEN AND SPILLED OUT
Mark 14:3-9

Have you ever been misunderstood? Most people have at some time or another in life. It is difficult for people to understand that an act of worship to the Lord is costly. Society has been very effective to breed the mentality that life is "all about you." That is a scary place to be.

When Mary broke the box of expensive perfume, it is said to have been valued at a year's wages. Have you ever given a sacrifice to the Lord that compares to a year's wages? That was a truly amazing gift, and the men present did not understand how or why she would do such a thing. It was extravagant worship.

Worship is costly. Beyond the perfume and the broken box, Mary was demonstrating her life to Jesus. She was living broken and spilled out, and living her life was for Christ's glory. What does it take for a person to be broken before the Lord? It involves a surrender of all one is to Christ. It involves willing to be misunderstood by religious people. It involves giving of self and substance that will not be restored to you. It involves honesty, humility, and genuine love for your Savior.

Mary's life was just as the box and the perfume. It was broken and poured out before the Lord for His glory. That is what God wants from every believer. That is what God wants from you.

Prayer and Praise:

Lord, I want my life to be broken and spilled out for You and for Your glory. Even if others do not understand me, let me live surrendered to You, spilled out and broken. In the mighty name of Jesus Christ, my Lord. Amen.

SURRENDER
Luke 1:38

The idea of surrender is not an appealing thought. Society exalts the individual who blazes his own trail, who pulls himself up by his bootstraps and succeeds. However, when you come to Jesus Christ, all of that is worthless. You come just as you are, in and with your sin, yielding your life to the Savior, or you do not come to Christ.

Often people want to come to Christ with conditions. You cannot come to Christ for salvation or walk with Christ when you have conditions of surrender. Surrender to Jesus Christ is absolute. You have no special deals worked out, no arrangements made and no favors you can call in. When you come to Christ, you come surrendering your life, your rights, and your will, or you cannot come to Christ.

When Mary was approached by the angel of the Lord, she surrendered all to God. She asked questions not with an accusative attitude or defiance, but questions of clarity. She accepted the will of God and surrendered. She said, "Behold the maidservant of the Lord." The maidservant was the person who would do all the jobs or tasks you did not want to do. She was a servant, and she did what she was told.

Have you surrendered in such a fashion to Christ that you do everything He tells you to do? Do you respond when He speaks to you? In church, when the invitation time comes, are you willing to leave your seat and go to the altar and pray when no one else has gone forward? When was the last time you responded and went to the altar to pray?

Surrender is not a popular topic, but it is crucial for a child of God to surrender everything he or she is to Christ. Surrender your rights, your family, your possessions, your job, your ambitions, and your desires. Surrender is not a onetime thing; daily you lay your life on the altar and confess to the Lord, not my will but Your will be done. Not my way but Your way be done.

It is only as you daily surrender to Christ that you are able to live under the lordship of Jesus Christ. Only as He is Lord of your life will your life have impact for God's glory and kingdom.

The song says, "All to Jesus I surrender. All to Him I freely give." Is that true of you?

Prayer and Praise:

Lord, show me any area of my life I have not surrendered by faith to You. Teach me to daily die to myself and live for Your glory and kingdom. In the mighty name of Jesus Christ, my Lord. Amen.

LED BY THE SPIRIT
Luke 4:1

After Jesus was baptized, He was led by the Spirit to the wilderness. After He fasted for forty days, the Devil came to tempt Him. Do you understand that you are to be led by the Spirit of God? Do you understand He will not always lead you to a place of ease and comfort? To be led by the Holy Spirit is crucial for a believer. It is the only way a child of God can live by faith and in obedience to the Father.

Once you are saved, the Holy Spirit takes up residence in your life for the purpose of teaching, guiding, and directing your life. It is crucial that you respond to the Holy Spirit's leading. Part of following the leading of the Spirit is living in agreement and obedience to God's Word. If the stewardship of your life is not in line with the Scriptures, you are not following the leading of the Holy Spirit, and you are not living by faith.

As you yield to the Word of God, the Holy Spirit guides you. He will lead your life. You may be surprised to find that He will lead you to a place of isolation, a wilderness, just as He did Jesus. If you read the Scriptures, it will amaze you to discover how many of the saints of God who had wilderness experiences. Joseph was in a dungeon (a wilderness), Elijah was three years in the wilderness, John the Baptist came preaching from the wilderness, and Jesus was led to the wilderness.

God leads His children to have wilderness experiences so that He can teach them dependency and faith in Him. If you resist the wilderness, you can miss God. The Holy Spirit leads you to the wilderness to teach you. The question is will you follow and stay put until God releases you?

Do not be surprised when you find yourself in a wilderness. In those times, God is preparing you for future service. When Jesus returned from the wilderness, He came forth in the power of the Holy Spirit (v. 14), and doors of opportunity opened for Him (He taught in their synagogues).

Prayer and Praise:

Lord, I praise You for how You prepare me for service. Wilderness times are difficult, but You enable me in those times, and I thank You. Keep me sensitive to the Holy Spirit as He leads me. In the mighty name of Jesus Christ, my Lord. Amen.

WHAT IS YOUR PLAN?
Luke 9:10-17

This is one of the stories you learn as a child in Sunday school. Jesus, with His disciples, after a long day of ministry, went to a secluded place, but the crowd followed them. Jesus received them and taught them about the kingdom of God, and He healed those who needed healing.

The disciples came to Christ as the day turned into evening and said to Jesus, send the crowd away. We are in a desert place, and there are no provisions here. Send them home. Is that how you react to people who have been hungry for the truths of the kingdom of God? Is that your plan, to send them home?

Jesus told the disciples to give them something to eat. The disciples protested, "We have nothing. Only five biscuits and two fish, a boy's snack is all we have." Yet, as Jesus commanded the disciples and blessed the food, He fed five thousand men plus the women and children—all with a small lunch that had been given to Christ.

What is your plan when Jesus asks you to do something you cannot do? Do you make excuses? Do you hesitate and complain? Or do you simply give what you have in faith and walk in obedience to His Word?

Jesus does not want you to come up with a plan. Jesus wants you to trust Him explicitly. Jesus does not need your ideas or input, He wants you to trust Him with what you have and obey His words.

You do not need to come up with a plan; you need to be close enough to Jesus to hear His plan, His Word.

How close are you to Christ? Do you hear Him when He speaks challenging words? Are you presently obeying everything His Word teaches? Are you close enough to Jesus to hear Him when He whispers?

Prayer and Praise:

Lord, let me learn daily to obey Your Word. Teach me to listen to You without giving You ideas of how things should be done or worked out. In the mighty name of Jesus Christ, my Lord. Amen.

DISTRACTIONS
Luke 10:39-42

Have you lived long enough to realize that many things can distract you from the most important things of life? Have you lived long enough to recognize that everything that is good is not the best thing for you? Have you lived long enough to know you are responsible for the choices of your life?

Mary and Martha each made choices in the text. Martha's choice was like many choices you have to choose from today. It looked important and it appeared needful. The choice that Martha made was a major distraction in her life that kept her from being intimate with Jesus Christ.

Martha was distracted by the preparations. She was so busy preparing for Jesus that she missed her relationship with Jesus. Martha was deceived by her duties. She got distracted in what she thought God expected of her.

Martha was so busy that her priorities were in disorder. Have you ever had days like that? Part of Martha's issue was that she was driven to perform. In all that she did for Christ, she failed to meet with Christ and receive His Words.

Mary understood what was needful. Mary realized that being busy and serving can be a distraction from the most needful thing. What is the most needful thing? The most needful thing is to focus on the Word of God, as you are in the presence of Jesus.

Do you sit at the feet of Jesus daily and listen to receive His Word? Do you guard that time alone with Christ so that nothing distracts you from Him? It is only after you spend time with the Lord that you are equipped to serve in His strength and for His glory.

Prayer and Praise:

Lord, I thank You for the truth of Your Word that You give me every day. Teach me to guard my heart and my time so that nothing keeps me from spending time with You. In the mighty name of Jesus Christ, my Lord. Amen.

THE OTHER PRODIGAL
Luke 15:25-32

The story of the prodigal son is a very familiar passage. Sadly, there are two prodigals in the story; the prodigal who left home and the older brother who refused to go into the father's house. What an awful picture of a child of God.

What was the sin of the older brother? He did not care about his younger brother. He told his father in anger, "This son of yours ..." He did not even acknowledge him as his brother. His next sin was anger. He was angry at the father for his celebration of his brother's return and restoration. Anger is a terrible sin. It can consume you and control you.

The older brother refused to go into the father's house, and the father did for him what he had done for the younger brother; he went out to meet him. The father pleaded with him, but you never see the older brother going in with the father.

The father says to him in verse thirty-two, "your brother." The older brother was just as much in need of reconciliation as the younger brother had been. The story never tells us he went in.

Has God ever challenged you with the sin of anger? When you have refused to go to the Father, has He not come out to you? That is what Jesus does for every sinner. He takes the first step coming to you by His Spirit and by His Word, and He entreats you to come into the house of joy, the house of reconciliation. The Father comes to you. He entreats you, He begs you to trust, believe, and repent. Will you dig in your heels as this prodigal and refuse to go into the house of reconciliation? When the Father speaks, obey Him quickly.

Prayer and Praise:

Lord, I know I have played the role of the prodigal son and the older brother. Thank You for entreating me to come in. Thank You for restoring me. In the mighty name of Jesus Christ, my Lord. Amen.

PRAY AND NOT LOSE HEART
Luke 18:1

The phrase lose heart simply means "to faint." You do not think you can go on. You feel weary and tired in your faith walk. Many of Scripture's greatest men experienced times they felt faint, or they would lose heart. David, a man after God's own heart, grew faint. Had it not been for Abishi coming to his aid, he might not have survived.

Have you ever grown faint and weary in your walk of faith? Most true believers have. The text gives you the secret to continuing with God. It is a very simple word pray. The context is simple—if you do not want to lose heart, pray. The issue is how is your prayer life?

One of the main hindrances to your personal prayer life is that you can make it complicated. You want to come before God in prayer with confidence and competence. The world is impressed with intellect and ability. When you come before God with these intellectual sounding prayers, you impress only yourself. The focus is on the prayer and not God.

God wants you to come to him as a child, just as you are, in simplicity and frailty, but you come focused on God and not on how you sound. As you spend time with your heavenly Father, over time you learn how to pray and not lose heart. Over time is an oversimplified phrase, because learning to pray takes a lifetime. It is not a fifty-yard dash, but rather a marathon.

What is involved in becoming like a child? You have to lose the focus on yourself. You spend unhurried time with the Lord, talking and listening. You begin at some point to walk in rhythm with Him. Prayer becomes as natural as breathing.

Do you still face trials and difficulties? Yes, but you do not lose heart. Do you ever feel overwhelmed? Yes, but that feeling drives you to your knees, and you cry out to the Lord. Crying out does not always sound intellectual or even competent, but you cry out to your heavenly Father anyway.

Prayer and Praise:

Lord, teach me to come before You as a child. Teach me to cry out to You even when it sounds messy. Let me not lose heart. In the mighty name of Jesus Christ, my Lord. Amen.

AN OCCASION FOR TESTIMONY
Luke 21:13

Do you know what a testimony is? It is an open declaration of a person's faith in Christ. Christians have one testimony of faith in Christ, but Christians have many testimonies of the faithfulness of Christ. You have a testimony of when God answered your prayers. You have a testimony of when God moved mightily in your life. You have a testimony, so have you shared it?

Even difficult seasons of life will provide you opportunity to testify of the goodness and greatness of God. Even the difficulties of life offer you the chance to share with lost friends, family, and coworkers of the wonderful works of God.

When was the last time you shared your testimony of faith? Have you ever shared how you came to faith in Christ with your children or your family? They need to hear from you, of your experience of faith and how God has worked in your life.

Good days, bad days, and indifferent days all provide an opportunity for your testimony. You do not share just the good stuff; you have to learn to be open and transparent to share the hard things you have to face.

It is as you share your testimony that you become stronger. The words you express openly to others make you more accountable to your Lord. The book of Revelation says this, "And they overcame him [the Devil] by the blood of the Lamb and by the word of their testimony, and they did not love their lives to the death" (Revelation 12:11).

By the sharing of your testimony, you are enabled by God to be an overcomer. Do you want to live as an overcomer? That is the goal of true believer: living to the glory of God, reflecting Christ to a sin-filled world and being an overcomer.

Being an overcomer does not mean you have a problem-free life. It means in spite of the troubles and trials, you are faithful to the Lord. Hallelujah!

Prayer and Praise:

Lord, let me see the opportunities You give to me to share my personal testimony. Father, give me boldness to share my testimony. In the mighty name of Jesus Christ, my Lord. Amen.

SIFTED AS WHEAT
Luke 22:31-32

The idea of being sifted is difficult to comprehend for a person. When wheat was sifted, the husk and the kernel was first separated from the stalk and placed in a large shallow-type basket. The person would then pick up the basket and begin to toss the wheat kernel and husk in the air, catching it as it came down. This constant jarring of the wheat was how the husk was separated from the kernel.

Sifting was normally done on a day when the wind was blowing. Once the husk was loosened from the kernel of wheat by the constant jarring, the husk would be carried away with the wind, the husk being lighter than the kernel. The kernel that was left was pure.

In the text, Jesus told Peter that Satan had asked for permission to sift him, and God gave it. Why would God give permission to Satan? God uses what Satan intends for harm to purify you. Satan means it for evil, but God uses it for good.

Satan's desire is to kill, steal, and destroy the child of God. He wants to kill your testimony, steal your joy, and destroy your life, but greater is He that is in you than he that is in the world. Do not be surprised at Satan's attack. Realize God will use it to purify your faith.

Jesus told Peter He had prayed for him, that his faith failed not. How wonderful it is to know Jesus is praying for you. Jesus knew Peter would deny Him, and He was telling him once he repented of that sin, he was to strengthen others in the faith.

Realize you will go through times of sifting, and you may not always respond rightly, but Jesus is praying for you, and once you are restored through biblical repentance, you will help other struggling brothers.

Prayer and Praise:

Lord, help me when my sifting times come. Teach me to understand You are allowing this in order to purify my faith. In the mighty name of Jesus, my Lord. Amen.

WHATEVER HE SAYS, DO IT
John 2:5

Do you like to receive instructions? Is there a difference between receiving instructions and taking instructions? The only difference is in your attitude of how you hear them given. Many people do not like being told what to do, and so taking instructions is more challenging. The wisest thing you will ever learn to do is to take or receive instructions from Christ.

In the text, why do you think Mary took this need to Jesus? After all, it was not her wedding or responsibility. She was probably trying to help those responsible to not be embarrassed by running out of wine. Why did she tell Jesus? She was looking out for others. Do you look out for others, or do you live solely for self?

Mary told the servants to do whatever Jesus said to them. That is sound and solid advice. When you obey the Word of God, God assumes responsibility for the consequences of your obedience.

Obedience is doing what, when, and how much God tells you to do. Do you do all that God tells you to do?

Jesus Christ began His ministry by filling the water pots full. Jesus filled Peter's boat so full of fish it began to sink (Luke 5:7). He filled the house where the people met as the lame man was lowered from the roof. He wants to fill you, but you must be willing to do all that He tells you to do.

Prayer and Praise:

Lord, teach me to listen ever so carefully to Your Word so I may obey all that You tell me to do. Fill my life with Your Holy Spirit. In the mighty name of Jesus Christ, my Lord. Amen.

HE NEEDED TO GO THROUGH SAMARIA
John 4:4

As you read this passage of Scripture, does it strike you that Jesus needed to go through Samaria? You read the Scriptures, you study theology, and you pray to the Almighty God for salvation and direction. How is it possible Jesus needed anything? He is God incarnate. Yet, the text clearly says that Jesus needed to go through Samaria.

Why was Samaria so important? It was not that Samaria was that important, but it was who lived in Samaria that was important. There was a woman who lived in that town. She was an outcast, an adulteress, a rejected and despised woman, but she was a kingpin. She had within her the ability to bring this entire town to their knees before Jesus Christ.

This was not a job for a rookie; this was a job for Jesus. When Jesus won her, He won the entire town. As Jesus waited there at Jacob's well, she came by and Jesus asked her for a drink of water. The pursuit was on. They talked about traditions, they talked about religion, until finally Jesus asked her about her sin. The man she was living with was not her husband. They talked about how thirsty she was for life.

Do you know anybody like this woman? A person trying to find fulfillment in the world but is always coming up short? Jesus told the Samaritan woman about His living water. She wanted it, but before she could have it, she had to deal with her sin. Jesus confronted her with her sin. Before a person can drink of the living water, there must be repentance of sin.

This lady, who was an outcast, hurried back into town, leaving her water pot, and told the men, the leaders, "Come see a Man who told me everything." The whole town went out to meet Jesus. She was a kingpin— you won her, you won the town. There are still others like her today. Jesus still offers His living water.

Prayer and Praise:

Lord, show me who the kingpin is in my town and use me to win that person to You. In the mighty name of Jesus Christ, my Lord. Amen.

NOVEMBER

November 1........John 8:32, Truth and Freedom
November 2........John 11:39, The Stone Removed
November 3........John 13:4-5, Foot Washing
November 4........John 17, The Lord's Prayer
November 5........John 21:15-17, Do You Love Me
November 6........Acts 1:8, Receiving the Power Of God
November 7........Acts 4:24-33, Praying for Boldness
November 8........Acts 7:55-56, Jesus Christ Standing
November 9........Acts 12:5, Sentenced
November 10......Acts 13:36, Serving Your Generation
November 11......Acts 16:6, Forbidden by the Holy Spirit
November 12......Acts 19:13-16, Being Known in Hell
November 13......Acts 24:25, A Convenient Time
November 14......Acts 27:39-44, Shipwrecked
November 15......Romans 1:1, Separated unto the Gospel
November 16......Romans 4:18-21, Marks of Faith
November 17......Romans 8:1, Walking After the Spirit
November 18......Romans 10:1, My Heart's Desire
November 19......Romans 14:19-23, How to Know Right from Wrong
November 20......1 Corinthians 3:3, Carnal Minded
November 21......1 Corinthians 5:5, Delivered to Satan
November 22......1 Corinthians 9:27, Castaway
November 23......1 Corinthians 10:13, Temptation
November 24......1 Corinthians 15:2, Believing in Vain
November 25......2 Corinthians 1:3, God of All Comfort
November 26......2 Corinthians 4:1, Faint Not
November 27......2 Corinthians 7:10-11, Godly Sorrow Worketh Repentance
November 28......2 Corinthians 13:5, Examine Yourselves
November 29......Galatians 2:20, Crucified with Christ
November 30......Galatians 6:1-2, Burden Bearing

TRUTH AND FREEDOM
John 8:32

This is one of the most wonderful promises in the entire Bible. Most people are pursuing happiness because they have a type of liberty and because they live in the United States. The Constitution of the United States promises this right—the pursuit of life, liberty, and happiness.

Jesus told those who followed Him, those who believed on Him, "If you abide in My word, you are My disciples indeed." To believe in Christ is for salvation. This is not an intellectual assent, but rather believing with your whole heart as you surrender your life to Christ. Then Jesus says you must continue in His Word.

If you are to know true freedom, you must commit to a personal and abiding relationship with Jesus. You will only abide in Christ to the degree you receive His Word into your life. How much time do you spend daily receiving His truth, His Word?

The truth of Christ will set you free. When you act in strict obedience to the truth revealed in the Bible, the truth will behave, and the end effect will be righteousness and godliness in your life. When you act in obedience to a lie (the world), the lie behaves and produces iniquity and sin in your life. To behave according to the lie is an act of independence from God, and this is an act of unbelief.

What are some things that hinder a Christian from accepting truth after he or she has been saved? Feelings, guilt, and doubt. Satan still attacks your mind to render you useless. That is why the intake of truth is so important. Plus, take every thought captive to the glory of God. If a negative, bad, or doubtful thought comes through your mind, reject it in the name of Jesus, and replace it with the Word of God.

Prayer and Praise:

Lord, thank You for the freedom that is given as I continue in Your Word. Let me be so surrendered to Your truth so that it behaves in my life, showing forth righteousness and godliness. In the mighty name of Jesus Christ, my Lord. Amen.

THE STONE REMOVED
John 11:39

The story of the raising from the dead of Lazarus is powerful. It reinforces the truth that Jesus Christ has the power to meet any need you have. He raised the dead. Do you know of anything greater than that?

When Jesus told them to take the stone away, Martha, Lazarus's sister, protested. She could not conceive of the power that Christ had. She thought Lazarus's body would be decomposing and smelling after four days. Jesus insisted the stone was to be taken away.

The stone had to be removed to let in life. Without life, there would be no truth or new life. The stone represents the many ways you try to keep things covered up, because you do not want to know the truth. To remove the stone is an unpleasant and painful process.

Light and life always connect. To walk in the light is a conscious decision to not keep any area of your life in darkness. Martha did not want to face the decay, despair, humiliation, and pain. She had soon forgotten the weeping of Christ, and that He identified with her. Jesus still identifies with you.

To remove the stone was an act of obedience to Christ, but also, a demonstration of faith. If you fail in this area of faith and obedience, you will miss the glory of God on this side. Do you want to see and experience God's glory? Then you must be willing to remove the stones from your life.

Prayer and Praise:

Lord, show me any area I have stones hiding and concealing the stink of sin. I want to walk in the light, Your light. Expose any area that is in darkness and allow me, by faith, to remove the stone and know Your cleansing. Let no area of my life remain in the dark. In the mighty name of Jesus Christ, my Lord. Amen.

FOOT WASHING
John 13:4-5

Most Christians read this passage of Scripture and interpret it to mean you are to minister refreshment and renewal to other believers. They fail to see the deeper meaning that the text teaches. However, there are a few churches and some denominations that still practice foot washing as an ordinance that Jesus established.

When Jesus took a towel and began to wash the feet of His disciples, He was teaching them a lesson in service, but more so, He was teaching them a lesson in humility. To physically remove your shoes and socks from your feet and allow another person to touch, clean, dry them, and pray over you is very humbling. In fact, it is easier to wash others' feet than to have your own feet washed.

This is why Peter protested. He knew he was undeserving of this act. He knew he should be the one washing the feet of Christ. However, Jesus was teaching. Jesus always is teaching the one lesson that receiving is as important as giving in this area. You must be clothed in humility to wash another's foot or to receive your feet being washed.

A man once shared he had participated in such a service. Another man, with which the first man had had a dispute, came and washed his feet. This man said, "All hard feelings were dissolved in that moment." Refreshment came, renewal came, and with those the enablement to continue came.

The question you must answer is, are you so clothed in humility that you would be willing to allow someone to wash your feet? Someone with whom you may have had a disagreement? Are you so clothed in humility you would wash someone else's feet? Someone who does not even deserve it, but desperately needs to be refreshed?

Prayer and Praise:

Lord, clothe me in humility day by day, so that I am willing to allow others to wash my feet. Clothe me in humility so that I am willing to wash others' feet. Use me to bring Your refreshment to others. Let me be sensitive to these opportunities. In the mighty name of Jesus Christ, my Lord. Amen.

THE LORD'S PRAYER
John 17

Most people think the Lord's Prayer is when the disci and asked him to teach them to pray. That is the moo contains true prayer of the Lord. It is interesting to note t. ......ever asked Jesus to teach them to preach, or to praise, or eve ... w to disciple someone. The disciples asked Jesus to teach them to pray.

Jesus taught the disciples the elements of prayer, and then He demonstrated to the disciples prayer—Jesus prayed. If Jesus prayed to the Father, how much more do you need to pray? In prayer Jesus was showing His reliance on God. If your reliance on God is measured by your prayer time, how much do you rely on the Father?

Jesus was depending on the Father's power (v. 2), not human strength. Prayer unleashes the power of God in a life that depends on God. Next, you see God's name was made known and evidenced in all Jesus did (v. 6).

Jesus then spoke God's word to men (v. 8), and men received it. When God's Word comes to you, do you receive it, or do you ignore it? One of the greatest verses is verse nine. We see Jesus praying for us. We are told that Christ ever lives to make intercession for us (Hebrews 7:25).

Part of the intercession Jesus makes is for you to be protected from the evil one while in the world. Next, He prays for your sanctification through truth. God's Word is truth. Finally, Jesus prays for oneness and unity, in order that a lost world can see and be saved (v. 23).

Every time you pray, it is because Jesus is praying for you. He is still interceding for you. The Holy Spirit is making intercession for you (Romans 8:27). You cannot fail with that combination interceding on your behalf. Hallelujah!

Prayer and Praise:

Lord, thank You for still interceding for me. Thank You for the Holy Spirit interceding for me. Teach me how to intercede in prayer for others. In the mighty name of Jesus Christ, my Lord. Amen.

DO YOU LOVE ME
John 21:15-17

When Jesus asked Peter, "Do you love Me?" what do you think was going on in his mind? Perhaps it's the same thing that has gone on in your mind at times. Peter remembered his boasting of how he would never deny Christ. He remembered how he said he was ready to die for Christ. He remembered how he betrayed, denied, and forsook Christ.

Have you ever made statements of your faith, your commitment, that have come back to haunt you? Most believers have, and still Christ loves you and seeks you to return. Just as Jesus prepared breakfast for the disciples who had gone fishing, Jesus invites you, also, to come back to Him and experience His fresh provision.

Jesus asked Peter the specific question, "Do you love Me more than these?" What are "these" He is referring to? Jesus was asking Peter if he loved Him more than his fishing boats. Has Jesus ever asked if you love Him more than your career? More than your boats and cars? Have you lived in such a fashion that Jesus needed for you to hear yourself answer this pointed question?

Getting honest about how a person loves the Lord is crucial. The way you know what you love is by what you give your time, attention, and your resources to. Many people say with their mouths they love the Lord, but their lifestyle denies Him. If a person does not determine to give his time to Christ, he will not. Time robbers come and steal away your time. The best intentions are wasted, because time is not guarded that belongs to the Lord.

It is very easy to mean to read the Bible and pray, only to be sidetracked by a television show that wastes one hour or longer. The establishment of priorities is crucial. The Devil is very subtle, and he allows little things to occupy your mind, your attention, and consume your time, so that you will not seek the Lord with all your heart, soul, strength, and mind.

Do you love Jesus more than your stuff? It is proven by how you spend your time.

Prayer and Praise:

Lord, teach me to guard my time and to prioritize my time with You being first and foremost. Show me what time robbers are in my life. In the mighty name of Jesus Christ, my Lord. Amen.

RECEIVING THE POWER OF GOD
Acts 1:8

The world desires power and control. There are a lot of different types of power. There is political power. There is financial power. There is emotional and relational power. There is military power and physical power. All of these pale in comparison to God's power. God has promised to give you His power if you will respond obediently to Him.

When Jesus Christ saved you, He enabled you to live the Christian life. He did not save you for you to live the Christian life in your own strength. It is humanly impossible to live the Christian life in your own strength. If you could live the Christian life in your own strength, then Jesus Christ did not need to die for your sin. Jesus died for your sin to pay the sin debt and to release to you the enabling power of the Holy Spirit.

That is the essence of Acts 1:8. The Holy Spirit comes upon a person who is born again to give him what he does not have, in order to do what God wants him to do. The Holy Spirit comes on a believer's life with power to live the Christian life. It is Christ in you, who lives through you, and enables you to live the Christian life.

The evidence that a person is truly filled with the Holy Spirit is not in some gift, but the power of God is on the person's life. When the power of God is on your life you will be a witness to Christ. Are you a witness to Christ? If not, you are not living filled with the Holy Spirit, and the power of God is not moving through you.

The power of God comes upon the person who is saved and filled with the Holy Spirit. It is this power that enables you to live the Christian life effectively and impact others with the message of Christ.

Prayer and Praise:

Lord, thank You for the promise of Your Holy Spirit. Thank You for the reality of the Holy Spirit in my life. Thank You for Your power released in me to live for You. In the mighty name of Jesus Christ, my Lord. Amen.

PRAYING FOR BOLDNESS
Acts 4:24-33

In this passage of Scripture, does it surprise you to find the early Christians praying for boldness? If they had boldness, they would not be asking for boldness. Because they were asking for boldness shows that they were in need of boldness. How about you? Have you ever prayed for boldness? You should, because the Lord loves to pour out boldness for Him in answer to your prayer.

Is boldness something that comes naturally, or is it something that is learned and you choose to participate in? To a small degree, boldness is related to confidence. When a person's confidence is strong, he tends to exhibit boldness. When his confidence is weak, he tends to be less bold.

One of the keys to boldness is having strong confidence.

What should your confidence to be in? Yourself, your abilities, your intellect, or your resources? Not necessarily. These things will give a person self-confidence, but the boldness a Christian needs is a God-confidence. Therefore, if you are to have boldness, your confidence in God must be strong. Strong confidence in God is related to faith in God. How do you increase your faith in God? Faith comes by hearing the Word of God (Romans 10:17). How is the intake of the Word of God in your life?

Every true child of God will need boldness at one time or another, boldness to stand for Christ when everyone else is denying Him. This may take place at your work, school, or even among family members. Pray for boldness. Build yourself up in the Word of God, and let faith spring forth. Strong confidence in God is a blessing for all believers. They can know this confidence if they will seek the Lord first and foremost in every area of their lives.

Prayer and Praise:

Lord, I need boldness to stand for truth; teach me how to position myself to receive this, as I ask for strong confidence in You. Give me boldness to not back away from a world that refuses You. Give me boldness so that I may glorify You. In the mighty name of Jesus Christ, my Lord. Amen.

JESUS CHRIST STANDING
Acts 7:55-56

When the president of the United States enters a room, people stand. Why do people stand for the president or dignitaries? It is a show of respect to the office held. The dignitary does not stand for the common person, but the common person stands for the dignitary.

In the passage of Scripture, the dignitary, Jesus Christ, is standing at the death, the martyrdom, of Stephen. Why would Christ stand? Jesus is the Savior of the world. Jesus is the Lord God Almighty. Jesus is the King of kings and Lord of lords, so why would He stand at the death of Stephen?

Stephen was the first martyr in the Bible. He laid his life down for Christ. He stood boldly before the God haters and proclaimed the Word of God, and they hated him and took up stones and stoned Stephen to death. When Stephen died, he died praying for the ones who were killing him. He prayed the same prayer Jesus prayed on the cross for those who nailed Him there. Stephen prayed, Father, forgive them.

In that moment, that glorious moment, Jesus Christ the Son of the living God, who is seated at the right hand of the Father, stood to receive Stephen into His presence. Jesus stood to receive one who was faithful to the death. Hallelujah to the Lamb!

Do you think you would be faithful to the death? It is a difficult question, maybe an impossible question to answer, but it is something every believer needs to give thought to. However, if you do not live for Him now, do not think you would die for Him? If you are not faithful in the stewardship of your life now, do not think you would die for Christ.

If you can ignore something as basic as tithing, do not think you would die for Christ. Before you die for Christ, you must live for Christ. Martyrs are not made at their willingness to die for Christ; they are discovered at that moment. Jesus Christ stands for those who give the ultimate sacrifice.

Prayer and Praise:

Lord, let me live in such a fashion that I could die for You. In the mighty name of Jesus Christ, my Lord. Amen.

SENTENCED
Acts 12:5

In order to stop the progress of the church, James the Apostle was killed with the sword. He became a martyr just as Stephen did. He died for his faith for the Lord Jesus Christ. When the worldly leader saw how it pleased the Jews, those who opposed the gospel, Peter was arrested and sentenced to die.

While Peter was in jail, the church did not cease to pray for him. What do you think they prayed? Certainly they prayed for his release and deliverance. They probably prayed for him to be bold, courageous, and faithful. They may have even prayed for those who guarded him that they would listen to the gospel and be saved. The church prayed. The church prayed without ceasing. The church gathered together to pray. Does your church gather together, specifically just to pray?

The amazing thing in this story is Peter's reaction to his death sentence. The night before his execution, Scripture tells that he was sleeping. How does a man sleep the night before the day he has been sentenced to die? How could he be so calm? Would you be calm?

If you remember the Word of God, if you know the Word of God, it enables calmness. At the end of John's gospel, Jesus told Peter a specific word concerning Peter's future. Jesus told Peter, "When you are old ..." (John 21:18). A simple word from Jesus made all the difference in the world to Peter. Jesus had told Peter he would be an old man. Since Jesus had given Peter a specific word concerning his age, Peter knew he would not die the next day, so he slept instead of panicking.

What specific word has God spoken to you that you need to hang onto and remember? To receive a word from God, you need to be in the Word of God. How does God give a person a specific word? As you read the Scriptures, the Holy Spirit pulls a verse or a passage off the page and He implants it in your heart. The Holy Spirit of God burns it inside of you, and it becomes engrafted to you; it becomes your word from God. In that word you have rest and calmness; you have hope.

Has God given you a specific word lately? Have you asked Him for a word? The Word of God makes all the difference in the world for a believer going through trials and difficulties. The Word of God gives forth life. Praise the Lord for His infallible Word!

Prayer and Praise:

Lord, thank You for Your Word. Give me a specific word and let it cling to me, as I cling to it. In the mighty name of Jesus Christ, my Lord. Amen.

SERVING YOUR GENERATION
Acts 13:36

All of us want to be relevant to our peers and in all our relationships. All of us want our lives to be understood and to have impact. How far will you go to be relevant to others? Would you cross the line of obedience to God in order to be "relevant" to peers? Would you compromise the Word of God in order to be relevant to society?

The church is challenged today to be "relevant" to culture. Do you think this is a correct concept, "to be culturally relevant?" It is a scary thought that the church today is culturally relevant to society. The church is to be biblically relevant. The church, the body of Christ, is to be different than the world. The Word of God is always relevant because of the author, God, and because of the message of salvation to a lost and dying world.

The text tells that, "For David, after he had served his own generation by the will of God ..." David was faithful to God and God's Word; therefore, he was relevant to his generation. Being relevant starts with being in and doing the will of God. To compromise the Word of God is not to be in the will of God.

You are called to be in the will of God, and once you do this, God will make relevant to a lost world His message of forgiveness and salvation. When a person thinks he must meet "felt" needs of individuals, compromising Scripture along the way, he will be culturally relevant, but not biblically relevant or right with God.

The message of Jesus Christ never changes. He came to seek and save sinners. Sinners must respond to Christ in repentance and faith. Methods may change. You need not use a telegraph machine to spread the Word of God. You have Internet access that takes the message instantly to others. Methods may change, but the message never changes.

Are you faithful to serve your generation being in the will of God? The message is always relevant. The messenger must be in the will of God. God will honor the faithfulness of His children.

Prayer and Praise:

Lord, let me strive always to be biblically relevant. For without biblical relevance, we have no message. In the mighty name of Jesus Christ, my Lord. Amen.

FORBIDDEN BY THE HOLY SPIRIT
Acts 16:6

There has never been a question whether or not the apostle Paul wanted to do the will of the Lord. With all his heart, mind, and strength he sought to advance the kingdom of God. Most would do well to learn this lesson. You would do well to seek the guidance of God as you live your life and how to advance and expand His kingdom.

The amazing thing in the text is that the Holy Spirit stopped Paul and forbade Paul to preach the word in Asia. Do you understand that? Does it make sense that the Holy Spirit would "forbid" the word to be preached anywhere? What is the lesson?

One thing that can be learned is that good intentions and good ideas are not always the will of God. You can become so driven to do, or to fulfill, a task that you fail to seek the mind of God, the will of God, and the permission of God.

Another lesson is that you are completely dependent upon the Holy Spirit. You can preach, teach, witness, and testify, but unless the Holy Spirit of God takes and breathes God's life into the words, it is as nothing. You must understand dependency on the Holy Spirit.

The next obvious question would be, are you sensitive to the Holy Spirit? When He says go, you go. When He says stop, you stop. Are you walking in such rhythm with God and abiding in His Word that you hear Him directing your life? Or do you presume on the Father, going about doing your religious Christian "stuff," but failing to live in true dependency on God?

God orders your goings and your stops. Be sensitive to the Holy Spirit. When He stops you, He may be redirecting your entire life.

Prayer and Praise:

Lord, You are my God and King; teach me to know Your ways. Teach me to yield to Your stops. Let me not be so headstrong that I miss You as I attempt to do "Your will." In the mighty name of Jesus Christ, my Lord. Amen.

BEING KNOWN IN HELL
Acts 19:13-16

As Paul ministered the word of God, many miracles took place. As these miracles were manifested the people took notice. One group was some of the "itinerant Jewish exorcists." They began to call upon the name of the Lord Jesus over those who had evil spirits. This sounds like a noble thing, trying to help those in bondage to the Devil. However, to confront the demonic takes more than a second-hand understanding of Jesus Christ.

Have you ever wished to have the same authority that the apostle Paul had? Many believers have wanted this, and the truth is it is available just as it was to Paul. Paul carried the authority of Jesus Christ because he lived surrendered to the lordship of Jesus Christ. He lived abiding, drawing his strength and direction from Christ.

Being known in hell is not for the spiritually elite. It is for all God's children who will walk by faith in a surrendered life to Christ. Being known in hell is a product of a life lived to and for the glory of God. It is not because your father or grandfather was a preacher. It is because you choose to bend your knee in submission and bow your heart to Almighty God. The Devil does not tremble at you because you are so good; he trembles only when you bend before the Father in the prayer of utter dependency: Christ in you, the hope of glory.

Being known in hell is not for bragging or boasting. It is because of a life of surrender and a life that seeks God with all its heart. Are you truly surrendered to Christ? Is there any area you have never laid on the altar to God? Do you seek the Lord with all your heart? If so, in what ways are you seeking God?

Prayer and Praise:

Lord, my desire is not to be known in hell, but to be known by You. As I am known by You, You will enable me in everything I need. In the mighty name of Jesus Christ, my Lord. Amen.

A CONVENIENT TIME
Acts 24:25

It is very easy to fall into the trap of wanting things to fit your schedule. When things come into your life which take you away from things you have planned, it can be stressful. However, you can so want to preserve your time and routine that you miss many things God has for your life which are tremendously more valuable than your agenda.

When it comes to the matter of salvation, many have pushed away the convicting power of the Holy Spirit, wishing to wait for a more convenient time. The sad truth is you are never promised tomorrow, you are never promised another opportunity to respond to God other than the present moment. When God speaks to you, that is the only opportunity you have to respond. You are not promised that He will speak to you or bring conviction to your soul another time. You only have the moment He is speaking.

This goes against what many would tell you. They say, "You can respond to God any time you want." Such a statement is inconsistent with Scripture. The Bible does not teach "decisionism" salvation, where you decide when you will respond to God. The Bible says, "But the word which they heard did not profit them, not being mixed with faith in those who heard it" (Hebrews 4:2b); and, "Today if you will hear His voice, do not harden your hearts" (Hebrews 4:7b).

Felix waited for a more convenient time, and it never came. What are you waiting for?

Prayer and Praise:

Lord, let me understand the time to do Your will is now. The time to obey You is today. Teach me to obey You quickly. In the mighty name of Jesus Christ, my Lord. Amen.

SHIPWRECKED
Acts 27:39-44

You read this passage of Paul's shipwreck and could easily think, "How does this apply to a person's life?" The truth of the matter is many people have shipwrecked their lives and never once been on a ship or a boat. People make poor decisions, and they shipwreck themselves financially; and they can shipwreck themselves emotionally by never learning to process feelings.

People also shipwreck themselves spiritually. Demas loved the world, left Paul for the world, and he is never heard of again (2 Timothy 4:10). It is amazing how people believe their choices will not have ramifications in the present and in eternity.

The good news is you do not have to let a shipwreck be the defining factor in your life. Everyone makes mistakes, but you must learn from your mistakes and move forward in faith. Paul faced more hardships than any other person in the New Testament, save Jesus Christ. He was beaten, stoned, shipwrecked, left for dead, and constantly opposed. One man said, "Everywhere Paul went and preached there was either a revival or a revolt." Paul never stopped. He never let his situation or circumstance detour him from the cause of Christ.

When Paul was literally shipwrecked, he remained faithful to Christ. You sense no panic in his words or deeds. How could he be so calm? He knew the word of God for his life. He knew he must go to Rome and nothing, not a storm or a shipwreck would, or could, stop the will of God.

Do you have that same confidence in your life? Do you know the will of God to such a degree that you are obeying it, that your life demonstrates such faith and confidence? If you do not, you may need to ask yourself why not.

Every Christian will face challenges, trials, and difficulties if they follow Christ. A shipwreck does not have to be fatal, if you are following Christ with all your heart, soul, mind, and strength.

Prayer and Praise:

Lord, whenever stormy waters come, let me stand on Your Word. Enable me to be faithful, even amidst opposition and trial. In the mighty name of Jesus Christ, my Lord. Amen.

SEPARATED UNTO THE GOSPEL
Romans 1:1

Paul starts the letter to the Romans saying he is "separated to the gospel of God." Have you ever considered what you have been separated to? Or are you separated to anything of the kingdom of God?

Most homes have in their possession a small knife called a paring knife. It is a knife designed to be used in cutting vegetables so close that you actually cut to the very edge of the produce. They are small, sharp and very useful. You take the paring knife, and you prepare fruits or vegetables in advance, separating them so they will be ready when needed.

That is what God wants for your life. He wants you separated from the world and the things of the world, prepared for Him, when He calls upon you. The question remains, are you separated unto God?

People are separated to many things, but not unto the Lord. It takes intentional effort to be separated to the gospel of God. Just as a paring knife cuts the produce, God by His Word and the Holy Spirit will cut you to the edge or the core of your being, as you yield to Him.

How does a person know if he or she is separated to the Lord? It is determined and seen by how a person spends his time and to what he gives his time. Everything about life is about time. If a person has no time for God, that person is a godless person, no matter what his or her profession of faith may be.

If you do not choose to give God your time, you will never be separated unto Him. Do you give God time every day in prayer, in Bible reading and study, in personal worship? Do you make every effort to be with the church in worship, praise, and prayer?

If all a person does is attend church on Sunday, that still does not make him godly. One hour out of one hundred and sixty-eight hours a week is by no means a mark of a true child of God. When a person is too busy to pray or read the Bible, yet he spends hours watching television, playing sports, or online, this person has a spiritual problem.

Everybody will be separated to something, either things of this world or the kingdom of God. What are you separated to? Are you living in such a fashion that you are separated unto God? Are you living for the moment, or are you living for eternity? It is determined by how and to what you give your time.

Prayer and Praise:

Lord, my desire is to be separated unto You and the gospel. Teach me to examine how I spend my time and to what I give my attention. Let me see how my free time is used. In the mighty name of Jesus Christ, my Lord. Amen.

MARKS OF FAITH
Romans 4:18-21

The King James translation reads, "Who against hope believed in hope." That is such a powerful definition of faith. Abraham was a man of true faith. When you realize what he did not have that is available today, it is even more amazing. Today, you have the Holy Bible, God's Word, in your possession. What a benefit for faith. Today, you live on the other side of Jesus's birth, life, death, and resurrection. These are all divinely tied to one's faith. Abraham did not have a Bible, and he lived before the birth of Christ, yet he had amazing faith.

How did Abraham have such faith? God initiated and called Abraham. God still does that today. God takes the initiative and speaks to hearts and minds, calling individuals to salvation and to obedience. Obedience is not just doing the will and command of God, obedience is done by faith.

Notice the marks of Abraham's faith. First, he believed. He had hope against hope; he believed. Abraham had firm confidence in God, Next, he did not become weak in faith. Abraham refused to doubt. Third, Abraham's faith prevented him from becoming discouraged by natural weakness. When he was eighty-six, he still had the natural capacity to produce Ishmael. Now, at one hundred, his ability to reproduce was dead. He was powerless in self.

Next, you see that he did not doubt God's promises, even when circumstances looked impossible. Fifth, he did not vacillate between faith and sight. He grasped personally the promise of God, Sixth, Abraham's faith was chorused by giving God glory. Finally, Abraham was fully persuaded: God's promises were certain and His power was sufficient.

As you read over these seven characteristics of Abraham's faith, how does yours measure up?

Prayer and Praise:

Lord, I want my faith to be as strong and bold as Abraham's faith. Show me what I am lacking in faith and why. Let my faith develop into full faith, just as Abraham's did. In the mighty name of Jesus Christ, my Lord. Amen.

WALKING AFTER THE SPIRIT
Romans 8:1

In this one verse (Romans 8:1) Paul gives the key to Christian victory—walking after or in the Holy Spirit. Some translations leave out the last half of verse 1, but it is most needed in the verse. It is repeated in Paul's letter to the Galatians (Galatians 5:16).

When a person is saved, he or she is changed by the power of God; the old passes away, and all things are new. The constant struggle is to put on the new man in Christ every day. There is no condemnation to those who are in Christ Jesus.

Eternally, this is the promise of God to those who are saved. Hallelujah! However, in day-to-day living, if you fail to put on the new man (done by faith just as you were saved), it is easy to begin to drift with the world. When one is drifting with the world, one is influenced by the world. When a believer drifts with the world, he loses many things. He loses full assurance, he forfeits the peace of God, and he opens himself to the subtle attacks of the Devil. Though he is eternally saved, he feels and senses condemnation.

It is crucially important to learn to walk after the Spirit. In doing this, you must understand it is a walk, not a labor. You adjust your life to seeking the things of God and pleasing God, and this is done every day. It is a walk, not a labor.

Also, to walk after the Spirit means to follow. To follow implies subjection. You must subject your life to Christ, to His Word and to His leading. Without subjection, or submission, you will never know the sweetness of Christ this side of eternity.

Verses 4 and 5 give more understanding of this Scriptural principle. The simple question emerges: Are you more mindful of the things of the flesh or the things of the Spirit of God?

Watch your walk.

Prayer and Praise:

Lord, teach me daily to seek to walk after the Spirit and not the flesh. Show me what my mind is mindful of. In the mighty name of Jesus Christ, my Lord. Amen.

MY HEART'S DESIRE
Romans 10:1

Have you ever stopped to consider what actually is your heart's desire? If you have a difficult time discerning the answer, then ask someone who is close to you; your spouse, best friend, or a family member. What you may not be able to realize yourself, others may readily have noticed in you.

Many people, even believers, may be surprised to realize exactly what is their hearts' desire. It always comes down to the same issues: it is to what you give your time, resources, and attention. Paul's heart's desire was to see his fellow countrymen saved. Do you desire to see this nation come under the salvation and lordship of Jesus Christ?

You understand a person is not saved because of his race. To be a Jew does not automatically mean you are right with God and saved. It is not by race. A person is not saved by religion. You can go to church every week and not be saved. You can have a church preference and a denominational preference and not be saved. A person is not saved by right living. Salvation is not merely being "moral" and "good." If that were the case, Jesus Christ would not have had to die on the cross.

A person is saved because he or she has been redeemed by Jesus Christ. The word redeemed means "purchased." When Jesus died on the cross, He died purchasing you from your sin. He shed His life's blood to pay for your sins and pardon you. Your responsibility is to call on the name of the Lord for salvation.

Once Jesus saves a person, He changes the person. The Holy Spirit comes into your life to teach, guide, and direct your life, and you are to daily yield to His direction.

Paul's heart's desire was to see his fellow Jewish countrymen saved. Is that your heart's desire? Do you pray as Paul prayed for family, friends, and coworkers to be saved? Do you verbally witness to them? Do you live your faith before them?

The quickest way to kill a witness is to live like the world and act like the world. Are you different than the people of the world, or do you pursue the same things they do?

Prayer and Praise:

Lord, my heart's desire is for Your glory. I long to see others come to a saving faith in Jesus Christ. Let me live out my faith every day before the world in which I live. In the mighty name of Jesus, my Lord. Amen.

HOW TO KNOW RIGHT FROM WRONG
Romans 14:19-23

Most people assume that everyone will know right from wrong. Many things contribute to one's understanding of what is right and what is wrong. Parents are major influencers. If parents compromise with the world, children will not know the difference between right and wrong.

Media is another major influencer. What people watch and observe impacts their ability to discern between what is right and wrong. Arts and entertainment is still another arena that will impact how a person defines right and wrong. When a sports figure or a musician lives for the world, and you follow that person as a fan, your standards are challenged.

When one talks about right and wrong for the Christian, it is always based on the Word of God. You will not properly discern right from wrong without knowing the biblical standard. God is a moral God. He gives the principles of right and wrong throughout Scripture. In this passage, in Romans, you are shown how to determine right from wrong.

The first test in discerning right from wrong is the test of Scripture. God's Word, the Bible, is absolute truth. Jesus said, "I am the way, the truth and the life (John 14:6)." In John 8:31-32, Jesus said, "If you abide in My word you are my disciples indeed; And you shall know the truth, and the truth shall make you free."

If you are trying to discern what is right or wrong, and it fails the test of Scripture, then it is wrong. Flee from it. The next test is influence. How will what you are doing or participating in have an impact on others? Will a young Christian stumble because of your involvement? Your influence on others is critical. If what you do is not in line with Scripture, stop it; if it is going to harm others in their walk with Christ, stop it.

Finally, the third test is that of conscience (Romans 14:22-23). This is the least effective test, but it is still a test. If your conscience has been seared by outside influences, your conscience will not recognize things as wrong. However, when your conscience rebukes something, stop it. It is when you ignore these rebukes and continue that a calloused heart develops. A calloused heart desensitizes you from God and His Word.

The last sentence in verse twenty-three is an eye opener: "Whatever is not from faith is sin." Is your life being lived by faith? Are you constantly adjusting your lifestyle to Scripture? If not, you will struggle with right and wrong, living by situation ethics, which is no ethics.

Prayer and Praise:

Lord, let me live so adjusted to You that I instantly know if what I am considering is right or wrong. Teach me to realize that my choices impact others greatly--for or against Christ. In the mighty name of Jesus Christ, my Lord. Amen.

CARNAL MINDED
1 Corinthians 3:3

The word carnal is not a word one uses often in his everyday conversations. Some younger people may not even be aware of the word or what it means. To be carnal is to be given to crude physical and bodily pleasures. Carnality is not a state of Christianity Paul was intending to create in writing this text. However, many have taken this concept and talk of "carnal Christians."

If a person finds himself as a carnal Christian, that is a call to repent. God never intended a Christian to live in carnality for any extended period of time.

There are characteristics of carnality. First, it is protracted infancy. You cannot serve self and others. Next, it is a state in which sin is supreme in your life. Third, carnality limits and denies spiritual gifts. Finally, a carnal person is sidetracked from receiving spiritual truth.

Carnality is about self—self-justification, self-elevation, self-indulgence, self-exaltation. Self must daily decrease, and Christ is to daily increase. This takes a conscious effort with deliberate activity. Do you feed your flesh, or do you feed your spirit? Do not be carnal. To be carnal is to be out of the will of God.

Prayer and Praise:

Lord, let me daily die to self and be alive unto Your glory. Empty me of me, and fill me afresh with Your Holy Spirit. Show me, convict me when self is unknowingly taking back control of my life. In the mighty name of Jesus Christ, my Lord. Amen.

DELIVERED TO SATAN
1 Corinthians 5:5

The very idea of someone being delivered over to Satan is gut-wrenching. How could a loving God, a God of grace and mercy, allow such a thing? Yes, God is a God of grace, but lest you forget He is a holy God and will not tolerate sin. Yes, He is a God of grace, but you must not forget that this is not His only attribute. He is a God of wrath, and His glory is many times magnified through His wrath.

Do not cheapen grace as a license to live any way you want apart from God. Sin separates one from God, and sin will be chastened and brought under judgment in a believer's life if it is not repented of.

When Paul wrote to "deliver such a one to Satan," he was showing how the grace of God would be demonstrated. It is far better to deal with your sin on this side of heaven and judgment than to carry your sin with you. To be delivered to Satan was for the purpose of allowing a sinning brother the opportunity to repent and return to the Father.

This is much like the prodigal son when he went and lived it up with riotous living, until his money ran out. He lived in the world, liked the world and was for the world, until he was bankrupted by the world. In essence, by his own choices, he allowed the Devil to blind him until he was at the bottom of the barrel. It was only then that he returned to his father's house with a genuinely repentant heart.

In life, when someone is playing the prodigal, the worst thing you can do is try to help him. In the act of trying to help him, you get in between him and God, and you prolong the process. Leave him to himself; let him come to the end crying out in desperation, only wanting mercy. This is the process God has ordained to return those who have gone astray.

Prayer and Praise:

Lord, teach me daily Your ways are always right. Let me not try to fix people by helping. Let me let You bring them to an end of themselves. In the mighty name of Jesus Christ, my Lord. Amen.

CASTAWAY
1 Corinthians 9:27

The Corinthian church was not the best model of a true God-fearing body of believers. They gave the impression they wanted to live Christian lives and be worldly at the same time. Nobody wanted to stand up for God's truth. They seemed to treat the Scriptures as God's suggestions instead of God's Word.

Paul, one of the greatest Christians who ever lived, said, "I want to be careful that I am not a castaway," or disqualified. What does it mean to be a castaway or disqualified? To be a castaway or disqualified was the greatest shame and dishonor.

There are two ways a Christian can be disqualified or a castaway. First, he may be disqualified by breaking the rules. Have you kept God's rules this week? God's rules are God's truth. Have you obeyed them? The second is that you could be a castaway for not giving your all. You did not put 100 percent in, and you did not give your best effort.

Being disqualified is not about going to heaven when you die. No, if you are truly saved you have the guarantee of heaven. It is about whether you are an honorable Christian, and when you get to heaven will you have anything to lay at the feet of Christ?

When you arrive in heaven you will receive an incorruptible crown based on how you ran the race of faith. You will place that crown at the feet of Jesus, if you were not disqualified and you received one. If you were disqualified, you will have nothing to lay at the feet of Christ for all eternity.

Last week is gone, and all you have is what is before you. By God's grace, this week, you should run to win so you will have a crown to lay at the feet of your precious Savior's feet.

Prayer and Praise:

Lord, teach me to obey Your truth and to always give 100 percent. Enable me to live in light of eternity and not just for the present. In the mighty name of Jesus Christ, my Lord. Amen.

TEMPTATION
1 Corinthians 10:13

As you read this verse of Scripture, it makes you want to thank the Lord for this wonderful promise. This verse shows how to overcome temptation. To be tempted is not the same as to sin; everyone is tempted at some point or another. It is when you give in to the temptation that you sin.

When you face a temptation, you face a choice. You have to decide if you will give in to the temptation or if you will make the choice and say no to the temptation. Temptation is common to man, but God is faithful and will make a way to escape the temptation. The key for overcoming temptation is in the faithfulness of God and not in your own strength or ability.

Temptation almost always comes when you least expect it. Your responsibility is to be daily abiding in Christ and drawing your strength from Him. Temptation is not sin, but God uses temptation to make His children stronger. As a temptation comes to your life and you respond in faith, spiritual muscle is developed, so you are stronger.

Why do you need to be stronger? The Devil will not leave you alone. He will come again and again with greater temptation and deception in the attempts to mess up your walk of faith. God is faithful. He allows spiritual muscle to develop before the next wave of temptation.

If you fail in the area of temptation, no spiritual muscle develops. If you fail in your walk with God, and you get out of rhythm with the Father (which is giving in to the temptation of the evil one), you will not be prepared to face the challenges and temptations of life.

One of the most subtle deceptions the Devil employs is distracting you from your daily quiet time with Christ. You are caught up the busyness of life and your devotion time gets pushed aside day after day, and you are not prepared spiritually.

Temptation is real, and it comes to all people, but God is faithful and provides the way of escape. Stay close to God. Look for the opportunity of escape and flee.

Prayer and Praise:

Lord, temptation sometimes comes at me like a giant wave of the ocean, and at other times it is so subtle I hardly recognize it. Lord, teach me to be aware of the subtlety of Satan and always to flee to You. In the mighty name of Jesus Christ, my Lord. Amen.

BELIEVING IN VAIN
1 Corinthians 15:2

As you read and study the Scriptures, you will find different types of faith. There is genuine saving faith; you will read of dead faith; there is demonic faith, and now you are introduced to vain, or empty, faith.

What does it mean when you have vain faith? If you remember the parable of the soils, there were four different types of soil. Wayside or hard soil, which the seed of the Word did not penetrate, and the birds of the air (the Devil) stole it away. This is a person who is knowingly lost.

Then you see the stony soil. The seed tried to take root, but there was no depth of soil, and the hard rock did not allow roots to go into the earth. This person is also lost, even though there was an initial response to the seed.

Next, the thorny soil—again the seed was responded to, but the cares of the world choked it out. This person is also lost. Finally, in the good soil, the person responds and fruit is brought forth.

Each person has every type of soil in him or her. Only the good soil is genuinely saved.

The stony ground and the thorny ground believed in vain. They made a response, but they failed to follow through, because the soil they allowed the seed to fall upon was wrong. Each person determines where the seed of the Word will fall.

Many receive it out of emotionalism or decisionism, but they never truly surrender to Christ. When faith is vain or empty it does not last, nor will it save. Paul warns us of believing in vain. It is a call to examine your faith to know if it is real or not. Does it have perseverance and follow-through?

Prayer and Praise:

Lord, thank You for giving me clear warnings to constantly examine my faith to see if it is real. Help me to be honest and know my faith is bearing fruit unto Your glory. In the mighty name of Jesus Christ, my Lord. Amen.

GOD OF ALL COMFORT
2 Corinthians 1:3

The word comfort means to sooth, to console, to cheer, even to encourage. Everyone likes comfort. Foods are even referred to as "comfort foods." That means they remind you of better days and times, such as when you were growing up with your family around you.

In the text, you read the phrase, "the God of all comfort," who has comforted you and will continue to comfort you amidst tribulations and troubles. That is such a wonderful promise. The key issue is to be in a position for God to comfort you.

God's promises are not automatic. Many of the promises of God are conditional upon your being obedient and faithful, even when times are difficult, in order to take advantage of God's comfort.

The word comfort is used twenty-nine times. It is the same word as Paraclete, or the word for the Holy Spirit. When God comforts you, it is the Holy Spirit strengthening you. God's comfort comes to you, not so much to make you comfortable, but to make you a comforter for others. Only those who have allowed God to comfort them are able to be of comfort to others.

It is about how you respond to adversity. When it comes, and it will come to everyone, do you respond by seeking God for comfort, or do you respond by complaining to God about your situation? Every difficulty you go through in life is preparing you to minister to someone else who will face a similar difficulty. Respond in faith to every trial and tribulation. Allow God to equip you to be an extension of His grace to someone else.

The God of all comfort will comfort you. Hallelujah to the Lamb! Praise God for His marvelous grace.

Prayer and Praise:

Lord, thank You for Your promise to comfort me. Teach me to respond to every difficult situation in faith, so I may in turn be a comfort to others who will face similar situations. In the mighty name of Jesus Christ, my Lord. Amen.

FAINT NOT
2 Corinthians 4:1

As Paul penned this letter, he made mention of having "this ministry." What ministry? It is a reference to the last chapter and the last three verses (3:16-18). It is the ministry of removing the veil, removing that which keeps people from seeing the truth.

The ministry you are to be about is taking away that which blocks, or hinders, from seeing the truth of God in others' lives. As you have been saved by the grace of God and the power of the Holy Spirit, you are never to quit, you are never to stop, and you are to never lose heart in doing the ministry of removing the veil that keeps people in darkness.

The key to not losing heart, or fainting not, is to keep your perspective properly focused on Christ. You are to preach Christ Jesus, not another message. God graces everyone who believes with the light of faith. The light of faith is given to you chiefly to enable you to behold the glory of God in Christ.

You must be careful that you are seeking the glory of Christ; longing for the glory of Christ. There are so many other things that call for your attention. All these other things are merely distractions the Devil uses to keep men in darkness.

Do not faint, do not lose heart; rather stay focused on Christ Jesus. Praise Him for allowing you the faith to behold His glory.

Prayer and Praise:

Lord, You are so wonderful. Enable me daily to focus on Your truth and Your plan. Let me behold Your glory. In the mighty name of Jesus Christ, my Lord.

GODLY SORROW WORKETH REPENTANCE
2 Corinthians 7:10-11

Most everyone knows what it is to be sorrowful; it is to be grieved, sad, or mournful. Human beings were created with emotions and can be very emotional over a variety of concerns. Emotions are not a bad thing; in fact, they are very helpful in the processing of feelings and pain.

However, just because a person expresses emotions does not mean she is right with God. Many a person has gone to an altar shedding tears of remorse, only continue doing the same things as before their altar experience.

Judas was saddened and had much sorrow after he betrayed Christ for thirty pieces of silver. His sorrow led him to take his own life, not to turn to Christ for forgiveness. The key to turning to God for mercy, forgiveness, and restoration is "godly sorrow."

Godly sorrow is not a mere emotion. Godly sorrow produces repentance, and no one can get right with God without practicing biblical repentance. Genuine biblical repentance produces fruit in keeping with repentance. It drives you closer to God. You become more reverent, passionate, and responsible. Purity of heart flows from your life.

Do you have godly sorrow? Or is your sorrow of the world and short lived?

Prayer and Praise:

Lord, teach me godly sorrow. Let it express itself in my life with a true passion for You and purity of heart. In the mighty name of Jesus Christ, my Lord. Amen.

EXAMINE YOURSELVES
2 Corinthians 13:5

After Paul has given words of encouragement and hope throughout this letter, he concludes by challenging professing believers to examine their faith. Why does a professing believer need to examine his faith? To be certain that his faith is real. The Bible tells of vain faith, demonic faith, and even weak faith. You have the responsibility to be sure your faith is genuine saving faith and effective faith.

How do you examine your faith? What questions must you ask and answer in order to know your faith is real and active? You must examine your faith based on the Word of God and not merely on your experience. Experience is always subject to Scripture. If you cannot substantiate your experience with Scripture, you must let go of the experience.

Emotions can cause confusion. Yes, God touches your emotions, but He will always be in agreement with the Word of God. Experience is always subject to Scripture.

Do you obey God's commandments? "By this we know that we know Him, if we keep His commandments" (1 John 2:3). Do you obey and keep the commandments of God, God's Word? Does the stewardship of your life prove this?

Do you confess that Jesus Christ is the Son of God? "Who is a liar but he who denies that Jesus is the Christ? He is antichrist who denies the Father and the Son. Whoever denies the Son does not have the Father either; he who acknowledges the Son has the Father also" (1 John 2:22-23).

Do you practice righteousness in your daily life? "In this the children of God and the children of the devil are manifest: Whoever does not practice righteousness is not of God, nor is he who does not love his brother (1 John 3:10)."

Do you love the brethren? Do you enjoy and seek out the company of believers, or are your best friends lost people? "We know that we have passed from death to life, because we love the brethren. He who does not love his brother abides in death" (1 John 3:14).

Do you pass all of these tests?

Prayer and Praise:

Lord, let me come before You daily examining my faith in light of Your Word. In the mighty name of Jesus Christ, my Lord. Amen.

CRUCIFIED WITH CHRIST
Galatians 2:20

Paul boldly and graciously declares, "I have been crucified with Christ." What a confession. Do you make this same confession? What does it mean to be crucified with Christ? How does the crucified life show itself in a believer's life?

The act of self-crucifixion is when you take up His cross and follow Christ. Jesus gave Himself for me in death. Now I give myself to Him in life. My passion is Him.

There are at least five marks of a crucified life. First, humility will be evidenced in your life. Second, you will be very much aware of your human inability, your helplessness. Third, you will be at rest in Christ. In abiding in Christ, you will know His peace and rest. Fourth, you will live separate from sin. Finally, you will practice and enjoy separateness from the world.

Prayer and Praise:

Lord, let the crucified life be evidenced in me. Let me know, enjoy, and abide in Your rest. In the mighty name of Jesus Christ, my Lord. Amen.

BURDEN BEARING
Galatians 6:1-2

Every person, saved or lost, experiences some degree of bearing burdens. However, for the child of God, burden bearing can be a ministry to others as you get under the load with them. As a child of God, you are commanded to bear the burdens of fellow believers. Just as you bear others' burdens, others will come alongside you and help bear your burdens in times of need.

When you are bearing burdens, the first thing you must identify is the source of the burden. Is this burden self-inflicted? Is this burden from Satan? Has God sent you this burden? Identifying the source enables you to understand adjustments that must be made to one's life or not.

What are the requirements to bear the burden of others? You must be aware of the need or issue. You must be available to get under the load with them. You need to be alert to the moving of God or the attacks of the Devil.

As you move through this process, you have to resist self. Self may want to quit, or self may want to try and fix something that God has allowed in order to teach you or someone else in this particular time. Do not get in between God and someone else. "Set your mind on things above, not on things on the earth" (Colossians 3:2). Finally, your motivation is always to die to self. This requires an act of faith and will.

Bearing burdens is an opportunity to minister Christ to others. There will be a day when you will need someone to get under your load with you and minister Christ to you.

Prayer and Praise:

Lord, burdens can be so heavy. Teach me how to get under the load with others in prayer to help them through these difficult times. In the mighty name of Jesus Christ, my Lord. Amen.

DECEMBER

December 1........Ephesians 1:17-18, What to Pray for Believers
December 2........Ephesians 5:15, Walking Circumspectly
December 3........Philippians 3:10, That I May Know Him
December 4........Colossians 1:9-12, Pray for One Another
December 5........1 Thessalonians 2:13, Receiving the Word
December 6........1 Thessalonians 5:17, Pray Always
December 7........2 Thessalonians 2:9-10, Satan's Power
December 8........1 Timothy 1:18-20, Shipwrecked Faith
December 9........1 Timothy 6:6, Growing in Contentment
December 10......2 Timothy 4:9-16, Cures for Loneliness
December 11......Titus 3:10-11, How to Deal with a Divisive Person
December 12......Philemon 1:10-16, Extending Forgiveness
December 13......Hebrews 3:15, Harden Not Your Heart
December 14......Hebrews 4:1-2, When the Word Is Not Profitable
December 15......Hebrews 8:8-10, The New Covenant
December 16......Hebrews 10:22, Preparing to Worship
December 17......James 1:21, The Implanted Word of God
December 18......James 4:7-8, Resist the Devil
December 19......1 Peter 2:4-5, Living Stones
December 20......1 Peter 4:19, Suffering According to the Will of God
December 21......2 Peter 3:3, Scoffers
December 22......1 John 1:5-10, Marks of True Salvation
December 23......1 John 5:12, Marks of True Salvation 2
December 24......2 John 1:4, Walking in Truth
December 25......3 John 1:9-11, Being Opposed
December 26......Jude 1:6-12, Root Sins
December 27......Revelation 4:11, You Are Worthy
December 28......Revelation 5:8, The Prayers of the Saints
December 29......Revelation 12:11, How to Overcome
December 30......Revelation 15:1-3, Your Works Follow You
December 31......Revelation 21:15-17, The Holy of Holies

WHAT TO PRAY FOR BELIEVERS
Ephesian 1:17-18

Oftentimes when you look at other believers, some of whom are in the midst of trials and are struggling, prayer comes easy for them. You know what they are facing and dealing with, and so you know how to bear their burden in prayer. There are other believers who appear to be handling life quite well, and you wonder how you are to pray for them. The most powerful prayers you can pray for anyone are when you pray Scripture.

Praying Scripture is the key to praying in the will of God. In these two verses, we are shown what to pray for other believers, whether they are struggling or not. Paul, writing under the inspiration of the Holy Spirit, tells you what to pray.

First, you are to pray that God will give them the spirit of wisdom. You are told in James 1 to ask for wisdom and God will give it to you. Believers need godly wisdom. Next, you are to pray that God will give them the spirit of revelation. Believers need revelation knowledge, understanding of Scripture and how it applies to them. Both of these requests are about knowing the Lord Jesus Christ and the Father better. It is about growing in intimacy with God.

You are also to pray that believers have their eyes of understanding enlightened. You are told in Hebrews 11:3, "By faith we understand." You need to see things from God's perspective, which gives true understanding.

Finally, as you pray for believers, pray they know the hope of their calling and the riches of God's glory. Hope is a tremendous confidence builder. Not hope in man, but hope based in the Lord Jesus Christ. When He saved you, He called you. To know His glory is what a believer lives for.

Prayer and Praise:

Lord, teach me daily how to pray Scripture for fellow believers. Show me the importance of praying Your Word on behalf of others who labor in service for You. In the mighty name of Jesus Christ, my Lord. Amen.

1. Pray that God gives the Spirit of Wisdom.
2. Pray that God gives the Spirit of Revelation
   Knowledge
   Understanding Scripture
   Appling that Wisdom

3. Pray for the eyes of understanding –
   to see Gods intentions and prospecti

WALKING CIRCUMSPECTLY
Ephesians 5:15

Circumspectly is not a word that is used very often in today's society. It is a word that means watchful, discreet, or prudent. The command of Scripture is for every believer to walk, to live, to behave circumspectly; be watchful. Why do you need to be watchful? The Devil prowls about trying to destroy you, your testimony, and your very life.

You are told three specific ways in which you are to walk in this chapter. In verse two, you are told to walk in love. In verse eight, you are told to walk in light. "Walk as children of light." Let the illumination of the Word of God and the Holy Spirit direct every step you take.

Lastly, you are told to walk circumspectly. The picture you can benefit from is of a house with a wall around it made of stones or concrete. On top of the wall has been placed, in the concrete, broken bottles and sharp rocks that would keep a person from trying to come across the wall.

As you look upon the wall, a cat appears and begins to walk ever so cautiously and tenderly. With precise form the cat raises her feet one after another and sets them down in between the shards of glass cautiously, never to step in the wrong place. That is how you are to walk and live in this world circumspectly.

Prayer and Praise:

Lord, teach me how to keep my eyes open to the snares of the Devil and my ears open to Your directing. Enable me to walk circumspectly in this world for Your glory. In the mighty name of Jesus Christ, my Lord. Amen.

THAT I MAY KNOW HIM
Philippians 3:10

When Paul writes this often-quoted verse, he was not encouraging you to merely know about Jesus Christ. No, he was encouraging you to know Jesus Christ with an intimacy and understanding that would direct your life.

To know Christ should be the goal of every true believer. It is easy to quote the first part of the verse, "that I may know Him and the power of His resurrection." The power is what is desired by so many, but there is a second part to the verse, and it teaches you how you will know Christ in power.

This part makes clear it is by experiencing the fellowship of His suffering, even to the point of death.

This is where many believers refuse to go. To know the power of the resurrected Christ in your life, you must also be willing to suffer for Christ, even to the point of death. Do you pray the entire verse or merely the first part of the verse?

Christ is strong in your life when you are your weakest and at your lowest point. It is then His grace is truly sufficient. Do you want to know Christ as the lover of your soul? Or is knowing a few facts and Bible verses enough?

Prayer and Praise:

Lord, I do want to know You in intimacy. I admit I do not understand all that entails, but I long to know You more. Teach me how to endure suffering, and even death, but let me know You. In the mighty name of Jesus Christ, I pray. Amen.

PRAY FOR ONE ANOTHER
Colossians 1:9-12

Prayer is the chief way in which a believer will grow in intimacy to the Lord Jesus Christ. Prayer moves through stages. You ask, seek, and knock. You pray for basic necessities and intercede on behalf of others. You have to learn to pray. The disciples never asked Jesus to teach them to preach or praise, but they did ask Jesus to teach them to pray.

Paul shows in this passage of Scripture how you are to pray for one another. Apparently this is a major concern, because Paul also spoke to this in the letter to the Ephesians. Paul does not stop praying for fellow believers. By praying for other believers, Paul is being used by God to encourage and enable others in the Lord.

As you read these verses, you are shown what to pray, as you pray these Scriptures for others.

First, pray that other believers will be filled with the knowledge of God's will in all wisdom and spiritual understanding. You must know God's direction and look at life from God's perspective. His understanding is crucial.

Next, you are to pray that others will walk worthy of the Lord, being pleasing to God in all they do. You are to pray they will bear fruit in every good work, and they will increase in the knowledge of God.

Finally, you are to pray they will be strengthened with all might, according to God's power. God's power is needed, not human strength and ingenuity. Pray for patience and longsuffering with joy. Joy is a believer's birthright in Christ Jesus. Often things are allowed to steal one's joy.

The prayer is ended by giving thanks to the Father for all He is and has done for the believer.

Prayer and Praise:

Lord, teach me to pray Scripture for other believers. In the mighty name of Jesus Christ, my Lord.

RECEIVING THE WORD
1 Thessalonians 2:13

Many times one will read the Bible, sit intently hearing the teacher in a class present the truths of God's Word, or listen, even taking notes, to the sermon that is being delivered. How certain are you that you are receiving the Word of God and not merely hearing?

To receive the Word of God one must yield to the Word of God, surrender to the Word of God, apply the Word of God, and live the Word of God in daily life. Just receiving instruction and not applying it to your life is useless.

The key to receiving the Word of God and continuing with Christ is in adjusting your life to the truth that you know and are receiving. If you fail to make adjustments of your life to the Scriptures, you stop receiving. You may gain head knowledge. You may be able to quote verses, even whole chapters or books, but it is all by rote.

When Paul wrote this verse about receiving the word of God, it was not a reference to the Old Testament or the reading of Scripture. It was a reference to a spoken or written message that God was anointing. No, the canon is closed, and there are no new Scripture additions. However, when a man of God preaches with the unction of the Holy Spirit, as that word goes forth, it will hit the mark. It will engage your spirit, and you will know you are in the presence of God, and you must respond to Him, not to man.

So many people sit in churches and hear men of God preach with power, boldness, and anointing, but they fail to respond. Why? They either have fear of others, or they think they are listening only to men. They never seem to realize they are hearing the word of God. They are accountable to respond and receive this word.

Have you ever sat in a church service and heard the preacher preach and sense that you needed to respond, but you did not? Why would you not? It is only as you respond that you will receive the word so that it will impact and change you. It is only as you respond that you are adjusting to the truth. Learn to receive God's word.

Prayer and Praise:

Lord, let me realize when I hear Your word preached that I must make adjustments of my life to the word, in order to receive Your word. It is so much more than hearing; it is about adjusting and obeying. In the mighty name of Jesus Christ, my Lord. Amen.

PRAY ALWAYS
1 Thessalonians 5:17

The command to pray without ceasing, at first glance, seems like an impossibility. You read this verse and you think, No one can pray 24/7. The command is not to be talking constantly to God all day and all night. The command to pray without ceasing is the command that you are always to be in a spirit of prayer. If you wake up at 2:00 a.m., you should be in a prayerful frame of mind. What is on your mind in the middle of the night, or who is on your mind? You must begin to realize God will wake you up in order to pray on behalf of others, even at 2:00 or 3:00 a.m.

In Ephesians 6:18, you are commanded to pray always. When you take this command to pray without ceasing and let God direct you, you will learn you can pray always.

The attitude of prayer is grounded by the act of prayer. You can talk about prayer. You can tell others how God answers prayer, but unless you start to pray, it is meaningless. If you are to develop an attitude of prayer, you must start praying. Do you have a specific time and place you pray? Do you have a prayer list? If you do not have a list, you end up after about five minutes, recycling what you have already prayed. The activity of prayer will eventuate into an attitude of prayer.

This will ultimately produce an atmosphere of prayer. The atmosphere of prayer will never be greater than the measured worth of the activity of prayer. It all begins with the right act of prayer. When a day begins with the right act it will continue in the right attitude of prayer all day.

Prayer and Praise:

Lord, teach me to start my day with prayer, true prayer, not rote or memorized prayers. Allow that act of prayer in the morning to continue throughout the day. Even as I sleep, wake me whenever You please to pray for specific needs. In the mighty name of Jesus Christ, my Lord. Amen.

SATAN'S POWER
2 Thessalonians 2:9-10

One topic that many people do not want to consider is the power that Satan has. He is stronger than any human being. Satan was created to be the one who protected the glory of God. He was the anointed cherub (Ezekiel 28). Pride entered him, his wisdom was corrupted, and Satan was cast down. Now he exists and waits on the final judgment when God sends him to the pit.

Satan's plan is to kill, steal, and destroy. He has power, nothing in comparison to God Almighty, but Satan has power. It was his power demonstrated when Pharaoh's magicians could turn their staffs into serpents. It was Satan's power when they replicated the first few miraculous signs that Moses did. Satan has power, but it is limited and always subject to Almighty God.

In this passage of 2 Thessalonians, you read of Satan's power: all power, signs, lying wonders, and all unrighteous deception. Be warned, Satan loves to deceive; he is a master of this. Whatever sign or wonder God does, Satan offers a counterfeit. You must be aware that every miracle may not be a miracle of God. If the message of Christ and the crucified life is denied, the sign is not from God.

In 2 Corinthians 11:14, you are told that Satan transforms himself into an angel of light. He is always attempting to deceive. Everything must be in agreement with Scripture; if it is not, Satan is on the prowl, and you must be very cautious. The more you know Scripture, the better you will be at recognizing Satan's attacks.

If you continue reading verse 10 (2 Thessalonians 2:10), Satan is able to deceive many because they "did not receive the love of the truth that they might be saved." Not receiving truth is why many fall into Satan's trap. Do you love the truth of God's Word? Do you adjust your life to the truth of God's Word?

You can measure your love for Christ by how much you love the Word of God. "The Word became flesh and dwelt among us" (John 1:14). Do you recognize the connection of loving truth and loving Christ?

How do you face and overcome Satan? Be a lover of the truth of God. Get the Word of God in your life every day. Feast upon it; take in massive quantities of it. The Word of God is the truth that is foundational for living. It is this truth that girds you daily for life and usefulness (Ephesians 6:14).

Prayer and Praise:

Lord, teach me to recognize the deception of Satan. Teach me to be so familiar with Your Word that I can easily spot a counterfeit. Let Your Word fill my life. In the mighty name of Jesus Christ, my Lord. Amen.

SHIPWRECKED FAITH
1 Timothy 1:18-20

What does it mean to shipwreck your faith? Paul said this had happened to at least two people, so it can happen to others. It could happen to you. How does it happen, and what are the consequences?

Paul defines fighting the good fight as "holding on to faith and a good conscience." These two things are connected. To hold fast to faith means you lean your entire human personality and being on God in complete trust and confidence. You do this with a clean, clear conscience. If your conscience has the conviction of God for some sin undealt with, your conscience is not good.

If your conscience condemns you, you will not be able to believe God. Condemnation is a faith killer. This is the point where you are in danger of shipwrecking your faith. Like a ship that is wrecked, when your faith is shipwrecked, you will fall short of all God has for you. This does not mean you will lose your salvation. It means you live a life of constant frustrations and failings.

Fight the good fight of faith. If your conscience is not good, if you sense conviction of sin, deal with it. Come again to the cross and freshly apply the blood of Jesus Christ. Make honest and complete confession to God and to another person who can hold you accountable. Make whatever adjustments necessary in your life to abide daily in Christ. Without adjustments, you will end up back like you were before.

Prayer and Praise:

Lord, show me if there is any area of my life that is not in agreement with You or Your Word. Let me examine the stewardship of my life and be sure I am right with You. The danger of shipwrecking my faith is real; show me how to feed my faith, so it can be all You intend for it to be. If I find myself in constant frustration, let me realize something may be wrong and that I must make adjustments to You. In the mighty name of Jesus Christ, my Lord. Amen.

GROWING IN CONTENTMENT
1 Timothy 6:6

In the Constitution of the United States of America, you are promised the right to pursue happiness. Have you achieved this right? Or have you realized happiness is based on happenings? The real thing you pursue when you are seeking happiness is contentment. Are you a contented person? Do you understand how contentment comes?

Contentment is the result of a godly life. In the Scriptures that you just read, you discovered the three ingredients of true contentment. First, do not be haughty. Stop demanding that life revolve around you and your interests (1 Timothy 6:5).

Next, put your hope in God and not uncertain riches (1 Timothy 6:9-10). If it is your desire to be rich, you will fall into temptation. To love money is to depart from the faith. Faith must always be in God and His Word.

Finally, do good with your money (1 Timothy 6:17-19). Money is not evil or bad in and of itself; it is your attitude toward money that is dangerous. This is why you are warned in the Scripture not to "love" money. Use money, not people. Use money to serve in the kingdom of God and help others in need.

To grow in contentment, you must remember life is more than bread and you recognize material things are secondary. Refuse the profit motive as the supreme drive of life. Always remember to use things to serve people. Love people and use things; you must keep that straight.

Prayer and Praise:

Lord, let me know contentment is always to be found in an abiding relationship with You. Please bring disturbing conviction to my life if I start to use people and serve things. In the mighty name of Jesus Christ, my Lord. Amen.

CURES FOR LONELINESS
2 Timothy 4:9-16

Most everyone has had moments of loneliness. Sometimes it is because you are geographically away from family and friends. Sometimes it is because you are misunderstood by family and friends. At some point in life everyone will face loneliness.

Paul certainly did. He was in a prison cell because of his faith. He was alone and lonely. As you read through 2 Timothy 4, you discover several things that caused Paul to feel this incredible sense of loneliness.

First, he was isolated in a dungeon. Why does God allow isolation like this? To allow you to be in a situation where all you can do is trust God? It was also winter, and therefore, cold. Are you aware how seasons affect people? Another contributing factor was that Paul's physical needs were not adequately met.

Possibly one of the two greatest causes for Paul's loneliness was he had been given a death sentence. With death being near, this can have a way of impacting one in a negative fashion. Finally, Paul had been forsaken by his friends. As you read these, do you see Jesus facing the same thing before the cross?

How can you get through loneliness? Gather select people around you (2 Timothy 4:9,11). Select people, not everyone, will be a help to you. Some individuals drain your life, while others build you up. Be selective.

Next, take care of your physical condition and needs (2 Timothy 4:13). Paul asked for a cloak so he could warm himself. When physical needs are met, it helps to have a good frame of mind. Also, get some good books to read (2 Timothy 4:13). Paul wanted the books and the parchments. Do you read very much? A good rule is not to try to read a book, only try to read a chapter. You will be amazed the books you read when you only read a chapter a day.

Lastly, engross yourself in the Word of God (2 Timothy 4:13). The parchments were the Old Testament and parts of the New Testament. Read your Bible. Sadly, many people have no interest in The Word of God; they have never read it in entirety. Loneliness comes to everybody. You can take these positive steps to overcome it.

Prayer and Praise:

Lord, thank You that You are my constant companion. Teach me daily to seek You and to allow You to govern my life, my time, and my choices. Let me daily fill my mind with Your truth so I can overcome loneliness when it comes. Let me be a builder to others and not a drainer. In the mighty name of Jesus Christ, my Lord. Amen.

HOW TO DEAL WITH A DIVISIVE PERSON
Titus 3:10-11

Life would be so much easier and simpler if people whom you come in contact with were respectful and honest. If people would show consideration of others, life would go along much more smoothly. You do not have to live very long to realize this is not the way things are. When your children start to school, they pick up attitudes from others that are not allowed in your home.

When you join the workforce you learn quickly what a "dog-eat-dog" world you live in. Even family members can cause much pain, grief, and frustration. It is always amazing to see how different two siblings can be even when raised with the same parental instruction and in the same home.

You do not have to live long until you encounter someone who is divisive. Sadly, it even occurs in the church. How do you deal with a divisive person? Scripture is not silent. You are told what to do, but only you can obey the Word of God for yourself.

The Bible tells you to "reject a divisive man after the first and second admonishment." If a person shows herself to cause division and discord among others, warn her, confront, and challenge her; if she heeds your warning, the divisiveness should stop. You determine if you warn her a second time. Scripturally, you only have to warn her up to two times.

If she refuses to heed the admonition, you are to reject her. This means you have nothing to do with her. This is where it gets challenging to you. Will you be like the father in the story of the prodigal son and let the son go without trying to help him or bail him out of trouble? Will you allow the person to come to an end of herself and come to her senses, turning back in genuine repentance to the Lord?

In today's culture, the grace of God is so emphasized in a way that you can easily overlook direct commands from the Word of God. The idea is prevalent that you can "love someone" into the kingdom of God. This idea is not taught in the Bible. The way you love someone is by your obeying Scripture and not merely by expressing a sentiment of feelings.

Many families and churches are torn apart because members refuse to "reject" the divisive person. You cannot continue life as normal with divisive people as long as their actions and attitudes cause division. The question remains, will you obey Scripture in this area?

Prayer and Praise:

Lord, You are God and You enable your people to live together in unity. Unity cannot be created by man; it comes only as Your people live in obedience to Your Word. Teach me how to love others as You love others. Teach me how to reject or rebuke others for the sake of unity in the body. In the mighty name of Jesus Christ, my Lord. Amen.

EXTENDING FORGIVENESS
Philemon 1:10-16

Onesimus was the slave of Philemon, and he stole something that belonged to Philemon and then fled. He now was a runaway slave, an act punishable by death. He ran to Rome and in God's providence, he met Paul, who is in prison. Onesimus was saved and became a servant to Paul, a helper. Paul was not just impressed with Onesimus, he saw him as a brother in the Lord. Onesimus was changed by the gospel. Paul wrote this letter and sent Onesimus back to Philemon.

Philemon had the right to bring charges against Onesimus, but Paul encouraged him to forgive Onesimus and restore him. He was asking for Philemon to receive Onesimus again as a brother in Christ. Onesimus had a debt he could not pay and now he returned to Philemon for forgiveness. Is that not how you came to Christ?

There are at least four steps to forgiveness. First, you must acknowledge someone has wronged you, even ruined your life. Second, you must declare to God, and to others if possible, you will not seek restitution, nor will you treat him as his sin deserves. Third, you choose to let him off the hook and for God to do with him as He sees fit. Finally, you pray blessings on him as Christ commands.

Is forgiveness easy? No. Does forgiving someone who has wronged you cost you? Yes. Do you only have to forgive the person one time? Probably not; every time the thought comes back into your mind you are to forgive again, and again, and again. Forgiveness is only as you yield to Christ and allow Him to supernaturally forgive through you.

Everyone will someday need forgiveness by someone. Husbands need to be forgiven by their wives and vice-versa. Parents need to forgive and be forgiven by children. If you choose not to forgive, you only harm yourself. Christ died to forgive you and to enable you to forgive others.

Prayer and Praise:

Lord, thank You for Your wonderful forgiveness. Let me not take it lightly or for granted. Teach me how to forgive others. In the mighty name of Jesus Christ, my Lord. Amen.

HARDEN NOT YOUR HEART
Hebrews 3:15

The children of Israel made it all the way to the edge of the Promised Land, and then they failed to go in. Do you find that amazing? They went through the plagues in Egypt, the desert, the Red Sea, the battle with the Amalekites, through all the challenges, and they got to the border and refused to go inside. Why did they hesitate and stop? Giants occupied the land.

Have you lived long enough to realize giants still occupy the land? Giants still confront and challenge believers every day. When you focus on the giants and not the promise, the provision and the leading of Almighty God, they can cause you to stop. In the process of stopping, your heart grows hard.

To harden your heart, simply neglect your duties and responsibilities as a believer. Just drift along with society, culture, materialism, and your heart will harden.

What are your responsibilities to God? You are commanded to seek the Lord first and foremost above everything else. Do you? How do you do this? Next, Scripture tells you that you are to fear God. You are responsible for cultivating a healthy fear of God in your life. You are to reverence, respect, and even be afraid if disobedience merits it, of Almighty God. Do you fear God, or do you fear man?

It is your duty as a believer to live in obedience to God. You are to practice complete obedience without complaint. Is the stewardship of your life that of complete obedience? Not partial obedience or delayed obedience. If you hold on to things that compete with Christ, your heart will harden.

The children of Israel did not set out from Egypt with the intent to get to the border of the Promised Land and then not go inside. Neither do believers today; but when you fail to keep your heart soft to God, it will harden. When you fail to listen to the voice of God, the Word of God, you will become distracted and your heart will harden. You have the warning; harden not your hearts.

Prayer and Praise:

Lord, teach me daily to seek You and to fear You. Let me hear Your Word, Your voice above the voices of man, and let me adjust to You. In the mighty name of Jesus Christ, my Lord. Amen.

WHEN THE WORD IS NOT PROFITABLE
Hebrews 4:1-2

All through life you will discover things that are not profitable. When you cannot find the matching sock, the one you have is not profitable. When you only have one hour to finish a task that will require ten hours, the task will go unfinished and the one hour will be wasted and unprofitable. Things can be unprofitable and time wasted can be unprofitable. However, how can the Word of God not be profitable?

The Word of God is life-giving and life-changing. The Word of God will set a person free from a life of sin and meaninglessness. The Word of God is sharp and powerful. How can it be unprofitable? The key to understanding this is in your response to the Word of God. Unless you respond to the Word of God with faith, it will not be profitable to your salvation, your deliverance, or your soul. How do you respond to the Word of God?

Faith, which is a gift from God to you, enables you to receive the Word of God. Faith is what enables you to believe God and to believe His Word. In the passage of Scripture, you see why the first generation of the children of Israel did not enter into the Promised Land. They heard the Word of God. They knew the promise of God, but they failed to respond to the Word of God with faith. They failed to obey God.

Today, when the Word of God is set forth and you only hear it, but you do not activate faith to obey, that Word of God to you is unprofitable. James tells that you are to be "doers of the Word and not hearers only." Do you do the Word of God? Do you feed your soul daily with God's truth? Do you adjust your life and your lifestyle to God's Word?

Tithing tells a lot about a person. Tithing is giving ten percent of one's income to the local church, the storehouse, as to obey God. There are many promises related to how you give and whether or not you give obediently, with a tithe to the Lord. Malachi 3 says you are under a curse if you do not tithe, and God will bless you if you do. Philippians 4 teaches God will supply all your needs if you give obediently (tithe) to the Lord.

These promises are of no value if you fail to act in faith on them; the Word of God is profitless. When you mix faith with the promises of God and obedience flows from your life to God, the Word of God is profitable for all things. It is profitable to you for holiness and godliness. It is profitable for usefulness and service. Always mix the Word of God with faith and miss none of the promises God has for you.

Prayer and Praise:

Lord, teach me how to mix faith with Your Word. Enable me to never hesitate once I know Your truth, but to obey You regardless of the cost. In the mighty name of Jesus Christ, my Lord. Amen.

THE NEW COVENANT
Hebrews 8:8-10

A covenant is an agreement made between two parties. It is a guarantee, a pledge, or a promise. How thankful are you that Holy God established a covenant with you? In the passage of Scripture, you read God promised, based on a new covenant, that He would put his laws "in their mind and write them on their heart."

This is a reference to Ezekiel 36:26-27, where God said, "I will give you a new heart and put a new spirit within you ... I will put My Spirit within you and cause you to walk in My statutes, and you will keep My judgments and do them."

God knows you cannot do His will, keep His commandments, or even love Him by simply commanding it. He now says that He is going to put His Spirit in you that will make you, compel you, to do His will and to love Him how He wants you to love Him. What a tremendous promise.

Do you sense a compelling force to obey Christ? Do you sense a compelling force to do God's will? Do you truly love God? If these are not true, you need to check and see if you have only added a religious preference to your life, or have you truly been born again by the Spirit of God.

The new covenant is amazing. It is the means by which God lives in you and accomplishes His will through you. As you yield daily to Christ and His Word, God is glorified by your life. This does not mean a problem-free existence; it means a life lived by faith.

Prayer and Praise:

Lord, thank You for the New Covenant. What I am unable to do, You do through me. I love You. In the mighty name of Jesus Christ, my Lord. Amen.

PREPARING TO WORSHIP
Hebrews 10:22

You prepare for many things. You prepare to go to work. You prepare a meal. You prepare to take a test. You prepare to get away for a few days. Do you prepare to worship Almighty God? How do you prepare to worship Almighty God?

One of the saddest commentaries on one's faith is not preparing to worship Jesus Christ. Many will spend no private time worshipping the Lord Jesus Christ during the week, and they show up for "church" on Sunday not prepared to worship.

Many in today's church have turned worship of Almighty God into merely "going to church." When all a person does is go to church, it is easy to miss God, it is easy to not prepare one's heart. It is easy to make an idol of "church" and have social interaction with people but still miss God.

How do you prepare to worship God? The first thing you notice is the call, "Let us draw near." God initiates; He calls you to come before Him. How are you to come before God? He gives you four check points.

First, you come with sincerity. Sincerity means "without wax." Sculptors in New Testament days would often fill cracks of a sculpted piece with wax. No one could tell the difference until it was placed in the sun and it began to melt. When you come before God with sincerity, you come without wax, and you come as you are with a true, honest heart.

You also are to come to worship with fidelity. You come with full assurance of faith. You come knowing you are saved and that your sins are covered by the blood of Christ. You have no sin undealt with.

You come with humility. Your heart has been sprinkled from an evil conscious. You come to worship, and you have nothing hindering your mind. Finally, you come in purity. Your body has been washed with pure water. You are clean spiritually, and you can come before the throne of grace worshipping Almighty God.

Prayer and Praise:

Lord, teach me daily how to prepare myself on how to come before You to worship You. In the mighty name of Jesus Christ, my Lord. Amen.

THE IMPLANTED WORD OF GOD
James 1:21

This verse contains the key to victory in your daily Christian life. The key is found in the word implanted. The King James Version reads "engrafted." With that word, it is easy to picture a tree branch being grafted to another tree. The key understanding is this is how you are to receive the Word of God.

How do you receive the engrafted Word of God? It is more than merely listening. There are three elements to hearing and receiving the Word of God.

First is submissiveness. Are you submissive to Christ? Do you yield to what the Word of God teaches? Do you practice forgiveness, or do you hold a grudge? Submissiveness is allowing God's Word to be the authority in one's life. Submissiveness goes against human nature, but it is still God's truth. You are not to live by human nature; you are to live by God's new nature that He places in you at salvation.

Next is purity. You are to lay aside all those things that pollute your life with sin. All those things you may think are not really bad, but are questionable. Purity of life is a life lived filled with and controlled by the Holy Spirit. By faith, lay aside all known sin. Confess and forsake it. Do you strive for purity in your life? How does what you view online or on television affect you? Are you faithful to church attendance, or do you make excuses why you forsake the assembling of yourself with the body of Christ? There must be purity in act and attitude.

Finally, humility is a key. You have to humble yourself to be submissive and to strive to live a pure life. You have to give up your rights and allow Jesus Christ to be your life. Daily, you must ask God to clothe you in humility, and then you must choose to allow humility to flow through you.

Once these three conditions are met, you are in a position to apply the Word of God, so that it does become engrafted into your life. The Word becomes real to you and you live the Word, you pray the Word, and you feast on the Word.

Prayer and Praise:

Lord, thank You for Your Word. Teach me daily how to allow my life to be engrafted with Your Word. Let me live Your truth. In the mighty name of Jesus Christ, my Lord. Amen.

RESIST THE DEVIL
James 4:7-8

Many a believer has an ongoing love affair with pride, self-centeredness, arrogance, meanness, blindness, and even dishonesty. These issues embrace you so seductively it takes more than good intentions to break them.

The key to resisting the Devil is found in the words that precede this command. They are found in the command to "submit to God." If you will not submit to God, you will never resist the Devil. How do you submit to God? You adjust your life, your lifestyle, your time, your attention, and your attitude to God and God's Word. You adjust yourself to God.

You give God time and space in your life. You put God before things—things that consume your time, attention, resources, and energy. You live the Word of God. When the Word of God speaks and your lifestyle or attitude is contrary, you make the adjustment, whether you feel like it or not. You learn to walk in the Spirit and not the flesh. You give no room for the Devil to get a foothold on your life.

This is not something that is going to happen overnight, but you start and you consciously make the adjustments of time and resources to God. If you choose not to submit to God, then the Devil will not flee. Jesus Christ faced the temptation of the Devil in the wilderness, and with each temptation, He chose God and God's Word, and the Devil left him for a season.

The same is true still—the Devil will flee, but he will come again and again trying to tempt you to fall. That is why you must daily and consciously adjust your life and your time to God. What you give your time to is what you live for.

A practical suggestion would be in reading Scripture. How many chapters a day do you read? As you go through this devotion, you are asked to read from one to five chapters. When you do not have a devotional to guide you, how many chapters a day will you read? If you read three chapters a day, you will read the Bible through in a year.

As you reflect on your day, did you read that many chapters? Did you spend time in prayer away from the distractions of life until you connected to God in prayer? Have you spent any time writing out verses in an attempt to memorize Scripture? If you have no plan to measure your activity with God, it is easy to fall into no activity with God and assume you are okay.

Prayer and Praise:

Lord, teach me daily to recognize when I have failed to give You time and space. Prompt me when I am wasting time with television or the Internet to realize I have not given you ample time and space. In the mighty name of Jesus Christ, my Lord. Amen.

LIVING STONES
1 Peter 2:4-5

You read this and your mind asks the question, how can a stone be living? You are right; a stone is an inanimate object. It does not need oxygen, food, shelter, or clothing. Yet you remember Jesus said if you keep silent "the stones will immediately cry out." You should never allow a rock to do your praising.

The reference here to living stones is a reference to the temple in Jerusalem. The stones of the temple were huge. The sound of hammering or chiseling was not allowed in the temple area. These stones had to be shaped at the quarry to exact specifications.

What Christ seeks to do for you is to shape you to the exact specification where you fit into His temple, into His body, the church. Christ has a specific place for you in His spiritual house. By yielding to Him and taking your priesthood seriously, you allow Christ to shape you until you fit His plan perfectly.

Christ is the chief cornerstone. This means He bears the weight of the entire building. This means He determines the size, shape, and place of all the other stones.

When you feel like you are being hammered upon, realize Christ is at work in you. When you sense your life is being chiseled upon, realize Christ is working in you to fit you to your exact place in Him.

As you take seriously your priesthood, God uses you. What does a priest do? He intercedes in prayer for others. He studies the Word of God, applying it to his own life and teaching it to others. Do you take your priesthood seriously?

Prayer and Praise:

Lord, thank you for hammering and chiseling my life so I will fit into Your body where I am supposed to fit. Let me take seriously my priesthood, and let me be a man of prayer and the Word. In the mighty name of Jesus Christ, my Lord. Amen.

SUFFERING ACCORDING TO THE WILL OF GOD
1 Peter 4:19

The idea of suffering is not appealing to anyone, especially living in the United States of America with all the freedoms and opportunities that are afforded to you. Everyone seems to do everything they can to keep from suffering. Yet people in America suffer. People go to bed hungry, cold, and penniless. People experience storms and floods. People lose jobs and family. This is not the suffering Peter is talking about.

To suffer for one's faith and this being the will of God is a difficult concept to grasp. There is a suffering that comes from doing wrong, and there is a suffering from doing right. You will suffer because you are a child of God because you are different than the world. The Holy Spirit resides in your life, and you have been changed, transformed into a new creation.

Nothing makes other people more uncomfortable than a changed life. There are things non-Christians do that Christians cannot do because of your walk and relationship with Jesus Christ. If you live to be accepted by the world, you have a problem. Paul told Timothy that the godly will suffer persecution.

If you live for Christ a life of holiness and separation from the things of the world, you will suffer according to the will of God. The question remains, do you suffer because of your faith in Christ? Do you face persecution at work because of your obedience to Christ? Or does anyone notice any difference in your life?

Do you do what the world does? Do you get entertained by what entertains the world? Do you dress, act, and sound like the world? If so, you will not suffer for your faith, because you are not living by faith.

Prayer and Praise:

Lord, teach me daily to recognize if I am like the world or if I am living by faith. Teach me to pursue You at all costs. In the mighty name of Jesus Christ, my Lord. Amen.

SCOFFERS
2 Peter 3:3

A church man came to his pastor one Sunday after the morning service, in an attempt to challenge the pastor, and said, "I am a scoffer." When the man, who was a member and faithful to attend every service that the church offered, said this, the pastor was stunned. To admit you are a scoffer means you are one who mocks and disbelieves.

The Bible is clear that in the last days scoffers will be present. Does the idea of a scoffer concern you? It should, because a scoffer is a false witness. He is one who will attempt to lead people away from the truth of God's Word. The key for you when dealing with a scoffer is to remember the Word of God.

In the last days, your mind will be challenged to think like the world and to embrace the world view, but you have been bought with a price. The precious blood of Jesus was shed for you. Remember the Word of God and when scoffers confront you, cling to the Word of God.

God has given you the tremendous gift of memory. Use it for His glory and the strengthening of your faith. Remember the moments when God worked on your behalf. Remember the times God spoke His truth into your life, making it personalized to you. Remember He is God, and you are not. Pay no attention to scoffers who only want to pull you down and deny the truth.

When you go to your workplace, or school, or marketplace, be prepared to encounter scoffers. Your job is not to convince them; that is the job of the Holy Spirit. Your job is to make Jesus look good. Your job is to live a life of trust and obedience before them, no matter what they say.

Scoffers are coming; in fact they are already here. Know the Word of God and live according to it, whether you understand it all or not, and live out your faith. To live out your faith, you have to live in agreement with Scripture.

Prayer and Praise:

Lord, enable me to recognize a scoffer and not run from him, but let me live my faith in front of him. Enable me not to get drawn into an argument, but to live by Your Word regardless of what they say. In the mighty name of Jesus Christ, my Lord. Amen.

MARKS OF TRUE SALVATION
1 John 1:5-10

Salvation is the greatest gift God extends to man. It comes only through a personal response and relationship with Jesus Christ. "For by grace you have been saved through faith; and that not of yourselves; it is the gift of God" (Ephesians 2:8). However, in today's culture, it appears salvation has become man-centered salvation and not Christ-centered salvation.

The book of 1 John was written to give a series of tests to show if a person is truly saved. The doctrine of the security of the believer is God is the One who keeps you saved. The doctrine of assurance of true salvation is how a person knows biblically if he or she is saved.

From the jailhouse to the drinking house a lot of people will tell you they are saved. How do you know for certain? Ask questions. Since you have heard the gospel, has God done a work in your heart that you now have come to hate sin and the things of the world you once loved? The God you once ignored and warred against, do you now desire Him?

A true Christian can struggle with assurance of salvation and even doubt, but God gives you the witness of the Holy Spirit and the witness of the Word of God to have true assurance. A life characterized by obedience reinforces assurance of salvation.

There are ten tests of true salvation given in 1 John. If you pass these tests, you have the witness of Scripture of true salvation. First, a true believer will walk in the light (1 John 1:5). You will walk in God's revealed will and conform to His character.

Second, a true believer is sensitive about her sin and expresses brokenness over her sin, and is open to rebuke for her sin (1 John 1:8-9). If you want to know truth and walk in the truth of God, you must be reprovable and teachable.

Third, a true Christian keeps God's commandments (1 John 2:3-5). You strive and struggle, maybe not perfectly, but push on to obey the Lord. You do not make excuses about disobedience.

Fourth, a true believer lives in the same manner Jesus lived (1 John 2:6). To abide in Christ means you have the same passion as Christ. Are you passionate about Christ or the things of the world?

Prayer and Praise:

Lord, show me clearly if I pass these tests of true salvation. Let the witness of the Word and the Holy Spirit confirm this in me. In the mighty name of Jesus Christ, my Lord. Amen.

MARKS OF TRUE SALVATION (2)
1 John 5:12

Continuing with yesterday's study of the marks a person will have if she is genuinely saved, you have to go to 1 John 2:9. This verse tells you a true Christian loves the brethren. To love the brethren (other believers) you want to spend time with Christians; this is one reason you crave the fellowship of the church.

The sixth mark of a true Christian is, a true believer does not love the world, (1 John 2:15-17)—the "world" meaning the world's system and values. The "world" is anything that does not acknowledge the lordship of Jesus Christ. As you assess this, you must look at one's dress, one's actions, and what one allows himself to be entertained by. True Christians do not love the world.

Next, a true believer will persevere among other true believers (1 John 2:19). You continue in fellowship with the body of Christ, the church. You never quit. Number eight, a true Christian is going to acknowledge everything the Scripture teaches about the person of Jesus Christ (1 John 2:2-23). You may not understand perfectly, but Jesus Christ was fully man and fully God. He is Lord.

Number nine, a true believer practices righteousness (1 John 2:29). If you are saved, you will practice and live righteously. You will conform to God and God's Word. Finally, number ten, a true Christian knows and confesses salvation is through and by Christ alone (1 John 5:12). It is not by decisionism, trying harder, being baptized, or by taking communion.

Salvation is through the blood Jesus Christ shed for you. Do not trust in a mere profession of faith. You are to trust in Christ.

Prayer and Praise:

Lord, thank You that Your Word gives evidences of true salvation. Let my life always be in line with Your Word, and let me trust in You and not in a past experience. In the mighty name of Jesus Christ, my Lord. Amen.

WALKING IN TRUTH
2 John 1:4

As you read this short letter, you will notice that John mentions truth several times. The call for a Christian is to walk in truth and to act in love toward one another. In today's society, people tend to gravitate toward love, even at the expense of truth. The love they gravitate toward is superficial and not the true love of the Father, but people gravitate toward love. Love is never to overshadow truth or to overcome truth.

As a child of God, you are called to walk in truth first and then love. This may sound harsh, but if you allow truth to be compromised, then you lose your foundation of Christ. If the church allows truth to be compromised, the church forfeits her solid foundation of Christ.

You are told in Ephesians to put on the whole armor of God so that you will be able to stand against the attacks of the Devil. The first thing you are to appropriate is the truth of God and Scripture. You are to gird your waist with truth.

As you continue reading Ephesians 6:10-20 about the armor of God being applied to your life and appropriated, you never read of appropriating love. Not that the love of Christ in you is not important, but truth is essential to live the Christian life. Without truth you have no basis for love. The reason you have love is because of truth. When you know the truth of Jesus Christ and the Word of God, love will flow accordingly from your life, but it will not be a superficial love. Love and truth accompany each other. Truth is always first, it is foundational. Truth is to abide in you and to direct your life. When that happens, love will flow and flourish.

You live in a time when everybody cries out for love, but their definition of love does not meet the biblical standard. You live in a time when every person demands his own rights, but truth must always be the basis for rights.

Love will fill your life as a believer when you walk in truth. When you seek truth, you will want to share this truth with your family and friends because you love them. Truth is communicated because of love. Truth is foundational and first.

Prayer and Praise:

Lord, give me a hunger for Your truth, so that Your love will fill my life. In the mighty name of Jesus Christ, my Lord. Amen.

BEING OPPOSED
3 John 1:9-11

What do you do when a person is a problem to you? What do you do when this person is in the church? How do you handle opposition? This is part of what 3 John is addressing. The third letter to John is one of the shortest in the New Testament, but it has much to say. Where encouragement and commendation are deserved, they are given. Where unspirituality is evident, it is not glossed over.

You do not have to serve the Lord very long to realize you will be opposed. Sadly, opposition sometimes comes from people who are in the church. Diotrephes was such a man. He was a problem to the Elder, John, and to the church.

What characterized Diotrephes was self-love. He was proud and self-willed. John wrote these words so you can know the type of person you should avoid. Paul had warned Timothy of people connected with the Christian church that held a form of godliness but denied the power of it (2 Timothy 3:5). This reminds you that members of the visible church are not necessarily part of the true church, the body of Christ.

John had written to the local church with a message for the members, but Diotrephes, in his arrogance, had refused to acknowledge the writer's authority. He may have refused to read the letter to the church, or he may have destroyed it. Whatever happened, the effect was to reject the instructions issued by John.

John complained that Diotrephes was gossiping maliciously against us (3 John 1:10). Character assassination is very harmful to church fellowship. Not only that, he deliberately defied the elder by turning others away from the church. He refused to accept spiritual authority.

John exposed Diotrephes for who and what he was. He warned that he would be obligated to take some kind of disciplinary action. Does it amaze you what professed believers will do in the church? God has put spiritual authority in place in the church. Every believer will one day give an account to the Lord Jesus Christ for how he treated this authority and the church.

Every church will have those who want to oppose. They will do this often under the guise of protecting the church. Your responsibility is to recognize spiritual authority and yield to it. Do not become a "Diotrephes."

Prayer and Praise:

Lord, give me spiritual sensitivity to recognize when a person is a "Diotrephes." Let me always yield to Your established authorities in the church and be very sensitive to Your Holy Spirit. In the mighty name of Jesus Christ, my Lord. Amen.

ROOT SINS
Jude 1:6-12

The concept of sin is very much understandable to every person. However, sin is talked about with the terms of the sin of omission and commission. What does that mean? The sins of commission are sins you commit. Things you do that are wrong and sinful. Stealing or lying would be an example of a sin of commission. The sin of omission is sin because of what you failed to do; you failed to pause and pray. You omitted reading your Bible today.

When it comes to sin, every true believer feels as if he is an expert, just as Paul called himself "the chief of sinners." As you read the passage today you are confronted with three specific sins that are best understood as root sins: unbelief (v. 5), pride (v. 6), and stubborn rebellion (v. 8).

The Israelites came out of Egypt, but failed to enter the Promised Land because of unbelief. The angels were cast out of heaven because of pride. The people of Sodom and Gomorrah rejected authority, and this is rebellion.

These three sins, and possibly others, are classified as root sins. A root sin springs up and becomes fruit bearing. You see fruit sins, such as lying, cheating, and stealing. These are readily confessed, but you have to go to the root in order to get the sin dealt with completely.

The challenge you face is to look at your life and see what habitual sin or sins you constantly struggle with. Have you dealt with the root or merely the fruit? Unbelief, pride, and rebellion birth other sins in one's life.

Pause for a moment and ask God to expose any area of unbelief of God's Word or God in your life. Pause again and ask God to reveal to you any area of pride and how it is manifesting in your life. Finally, take some time and ask God to show you any rebellious attitude toward God or God-ordained authority.

Once you have completed this, make honest confession of root sins, praying the blood of Christ for fresh cleansing and restoration.

Prayer and Praise:

Lord, teach me to recognize root sins in my life so that I may bring them to You in honest confession. Teach me to deal quickly with this type of sin in my life, as it bears fruit in so many ways. In the mighty name of Jesus Christ, my Lord. Amen.

YOU ARE WORTHY
Revelation 4:11

No genuine believer would ever deny the worthiness of Jesus Christ. Worthy means good, important, and having value, or worth. When one is described as worthy, it means she is of excellent character and deserving. Truly, only Jesus Christ is worthy to receive "glory and honor and power."

In this passage, the elders of Revelation fall down before the throne of God and worship Him. When was the last time you fell on your knees or your face before the Lord and worshipped? You left your seat, the pew you occupied, and you prostrated yourself before the throne of the Lord, while others were present? Are you too dignified to do such a thing?

These elders of Revelation were clothed in white, which means they were dressed in the purity and holiness of Jesus Christ. Because of this purity, these elders were near the presence of God. The crowns of gold they had on their heads, they cast before the throne of God. These crowns would represent their authority they had in their service to God. They yielded all authority to the Father as they worshipped Him.

How do you ascribe to the Lord Jesus Christ His worth? How do you demonstrate that Christ alone is worthy? These elders demonstrate submission to Christ. They fall down before the throne, and they yield all they are and have to Him. This is a lesson each believer must learn and act upon.

As these elders of Revelation bow before the Lord and cast their crowns at His feet, they are also vocal to declare His worthiness. Are you vocal to declare the worthiness of God, the only true God, to whomever is around you? They declared, "You are worthy, O Lord."

Prayer and Praise:

Lord, show me daily Your worth. Teach me how to bow and yield all I am to You. Always let me be vocal in my ascribing to You Your Worth. In the mighty name of Jesus Christ, my Lord. Amen.

THE PRAYERS OF THE SAINTS
Revelation 5:8

Prayer is talking and listening to God. It is communing with the Father. Sometimes prayers are offered consistently with how Scripture teaches one to pray, and sometimes prayers are offered in a crisis moment and rise from the pain of one's life. Prayer is asking, prayer is seeking, and prayer is knocking at the throne of the Father.

Do you realize that prayers can be eternal? As you read this passage of Scripture, you see the reference to the "prayers of the saints." These prayers are in golden bowls represented by incense, which gives off a pleasant aroma to the nostrils of God. Your prayers are not only heard, they are also retained in heaven as incense to the Father.

Knowing that your prayers are kept or stored in heaven as incense offering to God, does that not motivate you to pray more, to seek God more with intensity? You pray now for an issue or a need, but your prayers are kept like intimate letters written to the love of your life, to be read and reread for eternity.

Praying is not merely talking to God. Praying is hosting the Father. It is preparing your heart and life for His presence. Just as you prepare your home to host a guest, you prepare your heart daily to entertain the Father, to minister to Him, to show your love, your respect, and your gratitude to Him.

Do you see the connection between entertaining God and knowing His presence? If not, you miss the intimacy of prayer. Pray because you love the Lord. Pray because Jesus demonstrated the necessity of prayer and teaches you how to pray. Pray because it is an act of humbling yourself before the Father. Pray because you cannot live without prayer.

Prayer and Praise:

Lord, continue to show me and teach me the bigger picture of praying. Give me a hunger to seek You, and if I have no desire to pray, show me the sin that has filled my life and has distracted me from seeking You in prayer. In the mighty name of Jesus Christ, my Lord. Amen.

HOW TO OVERCOME
Revelation 12:11

Every true child of God wants what this verse says—to be an overcomer. Every true child of God knows that an overcomer is one who has heard the voice of God and has responded to it, walking in obedience and perseverance. An overcomer is one who will abide faithfully in Christ to the end.

To overcome does not mean you gain worldly success or notoriety. It does not mean you will have the acceptance of man, wealth, or worldly prosperity. It means you will be faithful to Christ, no matter the cost. Seven times in Revelation 2 and 3, Jesus says, "To him who overcomes." This means there is a possibility to be overcome by the world.

How do you become an overcomer and continue in overcoming? Revelation 12:11 tells three things are necessary. First, you overcome by the blood of the Lamb. You have to know you are truly born again, and you can have no doubts about your salvation. The blood of the Lamb is your covering and cleansing agent, and it has to be personally applied to your life and abided in. Do you know without a doubt you are truly saved?

Second, you overcome by your testimony. You must be willing to share your faith. You must tell others of the grace and mercy of Jesus Christ. You talk to friends, family, and coworkers about how God provides and guides. You talk about Jesus. Do you talk about Jesus and the Bible to others?

Finally, you love not your life even to the death. By your abiding in Christ and the Word of God, you choose Christ over everything. You had rather die than to deny Him. This is easy to say, but much harder to live out. If you will not live for Him and obey Him, you definitely would not be willing to die for Him. Do you adjust your life to Christ, to the Word of God, and to the church, the body of Christ? This is evidenced in all of your love and obedience.

Every one of these commands starts with an attitude of complete submission to God. Without the attitude being correct, the action does not flow. What is your attitude toward Christ? The church? The Word of God?

Prayer and Praise:

Lord, teach me daily to position myself to live, even to die as an overcomer in You. Give me greater passion for Your glory. In the mighty name of Jesus Christ, my Lord. Amen.

YOUR WORKS FOLLOW YOU
Revelation 15:1-3

Everyone is going to face death. The wages of sin is death, and the moment you were born, you began the process of dying. For the true believer, death is not the end; it is the beginning of eternity with Christ Jesus. However, how you lived will impact your eternity.

This Scripture tells you that your works will follow you. How do you understand that? Your works, all those things you did in faith, will go with you to eternity. Paul said, "Therefore, my beloved brethren, be steadfast, immovable, always abounding in the work of the Lord, knowing that your labor is not in vain" (1 Corinthians 15:58).

Scripture tells that you will be judged according to what you have done—your actions, your works, your deeds, and the motive with which you did them. All of these will be rewarded in heaven (Revelation 20:12).

As you live this life, you must constantly be examining your life as whether or not you are building with precious stones, or wood, hay, and stubble (1 Corinthians 3:12). Wood, hay, and stubble will not survive. Only the precious stones, only those which are of eternal value will endure.

What is precious? Your faith is more precious than gold (1 Peter 1:7). Are you adding to your faith those things Scripture commands—virtue, knowledge, self-control, perseverance, godliness, brotherly kindness, and love (2 Peter 1:5-8)? If you lack these, the Bible says you are "shortsighted even to blindness" (2 Peter 1: 9).

Are you living for the moment or have you chosen to live for eternity? You make decisions every day with the choices of how you spend your time, resources, and abilities. Choose to live for Christ. Choose to live for eternity. Failure in this area has eternal ramifications.

Prayer and Praise:

Lord, give me understanding every day about the choices of what I do with my time, talents, and abilities. Enable me to make right decisions to store up treasures in heaven and not to squander everything by living in the moment. In the mighty name of Jesus Christ, my Lord. Amen.

THE HOLY OF HOLIES
Revelation 21:15-17

The book of Revelation is a challenging book to read and understand. It is apocalyptic literature, and the closest thing you have to that type literature is political satire. You show a picture of a bear and an eagle and many readily understand the concept of Russia and the United States. This type of literature also uses numbers and meanings, which makes it even more challenging.

In chapter 21, you are introduced to a new heaven and a new earth. Plus, the holy city, New Jerusalem, comes down. The chief good of the city is the fact that God Himself will be there. As you come to verses 16-17, you are told the measurements of the city of one hundred and forty-four cubits. It is a perfect square.1

The Jewish mind that reads this would automatically think of the brilliant cube, the Holy of Holies. The high priest would go in one time a year, offering sacrifice for sin. The Holy of Holies was the dwelling place of eternal God, but now, the heavenly city, New Jerusalem, is the dwelling place of Almighty God.

In this Holy of Holies, you do not go in one time a year, but you dwell there forever in the presence of God. All time and creation has been longing and looking for this day; the day the saints of God come forever into the presence of the Father to dwell forever and ever.

Does that not excite you? Do you not have a longing for that day? For the final consummation of the people of God and the glorification of His bride, the church? Forever, you will be with the God in that place Jesus went to prepare for you (John 14:2-4).

Hallelujah to the Lamb! He is worthy to receive praise, honor, and glory. Amen!

Prayer and Praise:

Lord, You are so wonderful. I exalt Your name on high. I praise You because You and You alone are worthy. I magnify Your holy name. In the mighty name of Jesus Christ, my Lord. Amen.

1 Jewish Annotated New Testament, Oxford University Press, New York, New York, 2011, pg. 496.

The 40 Day Reign of God

Was the experience a "Great Awakening?"...a spiritual movement?...the unleashing of God's power and glory?...God's Kingdom movement?...an experience of His Shekinah glory?...or was it just simply a revival?

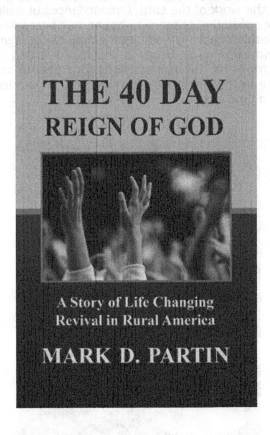

The experience in question occurred during October and November of 2006, at Indiana Avenue Baptist Church. It is challenging to explain; certainly impossible to define; and not easy to describe with mere words. For some it may even be difficult to comprehend. However, for all involved it is undeniable that God opened the heavens for forty days and poured upon us immense blessings. It is undeniable that God's breath entered each of us, causing us the rise in unity as a vast army. We became His army charged with changing the world, even if only in a small way.

Prices:

1 copy: $7.99

2-9 copies: $6.50 each

10 or more copies: $5.00 each

What's Faith Got to Do With It?
Everything!

There are seasons in the Christian life when we seem to grow weary and faint-hearted in the work of the Lord. Circumstances of daily living as well as the onslaughts of darkness seem to hound our every step and attempt to go forward. Setbacks have ways of interjecting discouragement and fear in our hearts and we long for freedom and rest. We find that our hands and hearts reach out for answers and long for freedom and fruitfulness. That is where the truths in the book you now hold in your hand have been written for such a time as this.

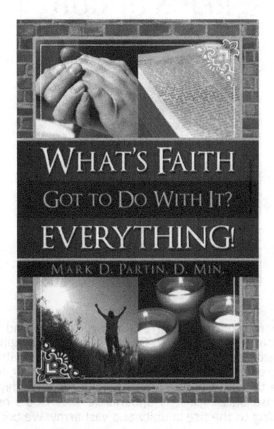

Prices:

1 copy: $7.99

2-9 copies: $6.50 each

10 or more copies: $5.00 each

The Power of Personal Testimony

A more open and mutual sharing-style of church fellowship together has traditionally been reserved for occasional weekend retreats, camp meetings, or small groups. This book shows, through living stories, actual circumstances, and documented history, how this has got to change-for revival's sake, for truth's sake, and for the world's sake. As you read this book you will take a giant step forward, seeing what happens when hidden blockages and unconscious hindrances are unexpectedly released in lives through the simple power of body-life witness testimony.

Price: 1 copy: $5.00

A Cry for Revival

As Moses was on the backside of the desert, before he could be used by God to deliver His people from bondage, he first had to hear God say to him, "put off your shoes from your feet, for the place on which you stand is holy ground." Moses needed cleansing, forgiveness, and a right relationship with a Holy God before he could be used as an instrument of revival and a blessing to others.

Price:

1 copy: $5.00

Praying With Fire

Do you have a desire for a fresh move of God in your own life and in your local fellowship? Do you hunger after more of God, but are not sure what to do to see it happen? Praying with Fire offers 21 principles about revival from revival passages of Scripture. Learn how to pray biblically for the presence of God in your life and church.

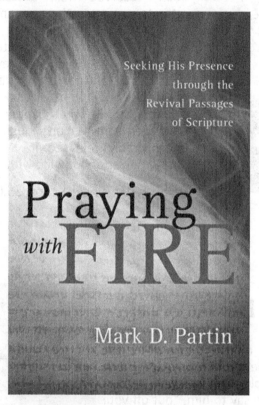

Prices:

1 copy: $12.99

5 or more copies: $9.99 each

For more information or to contact Mark for a Revival or Conference

Visit www.ministertominister.org
(423) 562-3420 or (423) 562-8981
markdpartin@yahoo.com